EDUCATIONAL THINKERS OF INDIA

EDUCATIONAL THINKERS OF INDIA

Shehzad Ahmed

ANMOL PUBLICATIONS PVT. LTD.
NEW DELHI - 110 002 (INDIA)

ANMOL PUBLICATIONS PVT. LTD.
H.O.: 4374/4B, Ansari Road, Darya Ganj,
New Delhi-110 002 (India)
Ph.: 23278000, 23261597

B.O.: No. 1015, Ist Main Road, BSK IIIrd Stage
IIIrd Phase, IIIrd Block,
Bangalore - 560 085 (India)
Visit us at: www.anmolpublications.com

Educational Thinkers of India

First Published, 2006

ISBN 81-261-3047-4

PRINTED IN INDIA

Printed at Mehra Offset Press, Delhi.

Contents

Preface

Education is the birthright of man, which has been emphasised not only in society, but also in all the religious and spiritual scriptures. Islam enjoins upon every man and woman to get education in spite of all the obstacles and bottlenecks. And, it is this quality of man which distinguishes him from other species of animals.

The growth and development of a nation largely depends upon its citizens' education. It benefits at both the levels: individually and cumulatively. Particularly, the education of woman is very essential as a mother lays the foundation of a child's education and instils in him all the qualities, which are expected of a great character.

As we know that education is a long and systematic process, different policies and programmes of study keep being formulated and executed. This important task of study is entrusted to the great scholars and renowned educationists of time.

Though the process of learning is uniform the world over, there have been experimented various techniques with a view to making the process more effective and less time-consuming. A number of educationists of international fame have chalked out different and distinct policies for the development of the course of education globally. Froebel, Rousseau, Mcluhan, Marx, Tagore, Iqbal, Gandhi, Abul Kalam Azad, Zakir Husain, Vivekananda, Radhakrishnan, K.G. Sayyaden and Krishnamurthi are to name a few.

From class Ist to Higher Studies, diverse approaches are adopted. The education think tank not only chisel the techniques of teaching and learning, but also shape the syllabi as per the need of the student groups and place, because different geographical and cultural backgrounds affect the process of learning to some extent or the other.

Similarly, the medium of education cannot be uniform in the entire country. That, too, is one of the major factors for different techniques and contents of study. Montessori, kindergarten, audio-visual, classroom study, correspondence study, etc. are all the instances of the efforts made by the educationists at different periods of time.

Encyclopaedia of Great Educationists and Thoughts is but an humble attempt to bring together the historical moves, recommendations, syllabi and various significant contributions ever made by the internationally known educationists to promote the cause of education.

This modest, comprehensive and exclusively prepared work is worth its salt. Hopefully, it would prove to be a great contribution in steering the afore-mentioned cause and benefiting scholars, students, researchers, academics and educationists, alike.

For further enhancement of its usefulness, readers' comments and suggestions are solicited and appreciated.

—Editor

Part-I
General

1

Introduction

Philosophy is related to all concepts of education, directly or indirectly. In fact, Philosophy and education are the two sides of the same coin. They present different views of the same thing. In other words one is implied in the other. Sir John Adams said education is the dynamic side of philosophy, the practical means of realizing ideals of life. Philosophy is the contemplative side and education is the active side of the same coin. Following is an account of some philosophies as they perceive and describe various aspects of education such as (i) aims of education, (ii) methods of education, (iii) curriculum of education, (iv) place of the child in education, (v) place of the teacher in education, etc.

Education vs Idealism

The fundamental proposition of idealism is that the mental or spiritual is more real and more important than the material. To the idealists reality is spiritual rather than material. This view of the idealists influences their educational thought. The aims and methods of education are particularly described to be different from what other philosophies consider them to be. In fact, idealism has contributed more to the aims and objectives of education.

Idealism and Aims of Education: The idealists consider education as a man-making process. In their scheme of education man is assigned the central position. All of them stress the dignity of man and the distinctiveness of his nature. They accept the doctrine of evolution of man, but assert that the biological account of man is inadequate and incomplete. They hold that realisation of ultimate values lies at the heart of the universe; man must become a moral being knowing what is good and what is evil. Man possesses a spiritual nature which enables him to apprehend moral values. Man's true environment consists of universal values realisation of which should be the ultimate goal of evolution. Man's spiritual nature is not something added to him; it is the essence of his being.

Hence, the goal of education must be self-realisation for all. This constitutes, according to idealists, a philosophical charter of universal education.

The idealists like Plato said that one fundamental aim of education is to enable the mankind through its culture to enter more and more into the spiritual realm, to enlarge the boundaries of the spiritual realm.

Education must help the individual to attain self-realisation through development of cultural values which guard man against any possible misunderstanding of self-realisation as an isolated or self-sufficient attitude of the individual. Man's higher or spiritual nature, according to them, is essentially social, as social is an expression of man's rational or spiritual and hence, of universal nature. The individual can realise his full potentialities only as a member of the human family. Thus, it follows that education should make efforts on children's social development and cultural development. Education for self-realisation does full justice to the social aim.

The idealists asserted that spiritual values are eternal and unchanging. Hence, this is one of the tasks of education to foster these values through educative process.

Plato said that the function of education is to help individuals in their exploration of the ultimate, universal values so that the truth of the universe may give power to their life.

The idealist hold that education must be religious, moral, intellectual and aesthetic. None of these aspects can be neglected if a harmoniously balanced personality is desired to be developed. They also say that physical development also can not be ignored.

Development of personality is the most prized aim of education according to the idealists. It is, defined by them as culmination in self-realisation. It is, to them, the end of ends, the goal of goals, realisation of the absolute idea. In the words of Rusk it means enhancement or enrichment of personality characterised by the embodiment of universal values. 'To some of the idealists self-realisation means development of divine qualities which are inherent in human beings but dormant at the time of his birth. Unfolding of these dormant qualities is the aim of education.

Development of will power essential for self-realisation is also said to be the aim of education according to idealists. Home has given eight points for the realisation of this ideal. These include:

(i) training of the will indirectly through activity rather than idea,
(ii) the object lesson method according to time and context,
(iii) self-suggestion, knowledge and practice,
(iv) proper discipline,
(v) providing knowledge of facts concerning nature and society,
(vi) development of moral character by ethical instruction,
(vii) freedom to make choice in most of the matters concerning the individual.

Another aspect of idealistic conception of education is the synthesis between nature and human beings. Education must aim at achieving an understanding of nature in human beings and educating them to achieve harmony with it. It is, as held by idealists, the essence of human nature to work towards a rational unity in himself. Education must lead the educand nearer reality, and towards his utmost possible perfection, "fine roses".

Great importance is attached to child's cultural development and preservation of social heritage. The individual should make his own contribution also to this. Education must enable the child to do so. For achieving this education must provide the child with cultural environment created by religion, morality, art, literature, mathematics science, etc. Teaching of humanities is more emphasised for this purpose. Plato said that moral principles had eternal validity and hence, education must help children develop qualities like rightness, justice, courage, and so on which were considered of permanent nature. Idealism places more emphasis upon more universal objects of education. Ross says that the function of education is to help us in our exploration of the ultimate universal values so that the truth of the universe may become our truth and give power to our life.

Idealism and the Method: Idealists suggest that the method of education must be oriented to achieving the complete development of all the innate abilities of the child and to train him for self realisation. Specific methods suggested are:

Instruction: It is the most important tool to impart information. But, it does not mean, as held by idealists, a tool for stuffing the child's mind with junk material. It implies modification and refinement of child's mind. It has to be, therefore, supplemented by sympathetic guidance. Idealists stress that training of all kinds must be provided in the school.

Activity: Like naturalists and the pragmatists, idealists also recommend activity based teaching learning. The child must learn through doing. Lectures must be followed by questioning by students. But, more important than this is the creative activity. The creative activity has to be natural, continuous and progressive. This helps in child's approaching nearer to self-realisation as through this child's innate tendencies are manifested. The instruction has to be active.

Experience: The child's own experience should be, as far as possible, the basis of his education. The task of the teacher is not to stuff his own experience in the educand's mind but to provide the child some insight through his own experience. Teacher's guidance must help the child to get rid of his frustrated and repressed tendencies. Independence and freedom is an essential pre-requisite for experience.

Idealism and Curriculum: The determinants of what should be taught in the schools, according to idealists, are the spiritual development of the child and the preservation and creation of cultural heritage of the human race. Hence, they said that curriculum has to be man-centred not child-centred, ideals and values-centred not freedom-centred, character and morality-centred not expediency centred. Ideals for chiidren should be the objective of curriculum transaction as asserted by Socrates, "Not man but reason is the measure of all things; not individuality but universality, not percepts but concepts and ideals are the norms for all human experience including that of children."

Idealism approaches the problem of curriculum from the domain of ideas rather than from the child and his present or future activities. To them present experience of the child is not very important. What is more important is the experience of the human race as a whole. Hence, the curriculum must reflect the civilisation, the capitalised experience of the race which gives two broad divisions of the curriculum (a) science and (b) humanities. T.P. Nunn (1923) said that a nation's schools should consolidate its spiritual strength, maintain its historic continuity, secure its past achievement and guarantee its future. To achieve this, the idealists stress that the curriculum must reflect those activities that are of greatest and most permanent significance in the wider world, and which are the grand expression of the human spirit. These activities are of two kinds: (a) those that safeguard the conditions and maintain the standards of individual and social life such as the care of health and body, manner, social life, morals and religion, and (b) creative activities. Hence, the curriculum must comprise (i) literature, (ii) art including music, (iii) handicrafts, (iv) science including mathematics, and (v) history.

From psychological point of view the idealists held a belief that the curriculum should reflect (a) what man knows, and (b) what man does or strives to do. Looking from this point of view the idealists curriculum should represent major modes of man's thinking enshrined in language and literature, science, mathematics, history and geography which constitute traditional intellectual studies. In addition to this art, poetry and music which represent man's modes of feelings should also be included in the scheme of studies. Representatives of what man does or strives to do such as major crafts should also form part of the curriculum.

Responsibility of a Teacher

The idealists attach much more importance to the role of the teacher in organizing education for the pupils. They consider educator and the educand two essential parts of an organic plan. They assign to the teacher the most important responsibility of creating a specific kind of environment for the desired development of the pupils. The teacher, as they say, must provide appropriate guidance to pupils, so that they may progress towards perfection and a well-rounded ideal personality. The teacher in the scheme of the idealists, is like a gardener who 'by his art' sees to it that both his cabbages and his roses achieve the finest form possible." The teacher by his efforts must help the pupils, who are developing according to the laws of their respective natures, to attain levels that would otherwise be denied to them. Ross (p. 12.2) says that the relation between the educator and the educand is such that both of them work out in the process of education, their own salvation achieving self-realisation by interaction with one another. Quoting Eucken Ross (p. 124) says that the educator can help the pupil towards true self-realisation by regarding him not as "a particular and exclusively individual being" but as "a being in whom a new and universal life seems to emerge".

Idealism and the Discipline: Just contrary to naturalism and pragmatism idealists stress the value of discipline as part of the educative process. However, this does not mean that pupils' freedom and liberty are not important to them. Freedom to follow any and every inclination of action is, certainly, not acceptable to them. Such freedom to the idealists is license, not true freedom. On the other hand, true freedom is "discipline" which means denying himself this kind of freedom one "becomes master in his own house" "achieving the higher freedom to follow the light that is in him, unhampered by the chains of his lower nature. Self-realisation is the only freedom worthy of the name. That man is free who is conscious of himself as the author of the law which he obeys" (Ross, p. 170). Thus, discipline not the freedom is the cry of the idealists. Ross (p. 171) further says, "if the educand is to succeed in realizing his spiritual possibilities, he must submit to a process of discipline which will enable him to apprehend the great values of life that are stressed by idealists."

Almost all idealists emphasise that the child should be taught to discipline himself and to contribute to the disciplined behaviour of others. Pupils' learning to be self-disciplined is an important educational value for the idealists. Punishment and strict external control to enforce discipline are not advocated. Idealists, on the other hand, recommend influence and impressions left on pupils by the teachers, parents and members of society, to be the most practical methods for this purpose. They emphasise that, for achieving this purpose, the educators themselves should be disciplined; in their own behaviour they must present the highest ideal of self-discipline. They stress that the entire natural, social and spiritual environment in which the child lives should be so fashioned that it should encourage the desire for self-discipline in the child.

Education vs Naturalism

As a philosophy naturalism has influenced the aims and objectives of education apart from discussing and describing its methods, curriculum, and a few other aspects of education. In the field of education, naturalism is neither the positivism of the physical world, nor mechanical positivism or even biological naturalism. It is entirely a different concept which seeks to base education on the experience of the child; and thus is a repudiation of all textbooks teaching. It adopts a scientific posture and seeks to base all education on psychology. Its motto is 'follow nature". Jean Jacques Rousseau (1712-1778) was the most important naturalistic philosopher of education. Another widely known such philosopher was Herbert Spencer (1820-1903) who published his book *Education* in 1861. This book is an excellent exposition of naturalism in education. Like Rousseau he also criticised the methods and curriculum of schools of his times. Rousseau's *negative education is* one concept which is sometimes very much misunderstood. Hence, before discussing other aspects of education, this concept is discussed in the following section:

Negative Dimensions

Rousseau said that the first education of the child ought to be purely negative. This he described as not teaching any virtue, value or do's or truth but shielding the heart of the child from vices and mind from errors. In other words it would mean imparting no education, no information of any kind to the child in the very early years of life. He said, "In childhood the aim of education is not to utilise time but to loose it". Elsewhere he said, "A 12-year old child should know nothing. Attention should be paid to the child only, not to knowledge."

The emphasis in negative education of Rousseau was on strengthening the sense organs and the power of reasoning. Rousseau said, "Nature wants that the child should remain a child before he becomes an adult." Rousseau criticised the system of education of his times saying that it was barbarous as it sacrificed child's present in favour of his uncertain future: It was trying to make the child an adult. He called this education of his times positive education. By negative education he would mean changing the old sequence of positive education by allowing the child to grow in his own way, own way of seeing, thinking and experiencing; and, thus, saving the child from groaning under the dead weight of the old imposed meaningless education. Explaining his new system of education Rousseau said, "give me a 12-year old child who does not know anything. By 15 years of age I will teach him so much as other children read in 15 years of early life."

Thus, negative education is self education. It is the education of sense organs and body. It is negative in the sense that it was a negation of the old system of teaching-learning, negation of classroom learning, negation of teacher's teaching in formal ways, negation of teaching morals and values. About morals Rousseau said that if you are all the time teaching morals to the child you will make him a fool; if you are all the time giving instruction, then child's mind will become useless. Whatever the child learns in the playground is four times more useful than what he learns in the classroom.

Naturalism and Aims of Education: Different philosophers have expressed and, emphasised different aims and objectives of education. Even among the different forms of naturalism, variations are found with regard to educational goals. Mechanical naturalism suggests that education should aim at the efficiency and perfection of the human being. This, however, is not the representative view of naturalism as a whole. Biological naturalism stresses proper adaptation or adjustment of the child to environment. Herbert Spencer described education to be a preparation and a training for complete life. As described by Ross the aim of education according to naturalism seems to be the present and future happiness, pleasure and happiness that are lasting and permanent are more worthwhile in the long run. But, McDougall denied the truth of this hedonistic view of aims of education. According to McDougall the aim of education is the sublimation of the energies of the propensities, the redirection, coordination and harmonious working of the native impulses. As described by McDougall education should enable the individual to attain the goals set for him by nature in ways that have individual and social value.

Naturalists also believe that education should prepare the pupils, equip them and through them the nation for the struggle for existence and survival. From another point of view, education is seen as the process of adjustment to environment, enabling the individual to be in harmony with and well adapted to his surroundings. Health of body and mind both is stressed and the ideal is a well adjusted happy being with no discontent. Bernard Shaw, another naturalist saw education as man's deliberate effort on accelerating the pace of evolution itself. To him the aim of education is the preservation, the handing on and the enhancement of racial gains from one generation to another.

Stagewise aims of education as stressed by Rousseau are:

(1) During the first five years the aim of education should be child's bodily development, development and

strengthening of every part of the body. The child should grow up healthy and strong through complete liberty.

(2) During childhood from 5th to 12th year the education should aim at developing child's sense organs through experience and observation.

(3) During adolescence from 12th to 15th year the child is ready for systematic education. At this stage education should aim at the development of adolescent's personality through hard work, guidance and study. The adolescent should be given knowledge of various kinds.

(4) The youth (15-20 yrs) as pointed out by Rousseau, should be taught moral and social qualities. The aim of education of the youth should be bodily, sensory, mental, social and moral development of the individual.

The aims of education according to Herbert Spencer another naturalistic philosopher of 19th century were as follows:

1. Self-preservation, i.e. preservation of body and mind.
2. Earning a living, i.e. education in all the sciences.
3. Establishing family and upbringing of children
4. Citizenship development
5. Use of leisure time devoted to study and practice of painting, music, sculpture, poetry and also recreation.
6. Moral development

The naturalists of nineteenth and twentieth century, however, believed that education should achieve a synthesis and adjustment between the individual and the society, between man and nature.

Naturalism and Curriculum: What should be taught in the school is the matter to which not all naturalists have the same answer. To have an all-embracing glimpse one has to extract a common factor from various views presented by several naturalists. The extreme form of naturalism emphasises the present experience, activities and interests of the child himself. So, they say, it is these which should determine the content of the curriculum. Their motto is "knowledge for the sake of knowledge."

The latest naturalistic movement in educational theory and practice had been expounded by A.S. Neill in a series of books. He tried to make *Summerhill* a residential school, the happiest school in the world, a place where the child's curriculum is dominated by play to the extent that if the child wishes he can play all the day, where teaching-learning matters little, books are of little value and examinations are hated. The school's curriculum consists of creative arts and activities having pottery room, wood and metal shop where children make whatever they want.

As a system of philosophy, naturalism has been exceptionally susceptible to the development of science. The naturalists attach greater importance to evolutionary theory, empirical teaching and scientific analysis. They recommended physical and social sciences to be taught at every level of education. They also said that language and mathematics being the tools for the learning of science should also be taught. The naturalists recommended that history should also be taught.

Yet, there are found differences and contradictions among the views of the naturalists with regard to the curriculum theory. For example, Comenius wanted the educand to study every subject without making selection, while Locke said every educand should not be required to learn every subject for reasons of individual differences. He emphasised that curriculum should be modified to suit the needs of the individuals. Similarly, Herbert Spencer wanted science to be the nucleus of the curriculum. The arts subjects were given, by him, secondary place in the curriculum. T.H. Huxley, another naturalist attached greater importance to cultural aspects of life in comparison to science.

Thus, it is very difficult to say what exactly the curriculum of the naturalism was. In fact, all eyes of the naturalists were fixed on the child and his freedom. About other aspects of education they only cursorily glanced.

Naturalism and Methods of Education: The naturalists conception of education was that it is the *Child* himself rather than the educator, the school, the book or the curriculum that occupies the central position. Stanley Hall calls this the paidocentric attitude which is said to be the keynote of 20th century movement and is essentially naturalistic. Naturalistic conception of education is based on psychology.

As regard the method of teaching, the naturalists stressed the direct experience of things. As Rousseau said, "give your scholar no verbal lessons; he should be taught by experience alone." "Things rather than words" was the slogan of the naturalists. They said that science should not be taught from readers or by "chalk and talk" lessons; it should rather be learnt by the pupil through his own work in the laboratory or wherever possible through a direct study of the natural phenomena. Similarly, geometry should be taught not by arguments and problems in the textbooks, but by means of actual survey of the school field, playground, etc. In the same way, geography should be taught through school journeys and actual excursions rather than taught from books and maps. Rights and duties of citizens should be taught not through talks but through the organisation of the school as a free natural society where every pupil is encouraged to participate. Students' self-governments should be the methods for teaching these qualities. Thus, most important method of teaching according to naturalists is to leave the child free to learn from nature.

Authoritarianism in teaching, rote learning, book-learning, classroom learning, theoretical teaching were denounced by the naturalists. Child's own experience was considered the most comprehensive book from which the child should learn according to naturalists.

Playway method of learning was very much emphasised by all naturalist philosophers. Artificiality of any kind was very much condemned by them. Informal atmosphere in the class and the school was considered important. Participation of children in extra-curricular activities was emphasised. The naturalists had a conviction that, left to himself the child will himself evolve the method which suits him best.

Naturalism and Discipline: Almost all naturalist philosophers discarded the traditional concept of discipline, which was imposed on the child from outside. Particularly, they opposed the method of physical punishment for they believed that this generated undesirable conflicts and strain in the mind of the child. Rousseau said, "Freedom and not the power is the greatest good. If the child makes a mistake he will get his reward from nature itself and thus he will learn to distinguish between right and wrong through the consequences of his own actions. Thus, discipline through consequences of behaviour was emphasised. This, however, should not be understood to mean giving license of doing anything and every thing to the child. As hinted by Dewey it becomes necessary sometimes to scold the child, to caution him or even to punish him.

Naturalism and the Teacher: Least important is the position of the teacher in the scheme of Naturalistic education. He is barely tolerated. His interference with child's education is deprecated. He is forbidden to resort to any coercive or didactic method. He may not even seek to influence the child. As said by Ross (p. 94) "His place, if any, is behind the scenes, he is an observer of the child's development rather than a giver of information, ideas, ideals and will power or a moulder of character. These the child will forge for himself." The teacher's role according to naturalists, is that of the setter of the stage, the supplier of materials and opportunities, the provider of an ideal environment, the creator of conditions under which natural development of the child may take place. Influenced by naturalism, several systems such as Montessori System, Dalton Plan, Project Method, etc. developed and they all assigned to the teacher a similar status. In Froebel's Kindergarten system the teacher is considered to have the same position which a gardener has in the garden. His only function is to make sure that the plants grow according to their own nature and that their development is not hindered.

Role of Naturalism

Naturalism has made important contributions to education as follows:

Paidocentric Movement: This tendency, as highlighted by John Adams means that it is the child himself rather than the educator, the school, the book on the subjects of study that is in the foreground of the educational picture.

Emphasis upon Psychology: Naturalists' emphasis on child's natural development resulted into psychological studies of the child's nature. Concepts like child's nature, his adjustment to the environment, individual differences with regard to their nature, etc. brought psychology into prominence.

Freedom of the Child: It was emphasised that the child must be given freedom to choose and learn. No predetermined design of growing up should be imposed on him.

Direct Experience of Things: Learning through one's own experience, an important principle of teaching-learning in education was an outgrowth of naturalistic philosophy. Rousseau said, "give your scholar no verbal lesson; he should be taught by experience alone.".

Playway Method: This is an important contribution of the naturalists towards children's growth and learning. The principle emphasises that young children be given enough opportunity to play. Through play activities children develop their creative and constructive powers.

Pragmatism under Influence

The term pragmatism has been derived from the Greek word "Pragma" which means use. Thus, pragmatism means a philosophy which emphasises usefulness of anything, use being the criterion of reality. It was born around 1878 and Charles Pierce was the person who, first, gave its clearcut formulation. This is the doctrine that evaluates any assertion solely by its practical consequences, and its bearing on human interests. It has several forms. It is a philosophy which may be said to be corrective of naturalism and toned down idealism, a midway house between idealism and naturalism. Charles Sanders Pierce (1832-1914), William James (1842-1910), John Dewey (1859-1952) and Bertrand Russell (1872-1970) happen to be some of the eminent philosophers of pragmatism. According to emphasis there are four important forms of pragmatism: (1) Humanistic Pragmatism, (2) Experimental Pragmatism, (3) Nominalistic Pragmatism, (4) Biological Pragmatism. Humanistic Pragmatism asserts that all truths are human truths; Satisfaction of human nature is the criterion of utility. Experimental Pragmatism said that truth is that which can be ascertained by experiment, and is useful in practice. According to nominalistic pragmatism the results of an experiment are always particular and concrete, never general and abstract. According to Biological Pragmatism, the ultimate aim of all knowledge is harmony of man with his environment. It further asserts that the school is a miniature society which prepares the child for future life.

Pragmatism and Aims of Education: The pragmatists do not accept development of eternal spiritual values, discovery of pre-existing reality and universals and teaching of moral standards to pupils, as the aims of education which were the heart of the idealists' scheme of education. They assert that any effort on the part of the educator to prescribe specific goals or to decide the child's purposes for him stultifies true education.

The aims of education as described by most pragmatists are the cultivation of a dynamic, adaptable mind which is resourceful and enterprising in all situations, one which is powerful enough to create values in an unknown future. The pragmatists accept growth or development of the child as the aim of education. But, the forms and standards of these are not pre-existing, not permanent and fixed. They are to be discovered in future. All the aims of education, they say, must be concerned with the present and the future and must be subject to modification.

According to Dewey education as such has no aims; education is an abstract idea. Only persons have aims. And the aims of persons are indefinitely varied differing with different children, changing as children and their teachers grow. Stated aims do more harm than good unless they are taken only as suggestions. Thus, aims of education, for the pragmatists, are mere suggestions, not to be taken literally. Even these aims must possess three elements in order to be useful. These elements are: (i) based on educand's actions and needs, (ii) they must elicit educand's cooperation, (iii) they are specific and temporary, not permanent and general.

American pragmatism, however, is certainly not guilty of neglecting the social aspects of education, as it emphasises that education must aim at realizing democratic values in life. It should instill in the educand a respect for democratic institutions. Kilpatrick said, "The classrooms must become living democracies; in a democracy it is self-directing personalities that we try to build; the kind that can carry forward life even more successfully in a developing world; and the progressive development of a better life for all men is the basis out of which morality and moral conduct arise".

Thus, it may be concluded that the pragmatists favour the democratic ideals of education.

Pragmatism is emphatically humanistic. It also assumes, like Protagoras, the sophist that "man is the measure of all things" and emphasises human purposes and the satisfaction of human wants rather than "one grand purpose towards which the universe is to move".

Pragmatism and Curriculum: The pragmatists favour that curriculum which satisfies the following criteria:

Utility Criterion: This criterion would mean that whatever is put in the curriculum, it should do good to the pupils, it should be of some utility, some use for the child. The knowledge that is provided to the child must help him in his later life in solving his problems and adjusting to his environment. "The school must store up experience that is to stand the child in good stead" (Ross, p.195). The curriculum must include the knowledge and skills that the child requires not only for his present life as a child, but also for his future life as an adult. In view of this criterion it was suggested that the curriculum for the young child of elementary school must include language, arithmetic, health and physical training, history, geography, domestic science for girls, agriculture for boys and training for some vocation.

Reality Criterion: The curriculum should be real, i.e. it should be concerned with the realities of child's nature and of life. Hence, its content should be selected from different activities of real life. The determining principle should be the natural interests of the child.

Child's Experience as the Criterion: This principle implies that the curriculum should be based on child's experience. It means that practical work should constitute an essential ingredient of the curriculum. Teaching through books should be supplemented by programmes which provide actual experience to the child.

Child's Interest as the Criterion: This criterion implies that while selecting material for constructing curriculum, child's own interests must be taken into account. Genetically, children have four kinds of interests-talking, searching or discovering, creative and artistic. Hence, the curriculum should include reading, counting, handicraft, painting, etc.

Purposiveness Criterion: The curriculum, according to pragmatist should be purposive. It means knowledge to be incorporated in the curriculum should be such as it must serve some purpose in the life of the child.

Integration Criterion: This criterion emphasises that the different subjects should not be completely segregated from each other as knowledge is one single whole. This is an important criterion which has been much emphasised by the pragmatists. Knowledge contained under various subjects should be organised in the curriculum in an integrated manner as far as possible.

Pragmatism and the Method: Pragmatic methods of education are based on psychology and sociology subject to the conditions that they give adequate scope for active participation by the educand and also that the method adopted must be dynamic and changeable. The method suggested is the "project method' which is the most characteristic and valuable contribution of the pragmatists. This method focuses on the learning process which involves some practical problem to be solved by the child.

The project as defined by Stevenson as a "problematic act carried to completion in its natural setting". Thomas and Lang define it as "a voluntary undertaking which involves constructive effort or thought and eventuates into objective results." Educational projects may be of individual or social character. Social projects are a sort of "socialised activities" and they are preferred to individual projects. In case of very young children, projects may take the form of play such as playing the roles of the school teacher, or running a family or a post office, etc. At higher levels more complicated activities such as production of a play, or a concert involving elocution, music, literature, craft work, needle work, etc. may be organised in the form of projects. In all subjects such projects may be prepared. But, it is not like this that the whole of teaching may be done through projects. Nor projects can be suggested readymade from outside. It is educator's insight that is needed for successful selection and completion of the project. What is more important is not the project itself but the incidental learning that takes place as a byproduct of the project method.

The great principle involved in project method of teaching is learning by doing, experience-based learning, one's own learning. Pragmatism offers more help in the methods than in the aims of education. The pragmatists assert that education is not so much teaching the child things he ought to know, as encouraging him to learn for himself through experimental creative activity. It is action which is emphasised by them rather than reflection. It was the belief of the pragmatists that true knowledge does not come from books; it, comes from child's own doing. The most general method of education according to pragmatists is putting the child into situation with which he wants to grapple and providing him, at the same time, with the means of dealing with them successfully.

Contribution of Educators

The pragmatists consider the role of the educator important unlike the naturalists who like him to banish from the scene. The educator has to be there in the capacity of an adviser and a guide of the pupils as well as a servant of society. His job is to create in the school an environment which may help in the development of the child's social personality and enable him to become a responsible democratic citizen. Dewey gives the educator so great an importance as he calls him God's representative on earth. But, unlike the idealists he has not to impose himself on pupils, Rather he has to see how best he can help the pupils to grow and develop naturally in conformity with their interests and potentialities. He has to identify most appropriate educational projects, motivate and guide students to carry them out, facilitate and provide essential materials needed for completing the projects. How efficiently, successfully and fruitfully the project method is used depends very much on educator's insight and wisdom. He has to be a model for the pupils.

Pragmatism and Discipline: What is discipline and how discipline should be enforced are discussed in detail by the pragmatists. They stress self-discipline instead of discipline as control and restraint from outside. True discipline comes from child's own inner striving. Strict control imposed by authorities, ultimately, does harm to the child. True discipline is the result of developed social consciousness of the educand. It is this social consciousness which prevents the child from indulging in anti-social activity. Pragmatists believe that freedom is the root of true discipline. Freedom and discipline are inseparable according to them. Self-discipline is the best discipline to them.

For developing self-discipline it is essential that the educand must understand and realise the importance of discipline. This realisation emerges, according to the pragmatists, from educand's engagement and participation in those activities which lead to fulfilment of his social obligations. Through their participation in school activities the educand happens to develop such qualities as responsibility, inspiration, insight, cooperation, compassion, etc. which make him a good, responsible citizen. Blind obedience to rules is no discipline, they say. True discipline is responsible behaviour emerging from the sense of social responsibility. This developed sense leads the educand to be self-disciplined. Dewey maintained that discipline is not the sole function of child's personality; it is very much dependent upon the socio-psychological environment in which the child is placed. Hence, acquiring the habit of being self-disciplined is the consequence of environmental manipulation. School activities may generate the kind of environment needed. Free, happy and purposive activity of the pupil is likely to result in permanent attitudes, initiative and independence. Training in citizenship, character-formation, moral education come from school activities which, ultimately, lead to self-discipline on the part of the child.

Ross (p. 211) said that realism emerged as a reaction against curricula of studies which had become "bookish, sophisticated and abstruse". Realism is the theory that holds that the existence of objects is real. The main tenet of realism is that objects and their qualities are independent of and uninfluenced by the knower and the process of knowing or knowledge. There are four types of realism which are well known. These are: (1) Naive Realism, (2) Neo Realism, (3) Representationism, and (4) Critical Realism. The naive realism emphasises that the object is what it seems to be; its qualities are not affected by knowledge: objects are known directly and they are common for all. Neo Realism says that an object is what it is manifestly seen to be. The total object is not the subject of knowledge, but its aspects are and they are independent of knowledge. Representationism is Lock's theory and implies that objects have their representation in man's thought. Knowledge of the objects is direct in the case of simple thoughts, but indirect in the case of complex thought. Critical Realism was propounded in America at the end of the 19th century. It is critical in nature. This realism says that objects are not what they seem to be. When the object becomes an object of knowledge it is influenced by knowledge. Knowledge of objects may be direct as well as indirect. The relationship between the knower and the known is not direct but takes place through the medium of thought which is the subject matter or knowledge.

In educational theory two forms of realism, *social realism* and *sense realism* emerged after the enthusiasm of Renaissance had been over. The social realism opposed bookish studies and stressed the value of direct studies of men and things. They advocated tours and travels as methods of teaching-learning. Sense realism stressed observation and scientific study of natural phenomena maintaining that all knowledge comes from the senses.

Realism and Aims of Education: It was the oft-repeated cry of realism that education should be made to conform to the social and individual needs of the child so that he may lead a happy and contented life in future. Its primary purpose was to prepare the child for real life, to prepare the child for adult life. An implication of this broad objective was that education should be directed towards a particular calling in life. Thus, preparing pupils for a career in life was one of the most sought for aim of the realists. Besides this the realists asserted that education should impart to the pupils a training that aims at the development in the pupil of certain attributes, habits, skills, sentiments and attitudes of mind as well as the possession and use of knowledge. This should be the training which is suitable for every future occupation, not fit only for one particular calling. The realists emphasised that education should fit a man to perform justly, skillfully and magnanimously all the offices both private and public. In a way it may be concluded that the aim of education as advocated by the realists was to give all round training of the mental faculties. It was emphasised that the main function of education should be to develop the qualities, in the educand, of determination, reason and intelligence so that he may successfully solve the problems of life.

Thus, vocational aims, social development aims and personality development aims of education were mainly advocated and emphasised by the realists.

Realism and Curriculum: As mentioned earlier realism was a reaction against curricula consisting of studies that had become "bookish, sophisticated and abstruse". To escape from this state of affairs some realists, particularly, the sense realists advocated the study of natural phenomena of which the senses could give first-hand knowledge. This resulted into displacing literary, and linguistic work by scientific studies including studies of real things by inductive method. Spencer said that scientific studies are of much greater value than linguistic studies. He further said that the study of surrounding phenomena is more valuable than the study of grammar and lexicons irrespective of the fact whether it is intellectual, moral or religious training. Huxley also vehemently pleaded for incorporating into the school curricula "a complete and thorough scientific culture."

The other subjects constituting elements of curriculum were given a new treatment. History should incorporate contemporary events to be studied in the light of past events. The study of civics should be included in the curriculum. Literature should be taught as a criticism of life. Mathematics must aim at understanding of the world. Application must be emphasised in the case of study of science.

Realism and Educational Method: The social realists stressed the value of direct studies of men and things and hence, recommended that educational tours and travels which would give real experience of varied aspects of life should be an essential component of the curriculum. Sense realists also advocated study of natural phenomena through actual observation and study of real things by the inductive method.

For teaching science, experimentation and application of knowledge were considered important. The realist supported fact-centred or knowledge-centred method of teaching. The inductive method of teaching emphasised teaching to begin with the parts and leading to the whole gradually. This is the same as the main "from part to whole " The realists said that knowledge should be analysed into principles and principles into hypotheses: and facts should be analysed into propositions. Thus, the method of teaching should be analytical and rational.

The realists also advocated that all teaching in the class and outside the class should be child-centred and purposeful. The realistic doctrine stressed that the teacher should think not only about his method of teaching but also about the value and significance of its content.

Education vs Existentialism

All philosophies have grappled with the problem of existence. In that sense all philosophies can be said to be existentialists. Modern existentialism, however, is concerned unlike other philosophers more with the problem of becoming than with the problem of being, more with particulars than universals, more with existence than essence. Kierkegaard is said to be the father of existentialism. The problem before the modern existentialists is "how to become Authentic Being". They emphasise "Action" and "Choice", instead of usual emphasis on knowledge and explanation. "How", not "What" is their main concern.

The contemporary existentialists hold that mans' existence is real in the sense that he is unavoidably a participant in the affairs of the world outside: he can not stand alone: he interacts with man, things and events of the outside world. He can not keep himself away from this bondage and hence his most common despair is not to be able to "choose", not to be able "willingly to be himself'. More serious type of despair is that he has to choose to be another than himself. Hence, they advocate that the aim of man's life ought "to be that which one truly is". Sorer Kierkegaard was a staunch religious person and had great faith in God's existence. Later existentialists, however, did not consider God to be a necessity. Jean Paul Sartre, for example, said that human life has no purpose: existence is ultimate: man should be free to choose: through freedom to choose man becomes himself.

Following are the assumptions of existentialists: (1) centre of existence is man, not the truth. (2) man is unique, being a composite of emotions, feelings, perceptions and thinking, (3) Man makes the universe meaningful. (4) man is not alone in the universe and, hence, the real living person is more important than anything else. (5) man is free capable of shaping his own life and choosing his own destiny.

The existentialists criticise idealism saying that there is nothing like universals and spiritual elements in life. Man's existence as it is and practical problems of life are more important. Truth is not God but existence. They criticised Naturalism also saying that man is completely free and can not be subjected to psycho-biochemical laws of causation operating universally as was advocated by the naturalists. They bitterly criticised scientific philosophy and developments saying that science has abrogated the value of man. It has dehumanised him. Scientific developments and technological progress leading to industrialisation and urbanisation have resulted into deprivation of man's freedom and a threat to his real existence. Everywhere man is found groaning under the weight of numerous constraints. He is not free: There is growing despair in the mind and heart of men. "Life is becoming like a raft on the open sea which is carried hither and thither without any definite direction." Man is the centre of universe and nothing else is equal to it. Man can not be subjected to any law, rule or principle, be it a universal, natural or social or political. Any external encroachment upon man's freedom is unjustified.

The existentialist philosophy asserts that the most serious problem of modern highly complex life is not ideological, but practical, such as how to inspire in man a sense of responsibility and freedom, removing feelings of alienation from the world, society and the self of the man.

Existentialism and Aim of Education: The aim of education according to existentialists, is humanitarian and humanist, which means inner development of man, development of real consciousness, i.e. consciousness of real self. The individual must understand and realise what it means for him "to be", "to exist". Thus, to impart knowledge of self-existence is the fundamental aim of education.

The existentialists emphasise education of the whole man, i.e. development of all aspects of his inner self, his feelings, emotions, thinking, etc. realizing ultimately what he is, what his purpose of living is, i.e. what he has to become. Education should create an environment which is conducive to this kind of realisation. The existentialists want the schools to lay emphasis on subjective knowledge, i.e. inward thinking rather than objective knowledge, the knowledge of subjects. For this reason teaching-learning of literature and arts is emphasised. They want that development of materialistic interests should be discouraged and self-realisation should be encouraged. They, particularly, favour religious and moral education.

Existentialism and Curriculum: Existentialism is averse to study of science subjects which impart objective knowledge because they think that this kind of objective knowledge displaces man away from his own self. Their belief is that science does not help in achieving inner peace and realisation of real self. Yet, they do not expressly say that science should not be taught. They only say that alongwith study of sciences more emphasis should be on arts and literature, ethics and religion. Character and personality development as aims of education can not be achieved without having a synthesis of both sciences and other subjects. At the elementary stage, they say the three Rs. should be mastered. They also say that foreign language, logic, mathematics, and philosophy should be taught at higher level. They prefer liberal education to vocational education.

Existentialism and Discipline: The key idea of existentialism is the freedom of the child, complete freedom.

But, this should not mean giving license to the child to do whatever he wants and is free to do. It only means that the child should not be so restricted as he is constrained to develop his inner self. The existentialists do not talk about discipline. They only talk about child's freedom to choose and grow in self-consciousness.

Existentialism and the Teacher: In the scheme of existentialists' scheme of education the teacher is given an important position to occupy. He is required not only to teach, but also to create an environment in the school which provides freedom to the child and, at the same time, stimulates his thinking. The whole purpose of existentialist education is realisation of inner-self through his free existence. The teacher has an important role to play in this context. He has to guide and counsel the students to this effect apart from teaching the subject. Through the impact of his personality he has to make the students realise what his inner self is, what he has to become and how. This is the most delicate but very important role that the teacher has to play.

2

Philosophy of Education

Various Views

There are three important aspects of human life and development that philosophy is concerned with. They are:

Ontology: This is concerned with the theory of being. It is concerned with the problem/nature of ultimate reality of Me and the end of life. This branch of philosophy is also related to metaphysics which deals with questions beyond physical reality such as who am I? What is the purpose of life? What is God? What is the design of God? and so on.

Epistemology: This is concerned with the theory of knowledge. The aim of knowledge is to find the 'truth'. How can we discern the truth from falsehood? Theory of knowledge deals with various methods of drawing the truth. We shall discuss this branch of philosophy in detail at a later stage.

Axiology: This is concerned with the theory of values. Ethics, aesthetics and logic are the three normative sciences that deal with intrinsic values. Ethics is concerned with moral behaviour or conduct of man. Aesthetics deals with the appreciation of beauty. Logical analysis which deals with reasoning, is of two types—induction and deduction. Axiology that is, theory of values or nature of values.

Philosophy of Knowledge

There are three terms which are inter-related—information, knowledge and wisdom. Information is related to bare facts which form data. It can be quantitative or qualitative or both. Knowledge is a meaningful structure of facts into some relationship. It reflects truth about reality. From Indian point of view, it is named as Vidya which involves—facts about reality and cognitive (mental) changes as well. There is mental growth in the process. Wisdom is the outcome of the process of realisation of reality related to life, universe and relationship between the two. It is based both on information and knowledge. Wisdom is the culmination of human experience and realisation in life.

There are certain questions related to knowledge which need thinking and reflection. They are given below:

(i) Can human knowledge acquire real knowledge?
(ii) To what extent can man acquire the knowledge of the supreme?
(iii) What is truth?
(iv) What is falsehood?
(v) In what manner, the truth can be differentiated from falsehood?
(vi) What is the evidence of knowledge?
(vii) What is doubt?
(viii) What are the sources of knowledge?
(ix) What are the types of knowledge?
(x) What are the theories of knowledge?

These questions are discussed under appropriate places in the ensuring paragraphs. But all these questions have direct bearing on discovery of truth, manufacturing of new knowledge human understanding and construction of curriculum and methods of teaching in education.

The Factors

Theory of knowledge attempts to define knowledge and explain its specific characteristics. The dictionary meaning of knowledge refers to assured belief; that which is known; information, instruction; enlightenment; learning; practical skill.

The nature of knowledge can also be understood with the help of its characteristics which are given below:

(i) Knowledge is a means to reach truth.

(ii) Thought is the raw material for knowledge.

(iii) Language is the vehicle of knowledge.

(iv) Meaning of words, terms, concepts form the foundation of knowledge.

(v) Knowledge is certain.

(vi) It is verifiable.

(vii) Its structure is based on facts and values. Knowledge is a structure of information into a meaningful whole. It is well organised system of facts giving meaning to it.

Different Kinds

General Types of Knowledge: Based on nature and criteria of knowledge, we can understand its types. Broadly speaking knowledge is categorised into the following types:

(a) a priori, and

(b) empirical

A priori knowledge is obtained by simply thinking. Its chief examplications are to be found in 'logic' and 'mathematics'. In order to see that 5 + 7 = 12, we do not need to take five things and seven things, put them together, and then count the total number. We can know what the total number will be simply by thinking. Propositions, maxims and postulates belong to a priori knowledge.

Unlike a priori knowledge, we obtain empirical knowledge by observation of external world (sense-perception) and of ourselves (introspection). This is based on sensations or sensory awareness. Five senses which are the gateways of knowledge, help to know our surroundings and individual self. All scientific knowledge derived through senses and observations belong to empirical knowledge.

According to Indian view, knowledge is of two types:

(a) para vidya

(b) apara vidya

Para vidya is related to physical world (external nature). It can be derived through five senses and reasoning. Apara Vidya is related to other worldliness, spiritual in nature. It is most elevated part of human nature. It is related to self, soul, spirit and God and their relationship.

Specific Types of Knowledge: Specific types of knowledge are determined through 'source' as criterion. The nature of source of knowledge leads to a type of it. Following are the specific types of knowledge:

Authoritative: This knowledge emanates from an authority or a specialist. All research based knowledge can be authoritative knowledge.

Empirical (Perceptual) Knowledge: Knowledge drawn through senses, observations is named as empirical knowledge.

Rational Knowledge: Knowledge drawn from reason is known as rational knowledge. Reasoning and critical thinking paves the way to rational knowledge.

Scientific Knowledge: That knowledge which is gained through observation and experimentation is known as scientific knowledge. It can be verified and tested by others. Here both empirical and rational knowledge are involved. They help in bringing out scientific knowledge.

Pragmatic Knowledge: The knowledge which is useful and of utility is known as pragmatic knowledge. This knowledge is personalised, relativistic. And it is based on observation, experience and experimentation. This knowledge is instrumental in one's adjustment.

Intuitive Knowledge: That knowledge which is subjective and spontaneous in nature is known as intuitive. It is neither related to senses nor related to reason, nor related to personal experience which can be repeated nor it is scientifically verified.

Revealed Knowledge: That knowledge which comes from a divine source and is communicated through man, is known as revealed knowledge. The knowledge contained in scriptures or religious books like Gita, Quran, Bible, Guru Granth Sahib and others is revealed knowledge. This knowledge is classical and universal in nature. It is not modifiable or subject to change.

Special Means

Knowledge is drawn from a variety of sources in human experience. Source of knowledge is related to either human self or cognitive process or external agent. Let us briefly discuss different sources of knowledge.

Revelation: This knowledge is conveyed to man by an external and more powerful agent like God or super-power. Knowledge contained in vedas or world scriptures (religious/ philosophical books) is revealed knowledge. Some super-natural or divine power conveys knowledge to man. Man is the receiver of knowledge. This type of knowledge is accepted as universal knowledge. It is not limited to time and space. It holds good at all times and at all places.

Authority: This type of knowledge comes from an authority or a specialist in a particular field of knowledge. A philosopher, scientist, economist, psychologist, etc. are different examples related to special field of study or knowledge. Whatever is said or written by an expert or specialist is accepted as final and of a standard. A teacher for a learner is an authority. Learner accepts teacher as a great source of knowledge.

Intuition: This type of knowledge is spontaneous and sudden. There is no involvement either of the senses or the mind. A flash of message is experienced or listened by a person. That special experience is realised by man. It comes true. It is said to be revealed but to certain persons having purity of heart and mind. Or all persons at different point of time experience this.

Reason: This refers to mind. The function of mind is to imagine, think, reason out. Reasoning is a mental process in which one draws out inferences or results. To enable a person to reason out there are certain well tried techniques like induction and deduction. Induction is based on inductive thinking that is drawing out a fact or generalising an experience based on different examples (from examples to generalisation) whereas deduction is the reverse of it. Here one moves from generalisation to particular examples (from generalisation to examples). Law of gravitation is generalised while observing fall of all things towards earth. This is an example of inductive reasoning. Solving particular sum based on algebraic formulae is an example of deductive reasoning.

Senses: Knowledge is drawn through five senses. In this regard, senses are the sources of knowledge. All scientific knowledge or empirical (based on senses) is drawn through observation and experiences related to senses. The knowledge drawn through senses is immediate, first hand, real and concrete in nature. We believe when we see with our eyes or hear with our ears, or taste with our tongue or smoothness/roughness with our skin or smell with our nose. More are senses involved in the process, more comprehensive would be the knowledge.

Experimentation: Man draws knowledge while making experiments either under controlled situation (laboratory) or otherwise. This knowledge is verifiable. One can verify or validate facts of knowledge through making experiment. Experiment can be repeated in order to check the reliability of facts. Therefore experimentation is a way or mode of drawing out knowledge. This technique can be availed in physical sciences and other social sciences. These days knowledge is becoming double after every 3/4 years especially in sciences. So there is an explosion of knowledge since the technique of experimentation has been instrumental for drawing new knowledge.

Basic Intelligence

Different schools of philosophy like Naturalism, Idealism and Pragmatism paved different ways to discover truth. They have enabled us to form new concepts, terms, ideas, thoughts leading to new structures of knowledge. Most popular theories of truth are as:

Correspondence Theory: This theory is based on the assumption that our ideas and thoughts have certain external objects or reality with which they correspond. Without external reality, ideas or thoughts do not have then existence. Therefore, every concrete object does have an idea or a thought about it. There is specific relationship between the two identities, i.e. object and idea or thought.

Characteristics of this theory are listed below:

- — Correspondence is a matter of external relations.
- — Truth is objective and specific fact having external basis.
- — Relation is pre-existent to the search for it.
- — Observer/subject does not add or subtract anything of his own.
- — Truth is researchable or verifiable at any point of time.
- — Truth exists in relation to object only. Schools of Naturalism and Realism are based on the theory of correspondence in respect of truth and knowledge.

Coherence Theory: This theory is based on the assumption that ideas or thoughts are interrelated and consistent. There is cohesiveness, logical connection and relatedness in ideas. Hence truth and knowledge are coherent in nature. It is believed that criterion of truth is more than correspondence to external reality as in the case of correspondence theory.

Characteristics of coherence theory are listed below:

— Coherence theory is a statement of test of truth.

— Consistency is the quality of this theory.

— There is logical interrelation between facts revealing the truth.

— There is hierarchy and structure resulting to a form of truth.

School of Idealism and constitutionalism are based on the theory of coherence in respect of truth and knowledge.

Instrumental Theory or Pragmatic Theory of Truth: This theory is based on the assumption of utility and usefulness. That knowledge is true which enables a person to know about the situation and adjust with it. This personal adjustment is the main criterion.

Characteristics of this theory are listed below:

— Truth is revealed through one's personal experience.

— Truth has no relationship with external objective reality.

— Experience is personal.

— Experience acts/works as an instrument for personal adjustment.

School of Pragmatism or Instrumentalism or Experimentalism is based on instrumental theory in respect of truth and knowledge.

Theories of truth and knowledge work as foundation to work out a scheme of acquiring knowledge. A theory is an approach as how to receive it, how to process it, how to assimilate it as part of human experience and how to make it part of curriculum at institutional level for imparting knowledge.

Basis of Intelligence

Knowledge is acquired at three stages of human experience while involving one aspect or component which predominates at that stage. These stages are:

(i) Sensory knowledge based on senses.

(ii) Rational knowledge based on reasoning and logical thinking.

(iii) Spiritual knowledge based on divine wisdom revelation and intuition.

Senses are the primary means to receive knowledge. This knowledge is known as perceptual or empirical. One draws knowledge through concrete objects or natural phenomena. It leads to formation of impressions, perceptions and sensory awareness about physical world.

Rational knowledge is of higher level than that of sensory knowledge. Here mind being at the centre-stage, rational thinking and reasoning are the means to attain this knowledge. Formation of ideas and attainment of concepts are the building material for critical thinking and awareness.

Spiritual knowledge is of highest order than the first two, that is, sensory and rational knowledge. Here spirit is at the centre—stage and self-knowledge, self-awareness, self-transformation and self-realisation are the end points. Divine wisdom is based on spiritual consciousness and awareness of man.

Methods of acquiring knowledge are worked out at three levels as per the stage of development and evolution of human experience. Besides instruction in classroom can be designed and programmed as per the nature and the level of knowledge by teachers and curriculum framers.

Attaining Knowledge

Based on senses, reason and spirit for attaining knowledge, philosophers and educationists have brought out specific methods. We discuss below these methods of acquiring knowledge:

Appeal to Authority: The knowledge which is attained while having confidence in authority or a specialist in a particular field of knowledge, is known as authoritative knowledge. This method of acquiring knowledge is related to the special fields of knowledge and the specialists working in those fields. That body of knowledge is accepted as true knowledge. One believes and has faith in it. In critical situations with regard to right knowledge, we refer to it.

Appeal to Senses: In this case, senses are the main sources of knowledge. One's awareness about immediate surroundings and of self takes place through senses. In this method, the intake of knowledge can be coloured by environmental factors and physical state of the body. Therefore the reliability of knowledge in this method, depends upon certain extrinsic/ external factors, originating from the environment.

Appeal to Observation and Related Processes: In this case, there are four sub-processes of attaining knowledge. These sub-processes which enable us to acquire knowledge are:

- *Observation:* It can be external or internal.
- It can also be natural observation or with the help of scientific instruments.
- *Explanation*: Here facts of knowledge are elaborated in a logical manner. Knowledge is accepted in a cohesive order.
- *Prediction*: This process is related to the principle of cause and effect relationship. Consequences are fore told or

predicted while conceptualising the causal factors. Both cause and effect need to be understood in a specific relationship.

— *Control*: In an experiments, the element of control plays a vital role. There are certain factors or variables which a scientist supposed to be controlled. In this case the ensuing results are precisely and accurately filtered out because of effective control on factors or variables.

All the four sub-processes contribute to draw a systematic body of facts or knowledge. They are mostly followed in natural, behavioural and social sciences.

Inductive and Deductive Methods: In case of inductive method one starts with particular cases or examples. And he tries to arrive at certain conclusion which is known as generalisation. This further leads to formulate a law or principle. Whereas in case of deductive method, one starts with generalisation or rule and comes to particular examples. Therefore knowledge is gathered both inductively and deductively. These methods are more applicable in teaching of logic, mathematics and sciences.

Institution: The elements which help to attain knowledge in intuitive method are preparation, incubation, inspiration and illumination. Each element is contributive to reach a significant knowledge. These elements bring a structural change in cognition (mental faculties).

Concentration and Meditation: Concentration is an activity of mind in which mental energy is focused with the help of physical aid like candle light flame or object. In case of meditation, one concentrates for a longer time on any idea or image or Mantra. Both concentration and meditation are the foundation of attaining knowledge. They empower the individual to conceptualise, infer and make link of the facts of knowledge in leading to a meaningful whole.

Problem Solving: The steps involved in the process of problem solving lead to a solution. This solution of a problem becomes part of knowledge. All the solutions of such problems or learnings form a significant part of knowledge. Therefore problem solving is an effective tool to acquire new knowledge.

The Impacts

A variety of methods of instruction have been worked out in education and they are put to practice while taking into cognizance the level and stage of child's experience. Such methods of instruction have corresponding relationship with specific type, source and method of acquiring knowledge. These methods are discussed below:

Methods of Instruction Related to Senses: Playway methods at early stage of schooling are developed on multiple sensory involvement. Child gathers knowledge of surrounding world through his five senses. He makes a structure of truth in the background of his personal awareness. Interacting with outside world and objects in the form of physical activities, modes of play and types of works, enable the child to draw knowledge. Maxims of instruction like concrete to abstract, hold good to draw concepts and understandings.

Methods Related to Reason: There are certain methods of instruction which seem to help the learner to draw knowledge and form concepts. These methods empower the mind. New ideas are reasoned out through inductive, deductive and other logical approaches.

Ideas, thoughts and new awareness are made while introducing certain ways and techniques based on reasoning and reflective thinking. Intellectual involvement, discussions, debates, brain storming, quiz, mental teasers, reflections are some of the examples of this category.

Methods Related to Spirit: Spirit/soul is the third level of human experience. Apart from sense and reason, there is another level or stage where spirit is involved. Knowledge related to spirit and divinity is realised through certain methods alongwith the growth of senses and mind. One is in a position to gather knowledge related to self and his inner being. This is the highest stage of one's experience and knowledge. Here intuition, revelations and illuminations work very effectively. A teacher should often take the learner to this stage of experience during his teaching.

Silent sitting, meditation, reading philosophical books and scriptures, devotional music, poems, classical and folk dances, discourses on how to live life, are some of the ways to reach spiritual wisdom and knowledge. Perhaps this is the end of education in educational institutions which needs to be practised.

Future Problems

Nowadays there is an explosion of knowledge due to unprecedented advancements in the fields of science and technology. These advancements have resulted into making a successful trip even to the moon. Old ideas are gradually changing giving place to new ones. Values and traditions are in the process of transformation. New knowledge has been discovered in each subject. Man's mind is disturbed with the question whether he should teach the new knowledge or the old. Should we teach the old for helping the student to learn the new? How should we present the old and new knowledge in an interconnected manner? What type of knowledge should be imparted at a particular stage? How should the knowledge given at the various stages of education be made as one connected whole? What methods should be adopted to facilitate the achievement of the objectives of teaching? Under such a situation only that person can successfully give solutions to these issues who is thoroughly conversant with the knowledge we want to impart. This ever increasing store of knowledge has created following problems for education:

1. What should we teach?
2. What is the purpose of teaching?
3. When should we teach?
4. How should we teach?

Rulings and Regulations

Structure of Knowledge: In the methods of teaching today one finds emphasis on acquainting the student with the structure of knowledge and not to impart informations. This means that the student should be helped to grasp the structure of subject in such a way as to enable him to understand things related to it in a meaningful context. The student has to be taught how things are related. If he understands the inter-relationship between things, he will be able to grasp many other relevant things in a meaningful manner.

Readiness for Learning: Today it is believed that any subject may be taught at any stage of education. The basic idea is that the fundamental principles of any subject may be taught in some form to a child of any age group. Many scientists, technicians and machinists could be produced in USSR through the theory of learning by conditioned response. This could be possible by creating a readiness in the individual for learning. Thus, education in USSR may be as an example of readiness for learning.

Use of Intuitive Analytical Method: Intuition is the method through which one reaches a relevant conclusion without analysing the situation. After reaching the conclusion one verifies it by analysis. Training should be given in hunches for developing intuition. Intuition is important in intellectual work, as well as in daily work. When a person tries to think intuitively and reach a possible conclusion, this habit refers to his intuitive ability. He at once grasps the intricacies of a situation and is able to go ahead in his chosen sphere of activity. Several great scientists and great persons base their thinking process on intuition in their respective fields. Intuition may be received in any mental activity higher or lower. The difference being only of the degree and not of the kind. Hence, training should be given in intuition in every school.

Motivation: In order to enable the student to learn, he must be motivated to learn. This motive may be a desire to learn or to win some reward or to get promotion to another higher class. The external incentives, like reward and promotion is not always helpful in stimulating the child to learn. One should depend upon the principles of child psychology, teaching methods and reorganizing the curriculum in an integrated manner for creating motivation in the child.

Use of Teaching Aids: A number of teaching aids have been developed these days. In order to be more effective, the teacher is now expected to select a proper teaching aid and use it relevantly. As there are so many aids to teach, the teacher naturally feels a problem of selecting the right one out of many before him.

Structure of Knowledge: A man studies not only for self-pleasure but also to benefit himself in such a way that he may use the earned knowledge in future for his betterment. In the process of learning he may acquire many such skills by virtue of which he may do many identical things later. In the same way through his studies he learnt many things and acquire many attitudes. These learnt things and attitudes are used later in various situations of life. The main purpose of various methods of education is to help the students to acquire certain useful principles of work, desirable attitudes and modes of good behaviour according to the accepted social norms. This will be achieved only when he acquires a grip over the structure of knowledge. Therefore, the major emphasis should be on helping the student to enter into the basic structural elements of the subject placed before him to learn. This creates the following two main problems before the teacher:

(i) How to reorganise the curriculum of the basic subjects in such a manner as to help the student to acquire the basic ideas effectively in order to develop the desired attitudes which may work as propellers of good behaviour.

(ii) The second problem is how to tailor the curriculum to suit each and every stage of education.

In order to solve in the above problems, the experts in the various subjects should sit together and reorganise the curriculum for the primary and secondary levels. These experts should be helped by experienced teachers of various primary and secondary classes. Experienced authors, film-producers and other experts may also be consulted in this work. Such a procedure has been followed in many advanced countries in the reorganising of the curriculum in mathematics, natural sciences, social sciences and literature.

When the general principles of a subject are learnt by a student he should be able to arrange the learnt things in a systematic and meaningful manner in his mind so that he may use the same when an occasion arises.

Readiness to Learning: It is assumed that any subject may be taught to any child at any stage of his development. There are three following bases of this assumption:

The Process of Intellectual Development of the Child: In his process of development the child has his own characteristic way of viewing the world. He understands the world in his own way. Hence, a subject should be taught to the child according to his point of view.

The teacher has not to teach a subject to the child according to the adult point of view. According to the demands of the development of the child, the subject-matter may be made more inclusive and comprehensive gradually. At first the child is better able to understand concrete things through the help of concrete things or concrete examples. This is able to comprehend abstract ideas. At first the child absorbs only those ideas which are presented before him through some concrete instances.

The Psychology of Learning: There are three mental processes during the course of learning: (a) acquisition of knowledge or ideas, (b) transformation of the learnt knowledge of ideas in which the learner tries to arrange the learnt things in his mind in his own way. In this transformation he analyses the inherent points and introduces such changes in the same way which may be helpful to him later, (c) evaluation about whether the transformation made is such as to fulfil teaching purpose. All these three processes, acquisition, transformation and evaluation are involved in learning of any subject.

The Notion of Spiral Curriculum: In the spiral curriculum the contents of a certain subject-matter is arranged in such a logical and challenging manner that the learner is propelled to learn further about the subject once learnt. In this process even a small child is taught such things which will be suitable even for an adult to learn. Thus, through the spiral curriculum the child is helped to absorb many such basic and structural ideas which are challenging even to an adult. Therefore, those problems, principles, ideas and values should be incorporated in the spiral curriculum which the society consider suitable for adults to imbibe. As the problems, ideas and values prevailing in society are undergoing constant transformation the spiral curriculum should be continually changed and modified according to explicit or implicit demands of the society.

Intuitional Method: When one is working on a problem for a long time thinking about its solution, all of a sudden he gets the solution, though he has yet to provide a proof for it. This method of finding a sudden solution is a result of intuitional thinking. Hence, it is called intuitional method. L-analytical thinking one proceeds step by step and he is conscious of this step all the time. The operations and informations involved in the analytical thinking are deliberately chosen and decided upon. It may also involve deductive reasoning. In contrast to this procedure of analytical thinking, the intuitive thinking is not well-defined. It implies implicit perception of the total problem. The answer arrived at by intuitive thinking may be right or wrong, but the thinker cannot justify his conclusion immediately. Intuitive thinking is possible only if the thinker is familiar with the domain of knowledge and its structure. Due to this familiarity with the domain and structure of knowledge the thinker is able to leap about, skip steps and employ short cuts. Through intuitive thinking an individual may get a correct solution which he can never obtain by analytical method. But once the solution is obtained through intuition, the same must be checked and verified through analysis, induction and deduction. An intuitive thinker may discover or invent problems, but it is analysis that gives proper form to these problems. But unfortunately the formalism of the school atmosphere does not recognise the importance of intuition. As a result intuition appears to be devalued in the school. Hence, the teacher in the school must devise methods for developing intuitive thinking in his students. For this the curriculum has to be carefully reorganised.

How to Develop Intuitive Thinking: After giving an answer through his intuition, the teacher should subject his answer to critical analysis to be made by his students. This procedure shall encourage the students to do their own intuitive thinking at times. It will energise the students and will bring life in the monotonous atmosphere of the class. The teacher must not analyse everything for his students rather the analysis should be made by the students themselves. One should remember that the emphasis in teaching or helping the students to grasp the structure or connectedness of knowledge will immensely facilitate intuitive thinking because the comprehension of structure will help the student to increase his effectiveness in grasping problems intuitively. Self-confidence and courage should be developed because effective intuitive thinking may be developed in the student on the basis of these traits. For the development of intuitive thinking the intuitive thinker must never feel shy if he makes mistakes in his intuitive answers. On the contrary, he should be willing to make honest mistakes in his endeavour to find out solutions to problems.

Motivation for Learning: Today every human society is exposed to continual changes. After the World War II, these changes have been revolutionary. The various countries are afraid of each other. There is an arms race. The world is divided in aligned and non-aligned groups, big and small powers, developed, developing and underdeveloped countries. The politicians categorise the human race into three major groups—first world, second world and third world. Each country of the world is facing political, cultural or social crises. There has been the impact of automatic machines, new sources of energy and space investigations. Never was the human society so much mechanised. Never was it so near to annihilation which is dependent on the calculation of some super power. This state of affairs has revolutionised the very concept of the school offerings. People no more interested only in intellectual, cultural and physical activities in schools.

They are now emphasising the teaching of science and technical subjects. Students offer these subjects, because these assure them positions in some technical establishments. More brilliant students are encouraged to offer science or technical subject whether or not he has an aptitude for the same. This trend has brought in many students who are not deserving on intrinsic merits study science and technical subjects. Many students are being neglected.

The children whose growth is delayed or who are not able to complete their formal education because of adverse circumstances are totally neglected. One finds a new current of pursuit of excellence which has divided children into two classes—brilliant and dull. In every country there is a search of science talent and there is a test for it on in all country basis. National scholarships are being awarded to able students in science and technical subjects. This has led to the neglect of the studies of humanities and social sciences. It appears that a day will come, when there will be dearth of learned persons and really efficient teachers in these areas. Hence, the cultural traditions appear to be exposed to great harm.

Thus, it is necessary to reorganise the curriculum of humanities, social sciences and literature in the same manner in which it is being done for science and technical subjects. Necessary reforms should be introduced in the examination system so that one may be able to classify students of various abilities on a scientific basis. If sciences and technical subjects are to be saved from unhealthy competitive spirit and over-importance, the Government must pay the same attention to the studies of humanities and social sciences. Incentive for learning should be made more comprehensive. Incentives should be energised by making the ability the basis of deservingness. Education should be saved from the ill effects of unhealthy competition.

Aids of Teaching: Today one should find a number of aids to teaching and learning. Some of these enrich the students' experiences. Some help them to understand the basic structure of the curriculum. The various aids to teaching may be grouped into the following four categories:

(i) Devices of Vicarious Experiences;

(ii) Model Devices;

(iii) Dramatizing Devices; and

(iv) Automatizing Devices.

Devices of Vicarious Experiences: These include films, television, micro-photographic films, filmstrips, sound recording and the like which are ordinarily employed Through these devices students are generally given such matters which are outside the prescribed courses. They are given experience pertaining to certain events directly. These devices enrich the experiences of the students and they also bring life in the educational procedure.

Model Devices: Through these the student grasps the fundamentals of an event or a certain context. These modes are generally shown as laboratory exercises. Certain wooden blocks have been devised for this purpose. Pictures and charts are also used for helping students to understand the basic structure.

Dramatizing Devices: These devices help the student in identifying a certain idea or phenomenon more closely. Some historical event or the life pattern of some great men may be dramatised. In the process of teaching the teacher himself may dramatise certain aspects of the subject-matter or may read out certain portions of the textbook in a dramatic tone. This may bring life in the classroom. It may also help the student to grasp the essentials in a better way.

Automatising Devices: These include machines to aid in teaching. Through these machines certain problems are presented in a systematic manner. Alternative answers are also associated with the problems. The student is required to select the correct answer. With the selection the machine begins to respond. If the selected answer is correct, the machine moves on further and presents another problem or exercise. The exercises for the machines are so arranged that the student encounters both easy and difficult ones. So if he fails in case of difficult exercises, in an easier exercise he succeeds immediately. Therefore, he is not discouraged.

Part-II
The Educationists

3

Dayanand Saraswati

The Position

Mulshankar who came to be later known as Swami Dayanand was born at Tankara (Gujarat) in 1824. He was born of very devout Brahmin parents. He was brought up on strict orthodox lines. When he was fourteen years of age, his father asked him to keep a complete fast on the Shivratri day and to observe an all night vigil in honour of Lord Shiva. As Mulshankar sat through the night, in front of the idol (of Siva), making many efforts to keep himself awake, a serious doubt crept into his mind. Could the stone image before him really be the great God of Kailash? The immediate cause was the sight of mice running freely on the idol and taking away the offerings placed before it. He sought explanations for this but the explanations failed to satisfy him and he vowed not to visit a temple again for worship. These events also aroused in him a keen desire in his mind to devote himself to search the solution of great mysteries of life. He studied Sanskrit to know the Vedas. The parents were worried about him. They tried to marry Mulshankar. He ran away from home. The year was 1845.

Dayanand wandered for fifteen years all over India, visited all places of religious interest. He gave himself to the study of Vedanta philosophy and the practice of Yoga under very able teachers. He became adept in Yoga.

After wandering for fifteen years from place to place, during which he acquired a deep insight into the various aspects of Hinduism, he came to Mathura where he became the disciple of Swami Virjanand, a profound scholar of Sanskrit language and a severe critic of the popular Hinduism of the day. It was under the guidance of Swami Virjanand that the future programme of Dayanand took definite shape.

He founded Arya Samaj in 1875—a movement to reform dogmatic Hinduism. He denounced idolatry as having no sanction in the Vedas and preached the worship of one God.

It was on 30th October (Diwali) 1883 that he died at Ajmer. He had been poisoned (glass in milk) by his trusted cook whom he pardoned and even gave money to escape to a place where the police should not catch him. Dayanand gave to us Satyarth Prakash.

We shall examine the philosophy of Dayanand in detail:

The Thinking

Faith in Vedic Truth and Righteousness: The philosophy of Swami Dayanand stands on Vedas. According to him, time-old wisdom contained in Vedas holds key to all our social and religious problems. To him, the Vedas are the source of all knowledge and this knowledge is final. And it is these Vedas which teach one one's character or righteous living.

Concept of Religion: Swami Dayanand regarded religion as the true conduct of life. Equitable dealings, the acceptance of truth and the rejection of untruth constitute the true conduct of life, or religion, and the reverse of this is irreligion. The religion of Dayanand was a simple affair. It was not idol worship but meditation.

Also Swami Dayanand believed that reason and faith are

not hostile to each other. Of course, in many ways faith goes beyond reason, but no belief is to be accepted if it contradicts the findings of the reason. He wanted that religion should be free from irrational beliefs and superstitions. The repudiation of superstition in all its forms found the negative aspect of his teaching on religion. Many sensitive people criticise him for having exposed the superstitions inherent in all religions and thereby wounding the religious susceptibilities of his followers.

To Dayanand, all men were equal. He made no distinction between the followers of Hinduism. Christianity and Islam and other religions. But he wanted all irrational beliefs in religions to go so that the people realise the priceless gem of religion.

Prayer and meditation are best means of worship. Swami Dayanand prepared a Sandhya or a collection of Vedic verses for daily worship for he laid a great emphasis on the daily need of worship. He was against idol worship, to repeat.

Concept of God: The Swami held that the ancient Aryans accepted the oneness of God, and that the worship of numerous Gods and Goddesses were introduced in later time. There are many verses in the Vedas, which clearly teach the oneness of God. "They call him Indra, Mitra, Varuna, Agni and He is the heavenly, noble winged Gurutman (i.e. the Sun). He is one, sages call him by various names."

> "He watches over creatures, those that breathe and
> those that breathe not. He is the sole, the one alone.
> In Him all gods become one".
>
> (Atharva Veda, XIII, 4. 14-21)

Dr. Radhakrishnan and Sri Aurobindo fully support the teachings of Dayanand. Thus Dayanand believed in the oneness of God. God is pure universal spirit. God has no form. Swami Dayanand holds that God permits the whole universe. He creates, sustains, and dissolves the universe.

Belief in Yoga: Dayanand believed that Yogic exercises were a must for life. These exercises are of great help in the process of mind transformation and are a part and parcel of religious Sadhana. These exercises should be invariably accompanied by disinterested performance of one's daily duties, of the cultivation of a pure, loving and compassionate heart.

Transmigration of Soul: According to Swami Dayanand attainment of moksha (or salvation)—which is the ultimate desire of all mortals is not an easy process and one may have to have pass through a number of births before one reaches the final goal of life. Thus Swamiji believed in the doctrine of transmigration of soul. It is a common belief with Hindus. The death of body does not mean the end of the soul and this is a belief which is also held by followers of Christianity and Islam but in a different sense. While Hindus believe that each soul passes through a succession of births till it qualifies for emancipation, the Christians or Muslims believe that each soul appears only once in the world and after death it remains in a state of quiescence till it is revived on the day of judgement. To Hindus this view does not appeal much.

The doctrine of transmigration goes alongwith the law of Karma which is an application of the universal law of causation in the domain of mind and consciousness.

The doctrine of transmigration explains, in more or less satisfactory manner, the existence of inequalities amongst living beings. Each one gets in the next birth what he deserves, as a result of his karma or action in the present life Soul thus is immortal and migrates.

Equal Rights for All: (Social and Political Philosophy):

Specific Characteristics

(i) While an individual should make every effort to make himself perfect physically, economically and spiritually, he should at the same time bend his energies to bring out the development of other members of the society. It is highly essential to develop social sense of human beings. Swami Dayanand says, "A person should not remain satisfied. He should seek good in the good of all others."

(ii) Swami Dayanand wants individuals to carry out their duties.

(iii) Swami Dayanand denounces caste system.

(iv) Dayanand believed in the equality of man. In the sight of the God, all persons are equal, and colour, community or sex makes no difference. And he gave equality to woman also. Educational opportunities were open to both boys and girls. Swami Dayanand advocated equal rights for men and women in all matters, in education and in marriage and in the holding of property. He was in favour of inter-caste, international marriages. Widow remarriage is also advocated by him. All respect must be given to women.

(v) State should maintain law and order. It should also look after the economic welfare of the individual.

(vi) He wanted men and women to observe Brahmacharya. He fixed age limits. For men; it was 25 years and for women, it was 16 years. The advantages of brahmacharya are known to us all.

Arya Samaj: He wanted to establish Arya Samaj with aims, firstly to protect Hinduism from the attacks of Islam and Christianity, and secondly, to reform the perverted Hinduism of Puranic age by reviving the original Hinduism as propounded in the Veda. Creation of Arya Samaj was a landmark in the socio-cultural history of India.

Ideas and Nations

Swamiji attached great value to the education of the people. The D.A.V. movement was his personal initiation. Certain basic ideas in his educational thought and practice can be referred as under:

Education as a Continuous Process: Dayanand holds that education begins in the mother's womb. During the whole period of pregnancy the mother has to be on her guard against all sorts of distractions and evil effects. It continues even in the later life. Dayanand has given details how education has to be imparted in accordance with each period of the child's physical and mental growth.

Compulsory Education: Being an Idealist, Dayanand believed in the compulsory education for all. Gandhi seems to have borrowed this principle from Dayanand. State and society should make it compulsory for all (both boys and girls). There should be no discrimination in educational institutions. All should be treated on equal footing. Social regeneration is only possible through universal and compulsory education.

Aims of Education: Development of Character or moral development. Dayanand advocated righteous life as the sole aim of life. Thus the main aim of education was moral aim. He advocated the fostering of ethical and moral virtues among the students. He believed that a true and sound system of education should have character formation as its main objective. Children should always speak the truth. In the matter of dress and diet also they should so conduct themselves as to gain in health, strength, general behaviour and knowledge.

The Curriculum: Dayanand emphasises the study of Vedas and allied Sanskrit literature. He says "..........those who read the Vedas do righteous deeds, practise Yoga and thereby know God, stabilize themselves in God and attain the highest happiness of salvation."

Syllabi of Study

1. Panini's Phonetics—to be taught for correct pronunciation.
2. Science of knowledge and Grammar—to be taught for 3 years.

3. Nighantu and Nikarata (Study of Vedic Vocabulary and Philosophy) duration 6 to 8 months.
4. Prosody (Rules governing poetry) duration 4 months.
5. Manusmriti, Vidurniti, and Mahabharata for one year.
6. Six Shastras (Philosophy) for 2 years.
7. Four Upvedas—for two years.
8. Jyotish-Shastra (Astronomy)—for two years.

Besides, he prescribed practical religious training, Sandhyopasana Yajna and Homa (Havana), etc.

Dayanand also favoured science and technology. He, however, prescribed a separate curriculum for women.

Dayanand did not make mention of any special method of teaching. But on the basis of his philosophy and educational principles, he seems to be in favour of discussion and lecture methods. Discipline is an essential element in the educational programme of Dayanand.

Teacher: Dayanand gave an important place to teachers. There should be male teachers for boys' school and female teachers for women institutions. Teachers must be men of high character and sound ideals. There should be close relationship between the teacher and the taught. The most important influence in the school should be the personality of the teacher—Guru. He must be dedicated to his profession.

Views about Women Education: As Dayanand advocated equal rights for women, he was strongly in favour of women education. He quoted the Vedas where women enjoyed equal right with men and were qualified for higher learning. Dayanand recommended for girls Grammar, Dharma, Medical Sciences and practical arts. The main sphere of duty of women is home. Thus he is the first Indian reformer who vehemently pleaded for their education.

The Evaluation

Primarily Dayanand was a socio-political reformer. He was a Sanyasi, a Brahmachari, a scholar and an educationist. In his quest to regenerate the society, he established the Arya Samaj, and advocated certain principles of education which became the guidelines for various institutions.

It can be said that Dayanand was not an educationist to be compared with Froebel, and Dewey as he did not give us any special system of education. He was an idealist and as an idealist, his educational principles were unpracticable like all other idealists. His emphasis on moral values, character development and democratic approach to education are the chief contributions to education.

4

Vivekanand

"Rooted in the past and full pride in India's prestige, Vivekanand was yet modern in his approach to life's problems and was a kind of a bridge between the past of India and her present. His mission was the service of mankind through social service, mass education, religious revival and social awakening through education." (Jawahar Lal Nehru). His call to the youth was "Arise, Awake, Rest not till the goal is achieved". Such was the dynamic impact of Vivekanand's personality and views, especially educational.

Personal Information

Swami Vivekanand was born in 1883 in a Kshatriya family in Calcutta. His real name was Narendra Nath Dutta. His father Shri Vishnu Nath Dutta was an advocate at Calcutta High Court. The atmosphere in his family was religious. Hence, from early childhood he was initiated into religious ceremonies with the result that he developed a keen eagerness for the study of religious scriptures. He possessed a keen intelligence. When he was five years of age, he was sent to a school. There he studied History and Literature as well as Indian philosophical traditions, and after becoming well-versed in these he studied in detail the Western Literature and Philosophy. Herbert Spencer and John Stuart Mill were his favourite philosophers and Wordsworth was his favourite poet. In this way, from early childhood Narendra Nath developed a sound and handsome physique and being endowed with a keen and penetrating intellect and pleasing art of conversation, he gained popularity very soon. Once his Headmaster Heasty said about him. "I have travelled far and wide, but I have not met such an intelligent, gifted and scholarly student even in German Universities". One day Heasty introduced him to Ram Krishna Paramhansa. Swami Rama Krishna had a profound impact upon Narendra Nath. Narendra Nath remained in close contact with Swami Ram Krishan Paramhans for more than six years and after satisfying Swamiji with his erudite scholarship and intense devotion to spiritual values, he got initiated into the saintly order and came to be known as Swami Vivekanand. In 1896 Rama Krishna Paramhans died. Swami Vivekanand established Ram Krishna mission in the sacred memory of his Guru and preached throughout his life in Asia, Europe, England and America the teachings of Vedanta as delivered by his Guru, Paramhans. He also toured extensively and by his untiring efforts established branches of Ram Krishan Mission throughout the world. By his organisational abilities and far-sight he could translate into practice the teachings of ancient Vedantic philosophy as interpreted and preached by his Guru. He showed the way that the ancient philosophy of Vedanta could successfully meet the various problems which the national life of India was facing in modern times. In short, Swami Vivekanand, by synthesising the idealistic philosophy of the west and creative philosophy of the ancient Hindu Dharma, brought glory and greatness to the Hindu thought and way of living. He died in 1902.

The Philosophy

1. Only study of books is not education.
2. Knowledge lies hidden in the mind of man. He uncovers and develops it by his own efforts.

3. Concentration is the key to all knowledge. For this, Brahmacharya is very essential.
4. Purity of thought, speech and deed is self-discipline.
5. Education should develop a child physically, mentally and spiritually.
6. Education should foster spiritual faith, devotion and self-surrender in the individual and should cause full development through service and sacrifice.
7. Education should develop character, mental power, intelligence and self-confidence coupled with self-reliance.
8. Religious education should be imparted by example.
9. No sex differences in the content of education.
10. Women should specially be imparted religious education.
11. Mass education schemes should be formulated and launched.
12. Provision for technical education.
13. Teacher to be a friend, philosopher and guide.
14. Closer relationship between teacher and students.
15. All subjects which promise the physical and spiritual advancement of a child, should be included in the curriculum.

Meaning of Education: "Education is the manifestation of perfection already in man".

Aims and Objectives

The Aim of Reaching Perfection: The prime aim of education is to achieve fullness of perfection already present in a child. According to Swamiji, all material and spiritual knowledge is already present in man covered by a curtain of ignorance. Education should tear off that veil so that the knowledge shines forth as an illuminating torch to enliven all the corners by and by. This is meant by achieving fullness of the latent perfection.

Physical and Mental Development Aim: The second aim of education is the physical and mental development of the child so that the child of today, after studying Gita, is able to promote national growth and advancement as a fearless and physically well-developed citizen of tomorrow. Stressing the mental development of the child, Swamiji wished education to enable the child to stand on his own feet economically rather than becoming a parasite on others.

Moral and Spiritual Development: According to Vivekanand, a nation's greatness is not only measured by its parliamentary institutions and activities, but also by the greatness of its citizens. But the greatness of citizens is possible only through their moral and spiritual development which education should foster.

Character Development Aim: According to him character development is a very important aim of any education. For this, he emphasised the practice of Brahmacharya which fosters development of mental, moral and spiritual powers leading to purity of thoughts, words and deeds.

The Aim of Development: Faith in one's own-self, Shradha and a Spirit of Renunciation-All through his life Swamiji exhorted the individuals to keep full confidence on their powers. They should inculcate a spirit of self-surrender, sacrifice and renunciation of material pleasures for the good of others. Education should foster all these qualities in the individual. He gave this call to his countrymen—"Arise, awake and stop not till the goal is achieved".

The Aim of Searching Unity in Diversity: The true aim of education is to develop insight into the individuals so that they are able to search out and realise unity in diversity. Vivekanand has further asserted that physical and spiritual worlds are one, their distinctness is an illusion (Maya). Education should develop this sense which finds unity in diversity.

Religious Development Aim: To Swamiji, religious development is an essential aim of education. To him, each individual should be able to search out and develop the religious seed embedded in him and thus find the absolute truth or reality. Hence, he advocated the training of feelings and emotions so that the whole life is purified and sublimated. Then alone the capacities of obedience, social service and submission to the teachings and preachings of great saints and saviours will develop in the individual. Education should foster this development.

Books for Study

According to Vivekanand, the prime aim of education is spiritual growth and development. But this does not mean that he did not advocate material prosperity and physical well-being. He advocated the inclusion of all those subjects and activities in the curriculum which foster material welfare with spiritual advancement. For spiritual perfection he prescribed Religion, Philosophy, Puranic lore, Upanishads, company of saints and their preachings, and for material advancement and prosperity he recommended Languages, Geography, Science, Political Science, Economics, Psychology, Art, Agriculture, Industrial and Technical subjects together with Games, Sports and other Physical exercises.

Methods of Teaching

Swamiji prescribed the same ancient spiritual methods of teaching wherein the Guru and his disciples lived in close association as in a family. The essential characteristics of those religious and spiritual methods were as under:

(1) To control fleeting mental faculties by the practice of Yoga.

(2) To develop the mind by concentration and deep meditation.

(3) To gain knowledge through lectures, discussions, self-experience and creative activities.

(4) To imitate the qualities and character of teacher by intelligent and clear understanding.

(5) To lead the child on the right path by means of individual guidance by the teacher.

Place of Child: Like Froebel, Vivekanand emphasised the education to be child-centred. According to him, the child is the store and repositor of all learning-material and spiritual pursuit.

Education of Masses: "I consider that the greatest national sin is the neglect of the masses, and that is one of the causes of our downfall. No amount of politics would be of any avail until the masses of India are once more well-educated, well-fed and well-cared for."

Women's Education: A strong advocate of women's education, he emphasised that they should have the same curriculum as the boys.

The Analysis

Though an idealist to the core, Vivekanand's philosophy of education contains traces of Naturalism and Pragmatism. He insisted that the chief aim of education is to develop to the full the moral and spiritual nature of the child, the essence of which is already present in him. He ceaselessly strove that education should develop nationalism as well as international brotherhood. His educational philosophy is a mixture of the ancient Vedantic philosophy and the modern western philosophy, omitting the pitfalls of both."

According to Dr. R.S. Mani, "Vivekanand's life mission was to advocate that people should be possessed of Shradha (Faith), of Virya (Courage) to attain the knowledge of Atma, and to sacrifice their lives for the good of others."

The Position

Some call him (Swami Vivekananda) the Militant Hindu, others call him a great reformer and crusader and yet many others remember him with various other epithets. The fact remains that he was one of the great Indians who refused to be placed second to any one in any sphere. He shook the world with his discourses on philosophy and religion. He wanted to establish the supremacy of Hinduism and he wanted to set and reset the glorious traditions of our great motherland. Swami Vivekananda was a great teacher. He wanted to strike a balance between the spiritualism of the east on one hand and materialism of the west on the other. Unfortunately, his life was short but he did his days' work.

Swami Vivekananda (a name he took in 1893 while sailing to USA) was born as Narendra Nath Dutt in a family at Calcutta in 1863. During his student days (he was an ardent student of philosophy and poetry), he came in contact with another great teacher-Swami Ram Krishna Paramhansa who made him incharge of his seminary with the words, "Take care of these boys." Narendra Nath resolutely undertook the conduct of young seminary and did not permit it to indulge in the idleness of God. He kept its members ever on the alert, he harried their minds without pity; he read them the great books of human thought, he led them indefatigably towards the wide horizons of boundless truth. Narendra Nath became a monk and preached the Gospel of Vedanta throughout the world. He participated in the Parliament of Religions held in USA in 1893. He toured India—its length and breadth. He even went to Ceylon. On Dec. 25, 1896, he swam the Indian Ocean and meditated on the rock at Kanyakumari. Swami Vivekananda died in 1902.

Staunch Individualist: In Swamiji we had a staunch individualist. "Individuality is my motto," he wrote to Abhayananda. "I have no ambition beyond training individuals."

He said again:

"If I succeed in my life to help one single man to attain freedom, my labours will not have been in vain."

That he was an individualist can be known from one more fact. The subjects of his interviews were 'Liberty', 'Courage', 'Charity', humane treatment of delinquents and so on.

Dignity of Humanity/Faith in Man: From the above point, it can be easily concluded that Swamiji had immense faith in man and in the dignity of humanity. About it he said, "No religion on earth preaches the dignity of humanity in such a lofty strain as Hinduism." He regretted that it is again Hinduism which treads upon the necks of poor and the low but then the fault is not of Hinduism but of Pharisees, and Sadducees. And about the faith in man, the quotation given in the beginning is an indicator enough. He says, "The only God to worship is the human soul, in the human body. Of course, all animals are temples too but human is the highest—The Taj Mahal of temples. If I can not worship in that, no other temple will be of any advantage. The moment 1 have realised God sitting in the temple of every human body, the moment I stand in reverence before every human being and see God in him-that moment I am free from bondage, everything that binds vanishes, and I am free". Know the man, he says. That is also the message of Vedanata.

Doctrine of Divinity/Concept of God: Like Swami Dayananda, Swami Vivekananda believed in the immortality of soul. That is also the message of Vedas, Swamiji says, "Each soul is a star, Man is potentially divine." And then God is omni present. He is Supreme. He creates man in His own image. The manifestation of God is in man. According to Swamiji, the worship of man is the worship of God.

And all religions are equal. No religion is inferior to the other. To quote him, "If God exists it must be possible to reach him. Religion is neither word nor doctrine. It is realisation. It is not hearing and accepting. It is being and becoming. It begins with the exercise of the faculty of religious realisations."

The Four Great Paths: In order to achieve salvation (freedom and liberation) Swami showed four paths: Paths of work, worship, contemplation and knowledge. It could be Karma, Bhakti and Jnana and the Propylacum. The motive force of all three is the science of inner forces, consciously controlled and mastered: the Science of Raja Yoga. Of these four Gospels of Vivekananda, his four Yogas, the most deep and moving is the Gospel of Work-Karma Yoga although to many others, it is the lowest of the three ways to achieve salvation but there is no 'high road' or a 'low road' for this purpose. Karma Yoga says, "Work incessantly but give up all attachment to work......Hold your mind free. Do not project into it the tentacle of selfishness, 'I' and 'mine'.

We learn from Karma Yoga the secret of work, the organising power of work, work is inevitable, but we should work to the highest purpose. All duties are His! Doctrine of service is the essential part of Vivekananda's teaching and practice.

Swami Vivekananda also made masterly analysis of three other paths leading to freedom and liberty. He dwelt in detail on Bhakti Yoga, Raja Yoga, and Jnana Yoga.

Swami Vivekananda was patriot of the first order. He wanted every resident of this land to be first and last an Indian, He sang the Glory of the motherland. He wanted all of us to sink our differences-religious, linguistic, cultural and to lead a life as citizens of this great land. India has rich cultural traditions and these be cherished by us all. India is also spiritual leader of the world. He states it emphatically.

Universalism and Science-Religion: He believed in religion which is of universal acceptance and which is science based.

He says, "All narrow, limited, fighting ideas of religion must be given up. The religious ideals of future must embrace all that exists in the world and is good and great, and at the same time have infinite scope for future development. Religion is synonymous with universalism. And it is not until "religious" conceptions have attained to this universalism that religion is fully realised. He advocated rationalistic religion.

On Women: He was all for them. He preached for equal rights between men and women. He made no distinction between man and woman. He asks, "Is there any sex distinction in Atman?" Again he said, "the best thermometer to the progress of a nation is treatment of its women."

Leading Position: The personal philosophy of Swami Vivekananda lies reflected in his educational philosophy and practice of education. Some points.

The Concepts

(a) Knowledge comes from within: (Rejection of Behaviourism which believes in everything external). Vivekananda says, "All knowledge that the world has ever received comes from mind: infinite library of universe is in your mind. The external world is only a suggestion, the occasion which sets you to study your mind. The falling of apple gave suggestion to Newton. He rearranged all the precious limits of thought in his mind and discovered a new link among them which, we call the Law of Gravitation. This is just an example to prove that knowledge resides within the individual."

(b) Education for all was creed with Swamiji. It hardly needs any elaboration.

(c) Swamiji was a Yogi. He believed in Brahmacharya. It was a must for concentration of mind which helped in education of the individual.

(d) Education must suit the needs of the child—psychological education. He says, "Their needs should be determined in terms of tendencies inherent in children and not according to what the parents of the children think". The point is that parents are not to determine the needs of children.

(e) Swamiji was in favour of women education. Their uplift, welfare was a part and parcel of his basic philosophy.

(f) *Concept of Education:* Swami Vivekananda defined education as: Education is the manifestation of the perfection already in the man. Swamiji believed in the development of inner powers. He did not believe in book learning. To him, book learning was not education.

What is education? Is it book learning? No. Is it diverse knowledge? Not even that. The training by which the current and expression of will are brought under control and become beautiful is called education.

Targets and Motives

In some books, you will find that about ten aim education according to Swami Vivekananda have been listed and Swamiji was not an educational theorist. That listing is mere irrational. From the philosophy of Swamiji and his teaching, the following aims of education can be deduced:

(a) Strong moral character should be developed through education. The main aim of education is this character building and not merely feeding information to the brain.

(b) *Self-realisation:* The education should enable one to realise one's self is the second aim of education. And before that it should create self-confidence. Only a self-confident man can realise oneself. Education should take man to freedom, to liberty, to salvation.

(c) Education should enable man to meet his needs. The economic aspect or the practical aspect of life can not be ignored. The education which does not help the common mass to equip themselves for the struggle for life, which does not bring out strength of character, a spirit of philanthrophy and the courage of a lion, is it worth the name? Real education is that which enables one to stand on his own legs.

(d) To promote universal brotherhood is another aim of education. He said, "Through education, we should gradually reach the idea of universal brotherhood by flinging down the walls of separation and inequality. In everyman, in every animal, however weak or miserable, great or small, resides the same omnipresent and omniscient soul. The difference is not in the soul but in the manifestation.

Content of Education: It cannot be purely western. Swamiji at the same time was born in modern times. Sciences could not be neglected. He did not specify any subjects to form the content of education-it was a broad approach-a sort of synthesis between Science and Vedanta. He also wanted Indian students to learn their own languages—particularly Sanskrit. He also wanted the students to learn Religion. Theology on one hand, English and technology on the other to keep with the current times, as already pointed out.

In the words of Swamiji, "My idea of education is personal contact with the teacher-gurugrha-vasa. Without the personal life of a teacher, there could be no education."

Functional Techniques

Swamiji was a monk. He also believed in inner knowledge. His methods of education would be determined by these two facts. You can at once say that the methods will be along the following lines:

(a) Meditation—for the concentration is a must.

(b) Faith or Shraddha.

(c) Discourse and Discussion.

(d) Self-study.

In Swami Vivekananda's own words, "To me the very essence of education is concentration of mind not the collection of facts. If I had to do my education once again I would not study facts at all, I would develop the power of concentration and detachment and then with a perfect instrument, I would collect facts at will." That speaks of his methodology.

Place of a Teacher

According to Swamiji, only few can become teachers. The personal life of a teacher is of much more importance than the knowledge a teacher possesses. He says that only a Tyagi can become a good teacher. A teacher must first be pure at heart and then a dedicated one.

Significant Contributions

Swami Vivekananda, original name Narendra Nath Dutta son of an eminent lawyer of Calcutta High Court was born in 1863 in Calcutta. He graduated with honours from Calcutta University. In the beginning he was a teacher for some time. But, his interest in philosophy and religion drove him to adopt the life of a monk. His contact with Sri Ram Krishna Param Hans in 1888 transformed his life. He left home and became a wandering monk. He travelled all over India preaching the vedantic scriptures and philosophy. In 1893 he was invited to participate in the deliberations of the world's Parliament of Religions at Chicago, America. He gave a soul-stirring address there. He was, then, invited to lecture on vedanta at several universities of the USA. In 1896, three years after, he was invited to lecture at Oxford University of England. He established Belur Math in 1899. The same year he was invited to lecture at California University and founded the Vedanta Society at San Francisco. He died in 1902 when he was only 39 years old.

Vedic Faith

Swami Vivekananda was a Vedantist. Hence, he was a teacher of spirituality preaching that every soul is destined to be perfect and that every being in the end will attain to that state. He also preached that whatever we are now, is the result of whatever we have been in the past; and whatever we will be in the future depends on whatever we do or think now. Spiritual perfection of man was the aim of life according to him for which one has to struggle. He believed in God, in the Vedas and in the birth-death-rebirth cycle. His belief was that this whole universe is one, that it is one Being manifesting itself in all the various forms. The human being has a divine nature. God is the material cause of this universe. It is only by name and form that one thing is differentiated from another. In reality they are one and the same. In the lowest worm as well as in the highest human being the same divine nature is present. When a person has realised his own nature, the whole world has vanished for him. His philosophy represents the highest spiritual and ethical values of mankind. His teachings having their roots in the upanishadas were believed by him to be helpful in solving social and political problems.

He advocated that spiritual knowledge is the only thing that can destroy our miseries for ever; helping man spiritually is the highest that can be given to him, because spirituality is the true basis of all our activities in life.

Good Character

Swami Vivekananda had an unflinching faith in eternal values. He said that these alone can ensure stability; they provide the driving power for progress. About education he said "There is no problem of modern India that can not be solved by that magic word *Education.*" He emphatically said that education is a man-making and nation-making process. It is the process which awakens the sleeping soul to self-conscious activity. It is the fundamental basis of human development, a means of human enlightenment and purification of human heart. He strongly pleaded for providing a spiritual orientation to education.

Vivekananda's concept of education was that "it is the manifestation of the perfection already in man" (*Education* by Vivekananda, chapter-I). He further said that education is not the amount of information that is put into the brain undigested all the life. We must have education which is life-building, man-making, character building, assimilation of ideas. True education is that which helps the common mass of people to equip themselves for the struggle of life, which brings out strength of character, a spirit of philanthropy and the courage of a lion. He said, "We want that education by which character is formed, strength of mind is increased, intellect is expanded, and by which one can stand on one's own feet, the end of all education, all training should be man-making. The end and aim of all training is to make the man grow. The training by which the current expression of will are brought under control, and become fruitful is called education" (Ranganathananda, p. 148). This is education that may be said to 'be true education, education which makes for growth and expansion of personality.'

Education, as stressed by Swami Vivekananda, must develop in man a sense of honour and dignity and also a sense of social responsibility, a respect for man as man and a respect for the dignity of man in their own persons. Character, efficiency and humanism should be the aim of all education. Vivekananda strongly pleaded that development of character through the service of his fellow men, the utilisation of his talents for ensuring the happiness and welfare of the millions of his less fortunate fellow-citizens should be the aim of the education (Ranganathananda, p. 163). Education for total human development was the vision of Vivekananda. He stressed the need to educate the millions of our common people as the national development depended on the "goodness and greatness of men to be achieved through education".

His approach to education was humanistic. He was highly spiritual and intensely human. His humanism in education centred around man emphasizing that man was the measure of all things. He held a belief that through education it was possible to develop in human beings qualities of 'heart and mind which make them tremendously powerful, full of hope, endowed with a firm mind and will, strength of muscle and nerves. It is these men and women who build a strong nation. Through education, he asserted, nations can unfold the humanistic and divine possibilities lying hidden within their people. To him, in fact, education, was the basic means for achieving human excellence and solving national problems.

Vivekananda stressed education for democracy, and national development. The strength of democracy was, to him, hidden in the young men and women who are free, responsible, politically aware, full of deep patriotic feelings and sensitive to human welfare. Education was thought to be a powerful instrument to achieve these developmental qualities in the people. He was a nationalist through and through and wanted that education should produce such enlightened democratic citizens who can build a strong and prosperous nation. "A nation is advanced in proportion as education and intelligence spread among the masses" said Swamiji.

Women education was considered by Vivekananda an essential component of India's national system of education. He said "daughters should be supported and educated with as much care as the sons". He further, held that it is only in the homes of educated and pious mothers that great men are born. He said that women should be taught History and Puranas, house-keeping and the art, the duties of home life and principles that make for the development of character.

Sewing, culinary art, rules of domestic work and upbringing of children, Japa, worship, meditation, development of the spirit of valour and heroism should form the content of women education.

National integration through education was one of the prominent objectives of Swamiji. He had a great faith in the youth of the country for national regeneration. For that reason he emphasised that they should get the right type of education which enables them to be endowed with an alert mind and full of hope strong in mind and firm in purpose and physically strong. Nation building through man-making was his precious dream. Swamiji said, "keep the motto before you: elevation of the masses without injuring their religion". He further said, "Teach yourselves, teach everyone his real nature; call upon the sleeping soul and see how it awakes. Power will come, glory will come, and everything that is excellent will come when this sleeping soul (of man) is roused to self-conscious activity".

On the basis of the foregoing discussion following aims of education may be inferred from Vivekananda's philosophy:

Individual Aims

(1) Physical development of the students

(2) Character development of students

(3) Spiritual development of students

(4) Development of total personality—i.e. developing self-confidence, self-reliance, self-discipline and self-sufficiency.

Social Aims

(1) Education for serving humanity

(2) Education for developing feelings of brotherhood, acquisition of the spirit of renunciation, i.e. giving up of

worldly pleasures as well as a life of arrogance, pomp and show.

(3) Education for enlightened citizenship and responsibility.

Selection of a Teacher

Vivekananda said that every soul is destined to be perfect and every being, in the end, will attain to that state. But, this does not preclude our receiving help from outside. The quickening influence comes from another soul, called the guru (Collected Works, p. 45).

He, then, stressed that the soul from which this influence comes must possess the power of transmitting it. He must be a real teacher knowing the secret of the scriptures. Knowing is not so important as to grasp the spirit of the scriptures. Again, Swamiji said that the real teacher is one who is sinless because it is impossible that there can be any spiritual light in that soul which is impure. A vision of God, glimpse of the Beyond never comes until the soul is pure. Hence, in the teacher, purity is the one thing indispensable.

Another important quality that a teacher should have is that he should not teach with any ulterior motive, for name or for fame or anything else, but simply for love, pure love. When spiritual forces are transmitted from the teacher to the taught, they can only be conveyed through the medium of love. In other words the teacher must have a high level of morality and spirituality..

The teacher, according to Vivekananda, has a great role to play in the task of educating the child. The relationship between the teacher and the student has to be that of the father and the son. *Guru grahavas* is recommended by Swamiji saying that this is one of the best ways a teacher can help the pupil. In this *Grahavas* the student has to live in the house of the teacher, under 24-hour guidance and supervision of the guru. The teacher during this period imparts knowledge and inspires his intellectual and spiritual development through his personality. The teacher has to be an enlightened person himself apart from being knowledgeable. He should have a great love of humanity.

Swami Vivekananda did not make any recommendation about any specific subject to be taught in the schools and colleges. He, however. stressed that children should be taught about their cultural heritage expressed in history, poetry, literature, grammar, languages and lives of the great men. It was also emphasised that the study of vedantic literature. *Ramayana* and *Mahabharata* should also be taught alongwith the story of India's past.

Swami Vivekananda was not against the teaching of science and technical subjects. He was aware of the advances in the field of science and technology. He said that scientific knowledge through a study of the various branches of modern science must find a place in the curriculum of schools. The same he recommended about technology and engineering subjects.

Vivekananda being a nationalist was very keen to see that India was economically prosperous and well-developed. So he stressed teaching of science and technology. He also said that the schools should produce self-reliant individuals who can earn their living after finishing their education. In a way he suggested that vocational courses should also form a part of the curriculum. The curriculum for girls, he said, should incorporate training in needle-craft, cookery, child-rearing and other useful subjects.

It was emphasised by Vivekananda that understanding and meaning are more important than just knowing. For that discussion, analysis, arguments and reaching the truth were considered essential. That was the way how students were made to learn at Guru's ashrama. The student would ask the question and the guru will answer.

This interaction between the teacher and the student would involve illustrations, analogies, reasoning, examples and sometimes further readings by the student till he was convinced of the teacher's answers. Self-learning was very much emphasised. Experience based learning was considered more valuable.

Aspects of Contribution: Vivekananda emphasised the importance of the following and contributed significant ideas as follows

(i) He stressed humanism in education

(ii) Advocated free and compulsory mass education.

(iii) Emphasised formulation of a national system of education.

(iv) Emphasised importance of women education.

(v) Emphasised national unity and national integration.

5

Gandhi

"There is no such thing as Gandhism and I do not want to leave any sect after me. I do not claim to have originated any new principle or doctrine. I have simply tried in my own way to apply the eternal truths to our daily life and problems. The opinions I have formed and the conclusions I have arrived at are not final. I have nothing to teach to the world. Truth and non-violence are as old as the hills. All I have done is to try my experiments in both on as vast a scale as I could do." Yet Gandhi insists that "there is no 'ism' about it."

Prominent Personality

Mohan Das Karam Chand Gandhi was born on October 2, 1869 at Porbandar, Kathiawar, Gujarat. His father was the Diwan of Rajkot. Gandhi's mother was a very courteous and kind hearted lady. Gandhiji was married with Kasturba at the age of 13 years. He passed the Matriculation Examination as an ordinary student. In the same year he was sent to England by sea voyage for studying Law where he spent three years and nine months as a student. On 10th June 1891, Gandhiji passed the Law Examination and returned to India as a Barrister. He practised law for some time, but did not do well here. In 1893, Gandhiji went to South Africa as a legal adviser where he resisted for twenty years the inhuman treatment of the British Government against the Indian subjects in a non-violent way. After his return from South Africa in 1915, he started a non-violent struggle against the British rule in India. In 1917 he established Sabarmati Ashram at Ahmadabad for propagating Harijan uplift, Village industries, other social reforms and launching creative programmes for national uplift. Not only this, in 1921, he launched his world famous non-violent civil disobedience movement against the British Government. Side by side, the Indian National Congress passed a resolution for complete independence. At this the English Government in India was forced to sign a pact known as 'Gandhi-Irwin Pact' to start negotiations for the independence of India.

Accordingly Gandhiji went to England to participate in the Round Table Conference, but nothing came out of that and the British Government in India continued its reign of terror in India. In 1942 Gandhiji was arrested and sent to jail. On his release from jail, he gave a 'Quit India' call to the British Government. The struggle for independence flared up tremendously and the whcle country rose in revolt against the alien rule. The British Government tried to crush the movement with cruelty and terror but later started negotiations for some agreement. Finally, on 15th August 1947 the British left India and declared its independence. Soon the country was enveloped into the fire of communal riots resulting in heavy loss of life and property. Gandhiji tried his best to pacify and stop this terrible carnage. He died on 30 January 1948.

The Thinking

Gandhi's philosophy is based on Idealism. He believes in God implicitly. The soul is the part of a bigger entity. Just as sunrays in the Sun which is absolute and one whole, so are the individual persons, innumerable, yet the same soul pervades in them. Reality for him is unity in diversity.

Important Dimensions

Truth: is the means to God realisation which is the ultimate aim of life. Reality for Gandhi is one and all encompassing. God is life, truth and light. He is Love. He is the supreme God. "God is Truth, i.e. Satya, and 'Satya' cannot be destroyed. The ultimate aim of one's life should be the realisation of God".

Non-violence: According to Gandhi devotion to truth can only be practised through devotion and strict adherence to Ahimsa. To him Truth and Ahimsa are the two sides of the same coin. "Ahimsa is complete absence of ill-will against all that lives. In its dynamic condition, it means conscious suffering. Non-violence in its active form is goodwill toward all life. It is pure life. "Ahimsa is the means, Truth the end."

Fearlessness: "Fearlessness connotes freedom from all external fear—fear of disease, bodily injury and death, or dispossession, of losing ones nearest and dearest, of losing reputation or giving offence, and so on."

Satyagraha: Satyagraha is change of heart by self-suffering, by adherence to truth and non-violence. The "doctrine came to mean vindication of truth not by inflicting suffering on the opponent but on one's self."

Concept of Education

Gandhi's philosophy of education is a dynamic concept. It provides for the fulfilment of man's needs, biological, sociological and psychological. He believed that education should bring about the development of the whole man. Such a thing can happen only when a man has his basic needs fulfilled.

Green had remarked that Pestalozzi was the starting point of modern educational theory. This may be true as far as western education is concerned. An impartial study of Gandhi's educational teachings will reveal that he is the starting point of the modern educational theory and practice in the East.

The Notion

Education, according to Gandhi, is a means to draw out the best from the child and the man, physically, intellectually and spiritually, Education should not confine itself to the teaching of 3 Rs. According to Gandhiji, teaching of 3 Rs, is neither the beginning nor the end of education. He paid greater attention toward the personality of the educand. He, in fact, intended at the balanced development of the child, physically, psychologically and intellectually, to enable him to achieve the ultimate aim, i.e. Truth.

He has expressed his thoughts about education in the 'Harijan' of 31st July, 1937 in the following words:

> "As a nation, we are so backward in education that we cannot hope to fulfil our obligation to the nation in this respect in a given time during this generation, if this programme is to depend on money. I have, therefore, made bold, even at the risk of losing reputation for constructive ability to suggest that education should be self-supporting. By education I mean an all-round drawing out of the best in child and man—body, mind and spirit. Literacy is not the end of education nor even the beginning. It is only one of the means whereby man and woman can be educated. Literacy in itself is no education. I would, therefore, begin the child's education by teaching it a useful handicraft and enabling it to produce from the moment it begins its training. Thus, every school can be made self-supporting, the condition being that the state take over the manufacture of those schools."

Gandhi called it Basic Education.

Basic Ideas

(1) From seven to fourteen years of age, education of each child should be free, compulsory and universal.

(2) The medium of instruction should be mother-tongue.

(3) There should be no place for English in the education of a child.

(4) Mere literacy cannot be equated with education.

(5) Education should develop human values in the child.

(6) Education should develop all the powers of child according to the community of which he is an integral part.

(7) Education should achieve the harmonious development of child's body, mind, heart and soul.

(8) Education should employ some craft as a medium of education so that the child gains economic self-reliance for his life.

(9) All education should be imparted through some productive craft or industry and a useful correlation should be established with that industry.

(10) Education of all subjects should be imparted through some local crafts or productive work.

(11) The industry should be such that the child is able to achieve gainful work experience through practical work.

(12) Education should be made self-supporting through some productive work.

(13) Education should lead to economic independence and self-reliance for livelihood.

(14) School should be a place of activity where the child gets busy in various experiments and gains newer and newer experiences bringing forth new researches.

(15) Education should create useful, responsible and dynamic citizens.

The Meaning

"Literacy is neither the beginning nor the end of education. This is only a means through which man or woman can be educated. By education I mean an all-round drawing out the best in child's and man's body, mind and spirit."

Specific Targets

Immediate Aims

Vocational Aim: Education for self-reliance, should be job-oriented to act as a safeguard against economic exploitation. Education should be self-supporting.

Cultural Aim: "I consider the cultural aspect of education as more essential than its academic aspect. Culture is the main foundation and an essential spirit of education. Hence, all types of human activities should bear the imprint of culture and refinement."

Perfect Development Aim: "The real education is that which fully develops the body, mind and soul of children."

Moral or Character Development Aim: "I have always given top position to culture, to heart and character development in the process of education. I consider character building as the main and essential basis of educational development."

Liberation Aim: Education should liberate body, mind and soul. By liberation he meant liberation from economic, social, political and natural slavery, as well as that of the soul from worldly pursuit and to devote itself to higher forms of spiritual living.

Ultimate Aim: Gandhi wished every child to grow into a divine human being by realising Godliness in his self. "Self-realisation is the summum bonum of life and education."

Books for Syllabi

The curriculum of Gandhi's system of education has been constructed with the definite view of achieving the aims and objectives laid down by him. His scheme of education is known as 'Basic Scheme of Education.' It aimed at the development of intellectual, physical and spiritual powers of a child in the best possible manner and make him grow into a whole man. With this point of view, he has suggested the teaching of the following subjects in his scheme of education:

1. *Basic Craft:* Education should be craft-centred and, therefore, teaching of craft has a primary place in Gandhiji's system of education. This craft should be related to the local conditions of life and society.
2. *Mother-tongue:* Gandhiji has stressed on the teaching of the mother-tongue, because it is effective instrument for the expression and communication of ideas and acquisition of knowledge. The mother-tongue is to be used as the medium of instruction in these schools.
3. *Arithmetic:* This is very useful subject for the day-to-day life.
4. Social studies.
5. *General Sciences:* This branch of subject shall include teaching of Nature study, Botany, Zoology, Phraseology, Chemistry, Hygiene and Physical education.
6. Art and music.
7. Domestic science for girls.

Guiding Principles

Gandhiji lays stress on the following principles in his methods of teaching:

(1) To achieve mental development, training of senses and parts of the body should be given.

(2) Reading should precede the teaching of writing.

(3) Before teaching of alphabets, art training should be given.

(4) More opportunities should be given to learning by doing.

(5) Encouragement should be given to learning by experience.

(6) Correlation should be established in the teaching methods and learning experiences.

In addition to the above, Gandhi emphasised the need of co-curricular activities, planning, realistic experiences, initiative and sense of individual responsibility to be associated with the craft-centred teaching methods.

The Discipline

1. Discipline should not be imposed.
2. Create conditions for self-discipline.
3. Stress on cooperation, hence craft-centred education. Craft should be related to local conditions.
4. *Social Discipline.* Education should build up ideal citizens capable of shouldering social responsibilities with success.

Distinct Features

1. Ideal of world citizenship.
2. Free and compulsory education.
3. Mother-tongue to be the medium of instruction.
4. Well equipped teachers.

Basic Education

Gandhiji had appointed a committee under Dr. Zakir Hussian in 1937 to draw up a scheme of education for free India. Nai Taleem or Basic Education was the outcome of these deliberations. The committee observed that "we feel very strongly the necessity for some organisation of pre-school education for children between the ages of three to seven years, it will go a long way forward helping the pre-school child to get a better home training than he gets now." However, the scheme initially aimed only for those children in the given age group who were either disadvantaged or/whose mothers went for work: more of a welfare measure. But the present day concept of pre-school, or early childhood education, goes far beyond that and covers all children of the said age group as a matter of necessity because the rate of intellectual development is at the highest acceleration during the child's early years, and education must capitalise on that. It was in 1944 when Gandhiji returned from jail, that he realised that the education of the child below seven, as earlier envisaged by Basic Education, cannot be neglected as it is an important stage in the period of human growth. It led to the emergence of Pre-Basic Education, which was experimented at Sevagram Ashram in 1945 under the supervision of Smt. Shanta Narulkar.

Stages of the Programme

(a) Stage 1: Conception to birth.

(b) Stage 2: Birth to two and a half years.

(c) Stage 3: 2½ years to 4 years.

(d) Stage 4: 4 years to 7 years.

Essentials of Pre-basic Education: According to Gandhiji, Pre-Basic education in its fullest sense is the education of children under seven for a development of all their faculties, conducted by the school teachers in cooperation with the parents and the community in school, in the home and in the village.

Essentials of Pre-Basic Education, therefore, be considered as under:

(a) The teacher and parents should cooperate in carrying out the education of young children.

(b) The home where the child is born and lives, influences him and that becomes the first centre of his education and learning.

(c) Pre-school education must not be expensive so that it can reach the millions in the villages.

(d) A child has to be active, creative and playful. He has to learn to do something through the medium of play.

(e) Though the child in pre-school cannot be self-sufficient or self-supporting, an attempt should be made to develop this quality. Self-sufficiency, according to Gandhiji, is an attitude of mind. One must not be a parasite.

Stages of Learning: As seen above, the Pre-Basic has four stages of learning spread over from conception to 7 years of age where basic education takes over. As a matter of fact, the first two stages are the real pre-school learning. In the first two stages, i.e. conception to 2½ years of age, it is all between the mother and the child where "opportunities are provided to the mothers to learn more about new and scientific trends and methods of child rearing, health, and hygiene, and mother craft.

Children are given custodial care and medical attention." The scheme still smacks of a welfare slant without showing any awareness of early interventions, environmental manipulation, and home stimulation, to enable a child to learn, as the stress is more on the care component rather than on education. Hence, a damp squib.

The next two stages, i.e. stages 3 and 4, from the age of 2½ to 7 years of age, cover an active period of learning where the children are left free so that an atmosphere is created toward doing something (how vague). They get full freedom to act, to move about, are free to choose their own activities, and a teacher only supervises so that a child handles the learning material correctly and effectively. Gandhiji's concept of early childhood education, therefore, upholds the principles of activity and freedom, manual work, and art and craft. It, however, lacks the sophistication and refinement of new learning techniques and procedures, as later envisaged by the missionary movement of Early Childhood Care and Education (ECCE).

Aims of Pre-Basic Education: The aim of the Pre-Basic education was "to cultivate good habits, character, cleanliness (personal and communal), discipline, good speech, self-expression, development of body and mind, and self-adaptation."

Programme Planning

(a) Community singing.

(b) Clean-up, personal and communal.

(c) Work play activity which included climbing the trees by using bamboo-made ladders; walking on a coconut tree trunk bridge and keep the body in balance; swinging with ropes; playing water games; playing with old tennis and rubber balls.

Free-Choice Activity Period: This included free choice, different types of play with educative apparatus-creative or constructive play, experimental play, imaginative and initiative play, picture making, clay modelling, picture book reading, cutting and pasting. Using apparatus bricks, blocks, cubes, sand, water, clay, tins and boxes of different sizes, funnel, bottles, wood hammer, saw and nails, dolls, toy cooking utensils, picture books, small boards, pieces of coloured chalks, paper paints, brush, scissors, old magazines, glue, beads, shells, toy measuring scale and some Montessori and Froebel apparatus.

The Evaluation

1. Psychologically, socially and biologically sound.
2. Emphasis on manual work.
3. Opportunities for self-expression.
4. Provision for affection and self-respect.
5. Pedagogically sound educational theory.
6. Combination of Naturalism, Pragmatism and Idealism.

Gandhiji's contribution to education is unique. He was the first Indian who advocated a scheme of education based upon the essential values of Indian culture and civilisation. The methods and techniques advocated by him and the environment he prescribed revolutionised Indian thinking and way of living. At heart he was devoted to Idealism. He wanted to translate his ideals and values into practice. His philosophy of education is a harmonious blending of Idealism, Naturalism and Pragmatism. It may be noted that there is no inherent conflict between the three philosophies.

They are contributory to one another. Idealism is the base of Gandhiji's philosophy whereas Naturalism and Pragmatism help translating that philosophy into practice. Gandhi advocated the ideals of truth, non-violence and moral values to achieve the ultimate truth of self-realisation. He is a devotee of Naturalism when he speaks about the development of the child according to his nature, and he becomes a Pragmatist when he advocates learning by doing and learning by experience. All these lead to an integration, so essential to effective education and development of the total personality. Dr. M.S. Patel remarked," The real greatness of Gandhiji as an educational philosopher consists in the fact that the dominant tendencies of Naturalism, Idealism and Pragmatism are not separate and independent in his philosophy, but they fuse into a unity, giving rise to a theory of education which would suit the needs of the day and satisfy the loftiest aspirations of the human soul."

Knowledge Gained

It was in January 1948 that M.K. Gandhi died. Much water has flown in Jhelum since then. More than 55 years have passed. Yet the ideas which he gave to us are still fresh and will continue to inspire us for the years to come because Gandhi was not a small man. Gandhi was a genius and had a multi-coloured and faceted personality.

Gandhiji, the Father for us or of the Indian Nation, the apostle of Truth and Non-violence was born at Porbander in Kathiawar. His full name was Mohandas Karam Chand Gandhi. Mohandas was indeed a Karamyogi and that was his plus point. What he said or preached, he did.

M.K. Gandhi did Law from UK. He started practice in Bombay but cases took him to South Africa where he spent lot of time. He led many movements there. His experiences in England, South Africa and in India made him bitter against the British rule. What he did for the liberation of the country after his return to India in 1915 at the age of 45 plus is known to all of us. We cannot repay his debt.

Other than being a politician, he was an educationist also. He gave to us his own system of education which is popularly called as Basic Scheme or Basic Education. In this question, we are concerned with his educational philosophy and background of it.

There are three important elements in the background of his educational philosophy:

1. Gandhi's philosophy of life.
2. His dissatisfaction with British system of education.
3. His educational experiments at Tolstoy Farm, Sabarmati Ashram and at Sewagram Ashram at Wardha. We shall mention in brief these three points here:

Special Characteristics

(a) He had firm faith in God. God is the creator. God is the ultimate reality according to Gandhi.

(b) Lover of Truth. He had absolute faith in Truth. In fact God is Truth and Truth is God. He was a seeker of Truth. He wanted everyone to idealise truth.

(c) Non-violence. This is a new element in his personality and philosophy. Absolute non-violence. It was his creed and he lived upto it. Non-violence is a weapon of the strong and not of the weak.

(d) Satyagraha. If you want to achieve something, suffer for it. It is the application of Non-violence or Ahimsa. If you want to be a satyagrahi then you have to live in discipline.

(e) Love for all, for all humanity.

(f) Gandhi believed in the dignity of labour. He worked with his own hands and compelled people to do so. It purified the spirit.

West no More

Long before he came to India, Gandhi had come to realise that the British system of education did not suit Indians or the Indian socio-economic conditions. Teeming millions of Indians were wrought in ignorance, superstition, inertia and illiteracy. The education which the British were providing was bookish and examination ridden. There was hardly any scope for originality. The education.was in a nutshell related to life. It made Indians foreigners in one's own home.

Fresh Trials

Very few people know that Gandhi had four sons. He never educated his sons in the British system of education. He educated them in his own way. He started experiments in education while he was in Africa. His first farm is known as Tolstoy farm (Gandhi was influenced by Russian story writer Leo Tolstoy) near Johansburg in South Africa. That was the year 1905. And when he came to India, his educational experiments continued at Sabarmati Ashram (Gujarat) and at Wardha (Sewagram Ashram). In these Ashrams, the inmates, living and working together, adopted certain codes. All the inmates were to work with their hands. There was no servant. Every job was performed by the inmates. Gandhi found that manual work has great virtues in its trait. One can earn and learn and can also be self-sufficient.

These experiments encouraged him to put forward the important principle of the educational philosophy: Education through a craft and self-sufficient education. This is how his educational philosophy took shape.

Conceptual Influence

Concept of Education: Education is not literacy. This is a point which should be understood once for all.

Gandhiji defined education thus, "By education I mean an all round drawing out of the best in child and man-body, mind and spirit." Through education, Gandhiji wanted to develop the whole personality and he wanted to ensure all round development. The British education was only intellect centred. Gandhi was concerned with body and spirit as well. And education should draw out the best. "True Education", says Gandhiji, "is that which draws out and stimulates the spiritual, intellectual and physical faculties of children."

Aims of Education

Aims of education are implied in the very meanings of education. He has given two sets of aims, viz. immediate and ultimate aims of education. Ultimate aim of education is identical with the goal of life, which is 'Self-realisation'. Self-realisation is the realisation of the self proper. True education should result not in the material gains but in spiritual uplift.

Gandhiji laid great stress on religious education which teaches fundamental virtues of truth, love, justice and non-violence. According to Gandhiji, "Life without religion is life without principles." Gandhiji is also of the opinion that God could be achieved not by returning into jungles but by living in a society and serving it. He preferred to call a student "Brahmachari", a searcher after God.

Self-realisation can take place through self-control, character and abstinence. Immediate aims, include 'bread and butter aims', the cultural aim, the harmonious development of all powers, the moral or character development aim, and sociological aim.

Bread and Butter Aims: This is also called utilitarian aim. It is due to this aim that he gave the principle of 'self-supporting education.' The educated should not only be made capable of earning his own livelihood in later life after school but also during the schooling. The child must be an earning unit who must be self-sufficient right from the beginning of his education. This aim is really an important aim of even modern education. No education can command the respect of the society if it does not enable its citizens to be economically efficient.

Cultural Aim: Cultural aim refers to the refinement of the personality. Mere knowledge is not enough. Education should lead to that quality of mind which may be reflected in daily conduct. Speech, behaviour and manner must be refined. Culture brings in humility and frankness. Education should not take Indian children away from its own culture. There is a need of synthesising cultures so that one could inherit world cultures. This aim enables the students to assimilate and appreciate other cultures.

Harmonious Development Aim: Harmonious development or perfection of nature is another aim that Gandhiji advocates. Harmoniously developed person is that who adjusts to his life and environment. He laid greater emphasis on the development of 3 H's, i.e. Head, Heart and Hand than on 3R's, i.e. reading, writing and arithmetic. Present system of education leads to unbalanced development.

Moral or Character Building Aim: It is the chief aim of education. The central purpose of education is to build character. If choice is to be made between character and other things in life, then everything else can be subordinate to the former.

Man must be a man of word. He must be ready to do something for the humanity at the first call to his conscience.

Sociological Aim or Training for Citizenship: Gandhiji reconciled the individual and social aim of education. In democracy the first slogan is 'Educate your Masters.' Thus Gandhiji advocated 'Universal education.' Every member of this Samaj should be educated so that he could uplift it. He must have qualities of a good citizen. Essential qualities are—spirit of courage, self-sacrifice and industry.

Gandhian curriculum includes following subjects:

1. Basic craft which may be agriculture or spinning and weaving or cardboard work and metal work.
2. Mother tongue both as a language and as medium of instruction.
3. Arithmetic/Mathematics: More emphasis is to be laid on numerical and geometrical problems connected with craft and commonly life.
4. Social Studies.
5. General Science.
6. Drawing, Painting and Music.
7. Domestic science for girls at higher stages. At lower stages same for boys and girls.

The Basic school curriculum is supposed to be a comprehensive one, covering all aspects of child's life.

In the Handbook for Teachers of Basic schools, K.G. Saiyidain wrote on Basic school curriculum. The framers of basic scheme or education have tried to make the syllabus coherent. This was organised around three centres:

(i) The child's physical environment.

(ii) The child's social environment.

(iii) The child's craft work.

The Child's Physical Environment: The child must know his physical environment. This helps him to adjust. The curriculum of basic school concerns itself with the study of the physical environment and aims at giving the child not only knowledge but a proper orientation towards it.

As such Physical sciences, Biological sciences, Hygiene and Geography, Astronomy are to be included in the syllabus to cover the physical environment of the child.

The Child's Social Environment: This section of the curriculum has been broadly named as "Social Studies."

This way you understand the interaction of groups, socio-economic and cultural life is also understood.

Craft Work: Education round and through a craft is perhaps the outstanding feature of basic scheme of Gandhiji. All subjects of curriculum are integrally related to craft.

Basic education curriculum thus means three things:

(a) Craft

(b) General Science.

(c) Social Studies.

(d) Special emphasis on mother tongue. Mother tongue is to be used as medium of instruction at all levels of Basic Education.

(e) Drawing: It is a medium of expression. It helps in developing aesthetic sense. It has utilisation value.

(f) Knowledge of mathematics. It is a must in any curriculum.

Techniques and Teaching

Gandhiji favoured teaching through physical and mental activities. Activity is the starting point of his methods of teaching. Gandhiji advocated education through a basic craft. Correlated knowledge should be given through a craft. This way of teaching has a number of advantages. Craft suits the nature of the child and is also socially useful being productive and all education is to be in mother tongue of the child.

Perhaps the things have got jumbled up in the para given above. The main points about methods of teaching are:

(a) Activity method or learning by self-experience. This way learning is very effective.

(b) Education through a craft. This has been repeatedly stressed that all education is to be through a craft. All subjects are to be woven round it.

(c) Correlation principle or Cross-subject principle is to be followed. Knowledge is one and as much should be given as one. There should be correlation with craft and with environment. Correlation should be natural and spontaneous. It should not be forced. Only expert teachers can do it.

(d) Questioning method can be applied.

(e) All education is to be in mother-tongue. It is easier to learn.

A Disciplined Life

Gandhian concept of discipline was that of discipline through self-control. It has to be Voluntary discipline. It has to be self-discipline. This is possible if you lead a life of self-restraint and self-sacrifice. This discipline is achieved through non-violent conduct of life. With Gandhi, non-violence was an article of faith.

Secondly, we have to work on a craft. That work is possible only when we have social discipline-otherwise not. He believed in social discipline also. That will make ideal citizens.

Position of a Teacher

Gandhiji had given to us Basic Scheme of Education or "Nai Talim" as he was tempted to call it. An ordinary teacher just does not fit into his scheme of education. In order to implement Basic Education, a special brand of teachers was required. He defined the duties of a teacher:

> "The teacher has to enable the students to understand the distinctions and qualities implied in various things. If the student does not learn to distinguish between things, there will be no difference between him and the machine. Man is a thinking animal. Therefore during the study period, we should be able to distinguish between truth and untruth, sweet and harsh language and clean and dirty things."

The teacher must have those qualities which he wants to promote in children. Gandhiji believed that students learnt more from the personality of a teacher than from books and lectures.

Gandhiji wanted the teacher to be one with his students. Gandhiji did not mean that students should imitate their teacher blindly. He gave full freedom to students. He recommends that the teacher should urge the students to think and ponder over everything told before they decide to follow a course of action. Teacher therefore has role to play in Gandhian Education. The teacher should be a virtuous person and should be able to establish a heart to heart contact with the students.

Quality of Definitiveness

Mahatma Gandhi was a unique personality. He was an idealist, naturalist—and a pragmatist—all rolled into one. He was a rare human being. In brief, we describe all the three facets of his wonderful personality.

An Idealist: Gandhi was an idealist and this is evident from the following points:

1. Gandhi believed in God. To Gandhi, God is the ultimate reality.

2. Gandhi believed in absolute values. There is such a thing known as truth, beauty and goodness. Gandhi always spoke the truth.
3. Non-violence was a creed with Gandhi as an idealist. He was ready to die for this ideal. Non-violence was a weapon of the strong.
4. His was a life of sacrifice.
5. Gandhi believed in earning one's own living. He loved to work with his own hands.
6. He believed in morality. Idealist only think of moral and religious education. Morality should be practised.
7. Gandhi was broad-minded in religious views. He was tolerant of all other religions and views.
8. His life was his message. Whatever he preached he practised. He set example before others to emulate.

A Naturalist

1. Gandhi believed that the nature of the child was good. Gandhi was simply following Rousseau.
2. Gandhi wanted that education should be child centred. He gave due importance to the child. The nature of the child is that the child is active. The child cannot sit still. The interests of the child must also be taken into consideration. We should not bore the child with lectures.
3. The child be free. Gandhi believed in the freedom of the child.
4. Natural Surroundings: Gandhiji wanted children to be educated in natural surroundings. The atmosphere should not be restricted.
5. Gandhi had his ashrams in open places. This very fact is reflected in his education. Let village children be educated in villages. This gives them the first hand experience.

A Pragmatist: The word Pragmatism has been derived from Greek word 'Pragma' which means action. It is an American School of Philosophy. Charles Pierce, William James and John Dewey are its founders. They believe in action and not in contemplation, and for them, reality is changing. There is no such thing as absolute values.

Let us now examine Gandhi and his philosophy in the light of the above para.

Gandhi comes out as a pragmatic thinker. Gandhi believed in action. This is reflected in his "Satyagrahas". That way Gandhi was a real Karamyogi.

Gandhi did not believe in verbal education. His scheme of education is based on activity. The craft centred education is pragmatic education. It is also self-supporting education.

Gandhi believed in learning by doing. It is activity all the way. Activity, expression and construction are the fundamental principles of their teaching methods. Gandhi was a democrat. He believed in the freedom of man.

Learning should be in co-operation with the society. It cannot take place in isolation.

So we can conclude that Gandhi was an idealist, naturalist and pragmatist-all rolled into one.

Fundamental Education

M.K. Gandhi was not a theoretical person. Whatever he propounded as an educational philosopher was reflected in his scheme of education known as Basic Education or Bunyadi Shiksha or Nai Talim. This shows that Gandhi was educationist in true sense. He was a practical man. We shall now make ourselves familiar with Gandhian System of Education known as Basic Education or as Wardha Scheme because it was 'born' at Wardha (Maharashtra).

In April 1935, Gandhiji founded what is called Sevagram Ashram, a village with an ideal 13 miles from Wardha towards the Nagpur side. It was here that Basic Education was born in October 1937 at a Conference convened by the Mahatma which was attended by the then leading educationist of the country. The following four resolutions were passed and these in themselves comprise Basic Education or Bunyadi Shiksha or Nai Talim. Those are:

1. That education be free and compulsory for all children between age group 7-14, i.e. for eight years.
2. That the medium of instruction be the mother tongue.
3. That the process of education throughout this period should centre round some form of manual work, and that all other abilities to be developed or training to be given should, as far as possible, be integrally related to the central handicraft chosen with due regard to the environment of the child.
4. That this system of education will be gradually able to cover the remuneration of teachers, i.e. a self-sufficient scheme. Gandhiji was not bothered about the school building.

Later Zakir Hussain Committee drafted the syllabus for said scheme and submitted it on December 2, 1937. To sum up, Mahatma Gandhi's educational theory was determined by the following factors:

(a) His educational experiments.

(b) His philosophy of life.

(c) His dissatisfaction with the prevailing system of education.

(d) Gandhiji's conviction that salvation of India lay in educated Indians.

Basic system of education is a national system of education in extent, scope and administration. It possesses the following distinguishing features:

Free and Compulsory Education: This resolution meant that education must be free and compulsory for all boys and girls between the age of 7-14 irrespective of caste or creed. As a concession, however, girls, if their guardians so desired, could be withdrawn from the school after their twelfth year. In all, a child will spend 8 years at school and during these eight years, the child will come up to the level of traditional matriculation minus English.

Mahatma Gandhi was convinced that what a child learnt in traditional schools in ten years will learn in eight years except English, which according to him was not required. This will also effect a saving of two years and the knowledge which the child will get in Basic schools will be solid one and related to the life of the child. It was the duty of the state to provide free and compulsory education to children.

Medium of Instruction: Mahatma Gandhi emphasised the mother tongue of the child both as a subject of study and as medium of instruction. In his own words, "It has been my conviction that Indian parents who train their children to think and talk in English from their infancy betray their children and country." He was of the opinion that the greatest defect in the existing system of education was the foreign medium of instruction. Learning through mother tongue has several advantages:

(i) Language is an essential tool of thought. We can think best in our own language. It is difficult to think critically and clearly in a foreign language.

(ii) Teaching through mother tongue meant saving of time also.

(iii) Having mother tongue as medium of instruction will make the child national minded and patriotic.

(iv) If education is carried out in mother tongue, parents also can help their children a lot in studies.

(v) It is economical. We do not have to employ English language teachers in our schools.

(vi) By having mother tongue as medium, tendency to learn things by rote learning is curbed. It is an obvious psychological advantage. There is no undue strain on the minds of little children.

(vii) It leads to quickness in conservation.

(viii) Children can appreciate things including others' views, better in their own language.

The Craft Centredness: As per the original resolution, education is to be provided through a craft or some purposeful activity. This craft or activity is to serve as the nucleus of all education or all other types of instruction. In fact, this clause, i.e. education through a craft gave a special status to basic education. The development of body and mind which Gandhiji aimed at was possible only through a craft and not otherwise. There are numerous advantages of this or it has been found out that craft centred education is (i) psychologically, (ii) sociologically, and (iii) physically sound.

As a result of exercise one becomes physically sound. A healthy mind exists in a healthy body. We get able citizens. Craft is in agreement with child's psychology. The child is active. When he works on a craft, he feels satisfied. Further it gives concrete shape to abstract knowledge.

Sociologically, craft is useful in teaching live and let one live. It teaches one co-operation.

Let us see in detail how craft is Physically, Psychologically and Sociologically sound.

Physical Aspect of Craft: It is good to develop children physically. These days we are having intellectual giants but very weak people on the physical side. In fact the healthy mind will exist only in healthy bodies and not otherwise. Physically healthy inhabitants are an asset. Able bodies citizens are all the more needed in a country which is threatened by the enemies. During these years after freedom, we have become so lethargic or have kept ourselves busy with intellectual pursuits that the very thought of enemy attacking us sends a chill down our spine. We get nervous breakdown and the business community especially runs for their lives. Education through activity or work or craft, thus, has numerous advantages. It will strengthen the muscles and build resistance power and stamina of the child and will keep numerous diseases away. Good physique also means less temptation to commit a crime as the power of resistance is much more.

Psychological Aspects: The introduction of craft in education is psychologically sound because of the following reasons:

(i) It is in agreement with child's psychology. The child is active. He likes to do things and roam about. It is simply criminal on our part to make him sit at a place or in a corner for hours together and bore him with what we call teaching in an attempt to put into his little brain at which is bookish and dry. Education through craft is based on the psychological principle of learning by doing.

(ii) Education through craft makes education interesting. Children get added pleasure if they can produce something of their own as a result of their own efforts.

(iii) Abstract thoughts are hard to learn. Learning by doing and through a craft, gives those ideas concrete shape and children learn quickly.

(iv) Craft suits children of all levels of intelligence. It appeals particularly to children of low intelligence. They will be enable to do something worthwhile in school instead of sitting like dump driven cattle and going home blank.

(v) Craft gives confidence to children in the sense of the success which they achieve while doing a work.

(vi) Craft work releases the children from the tyranny of hooks. They feel happy and refreshed while working. Being a book-worm sometimes affects one's health badly.

(vii) Through craft, children will also be sublimating their instincts and it will keep them mentally healthy and alert.

(viii) Lastly, one more principle which makes the introduction of craft in education psychologically sound is the principle of transfer of training. While educating through a craft we are going to instill many habits like cleanliness, orderliness, honesty, truthfulness, etc. in our students. They are bound to transfer these habits picked up during their school age into the other spheres of life later when they grow up.

Sociological Aspects

(i) We shall teach them the principle of live and let live. One for all and all for one.

(ii) Through craft, we shall teach them the dignity of labour. Self help is the best help. That babu type mentality must disappear and this way it can go. Teaching through craft be all the more stressed during the year 11-14 because it is here that children feel enchanted by the white collared professions and shirk manual work.

(iii) When all work together, barriers of caste, creed and religion amongst different human beings disappear. It will bring in kinship and solidarity. We shall not grow in isolation and be ready to help one another in time of need. It diminishes social prejudices.

(iv) It will teach us cooperation.

That is why craft is to form vehicle of all education. It is not present system of education plus a craft but education through craft. The former approach means that we want to give training in a special trade. It has not to be understood like that. Mahatma Gandhi suggested two crafts, i.e. Agriculture and Spinning and Weaving for education.

Self-sufficiency: To Gandhiji, self-sufficiency was the acid test of basic education. It may be noted that the traditional system of education being costly did not appeal to Gandhiji and that was why he laid stress on the fact that his system of education should be self-sufficient, i.e. the students do not have to pay anything for their education. The salaries of the teachers would be met by selling the produce which we get as a result of work on the craft. Every student will also get something, i.e. mid-day meal and two uniforms of khadi in a year. Naturally everybody would run for such type of education. By working on craft, children can pay in kind and that could be the only fees for their education. Gandhiji was never worried about the building of the school. He considered it a responsibility of the society to provide shelter for its children. By working for one another and for their benefit, children will learn the importance of money. It will also teach them to be economical and will also tell them that it is sin to exploit the poor ones. This type of approach will also prepare the individual for life. Further, it will also help us in realising Gandhiji's objective of educating each and every Indian.

Correlated Teaching: Mahatma Gandhi wanted all education to be imparted through craft. He had suggested two crafts for the purpose, i.e. agriculture and spinning and weaving. He wanted to present knowledge as a whole, as an integrated whole. He never wanted to pigeon hole it or give it in the shape of air-tight compartments. He wanted to relate knowledge to life and also correlated teaching to craft as the centre of education and the only means of doing so. Other advantages of correlated teaching are:

(i) It makes education easier.

(ii) It raises the standard of education.

(iii) It makes the subject interesting.

(iv) It checks and reduces note learning, and

(v) It increases love of environment in the child and makes him a good citizen.

A.B. Solanki has tried hand to tell us about the concept, etc. of correlation in his book, "This Technique of Correlation in Basic Education." He has given us various types of correlation, i.e. Unilateral, Bilateral and Multilateral type of correlation. There is another classification and which is more realistic and comprehensible, viz. natural and forced correlation. About this we shall talk more when we come to criticism part of this aspect.

Creed of Non-violence: Mahatma Gandhi was sick of the communal and international strife. He wanted to create a generation who knew to live in harmony and was based on mutual love, regard and admiration for members of different communities. He wanted to create a generation who should believe in non-violence and that was possible only when we taught that to little children from the very beginning. He saw that it could be realised through basic education.

Ideal of Citizenship: Gandhiji (as a corollary to the above feature) wanted to make children ideal citizens of the country. After all, a child of today is a potential citizen or citizen of tomorrow. He must know his duties and rights, responsibilities and privileges. In the set up of pre-partition days, education in this direction was not given, i.e. education to develop civic sense was completely ignored. Through basic education, he wanted to make children right type of citizens.

Basic Education and Teacher: In the traditional system of education, the teacher has got hardly anything to do at his own initiative except to follow and finish the rigid syllabus laid own for him by somebody else, sometimes not connected with education at all. There is little that the teacher can do on his own. His schedule is tight and his hands are full. In basic education, the things are the other way round. There is ample scope for experimentation. This system will keep the teacher active and will compel him to do something. Other than this, Gandhiji assigned to the teacher position of great responsibility and importance. The chief concern of the teacher is moral training or character building of the child and that only could make us a strong nation. The teacher is expected to be a selfless worker and ready to suffer consciously to any extent for truth and non-violence.

Positive Aspects

1. There is more of elasticity and variety in it.
2. It is child centred education.
3. Basic Education is not textbook ridden. To be precise, Gandhiji was dead against the use of text-books in basic education.
4. There is no importance of formal examinations. Day-to-day work of the child is to be assessed. It has radically changed the concept of evaluation in modern education.

This system was accepted as the National System of Education immediately after independence. And Shri G. Ramachandran has rightly called it the most dynamic educational concept in Indian educational history.

What Makes Basic Education Basic? It is indeed a very relevant question which needs an answer. Gandhiji's system of education is basic because of the following reasons:

(i) The word 'Basic' is derived from the word 'Base' which means the foundation of a thing on which the entire superstructure rests.

(ii) Gandhiji's system is basic because this much education is mere fundamental to individual's survival in the world. It is the minimum education which every Indian is expected to have or receive without any consideration whatsoever.

(iii) The system of Basic Education is closely reacted to the basic needs and interests of the child.

(iv) It is basic became it comes first in time, i.e. when it is the primary period of the education of the individual.

(v) It is basic because it takes into consideration Indian culture, basic potentialities of the person and professions of the community.

The Assessment

Free and Compulsory Education: Gandhiji told us that education for all children would be free in the age group of 7-14. Later on the Committee headed by Mr. B. G. Kher recommended that it should be so for all children between 6-14. The Punjab Government Passed an act in this direction. It also went further and made education upto the higher secondary level free. This created a lot of fuss for there was a mad-rush on the part of children who sought admission in government schools. The private management's felt strongly about this also as these schools too were badly hit by large scale migrations to the state-run schools. After a while, the Govt. also felt the economic strains of this step and it withdrew its order of making education upto the higher secondary level free. These days in Punjab, education is free for all children between the age group 6-11. The reasons as to why we have not been able to expand and make primary education free in the entire country have been discussed in the chapter on primary education.

Mother-Tongue as Medium of Instruction: In principle, it is an ideal thing to educate children in their own language which they comprehend and follow. But in practice, this is not possible as it has generated much heat in political quarters and we have with us what is known as language problem. Further, in a country like India by educating children through mother-tongue (in many cases the provincial-language) are we not creating unbreakable barriers on the basis of language? A

Tamilian will not be understood in Punjab and a Punjabi will not be followed at all in Assam. Is not it a step towards national disintegration? This criticism, though valid has been met. Mother-tongue is good, say excellent, as far as early education of the child is concerned but for higher education, we have to think of a medium which is understood all over the country. Further, in mother-tongue we may not have enough books for the child in a subject and sometimes suitable vocabulary for technical terms be not available in the mother-tongue. That is why we advocate the study of two languages or three languages. Unfortunately, we have not been able to ban English because of sentimental or other seasons. So mother-tongue be used as, medium of instruction for the early education of the child and then we shift to either English or Hindi unless the child has a mind to specialise in that language (his mother-tongue). (See also Language Problem).

Craft Centredness: Craft centredness is the only unique and distinguishing feature of basic education and befittingly, maximum criticism has been directed against this aspect of basic education. This aspect has been least understood and appreciated. Let us examine briefly the points of criticism and how those have been met with:

(a) Education through craft is nothing but child labour as through his handwork, we are going to pay off the teachers. This is true when the concept of self-sufficiency is understood in old context (pre-independence days) or stretched too far. Nowadays we are not so rigid about self-sufficiency and there is no harm if the child works a little on it.

(b) Working on a craft for sometimes or some hours in day may exhaust children. They may not be able to concentrate on their studies in the class later when they assemble for the purpose. They may get tired or fatigued early. This criticism is met by the saying that man is but a creature of habit. Soon, children will adjust to the routine and habit of working will be formed.

(c) By talking of craft and by making it a centre of all education, are we not going back to the cow dung age? Are we not putting the clock back when this is an atomic age and a century of rapid industrialisation? This point too stands contradicted. Well 'by installing the industry', what do we do? The answer is production. We are interested in production (other than 'population' of course) and through the craft, if we can produce something other than educating the children, well and good. It certainly goes to our advantage and our economy stands strengthened.

(d) Introduction of craft will make education all the more costly. After all to run the show successfully, we need tools and implements and also a room to store those and a chowkidar to take care of them. We have to spend money on their maintenance also in the years to come. Further, we need craft teachers also. All this adds to the cost of education. But then the question is which system of education is cheap system? In all systems of education, initial investment has to be made and what is the harm if we invest a little more in basic education when we know that this is a better system of education and the results are going to be splendid. You be the judge and decide.

(e) Introduction of craft leads to a compressed sort of atmosphere. There is no freedom. It is wrong allegation. We have to learn discipline and work as team to produce something useful.

(f) Craft makes basic system a rural system of education. Well, we can make some changes in its content to have its universal appeal.

(g) Teachers are lazy. They misuse (or 'use') craft to the maximum and have a lot of free time. Their attitude is bad attitude. They assign some task to children, i.e. to dig up a field and themselves enjoy the leisure thus afforded in idle gossip. It is indeed sad and I, being a teacher myself, hang my head in shame for all teaching community. It will be good if right attitude is inculcated in them towards craft work.

(h) Education through work does not appeal to intelligent and brilliant children. We can tell them the importance of work and the obvious advantages of physical labour and convert them to our side rather than force them. Further, there will be few such cases and they can be ignored also if no other way is available or let them do that work which is intellectual and is related to craft such as maintaining stock store register and accounts.

How to Select a Craft ?: We have to apply certain criteria while selecting a craft. The criteria suggested are:

(i) Select only that craft which has got educational potentialities, which has horizontal and vertical dimensions or deep enough so that all education could be provided through it.

(ii) It must be in accordance with the geographical conditions of the locality.

(iii) It must suit the needs of the people. It must be also interesting.

(iv) It must have productive aspect otherwise, the self-sufficiency aspect is bound to suffer.

(v) There must be availability of raw material-otherwise the students may sit idle and waste their time and energy.

(vi) It must suit the age of children so that they are able to handle it suitably and with confidence.

(vii) It must provide children with good experiences.

(viii) Tools must be available.

Urban Schools and Craft: Another problem is craft for urban schools. Gandhiji has suggested only two crafts, viz. agriculture and spinning and weaving. But these are suitable for rural schools or for those urban schools with which sufficient land is available. But what about craft for those schools which are located in congested localities or in big cities e.g. for schools in Bombay where children have not even seen real cows or buffaloes? To talk of agriculture to them will be like casting pearls before swine. So it was quite a lot of problem to think of a craft suited for urban cities. Answer is that we should not be rigid in having only in those two crafts as suggested by the Father of the Nation. Let us choose one in the light of the geographical conditions and educational potentialities. We can have wood-work or utensil making as craft in the city schools. Those can serve us well for the concept of teaching solely though craft has undergone a change as discussed in the next pages.

Self-sufficiency Aspect: Just like craft, this aspect of basic education has also been vehemently-criticised and naturally we had to change the concept. In fact the failure of basic education has been due to over-stress on this aspect. The chief points of criticism are:

(a) A basic school will be self-sufficient only when 15 acres of land is attached to it. It is thus next to impossible to have 15 acres of land attached to each and every school. Will it not thus check the opening of new schools and spread of education which we aim to provide to each and everyone?

(b) Tools and implements are required. Children cannot work with bare hands. It is said that sufficient number of tools are not available and in a number of places, those are not well maintained, or are out of order. In many teacher training colleges, for 100 students only 30 'Kahis' are available and during the agriculture period, 30 students are busy while the rest, i.e. 70 loaf about. The same is true at the school level. When workers are idle, how can you expect basic education to be self-sufficient?

(c) Self-sufficiency is possible only if we have all eight classes in the school and in every class there are thirty students. After all, we need workers to work and we are not going to employ outsider to work for us. This, i.e. to have eight classes and each having thirty students is next to impossible. It may be noted that we must have thirty students in the last two classes because it is the grown up children who are going to be of tremendous help in realising the target of their school being self-sufficient. This again is not possible, populated as our country is. In many of the modern high/higher secondary schools, the number of students in the last two classes is three sometimes. So, under these circumstances we cannot achieve self-sufficiency.

(d) The quality of the goods that we are going to produce in school be much better or should be favourably in comparison to the same produced in the factories or elsewhere only then people are going to buy it and we are going to earn something from it. We do not bother for quality and as such we suffer. The product manufactured in the school thus has to be thrown in the gutter. We may take the case of ink or chalk or soap which we make in our schools (even in colleges in the hobby classes). The quality is horribly inferior. This amounts to waste. Thus the self-sufficiency target cannot be realised.

(e) Further, if we remain obsessed by the aim or realising self-sufficiency in our schools, the quality of education stands lowered down. We achieve this at the cost of education. Our school then ceases to be a school, it becomes a factory and the students become factory workers. Is it not child labour? It is not exploitation?

Because of all this and because of changed circumstances (In 1937, Gandhiji never realised that we shall be free so soon), the concept of self-sufficiency has undergone a change. We have a national government—our own government, and education is its responsibility. It will pay the teachers. Children do not have to bother now. Further, we cannot do away at the same time with self-sufficiency. It will rob much of the charm of craft centredness of education. The only thing is now that we are not rigid about our schools being self-sufficient. These days, the concept of self-sufficiency is that if we can provide a child with one uniform in a year and mid-day meals, the school be taken as self-sufficient. Let us see how far we shall achieve this target though in many cases it stands practically abandoned.

Correlation and Basic Education: Correlation was indeed a unique feature of this scheme but correlated teaching somehow or other has not been possible. Gandhiji suggested craft as a centre or the only centre of correlation. This was not possible. All knowledge could not be correlated with the one centre, i.e. craft which was suggested. In later days two more centres, viz. Physical and Social Environments of correlation were added.

In all, there are now three centres of correlation—(i) Craft, (ii) Physical environment, and (iii) Social environment. But the tragedy is that we do not have those teachers who are experts in correlated teaching. If at all, there is any correlation, it is all forced, unnatural and foul. Ultimately, we had to make concessions in this direction also. Further correlation is possible only in lower stages but at higher stages say in post-graduate classes, this cannot be done. The 1963, version of correlation in basic education is, "Correlate what you can, where you cannot, do not bother." What it amounts to actually is basic education with all the changes highlighted earlier minus correlation. Other points of Criticism against Basic education are:

Confusion in the Understanding: The great master M.K. Gandhi, now being dead, there is hardly anyone left now who could clarify our doubts from time to time. There is a wild charge in some quarters that the founder himself, M.K. Gandhi, was not clear about his contribution. This is not so. He in fact, was so busy in other activities, that he could not devote much time in this direction in his life time.

More of Sentiment: Gandhi was a great man and we revered him, therefore all that he said or did was equally great and needs all attention from us all. It may be true as sentimentality makes one coward and he closes his eyes towards the defects of the scheme. But it is again our fault. Gandhiji never wanted us to be sentimental.

Attitude of Teachers: It is all the more painful when we come specially to teacher education because their attitude is picked up by those who are going to teach in basic schools. In a study conducted by the author in 1964, it was found out that most of the teacher educators teaching in Basic training colleges in erstwhile Punjab in 1963-64, were neutral or had no attitude towards Basic education. It is better to have negative attitude than to have no attitude towards thing. The conclusion is that they have many doubts in their minds and those very-doubts are being passed on to posterity and thus incalculable harm stands done to Basic education. It is a question of lack of faith and availability of right type of teachers.

Apathy of Parents: As the case with teachers, so is true of parents. By Basic education, parents understand work. This is how it has been interpreted to them. A parent sends a child to school to learn something and when on return from school, the child tells his parents that he did this much digging and that much spinning, the parent is flabbergasted. He prays that sooner the Basic scheme fails, the better.

Suitable Text Books not Available: But it has been found out that we cannot do without these. Text-books have to be used as an aid towards education. Those have to supplement the scheme. It will be unwise to outrightly reject the text-books. After all, the labour of man over the past so many centuries lies stored up in books and text-books. So we accept the use of text-books in basic education. Suitable text-books are not available.

Lack of Funds: It is better to keep quiet on this aspect. Much has already been said elsewhere.

Opposed by Certain Traditionalists: They do not want any change in the existing system of education. In the traditionalists, we may have some administrators also. They have crippled it. It is a vicious circle of blaming one another perhaps. Educationists and teachers blame the administrators and stand blamed in return. The thing stands where it was.

Lopsidedness of Reform: It only touches one aspect of Indian education and does not bother for other stages.

All said and done, Basic education in itself was something unique and good. We have given it a different colouring and instead of implementing it by making suitable changes in the scheme as originality conceived in order to achieve something positive we have played with it. It is tragic that we have given it our colouring and by making it a point of controversy we have rung its death knell. It as a topic, occupied an important place in postgraduate courses of many universities and now it has been reduced to the status of a mere educational problem which hardly merits anybody's attention. That was why because of the poor quality of basic schools, Dr. Zakir Hussain, one of the founders of Basic education scheme was led to remark that the system of Basic education as it was practised recently was a fraud. Other epithets which are associated with Basic education are FARCE, FAD, FAULTY. The sooner thus we correct our mistakes the better it would be but we must remember that the main contribution of Basic education has been to make us realise the fact that a system of book-centred education which the traditional schools have been providing so far is no good for the country. We are not going back to purely bookish learning at least in the primary stages, even if we have to abandon Basic education. We are to have work in our curriculum and that itself is the biggest success of Basic education. It has convinced us that for some more years to come, if we do not learn to work with our own hands and stick to white-collar attitude, we are going to perish.

Basic education exists as a fad at some places in the country. In reality, it has vanished from India especially after 1969-Gandhi Birth Centenary Year! Strange! No funds were allocated for Basic education in 4th Five Year Plan ending in 1974. The National Institute of Basic Education at New Delhi was also wound up in 1969.

Over all, the future holds no promise for Basic scheme unless we reaffirm our faith in the ideals of Basic scheme and rededicate ourselves to it. What is now important is to have Basic education attitude.

Gandhiji meant by education, "an all round drawing out of the best in child and man—body, mind and spirit". Harmonious development of all power-innate and acquired, was the chief goal of Gandhian education. "True education", he said, "must stimulate the spiritual, intellectual and physical faculties of the children." This all round education, he believed could be given through craft. His emphasis on it is composed, advancing, and conversely, no individual can advance without the nation of which it is a part, also advancing." Gandhiji held, "that the individual must work out his perfection in a spiritual society."

He did not agree with Rousseau that the individual can develop in a social vacuum. Self-realisation and social service must go hand in hand. An individual, according to him "can make the best of himself in a State and the State can achieve its highest development only on the condition that each of its citizens gives the best that is in him." The individual develops in a social atmosphere. It is there that it can have common interest and can engage himself in common activities. Like John Dewey, Gandhiji wanted to transform the schools into communities where individuals get abundant opportunities of social contact and co-operation.

Gandhiji synthesised the individual and the social aims of education. He proved it by example and precept that 'self-realisation' and 'social service' were not contradictory. A fusion of the two in a man made him complete.

6

Tagore

Education has been defined as a consciously controlled process whereby changes in behaviour are produced in a person, and through him in a group. It is a gradual adjustment of the individual to the spiritual possessions of the race. Hence, education is considered to be normative in that it explores various aspects of human personality so as to prescribe a generally suitable and acceptable programme of learning which should be conducive for the attainment of its objectives and goals. However, there has been a continuous change in the nature, extent and import of these objectives which are inversely related to the meaning and reality ascribed to human nature and to the environment in which education takes place. Hence, education is in dire need of some sort of a philosophy which may provide it with direction and roots, stability and purpose.

Life is dynamic, it is a continuous change. Since education invariably occurs in a social matrix, it also acquires the same characteristic. The ideals of life are eternally at variance, due to contemporary socio-economic conditions and political ideology, and their conflict, for whatever reason, reflects itself in educational theories. Hence, as long as life is what it is, in all ages the singular aim of education had been to educate man to achieve his complete self in accordance with the concepts prevalent from time to time. Education, therefore, is a means to achieve functions of philosophy.

As the field of education has been possessed by respective philosophies as the final means of shaping the young minds toward attainment of prescribed goals, education, in this sense, is an offshoot of philosophy and it translates those desirable objectives through its inherent processes and spells out means for doing so. Ross speaks of this "inevitable tendency of the philosophers to turn into educationist" as the great philosophers of all ages and of all countries, have also been great educators. This is but logical because if one does not preach his own philosophy who else would, and the best means of preaching one's philosophy is to ensure it as an instrument of human regeneration.

Rabindranath Tagore based his philosophy of education on human regeneration. The main tenet of his philosophy is the ultimate affinity between man, nature and God. His educational philosophy is an attempt at self-realisation by means of communion with nature and God. He lays special emphasis on education as a means of self-realisation which consists in the realisation of the universal soul in one's self. According to him the fundamental purpose of education is not merely to enrich ourselves through the fullness of knowledge but also to "establish the bond of love and friendship between man and man".

The spark of divinity that Tagore saw in man lends a special significance and import to his philosophy of education as it singles him out as a visionary who had his feet planted on firm ground. His philosophy is as much relevant today as it was during his time: it is a philosophy of love and compassion responsive to human hopes and despair. It is a philosophy of man in search of himself in this myriad of wonderland called universe. Man is not only the centre of this edifice but is the "measure and the sanction of all things". Tagore believes that the chief end of human life is to work for happiness of man upon this earth within the confines of nature which is his home. His philosophy of education is an elaboration of this central theme and provides ample opportunities to reconcile and resolve apparent anomalies in our day to day life. Tagore is a champion of humanity, of human values and ideals. His philosophy of education aims at producing enfranchised citizens who may hold their heads high without any fear in their hearts.

Significant Contribution

Rabindranath Tagore was one of those contemporary philosophers of education who may be called a humanist in the most strict sense of the term. His humanism is not naturalistic but is integral to the tradition of Indian humanism. His philosophy was cosmopolitan humanism of which his theory of education was a direct corollary.

His Purposes

The aim of education, according to Rabindranath, was self-realisation. He was a great poet and a saint who through his imagination and insight, realised the universal soul within himself and in Nature. This realisation by every one, according to him, was the goal of education. Self-realisation means the realisation of the universal soul in one's self. Man's aim in life is to achieve this status, a process which, cannot be realised without education. Education, therefore, is integral to life. In the absence of education the individual will be deprived of self-realisation. Rabindranath did not find any incompatibility between thought and life, philosophy and education, both are inversely related and are inclusive of each other.

Rabindranath believed that every one is potentially divine and every one can realise this potentiality. Man has a spark of divinity in him which inspires him for self-attainment, self-realisation, the realisation of his true nature. Education should, therefore, provide opportunities to harness these innate potentialities. His philosophy was influenced by the great Indian traditions contained in the Gita and the Upanishads, though Rabindranath had the added advantage of familiarity with the educational ideas prevalent in the West. Therefore, like other Indian humanists, he synthesised the ancient Vedic traditions with the modern western scientific attitude in formulating the goals of education.

Defining the aims of education Rabindranath said "the fundamental purpose of education is not merely to enrich ourselves through the fullness of knowledge but also to establish the bond of love and friendship between man and man." This shows the humanistic aim of education in his philosophy. His approach to ultimate reality was integral and therefore he believed in an inner harmony between man and nature, and nature and God. The trinity of man, Nature and God is in fact the three dimensional view of the same reality. In man again, the physical, the mental and the spiritual aspects are equally important and are internally related. Rabindranath, therefore, believed in multisided education with physical, intellectual, moral and religious overtones. He condemned the system of education "which partially exercised the intellect only to the entire neglect of the body." Education of the body in the real sense, according to him, "does not exist in play and exercise, but in applying the body systematically to some useful work". Thus, one of the aims of education, according to Rabindranath, is physical development and he gives it a special treatment and import.

The Progress

It was quite natural for Rabindranath to emphasise the role of games in the school education. Pointing out the value of physical activities in the children's education he said "even if they learnt nothing they would have had ample time for play, climbing trees, diving into ponds, plucking flowers, perpetuating thousand and one mischiefs on Mother Nature, they would have attained the nourishment of the body, happiness of mind, and the satisfaction of the natural impulses of childhood". It is the active process of familiarisation with nature, a sort of feeling it on their pulse, that is so central to his educational system. The physical fitness is the first cardinal principle in the child's development, which is possible through intimate contact with Nature.

As a poet Rabindranath well realised the life-giving value of Nature's contact with man. About this he said "I speak in very moderate terms: seven years till then let the child have nothing to do with clothes and shame. Till then let nature alone conduct the indispensable education of the savage. This is particularly relevant for the educational institutions in our society. Almost all contemporary Indian philosophers of education including Gandhi, Vivekanand, Dayanand, Aurobindo and Tagore point out the importance of setting educational institutions in natural environment so that the educands may learn by their touch with Nature. Rabindranath translated his faith in Nature by setting up his three institutions, Shantiniketan, Vishvabharti and Sriniketan in similar atmosphere.

Preparing the Land

Tagore lays equal emphasis on the mental aim of education. He was critical of the prevalent system of education which laid sole emphasis on bookish learning. Condemning this tendency Tagore said "we touch the world not with our minds, but with our books. Intellectualism takes us away from nature and creates a schism between man and man as we know only the people of the books, not those of the world.. Intellectual aim of education should be the development of the intellectual faculties such as logical thinking, critical appraisal and assimilation, sharpening of sensibility and imagination. Thinking and Imagination are the two faculties which should be developed through education as they are vital for adult life". The emphasis on the education of sensibility rings a familiar note contained in the philosophy of another great poet, John Keats who drew inspiration from the immortal system of Immanual Kant who made sensibility and imagination central to his critical philosophy.

Rabindranath criticised the prevalent system of education which puts unnatural premium on memory and cramming with too little left for thinking and imagination. He said "since childhood, instead of putting all the burden on the memory, the power of thinking and the power of imagination, should also be given opportunities for free exercise."

> "True education consists in knowing the use of any useful material that has been collected to know its real nature and to build alongwith life a real shelter for life". Education should facilitate assimilation of culture so that the educand, by means of education, is able to use it in his interaction with the environment. Explaining this aim of education, Rabindranath said "if we believe that the chief aim of education for an Indian is to initiate into the unique pursuit of infinite, then we must constantly remember that neither the education of the senses nor that of the intellect, but the education of feelings, that should receive the place of honour in our schools, our true education is possible only in the forest through intimate contact with nature and purifying austere pursuits".

Specific Targets

Tagore's approach toward aim of education was realistic. He was, however, not favourable to utilitarian aim of education which has permeated the present day philosophy of education. He objected to the imposition of the British system of education on India which has damaged the body structure of the Indian system of education to such an extent that in spite of concerted efforts since Independence nothing much could be done to minimise its influence on the ethos of Indian intelligentia. Tagore said "knowledge has two departments: one pure knowledge, and the other utilitarian knowledge, whatever is worth knowing is knowledge. It should be known equally by man and woman, not for practical utility but for the sake of knowing, the desire to know is the law of human nature."

But Rabindranath did not ignore the earning of livelihood aim of education. He appreciated the practical bias in the western system of education. Though he did not want to make education as an instrument or means for earning livelihood alone, he admitted that bread earning is a necessary part of any sound goal of education.

Therefore, he said that from the very beginning such education should be imparted, that one may know what mass welfare means, and which may facilitate earning a livelihood. He emphasised that the real aim of education is to develop man and woman who may be able to fulfil the needs of the country; "one of the main aims of education is to prepare the individuals for the service as future citizens by equipping them with such skills that enable them to take up their appointed role, as well as to foster socially desirable attitudes. Tagore, however, did not give as much importance to utilitarian aim of education as was done by Gandhi who considered education as an insurance against unemployment and exploitation.

New Ideology

Tagore's philosophy of education cannot be understood without understanding his metaphysical theory which revolves around the concept of Cosmic Man: a vision, a poet's dream which Tagore cherished and lived by. Referring to Cosmic Man as the ultimate reality Tagore said "truth is the infinite pursued by metaphysics, fact is the infinite pursued by science, while reality is the definition of the infinite which relates truth to the person. Reality is human: it is what we are conscious of, by which we are affected, that which we express". The Cosmic Man, is known by individual not by his reason or logic but through direct realisation, a sort of communion. In the words of Tagore "Reality, in all its manifestations, reveals itself in the emotional and imaginative background of our mind, we know it, not because we think of it, but because we directly feel it. It is not banished from our conscious mind". This further affirms Tagore's emphasis on the feeling aspect of human experience. He considered man more central to the scheme of things. Man is more than reason, a soul, a spirit, a finite-infinite being, an angel who seems to have lost his wings, and is now in the process of becoming.

The idea of Cosmic Man is in conformity with the message in the Gita: the message of Vishvaroopi Darshan. The cosmic man is at the back of all movements, all change, all order and system in the universe: he is the measure of everything and is central to all movement. The relation between him and Nature is panentheistic which finds meaning in the concept of God. Cosmic Man includes both Nature and God. Rabindranath admitted "I have never looked at God, Man and Nature as problems which can be considered in isolation from each other. I could never conceive of their occupying watertight compartments". Cosmic Man lives even in the humblest person, therefore, even the lowliest of the low should not suffer from personal and social neglect. The worship of the poor is the direct corollary of Tagore's vision of the Cosmic Man. He said "He is where the tiller is tilling the hard ground, where the path maker is breaking the stones. He is with them in sun and shower, and His garment is covered with dust (and sweat). Put off your holy mantle and like him come down on the dusty soil". That work is worship, was an essential tenet of Tagore's Cosmic Man, and he lived by it.

Concerning the metaphysical problem arising from assigning personality to the ultimate reality, it should be remembered that for Rabindranath personality is not something limited and mundane but unlimited and supra-mundane while in the man it is found in the first form, in Cosmic Man it may be seen in the second meaning. Elucidating this meaning of Cosmic Man he writes "This personality which is the conscious principle of oneness, the centre of relationships, is the reality, therefore the ultimate object of attainment, this world exists only in its relation to a central personality. When that centre is taken away, it falls to pieces, because a heap of abstractions, matter and force, logical symbols, and even those thinnest semblance of reality, would vanish if the logical person in the centre to whom they are related in some harmony of reason were nowhere".

He is more for the 'saguna' form of reality rather than 'nirguna' form of reality which blinds human mind and soul by its sheer brilliance.

God is the perfect person. Man is a person in an imperfect sense: he is always in the process of becoming, moving toward the attainment of his true self. He is an individual whereas God is a person. He is a Cosmic Man. He is the super person who is seen in different forms which are virtually all-inclusive. He is anthropomorphic and is endowed with human attributes which make Him intelligible to man. It is in Him that human beings share their experiences. "The relational world is for me both individual and universal. My world is mine but it is also yours, it is not in my own individual personality that Reality is contained, but in an infinite personality.

Tagore avoids the solipsistic and mentalistic tendencies inherent in the philosophy of Berkeley, as well as the pitfalls of the philosophy of Nietzsche whose Super Man is the negation of both man and reality. Tagore's idea of Cosmic Man is human, is in and through the work and toil that spells human life, is responsive to human hopes and despair, in short, is one with man, is humane.

Place of a Person

Reality according to Tagore is one in which God, Nature and Man reside in a spirit of intimate relationship. The three are, infact, three dimensions of the same reality. Man is intimately related to God and Nature. Man and Nature are but two expressions of the same Divine. Divinity is panentheistic, it runs in and through the fabric of all creation; it permeates the cosmos. In his philosophy of education, Rabindranath considers the intimate relationship of man and nature as the basis of self-realisation. His system accepts both in a spirit of mutual dependence and harmony. Nature is propitious, is conducive toward man's attainment of his spiritual and material excellence. Nature and Man are mutually amenable. Tagore says "In the west the prevalent feeling is that nature consists exclusively of inanimate things and beasts, that there is sudden unaccountable break where human nature begins. According to it, everything that is low in the scale of beings is merely Nature, and whatever has the stamp of perfection in it, intellectual and moral, is human nature. The Indian mind never had any hesitation in acknowledging its kinship with nature, its unbroken relation with all".

The intimate relationship between man and nature is the hal-mark of Indian philosophy. This relation is conceived as companionship, a permanent source of inspiration, a state of communion. A life divorced from nature cannot be a complete life, according to Tagore, even in the liberated state our relationship with Nature continues. "The soul's birth in the spiritual world does not coincide with severance of relationship with what we call nature, but freedom of relationship".

It was this firm conviction of the intimate relationship between man and nature that made Tagore emphasise so much on the natural environment in schools. He wanted that "young mind should be saturated with the idea that it has been born in a human world which is in harmony with the world around it". Even the superiority of man lies in his ability to be in union with nature, an ability which is not quite possessed by other living beings.

Human Dimensions

Derived from Latin 'Homo' meaning human being, Humanism is the philosophy in which man is the measure of everything. In historical retrospect whatever had been found to be useful for human welfare has been attached with the concept of humanism such as the ideas of social welfare, scientific attitude, progress of democratic institutions and other such concepts emerging out of the process of democratisation of man and society. As a philosophy, humanism has a definite notion regarding man, his problems and universe. Greatest good of the greatest number according to democratic means is the mainstay of this social and philosophical concept. Its major contributions have been:

(a) Belief in life in harmony with the noblest ideas and the highest values.

(b) Affirms the dignity of man.

(c) Faith in the necessity of establishing a social order based on peace, progress and democracy.

(d) Commitment to peace and a meaningful concept must have far reaching influences on the social and educational aspects of a society. The impact, in brief, is as under:

  (i) Education is considered an important part of man and society.

  (ii) Education has creative role in establishing an ideal society.

  (iii) Education is an agency of freedom and responsibility.

  (iv) Employment-oriented education.

To sum up, man is not only the centre, he is the measure and the sanction of all things. Humanism believes that the chief end of human life is to work for happiness of man upon this earth within the confines of nature which is his home.

Pointing out the human elements in Tagore's philosophy, Humayun Kabir wrote "Rabindranath Tagore was one of the greatest humanists that the world has known. The key-note of his life was resistance to tyranny in all forms. He struggled against economic exploitation, political subjugation, social inertia and injustice, and religious intolerance and insensitiveness". These words, however, do not convey the most important aspect of Tagore as a humanist. Undoubtedly he fought for human virtues but the more important point is that he presented a humanistic philosophy and a religion of man which again were the foundation stone of a gigantic system of humanistic education.

Tagore was essentially a poet, therefore, his Humanism is generally expressed in his literature. Pointing out this facet, he writes "Humanity is the very epitome of the wide and varied universe. To know it properly is to realise the highest manifestation of Brahma since all its world wide aspect of humanity is permeated with the spirit of God. This universal greatness of humanity has truly found its triumphant poetic expression in our age in the literature of Rabindranath".

Besides literature, Tagore's Humanism is expressed by his idea of religion of man. His works Dear testimony to his unstinted emphasis upon the uniqueness of the human individual, his greatness in the world of the living, and his intimate relationship with nature and God. It was due to his Humanism that while he opposed the British, he was not against the British people.

It was again this Humanism which made him work relentlessly for the establishment of a cosmopolitan educational institution in the form of Shantiniketan. His educational system is as much the embodiment of his Humanism as his literature is its expression.

Method of Education

The most important means of education, according to Tagore, is the environment of the child. The importance of natural environment has been accepted by almost all contemporary educational psychologists. It is through the natural environment that the child trains his senses by his contact with plants and trees, flowers and leaves. Education, according to Tagore, should be imparted, "in an institution where the first great lesson is the perfect union of man and nature, not only through love but through active communication, can be had unobstructed". It is only in a natural environment that the child can realise the presence of a universal soul which is the root of his existence and also that of nature. The teaching of different subjects is made natural through the intelligent utilisation of the child's environment. His knowledge of science may be helped by his observation of insects and animals, plants and training is helped by his observation and appreciation of forms and colours and movement to the development of the child's sense organs and mind. His creative powers are expressed through his contact with natural objects. His co-curricular activities in natural environment result in the development of different virtues.

Tagore regretted that, "Ours is the only country in recent history where the educational institutions stopped at their boundary walls and were dissociated from the wide world outside". Pointing out to the gulf between bookish knowledge and the child's environment, Tagore lamented that the current education does not help in making the educand either an efficient worker or a good citizen. "It is not enough for a farmer boy only to grow into a good farmer, but he should also grow into a good citizen of the country".

Besides natural environment, social environment is no less important in the development of the child, in fact it is more valuable. The social environment makes the surroundings of the children in which they fulfil their needs and drives and develop their beliefs and ideas. It is the knowledge of this environment which creates the feeling of essential unity of mankind in the child. The impact of the social environment is more explicit in the relationship between the teacher and the taught on the one hand and the educand and his companions on the other. If this relationship is based upon love, sympathy and mutual understanding, the educand adequately develops moral virtues. Every educated person should learn to play a role according to his particular qualities in the human society. The cultural environment again is a part of the social environment. In educational institutions this is created through co-curricular activities and cultural programmes.

The most important means of education is the medium of instruction. Almost all contemporary Indian philosophers of education pleaded for the adoption of mother-tongue as the medium of child's education. Tagore was no exception. He said, "if education does not enter into the deeper strata of the society and does not attain permanence through mingling with the living streams of the mother-tongue, then it can only become an object of temporary beauty but can never become a lasting foundation of life".

India needs education on a large scale particularly technical and vocational education. Tagore realised that this is possible only through the mother-tongue. The use of English language for this purpose had been the main cause of the poor state of education in India. Unless our educational institutions adopt regional languages and national language as medium of instruction and unless sufficient books are available in these languages, the aim of universal education in India will remain a distant dream.

Besides regular teaching in educational institutions through mother-tongue, Rabindranath discovered several other important means of education. He was very much in favour of reviving the old rural institutions in the villages. He attached much educational value to community entertainments, recitals of Ramayana and Mahabharata and religious education. Besides, the community fairs organised in villages from time to time are also useful means of education. The vocational education in the villages is very much helped by the fairs. To make education mass-oriented the means of education should also be indigenous and easily available in the rural areas.

His aim of education was the most comprehensive and included all aspects of human personality, different strata of Indian society, and the world community. Thus, his plan was developed on a very comprehensive perspective. His educational plan is activity-oriented. Its aim was to develop an all-round human personality by means of co-curricular activities besides bookish knowledge. He laid emphasis on physical, mental, oral, religious matters. The curriculum in his educational institutions was not fixed but would change according to the needs of the individual, of the rural masses, of the poor people, and that of man as a member of international community. He wanted to make student-life self-reliant. His aim was to develop a sort of communion between man and Nature. Freedom was the hallmark of his system of education.

Fight for Independence

Tagore believed in complete freedom of all types—intellect, decision-making, knowledge, action and worship—which could be achieved by the practice of equanimity, harmony, and balance. Through this practice the educand could learn to distinguish between true and false, natural and artificial, relevant and irrelevant, permanent and transient, liberal and narrow, universal and individual. Thus, the educand could achieve a harmony in the true and relevant elements. Once he acquired this ability he could progress by self-guidance. This, in fact, is the real meaning of self-education based on self-realisation. Education, according to Tagore, is a progress of self-realisation which lies in the attainment of freedom where intelligence, feeling and determination worked freely. It is not the absence of control but self-control. Once it is achieved there is no danger of straying away from right path because the senses, intelligence, emotions, feelings and mental powers of the educated person are guided by his own self.

Preferred Method

The ideal educational system should aim at man's perfection which means the development of all the aspects of human personality. This is the sole aim of education which again should be realised on a universal scale because an individual can realise itself by acquiring an abiding faith in the universal soul. Thus, education should lead to the realisation of universal man. It should enfranchise human beings. An enfranchised human being has the following virtues: wisdom, steadfastness, emancipation, courage of conviction, sense of discrimination, attitude of friendship and cooperation.

Tagore tried to utilise the findings of modern western educational psychology as well as the wisdom of the ancient Indian sages, in his ideal educational system with activity as its basis. It required both the educand and the educator to be always active. He fully exploited the principles of active responding and learning by doing. Learning and exercise went together. He was against the orthodox or formal discipline and punishment, as he had ardent faith that "only through freedom can man attain his fullness of growth". In his ideal system of education discipline was intrinsic and self-imposed. The educands were allowed to commit mistakes and learn through them as mistakes provide depth to the process of learning as later advocated by Norman Crowder while constructing his Branching programme as a strategy of teaching-learning process.

Tagore was against the prevalent system of evaluation. In this field also he applied the principle of self-determination.

Invigilation was absolutely unnecessary and the examinees themselves took their question papers and answered them. He tried to build up an ideal educational system and experimented in all its facets such as aims, medium, means, curriculum management and co-curricular activities. One may not agree with the details of his educational system and may not call it ideal, but nevertheless, the system bears the stamp of his genius and was a bold superstructure based on a comprehensive philosophy, with the best of intentions of developing perfect men and women as citizens of the world community.

Basic Education

Tagore's ideas about the early childhood education may be traced in his plays such as Kabuliwallah, and Home Coming where Mini and Phatak respectively play the role of a growing child, as well as in the Child's Return and, the Crescent Moon. Tagore wanted the children to grow up into a free and open world. He was convinced that in early years the child should arrive at truth through natural process spontaneously by coming into contact with things and persons. Learning for a child, according to Tagore, is explorative, active and full of joy, where the learning programme is activity-centred. Education "in play and activity precedes all else, and was followed by training through activity and play in order to develop hardy youth" (William Cenker). Tagore also stressed on the creative and artistic aspects of learning, crafts, work and play. "Art for Tagore, is the bridge between man and the world".

In conformity with Froebal and Montessori, Tagore emphasised on learning through movement and rhythm which establishes harmony between body and mind. " Children must express themselves with their whole bodies and education of the body must be in contact with air, water, earth and light. The body should sway with the inner movement of the thought. Employing the whole body, movement must accompany thoughts and emotions". (William Cenker)

Rabindranath Tagore's philosophy of education aimed at developing a system of education for human regeneration through literature, poetry, social activities and educational programmes. He was a humanist in the real sense of the term. Though not a rationalist, he believed in something higher than reason in man. He did not think science alone to be capable of delivering the human goods and, therefore, wanted to synthesise it with Vedanta. He was a nationalist yet transcended the barriers of narrow nationalism: in him the line where the two meet is invisible. As a matter of fact, the concept of internationalism finds meaning and clarity if viewed with reference to nationalism: nationalism should be the springboard to internationalism, and the two should be mutually inclusive. Short of this there shall always be gaps and contradictions.

In fact, the author has a firm belief that it was Tagore's spirit of Internationalism, so much evident in his literary works, that enabled him edge past another great poet and visionary of his time, Muhammad Iqbal, for the race toward the Nobel Prize for literature. A cursory comparison of the poems 'Where the heart is fearless and the head is held high' and 'My country, the most beautiful land', may reveal the two facets of nationalism, but whereas Tagore rises above himself, Iqbal is confounded in the shackles of narrow and parochial nationalism. To Tagore the ultimate God was the Cosmic Man, and the only aim of all the man's efforts was the realisation of God. Human regeneration was his sole aim, and the virtues such as freedom, purity, sympathy, perfection and world brotherhood. He possessed a philosophy which possessed him: the end result was one of the biggest experiments ever conducted in the field of education in contemporary India.

Character Sketch

Rabindra Nath Tagore was one of the fifteen children of Maharishi Davendra Nath Tagore, founder of Brahmo Samaj movement in Bengal. Rabindra Nath Tagore was the fourteenth child. He had six brothers and was youngest amongst brothers. Rabindra Nath Tagore was born in Calcutta on 6th May 1861.

Rabindra Nath Tagore was allergic to formal system of education. He had most of his education in his home at Calcutta through private tutors and private readings. For higher education. Rabindra Nath was sent to Bengal Academy but he was soon fed up with the rigid and lifeless education imparted there. He developed aversion for it and he left Bengal Academy. In 1877, he was sent to England to get education in Law, but, there too he did not complete this education and returned to India without getting the degree.

At the age of 8, he started composing verses and very early in life, he started writing for the Bengali magazines. Gradually love of learning increased by leaps and bounds in him and he wrote many stories, novels and poems. This earned him world wide reputation. He came to be affectionately called as Gurudev.

Rabindra Nath Tagore was married and had children. One of his children died during his life time and this shook him.

In 1913, Rabindra Nath Tagore was the first Indian to have won Nobel prize for literature for his work "Gitanjali". The same year Calcutta University adored him with the degree of D. Litt. In 1915, the Indian government adored him with knighthood which he returned after the notorious Jallianwala Bagh incident in 1919.

Dr. Rabindra Nath Tagore attended M.A. English Classes at the University of Oxford. He travelled widely. He went to Japan, Europe and USA. He had his own philosophy of life and education. To put this into practice, in 1921 he established the famous Vishwa Bharti at Shantiniketan Railway Station. Bolpar, about 140 miles from Calcutta? Vishwa Bharti is now a famous university and is a seat of learning of Indian philosophy and arts. He remained associated with it for nearly 20 years till his death on May 9 (some say May 6) 1941.

Tagore was a philosopher, poet, novelist, dramatist, short story writer, actor, painter and prophet all rolled into one. He enriched Bengali and English languages. He loved humanity and man was divine for him. His works are read all over the world. He has given to us classics.

1. Rabindranath Tagore was married at the age of 18 years to Mrinalini.
2. Tagore had five children three daughters and two sons. Two of them (one son and one daughter) died before they were 13 years. Tagore remained in grief.
3. His wife died in 1902.
4. Tagore started his school in 1901 at Shantiniketan with five teachers and five students.

Theory of Education

Concept of Reality/God: Tagore says. "I have never looked at God, Man and Nature as problems which can be considered in isolation from each other. I could never conceive of their occupying watertight compartment."

Therefore his philosophy presents an integral picture of God, man and nature. He says, "My mind is used to look at reality as an integral whole is being understood of course, that I am referring to the wholeness of the spirit not to material unity."

God is a postulate. It is axiomatic reality. No proofs for the existence of God are needed.

Man is always incomplete. He feels completeness only when he comes in touch with nature. But still he does not get complete satisfaction. "Our satisfaction in Nature, though real, is still incomplete. It is a satisfaction of our empirical ego. But we have our higher self which finds contentment only in infinite."

There are moral grounds for the existence of God. There is no such thing as 'personality of God.' Relationship between God and man must be that of joy and affection.

Independent reality is also self or self is also regarded as independent reality. To him, the independence of self is necessary for Reality as a whole, to quote Dr. S.P. Chaube. In Gitanjali, Tagore describe 'God' and 'man' as two separate realities floating 'at will'. It is true that the human self derives its contents from its affinity with the infinite. But his affinity does not imply that it is not free to have its own individual experiences. Therefore, Tagore does not like to undermine the independence of the self by making it entirely subsequent to the still of God. He believes that self has power to work on its own initiative as well. Reality thus means two things:

(a) Existence of God.

(b) Independence of self.

Concept of Man: He had his own way of looking at man and life was well versed in the teachings of Vedas and Upanishads. For him, supreme is all blissful and the cosmos and the individual as manifestation of the blissful asked of supreme reality. Everything in this world is harmonious and beautiful. Man's life is a saga of discovering and establishing this harmony between his own personality and the universal person and the supreme person. Harmony, beauty and bliss or ananda are the bay votes of his philosophy and approach to life. Tagore recognises absolute blisship between Man and Nature. And he says, "When a man does not realise his kinship with the world of nature, he lives in a prison house whose walls are alien to him." Man is indispensable element of Reality. Man and nature are independent. There is active communication between the two.

Man occupies a place of pride in universe. He gives high status to man. God himself may be considered in terms of humanity. "Reality is human." "Truth is human." We rank Tagore as humanist of first rank because he gives man the highest place within the phenomena of the world. Even ultimate Reality is depicted in human terms.

Concept of Mind: It is that of psychic mind. He believes in consciousness and he believes in raising it above the level of lower desires by austerity, but by healthy preoccupation with social or intellectual activity.

Theory of Knowledge: Opportunity for self-expression should be provided. This will develop creative faculties.

Values: His views on values are known from his views on ethics. To him, highest ethical ideal must satisfy the whole of human nature. Therefore he regards moral discrimination as an essential part of human nature. He says:

> "The life of an animal is immoral, for it is aware only of immediate present, The life of a man can be immoral but it cannot be immoral, it must have a moral basis."

Moral ideas have influenced the course of civilisation. Moral values are highest values. Morality makes us conscious of our personality as man.

Tagore also accepts humanistic values and attitude.

He criticises ego and the egoistic man.

Tagore does not reject pleasure but he does mean that it must be regulated by the higher or spiritual nature of man. Seeking of pleasure should never be the only value to cherished by man. Tagore accepts worldly values. Since he wants to live on amongst man, he believes in a life of action and to transcend himself beyond worldly wants. He also believes in freedom but not absolute freedom.

Various Aspects

Tagore is an individualist, idealist, humanist—all these rolled into one, we shall examine him from these angles.

Tagore as Individualist: Tagore was out and out an, individualist. He believed in the right and freedom of the individual to shape his life as the individual desired. Everyone knows that no two individuals are alike-so why bind all of them with the same rope? It was thus in the development of the individual that Tagore wanted the unity of the mankind. With the development of the individual that Tagore wanted the unity of the mankind. With the development of the individual the Creator will be realised by the individual. Some of us are likely to misunderstand Tagore. The development of individual is compatible with the growth of the social units! This is not to be forgotten.

Harmony with All Things: The basic principle of the philosophy of Tagore is "harmony with all things," harmony with nature, harmony with human surroundings and harmony in international relations. The highest education is that which does not merely give us information but our life in harmony with all existence. Education system should be in tune with the young growing life. He saw harmony between nature and man, man and man.

Tagore as Naturalist: Tagore's naturalism is based on the Indian belief in fundamental unity of creation and man's kinship with nature. The essential fact is that this world has a vital meaning for us and we have to know it, we cannot ignore it, we have to establish a contact with it. This way, we shall be happy. When a man does not realise his kinship with the world. Tagore says, "He lives in a prison house whose walls are alien to him." He loved nature immensely—the moon, the stars, the hills. Nature had deeply moved him-had stirred the poet in him. He stood inspired by the flowers, trees, fruits. And for its freshness, beauty of form and colour, nature attracts the child and develops his love of freedom. So know nature, realise your relationship with it.

Tagore's Humanism: According to Dr. R.L. Ahuja, the humanism of Tagore, has two aspects: the actuality of individual joy and suffering, and the reality of a world-culture of humanity as its background. He worked unwearingly, to relieve the distress due to flood and famine in his own villages of Bengal. Equally untiringly did he endeavour to spread to the four corners of the world the message of the coming together of the races of mankind of universal humanity.

Tagore as Spiritualist (Spiritualism of Tagore): Tagore's naturalism as described above, paves the way for spiritualism. Music is an aid to the process, he started the Shantiniketan school to give spiritual culture to Indians. His belief was that every Indian should attain spiritual perfection.

(i) *Tagore's Conception of Universe is Purely Human:* All values have their origin in man. Truth is realised through man; Beauty is felt as such by man. He says, "Reality is human and even Truth is human."

(ii) *Tagore's Conception of God is also Human:* To quote him, "He is there where the tiller is tilling the hard ground and where the pathmaker is breaking stone. This is the high point in Tagore's philosophy."

Tagore and Cultural Cosmopolitanism or Internationalism: Rabindranath Tagore was an internationalist. He looked at the world as a whole. He was for unity of mankind and its brotherhood. He hated distinctions made on caste, creed, sex. He was for the unity of soul between East and West. Thus in conformity with his culture and philosophy, he advocated a synthesis between East and West, so that the East should give its best to the West and in return assimilate the best that Western civilisation gives it. He faced the both-East and West. He was grateful to both—East and West. His University is "Vishwa Bharti". It is very much international.

Tagore Believe in Truth, Beauty, Peace and Non-violence: He was also a lover of art, painting and music.

Belief in Spontaneous Expression and Creativity: He never wanted to curb this. This again supports the first point in the philosophy—individualism. This forms the high mark of his educational philosophy which is now to follow:

The Background

His educational philosophy sprang up from two sources:

(a) hatred towards school.

(b) love of nature.

To quote, "Tagore's philosophy of education is, therefore, a result of the memory of his school days, when the school resembled an educational factory, lifeless, colourless, dissociated from the context of universe, within base white walls staring like the eye balls of the dead.

His contributions revolve round the two above.

Concept of Education: Education to be real must be of the whole man of the emotions and the sense as much as of the intellect. Man in his fullness, said Tagore, is not limited by the individual but overflows in his community. And so in his school, along with training in individual initiative and self-reliance, equal emphasis was laid on community service.

Nor is education a plant that can be made to grow as an exotic variety in the hot house. If it does not strike roots in the soil and adapt itself to the natural environments, it has little value for the people as a whole.

In short, education according to Tagore meant development of the individual. It meant enrichment of personality and education should be Indian one and not borrowed from the West.

Aims of Education: The aims of education according to Tagore are:

(1) *Emancipation and Perfection of Man:* About this Tagore says, "The highest education is that which does not merely give us information but makes our life in harmony with all existence." He aims at the emancipation of man from all kinds of bondages. He aims at a perfection not only that of body or mind but also that of soul. It is the fullest

growth and freedom of soul. In order to achieve that aim in his endeavours he makes education as broad based as possible.

(2) *Unity of Truth:* Another object of education, according to Tagore, was that of giving man the unity of truth. He says that physical, intellectual and spiritual life are one and we must give this idea to the children. This way harmony will prevail and when we do not do this, there is break between the intellectual, physical and spiritual life.

(3) Moral Development of the child is the third aim of education according to Tagore. Tagore attached far more significance to moral values in education than for mere results of science which produced a system and physical power.

(4) Education should develop international outlook is another aim.

(5) *Education should be Creative:* Tagore does not want education to be mere informative but desires that it should be creative also. He says, "The great use of education is not merely to collect facts, but to know man and to make oneself known to man."

(6) *Physical Development:* Tagore always believed that a healthy mind lived in a healthy body. Therefore physical development of the child is a must. This is possible only through some physical activities like swimming, diving in ponds, climbing on trees, plucking fruits, etc. A healthy diet was also prescribed.

The Curriculum: Tagore was a naturalist and also an idealist and he wants things of beauty and nice virtues to be taught in the curriculum. He lays stress on those subjects which make a child full and rich in knowledge. He also wants them to appreciate truth, beauty and goodness. This guides us towards the curriculum. Subjects recommended by him to be taught are: History, geography, nature study, language, science.

Activities or finer subjects will include music, art, poetry, dancing, dramatics.

He was very particular about Music and Drama. Music is essence of life and drama releases the children's tensions and anxieties.

Vishwa Bharti is known the world over for its wide and varied studies, hobbies and cultural refinements.

Methodology: Rabindranath Tagore does not believe in routine methods of teaching. He broke new ground in the methodology of teaching. His belief is not in routine methods of teaching. Even at the outset, to quote Dr. R.S. Main, when he opened his new school, he declared that the ordinary routine methods of teaching were not to be expected in his institution. To quota Tagore, "Those who still require an artificial method of feeding in their lessons, who need constant watching and goading from their teachers will find themselves out of place in Vishwa Bharti." He rejected mechanical methods of teaching. These methods were uninspiring. Tagore wanted the boys to progress at their own rate without being goaded by others. Tagore points out, "When I was young I gave up learning and ran away from my lessons. That saved me and I owe all that I possess today to that courageous step taken when I was young. I fled the classes which gave the instructions, but which did not inspire. One thing I have gained, a sensitivity to the touch of life and of nature who speak to me."

What then is his method?

It is clear that his method of teaching is method of freedom in teaching as well as learning and, therefore, does not like the lessons being forced upon the children.

Secondly, it is activity method. He wants teaching-learning to be a joyous adventure, full of thrills, wonders, surprises. It could be Heuristic approach. Let the child find out through activity. It is also sense training through and through. It is also naturalness in teaching. School is not to be a factory and learning has got to be enjoyable.

His approach is Gestalt approach. He believes that children learn their lessons with the aid of their whole body and mind, with all the senses fully active and eager. He thus believes whole methods of teaching rather than part methods.

He also believes the child's mind is quite sensitive and it will pick up things of its own.

And to quote him, "Teaching while walking is the best method of education."

The Discipline: Tagore does not want that we should be harsh to children. They should be treated with all sympathy and consideration. Discipline was never, in fact, a serious problem for Tagore.

Tagore says that if the atmosphere is good, discipline problems will not arise. It is only control that breeds in scandals and indiscipline. So where there is freedom, no question of indiscipline. He also believes in self-discipline. He wants children to experiment but not in undisciplined manner.

Tagore recognises that the boys are full of enthusiasm and when they find opportunities for self expression, they may be little uncontrollable. He could rather enjoy the children expressing themselves freely in their outbursts of playful spirit which may seem uncontrollable, but not tolerate the repression of the child with no freedom to expand. Therefore, after analysing the psychological cause of indiscipline, he gave the children unrestricted freedom to do whatever they liked. This way many psychological complexes are eliminated and "naughtiness" seldom occurs.

Tagore wants us to understand the natural inclinations of children. Then those are to be stimulated and encouraged because he believes that it is out of this encouragement that true freedom of man emerges.

He gave much freedom to children in his school. He tried to arouse their interest in the various aspects of universe in a natural manner and not only through class teaching.

Tagore is against the so—called traditional school discipline because it does not take into consideration the individual interests and abilities. About the traditional school, Tagore says:

> "It is a manufactory designed for finding out uniform results. It follows an imaginary straight line of the average in digging its channel of education. But life's line is not straight line."

Social traditions should not be imposed on children. According to S.P. Chaube, they interfere with their national freedom.

Tagore believes in self-imposed discipline. In Shantiniketan, he made a provision for boys 'own' court of justice wherein all breaches of conduct were dealt with.

Role of Teacher: Role of teacher is important. He is the Guru. He is to guide the students. He is to keep them on the track. He is also to keep in contact with them. Teacher is also to remain learner throughout his life. He who fails as a learner, fails as a teacher.

Tagore says, "A teacher can never truly teach unless he is learning himself. A lamp can never light another lamp unless it continues to burn its own flame. The teacher who has come to the end of his subject, who has no living traffic with his knowledge, but merely repeats his lessons to his students can only load their minds, he cannot quicken them. Truth not only must inform but also inspire......."

Tagore wants that the teacher should try to understand the relationship between their subjects and the human life and the same should be brought home to the students as well.

Role of Vishwa Bharti University

Vishwa Bharti University at Shantiniketan: To give his ideas and ideals a practical shape, Tagore founded what is now known as Vishwa Bharti University at Shantiniketan (Rly. Station Bolpar in West Bengal). It is an international university for Tagore believed in internationalism very much. Vishwa Bharti means a place where universal knowledge is given or gathered. Infact, Vishwa Bharti University has grown out of an ashram founded by father (Maharishi Dabendra Nath Tagore of the Brahmo Samaj Fame) of R.N. Tagore in 1863. Since 1921, it is recognised as a university. It is said that India needs more such type of universities.

Why of Shantiniketan? The Vishwa Bharti University at Shantiniketan was opened with the following aims:

(i) To bring learned people from East and West together.

(ii) To promote internationalism.

(iii) To help Indians create.

Tagore said that our knowledge was second-hand knowledge. There was nothing original in it. At Shantiniketan, all freedom will be given to create.

(iv) Lastly to provide for the fullest development of man.

According to Dr. S.P. Chaube, Tagore had three main purposes in establishing the Vishwa Bharati. He has described these as follows:

1. To teach the different cultures of the East, especially those that originated in India or found shelter within her stores.
2. To establish the Institute of 'Rural Reconstruction' in order to lay the foundation of a happy, contended and human life in villages and lastly.
3. To seek to establish a living relationship between East and West, to promote inter-cultural, inter-racial amity and understanding and fulfil the highest mission of the present age—the unification of mankind.

Chosen Departments

1. Vidya Bhawan is school of research. Here research is carried on in all languages and in Indian Philosophy.
2. Patha Bhawan (Just ordinary school).
3. Teacher's College.
4. Music and Drawing School (Kala Bhawan).
5. Hindu Bhawan.
6. Industrial Training School.

Different Factors

1. It is located in natural surroundings.
2. Classes are held in the open under the trees.
3. More stress is laid on teaching and learning of music, art, drama, poetry.
4. Unlike Gandhiji, Tagore did not lay much stress on manual work. He stressed on something fine and delicate. He did not reject gradual work altogether.
5. Individual attention is paid to each and every student.
6. Students themselves make rules and run the university.
7. Atmosphere is homely, prayers are sung, and due stress and place is given to extracurricular activities:

   In fact, what Tagore said is fully practised here. Students work hard here.

The Analysis

1. Religion and religious education were neglected by Tagore.
2. He was much influenced by Nature. According to him man and nature have original integration.
3. Love for nature does not make Tagore a Naturalist. He was basically an idealist and remained so.

4. He condemned British system of education and gave to us his own fresh system of education.
5. To quote H.B. Mukherjee, "Tagore was the greatest prophet of educational renaissance in modern India. He waged a careless battle to uphold the highest educational ideal before the country and conducted educational experiments at his own institution which made them living symbols of what an ideal should be."

Educational Influence

Tagore was the youngest son of Maharishi Devendranath and the grandson of Dwarikanath Tagore. He was born in 1861 in Calcutta. His family was famous for its progressive and enlightened views. He was taught Upnishads, Astronomy and Sanskrit by his father. In the school he was not able to adjust to the dead routine and its lifeless teaching. He, then, left the conventional studies and was sent to England in 1877 to study law. But, the study of law did not suit his taste and temperament. He developed interest in English Literature. He started writing for Bengali periodicals. After having stayed at London University for three months he returned to India and continued his writing work. His first collection of poems was published when he was only twenty. In 1901 he established a school at Bolpur which in 1921 became the famous Vishwabharati, an international university. In 1909 his. "Geetanjali" was published which in its English edition appeared in 1912. This was a turning point in his life as he was awarded the Nobel Prize for literature for this in 1913. He was on the side of the national leaders in the struggle for freedom from imperialist rule in India. He had renounced his title of "knighthood" in protest against the repression by the British government in India. Then, he devoted himself to the furtherance of the cause of education in India.

Tagore was a great humanist. He had a great faith in humanity. He believed and propagated that all men on this earth are alike in the eye of God who alone is the source of man and nature. He emphasised that there is unity between man and man, and also between man and nature. He said that every human being had the right to shape his life in his own way. Human dignity, his individuality and inner potentiality must be given due regard and full opportunity for development. In this way, he was an individualist.

Tagore was a Vedantist. He believed that all living beings are a manifestation of Brahma (God) though not in the perfect form. Human life, to him, was a continuous struggle for reaching nearer and nearer to perfection and realisation of Brahma (God). All living beings having a common source of origin and a common ending in Brahma represent a grand unity, unity of origin and purpose. Superiority of any individual on the basis of caste, race, religion, country, etc. was denied by him. He said that the doctrine of special creation is out of date. No culture is superior or inferior to any other one. All are born equal. He believed that spiritual unity was reigning supreme over all human and non-human living beings.

Current Fashion

On account of the children having sensitive receptivity, sub-consciously they learn many things from nature. The lessons from nature influence the mind without strain and have a lasting impression on the mind. He was pained to find that in city schools, nature, the greatest of all teachers, is thwarted at every step by the human teacher. Nature, the unseen educator, should, therefore, be given a free hand in educating children according to her own principles; what she alone can do can never be done by anybody else. Education in nature is knowledge through direct experience. Such knowledge is not only first hand but is also accurate and vivid. The direct experience stimulates more observation, experimentation and reasoning, while knowledge from books is second hand, dull and is passively assimilated.

Besides the physical and intellectual development of children by education in nature, they have the education in sympathy. "The highest education is that which does not merely give us information but makes our life in harmony with existence. Thus harmony is possible through the realisation of our kinship with all the forces and phenomena of the universe".

For education, he said, there should be a place where men have gathered for the highest end of life in the peace of nature, where life is not merely mediative but full in its activities, where men aspire to realise man's world as God's kingdom; they must aspire to be the citizens of the world. It should be a place where the young and the old, the teacher and the students sit at the same table to partake of their daily food and the food of their eternal life. He founded a school, which was not imposed upon the children by autocratic authorities. It was impressed upon their minds that it was their own world, upon which their life should fully and freely react. Freedom of mind, heart and will are the governing features of Tagore's institution—"The Shantiniketan".

Tagore wanted an equilibrium of the 'Natural' and the civilised forces in man. The art of education, according to him, should consist in training the child, to inhibit all those impulses that are anti-social. "For our perfection we have to be vitally savage and mentally civilised, we should have the gift to be natural with nature and human with human society." It was why he suggested that besides communion with nature there should be communion of man with man. This would enable them to learn social behaviour and cooperation in educational activities.

Tagore also advocated freedom for children. He was convinced that "only through freedom can man attain his fullness of growth". Freedom and joy are the key words of his educational philosophy.

7

Muhammad Iqbal

Brief Life History

Muhammad Iqbal, one of the greatest Urdu Poets was born in Sialkot on November 7, 1877. He was the youngest child of a tailor Sheikh Nur Muhammad and his wife Imam Bibi. Originally the family had been Kashmiri Brahmin, and became converts to Islam some generations previously. The young Iqbal learnt Urdu, Persian and English, and was brought up as an Orthodox Muslim. In his early life he learnt the Koran and studied commentaries on the text. He was a lover of sports and bird-watching was also his hobby. He completed High School in 1892 and won a Merit scholarship for College education. His parents got him married at the age of fifteen.

In 1895 when Iqbal was eighteen, and had passed his Intermediate from the Suthsh Mission College in Sialkot, he was admitted to the Government College Lahore, where he studied Arabic, English and Philosophy. He graduated in 1899, and was awarded a Gold Medal for his outstanding scholastic performance.

Iqbal used to compose poetry when he was at school. However, it was in Lahore that the young college student gained fame by his recitations at various poet symposia and mushairas. His friend Sheikh Abdul Kadir (Later Sir) encouraged him to write more poems and persuaded him to get them published in an Urdu Magazine Mukhzan. He became well known in Urdu literary circles, and Professor Thomas Arnold (Later Sir) composer of The Light of Asia took note of Iqbal's poetic ability, while he was studying for the Masters degree. Iqbal was appointed Reader in Arabic in the Islamia and Government Colleges, while studying law at the same time. He appeared for the Provincial Civil Service Examination, but due to medical reasons, he did not qualify.

Iqbal went to Europe in 1905, and took the Master's degree in Philosophy from the Cambridge University. Later he succeeded in learning German and obtained a Ph.D. from the University of Munich. At the same time, he was composing prose and poetry pries in Persian, and was held in high esteems by classical scholars. The three years that Iqbal spent in Europe, influenced Iqbal's ideas greatly. The impact of western ideology upon his Islamic background, brought about a change in his outlook. While he admired the philosophy of the Sufi Mystics, he now refused to consider life transitory or unreal. He detested the materialism of the West, and was upset by the decadence of Islamic values. Western ideology made him realise the importance of Will Power (KHUDI) and the development of the self. This self is to be merciful but assertive. Power and wealth are desirable but only if obtained by hard work and determination and not by inheritance on by chance or exploitation.

His education in Europe, made Iqbal believe strongly that intellectual and poetic endeavours are not in any way superior to a life of action. He even considered giving up writing, but was persuaded by his friends not to do so.

He was a member of the Punjab Legislative Council and was made a delegate to the First Round Table Conference in London in 1931.

He died in Lahore in 1938, after achieving great honour as a distinguished scholar and Urdu poet.

Thinking in Education

Although not an educator, in the professional sense of the word, Iqbal as a poet and a philosopher, has left a legacy of thoughts and ideas, that are useful to educators, and can give inspiration to young people.

It requires a proper knowledge of the Muslim heritage, to appreciate many of his ideas.

Just as Swami Dayanand, and Swami Vivekananda, gave a new understanding and appreciation of the thoughts and ideals embedded in Hinduism:

(i) Iqbal the poet gave new understanding and interpretation to the teachings of Islam. Iqbal was attracted to the teachings of the prophet, because of two fundamental beliefs:

  (a) The Oneness of God.

  (b) The Brotherhood of Man.

  He fervently believed that no religion other than Islam preached or practised these two ideas effectively.

(ii) Iqbal loved Hindustan and considered it the best country in the world, yet he denounced narrow nationalism. He believed that only nationalism, without an understanding of other nations, leads to conflicts and wars. He believed that "there is only one unity—the brotherhood of man which is above race, nationality, colour or language." He detested discrimination.

(iii) Iqbal had faith in the individual, and in the individual's ability to attain the highest level of development. He held that man's faith, his culture, his historical traditions are the things in life, for which one may sacrifice any thing.

(iv) According to Iqbal direct knowledge comes through the affective and not the cognitive process. Although Iqbal disliked Plato's idealism, yet his own view of art is platonic. Instead of dreaming, however, he is inclined to theorise. He does not discover or uncover the meanings of things, he assumes that he already knows them.

(v) A devout Muslim, Iqbal, criticised the Mullahs, and exhorted Hindus and Muslims to come together. He wanted them to build new shrines where they could worship together, and regarded every corner of India as sacred.

(vi) The world is real, life has a purpose to serve. Within every man is a superman, who can ceaselessly strive to make a better world. This aspect of Iqbal's philosophy appeared after his education in Europe and is termed the philosophy of KHUDI or self-hood. From Khud Ego to Khudi Super-Ego, Khudi, refers to an assertive will power which is charged with moral values.

(vii) Human beings should strive for perfection or Fakhr—a pride in what comes from the highest endeavour. They should constantly work for the good of humanity without an eye on material gains. The poor man who works for the betterment of humanity, is a truly wealthy man.

(viii) A ceaselessly agitated mind, and a state of tension within the individual are needed in man, if he is to achieve anything. Meditation and relaxation cannot lead to achievement. One of his Persian poems reads thus:

"May God bring or storm in your life

The sea of your life is placed, its waves

Devoid of humult"

In one of his Persian works Secrets of the Self—he says "Personality is a state of tension and can continue only if the state is maintained." He advocates that the state of tension is one of the most important attributes of man, and he should not fall into a state of relaxation.

Part in Education

From the ideas derived from a reading of the poetry of Iqbal, both in Urdu, and in Persian, we can see that he is indeed a very great poet, philosopher, and in a sense a revolutionary. He has many new ideas to offer, and these may be incorporated in education.

1. *Patriotic Fervour:* Iqbal loved Hindustan—and considered every part of it as sacred. He exhorted Hindus and Muslims to come together.
2. *Internationalism:* He decried narrow nationalism and urged equality between races, creeds and nations—He detested war and conflict.
3. He was not a Conventional Muslim but provided a new insight into the teachings of Islam. His faith in the Prophet-Muhammad was the mainspring of his thought. He believed in the Oneness of God and the Brotherhood of man.
4. He gave us the idea of KHUDI and Fakhr (Super Ego and Pride), which combination are very similar to the Hindu ideal of Nishikarma, or striving for perfection without hope of a reward. He urged mankind to have a pride in striving ceaselessly towards the goal of perfection.
5. Iqbal condemned the strong who exploited the weak. He advocated a better life for the poor people. His ideas may be regarded as Marxist revolutionary in a sense, because he urged the peasants to rise against their oppressors, to destroy the crops and the monsoons of the rich. Yet he was a supporter of the highest Muslim values and a pan-Islamist. He denounced Capitalism because he considered it cruel and heartless.

6. Iqbal had full faith in the individual and in his ability to rise to the highest pinnacle of development. He urgest ceaseless striving for perfection by the individual.
7. Iqbal urged universal, social reconstruction—He despised discrimination of groups, individuals and communities amongst themselves. All should be one, and no different treatment should be meted out to any one. "It is in the temple of love and compassion", he writes in his poems, that we can create a new world with new dawns and sunsets because there are new worlds beyond the stars we see". He was a humanist to the core.
8. Iqbal's perfect man is one who is truthful compassionate and fearless. He can face death with courage and without any fear whatsoever.

Place among Educationists

Iqbal has given us many valuable ideas, on the dignity of man, based on the ideals of Islam, as well as those of a humanist. He has stressed the importance of the Super Ego and Pride in the process of attaining fulfilment of one's goals as a human being.

Iqbal the nationalist with patriotic fervour, was yet an internationalist. People may question why he supported the idea of Pakistan. Iqbal wanted a Pakistan or Muslim homeland within India, he wanted a homeland based on humanitarian ideals within India, he wanted a homeland based on humanitarian ideals, which was not confined to any one region or territory.

According to one of his poems:

"God-possessed dervish is neither of the

East nor of the West.

My home is neither Delhi nor Isfahan nor Samarkand".

Again, in another poem he wrote:

"You are on the highway, How can you be confined to any particular place?

Pass through Egypt and Hijaz. Leave behind

Persia and Syria".

A few months before he died in Lahore he said "Only one unity is to be depended upon—that unity is the brotherhood of man."

Iqbal has left us many of the highest ideals of humanity through his beautiful poetry, and these may be incorporated in education.

Practical Knowledge

India is rightly proud of Dr. Muhammad Iqbal because he occupies a unique position in contemporary Indian thought. He applied academic philosophical standards to Islamic thought. Iqbal carries the Islamic tradition with him whereas Indian philosophers thought in the background of Hindu tradition.

Sir Muhammad Iqbal was born in 1876 at Sialkot. Others say that he was born in 1873. Ariyway, Iqbal got his early education at Sialkot and Lahore. His academic career was excellent. He obtained his M.A. in Philosophy from Govt. College, Lahore. He did his Ph.D. from Cambridge. He taught philosophy. He also practised law but primarily Iqbal was a poet and a philosopher. Poetry was his first love. While Tagore wrote in Bengali in East India, Iqbal wrote in Urdu in Western India. Both wrote and rose to great heights. Iqbal's books are well known. Iqbal wrote for children, for the youth, for the romantics and for the old. His "Saare Jehan Sey Achha" or "Tarana-i-Hindi" is well known. It was written in 1904 and published in a Kanpur paper for the first time.

In old age, Iqbal accepted a pension from the ruler of Bhopal which he enjoyed till his death. Iqbal died in 1938 at Lahore. Iqbal stands honoured all over the world.

Overall Information

Iqbal feels that the intimate truths are not known in an ordinary way which is the way of experience. Iqbal does not deny of experience but this only represents a normal level of knowledge. Reality can not be known directly. Experience approaches reality in a very indirect manner. Reality can be approached directly and Quran has spoken about such a process.

The Quran describes the source of knowledge—the one that can be known directly as Faud or Qalb-heart. To quote Iqbal, "The heart is a kind of inner intuition or insight which, in beautiful words of Rumi, feeds on the rays of the sun and brings us into contact with aspects of Reality other than those open to sense perception." It is according to Quran, something which "sees", and its reports if properly interpreted are never false. The "heart" thus is the seat of intuition.

(i) Immediacy—i.e. It is immediate knowledge of Reality or God because it knows it without the help of any medium. Iqbal says that intuition has the directions of sense-experience.

(ii) Intuitive experience is always as a whole. It is an unassailable unity.

(iii) Relation with Supreme. This experience, according to Iqbal, is a moment of very intimate relation with the supreme. It is an awareness of God, a feeling of the presence of the Divine.

(iv) There is an objectivity about Intuition. It transcends the individual and causes an awareness in which the individual feels that the object—the supreme self is there.

(v) According to Mr. Basant Kumar Lal, Iqbal asserts that this experience is incommunicable. It is sometimes, taken as a defect of intuition.

Concept of God: Islam believes in Monotheism. It conceives God as one omnipotent all, knowing and supremely good creator of the world. It believes that God is a personal God. In Islam we do not make any distinction between God and the Absolute.

Iqbal has conceived same attributes of God. His attributes are intellectual in nature like:

(i) Creativeness

(ii) Knowledge

(iii) Omnipotence

(iv) Eternity

(v) Immanence

(vi) Transcendence.

Creativeness: This attribute appears to be a necessary attribute of God on account of the fact that God has been conceived as an Ego. An Ego-life is always a creative life. The Supreme Ego is also creative in the ways in which Ego is creative.

Knowledge: "In Him thought and deed, the act of knowing and the act of creating are identical." Divine knowledge is creational, and as there outside God. He himself is the object of His knowledge. He knows as He creates and creates as He knows.

Omnipotence: Omnipotence is not to be conceived as a whimsical or arbitrary concept capable of doing everything and anything. It must appear to be "a reasonable" concept. It must be emotionally and intellectualy satisfying.

Eternity: Eternity has to conceived by Iqbal as a time concept, it is not an idea of endlessness in time. Real time is duration which leaves nothing behind and which potentially everything that is to happen. God is eternal because He is the possibility of all expressions. Basant Kumar Lal says of time-process is one of the expressions of the infinite possibilities contained in God. It is in this sense that God is eternal.

Power cf Prayer: Iqbal believes in prayer. He believes in patience. Prayer and patience are related. Patience hardens the self against every kind of ills, and enables him to cultivate the capacity of applying concentrated energy to every situation that confronts an individual. The purest example of concentration of patience is prayer.

Prayer intensifies life. It is the way in which ego is able to affirm itself even in the midst of adversity.

Man's Ego: Iqbal believes in Ego. Ego is two fold:

(i) Efficient Ego, and

(ii) Appreciative Ego.

Efficient ego means the worldly life or material life whereas appreciative ego is spiritual existence which is experienced when the efficient ego is in abeyance.

Concept of Man: Man is the apex and crown of all creations of God. Iqbal believes in freedom and liberty of man. Man is vice-regent of God. He believes in high destiny of man. Man on his part must strive towards perfection. If Man has bad habits and performs bad deeds, he must be able to justify these.

Man must develop all his powers. Man must exalt himself.

Good Man: Let us know Iqbal's concept of good man. A good man according to Sir Muhammad Iqbal must have the following characteristics:

(i) *Creative Life:* Man must lead creative life so that he is able to transform this crude world into beautiful world.

(ii) A good man is he who applies his intelligence.

(iii) *Subordination:* Man is subordinate to God. He must lead a humble life.

(iv) Good man refuses to compromise with evil.

(v) A good man is courageous.

(vi) *Active Contact.* A good man is in active contact with material and cultural environment.

Faith in Mankind: Man is the representative of God on earth. Iqbal has faith in man's high destiny. Man is to strive towards perfection only. And you can have perfection only when you develop all your powers.

Views on Religion: To quote Iqbal, "Religion in its higher manifestation is neither dogma nor priesthood nor ritual. It can alone ethically prepare the modern man for the burden of great responsibility which the advancement of natural science necessarily involves and restores to him that which makes him capable, of winning a personality here and retaining it hereafter?" It was the practical approach to religion.

Educational Philosophy: We have seen Iqbal's philosophy of life. From it, it can be easy to deduce his educational philosophy.

Iqbal was not an educationist in the strict sense but was a teacher throughout his life. He had the feel of education. Thus we can know about his educational philosophy from his personal or general philosophy and his experiences as a teacher.

Targets and Objectives

The aims of education according to Iqbal are:

Development of Self-hood or Individuality or Khudi: This is the chief aim of education according to Iqbal. As individuality develops, the power and capacities of man become sharpened and well defined. This growth of individuality is in no way isolated from the rest of the mankind. Iqbal quotes Quran,

"Blessed is he who hath made it grow and undone is he who has corrupted it."

Development of Creativity: Every individual has creative powers in him. These are to be developed. The process of education is to ignite these creative powers. Creativity is to be developed.

Morality and Character to be Developed: This is the next important aim of education. Morality is to be developed. Character is to be developed. He wanted the moral code which "arises out of willing cooperation of free egos." For him 'goodness is not a matter of compulsion.' True morality develops only when there is a choice, freedom and experiences acquired through social interaction.

Education Must Develop Patriotism and Nationalism in the Students: This is another aim of education according to Iqbal.

Social Development: Education should also develop a child socially. It means that one should be well adjusted with the society.

Cultural Values should also be Developed: The cultural values of community should be appreciated. To quote Iqbal, "Education enables a child to adhere to the highest on its cultural values enables and traditions. Any form of education which ignores this fundamental task is utterly superficial and sterile."

Study Books

Dr. Iqbal suggested that curriculum should be broad based. It is only this that will develop national self-respect and understanding. He also suggested that the curriculum should be life centred and realistic. It should be related to the needs and aspirations of the students. Accordingly, Dr. Muhammad Iqbal wanted the teaching of:

(i) Sciences—Physics and Chemistry must be taught. They help in saving life.

(ii) Morality and Religion are equally must. To quote him, "Religion has always elevated the individuals and transformed whole societies." The religion advocated by him was, "living nobly and adventurously in the name of God."

(iii) History should be taught. It helps in understanding the present.

(iv) Political Science and Economics are equally important.

(v) Languages like Urdu and Persian are a must. These help in understanding religious teachings.

(vi) Cultural heritage is equally a must.

(vii) Creative education and guidance should also be taught.

Teaching Methods

Freedom: The process of education should be free. We have already said in the main part that Iqbal valued freedom like anything. Freedom is an essential condition for the growth of man. There should be no dogmatic teaching. Freedom is the watch-word of Dr. Iqbal in the learning process. He rejects all external restraints.

He believes in intellectual freedom. Intellectual freedom assures of unlimited advances in knowledge. And he also believes in Moral freedom. Moral freedom is a freedom of choice between good and evil. Goodness is not a matter of compulsion—you are good because there is no way out. No! you are to be willingly good.

Principle of Experience: Like pragmatists, Iqbal values experience as a method of teaching. Experience is a great teacher. Man learns through first hand experience. Let there be errors. Never mind these errors. Error is indispensable factor in the building up of experience.

Principle of Activity: This means that education should be action-oriented. Action has great value in life. It helps in formation of character and personality.

Principle of Variety: Variety is the spice of life. You can't give the same activity to the child everyday. The child wants new activity, only then he will attend to it for long, otherwise the child will lose interest.

Memory should be encouraged. Let them remember verses.

Teacher to be a good model in teaching learning. These are some of the points highlighted by Iqbal in his Techniques of Teaching.

Women's Education

Equal opportunities should be provided to women for their education. He was all for the education of females. He wanted that moral, spiritual and religious education should be imparted to women as they inculcate and develop higher values of life in children. He was critical of the domination of women by men. He wanted equal place for women in society.

Action-oriented Education: Action has a place in life. He wanted education to be action-oriented. Action makes ideas valid. His doctrine was "the call to act, throw off lethargy and emerge, as supermen." He did not believe in defeatism. He did not believe in, "Those also serve who stand and wait"—a statement given by an English poet. Action and struggle form the keystone of the whole structure of life. Action, thus is all the more important in life.

Well Integrated Education: Iqbal believed in giving well integrated education. Integrated education helps in achieving balance between different aims—intellectual and spiritual activity and contemplation.

Humane Outlook: Education must promote humane outlook. Iqbal was a humanist to the core and he wanted education to be humane.

Package for Fair Sex

Dr. Iqbal thought and believed that education was a part of our life. You cannot run away from it. We are alive that is a chance otherwise what is life? It is a passage of thoughts, a series of deaths. Education has to be sensitive and oriented to this dynamic character of inner life of man. Education thus is a process of adjustment. It is to be properly conceived and properly directed.

Value of Prayer: We have already highlighted this. Iqbal had great faith in prayer. It has been elaborated by K.G. Saiyidain when he says, "Within the educative process room must be found for that silent, reverent communion with the self and with the nature in all her beauty and majesty which is often a prelude to communion with God."

On the basis of philosophy of Iqbal, we can say that the system of education advocated by Sir Muhammad Iqbal was comprehensive and well integrated. Through it he wanted to strike a balance between the material and spiritual activity and contemplation. Iqbal was indeed a great poet, philosopher and original thinker. India is rightly proud of him.

8

Sri Aurobindo

Life at a Glance

Aurobindo Ghosh was born in 1872 in Calcutta. His father sent him to England at the early age of six so that he grows up into an artificial Englishman. In England he not only mastered Greek and Latin languages to study the masterpiece creations of ancient philosophers, social thinkers and poets, but also became well-versed in many European languages namely, French, German, Italian, etc. Upto the age of fourteen he received purely Western education.

In 1890, Aurobindo passed the Indian Civil Service Examination but could not appear in the test of horse riding. As such, he found himself not qualified and returned to India in 1893 and served for thirteen years in the Baroda state under the Gaekwad ruler. Here he studied Sanskrit language and literature and prepared himself for his future mission. After the Bengal partition disturbances, he resigned from his job and jumped into the political struggle which was hotting up by leaps and bounds.

Gradually, through his papers namely 'Bandematram', 'Karmyogin', 'Dharm' and fiery speeches, he roused the intense feeling of nationalism in the people of India and finally declared complete independence as the goal of struggle of independence. He suffered imprisonment many a time because of his active involvement in the struggle of freedom. Once, while lodged in Alipur jail, he realised the presence of God in a dream. He was so much influenced by the Divine Vision that in 1915, after his release from prison, he quitted all political activities and retired to the French territory Pondicherry for penance and spiritual advancement. There he built an Ashram which is famous all over the world as Aurobindo Ashram. He spent the rest of his life in this Ashram doing Yoga Sadhna, meditation for spiritual growth and development. In this way, Aurobindo was transformed from a politician to a philosopher and preached to the world his philosophy of Dharm, spiritual growth, Brahmacharya Yoga and Educational ideology. He died in 1950.

The Concept

Aurobindo Ghosh was an Idealist to the core. His Idealistic philosophy of life was based upon Vedantic philosophy of Upnishads. He laid great stress on the spiritual penance, Yoga practice and Brahmacharya as necessary for the development of human soul. He exhorted that the sole aim of growth should be to achieve the all pervading Divine Power. According to him this principle of growth continues to operate always in all conditions and in all times and places. During this cultural growth, a stage arrives where by virtue of his supreme development of mental powers, a man attains the status of Superman himself. After this, he grows from knowledge to more knowledge and from light and enlightment to more enlightenment progressively where he experiences the supreme happiness and divine bliss and gains the insight into all creation.

Aurobindo Ghosh was not only a great philosopher but an eminent educationist as well. He showed to mankind the way to the highest spiritual growth. As such, he is acclaimed as a great solace giver to the people. Shri Aurobindo expressed his thoughts in his weekly newspaper 'Karam Yogin' in which he stressed that the main aid of a teacher is his conscience. This conscience has four stages namely: (1) Consciousness, (2) Mind, (3) Intelligence and (4) Knowledge.

Education should develop all these four stages as much as possible. As an Idealist, Aurobindo's philosophy of education is based on spiritual penance, yoga and brahmacharya. He held the view that education involving these three factors will definitely develop man to the fullest extent. According to Aurobindo a man does not possess a physical extent.

According to Aurobindo a man does not possess a physical spirit only as he is endowed with higher mental, godly intelligency and a very high spiritual soul element. Not only this, he has a capacity to recognise and realise God by training his powers of thinking, concentration and deep meditation together with other divine faculties to the fullest. According to Aurobindo, real education provides a free and creative environment to the child developing his interests, creativity, mental, moral and aesthetic senses leads to the development of his spiritual powers. Shri Aurobindo himself writes: "That alone would be true and living education which helps to bring out to full advantage all that is in an individual man."

Basic Things

The basic principles of Shri Aurobindo's educational philosophy are given below:

1. Education should be imparted through the medium of mother-tongue.
2. Education should be child-centred.
3. Education should be according to the mental aptitudes and psychological needs of the child.
4. Education should develop to the full the latent powers of the child.

5. Education should achieve the physical purification of a child.
6. Education should develop consciousness.
7. Education should train the senses.
8. Education should develop the soul substance of an individual.
9. Brahmacharya should be the basic foundation of education.
10. Subjects of education should be interesting.
11. Education should develop all the facilities of child to make him a complete man.
12. There should be religious tinge in education otherwise it will spread corruption.

The Philosophy

Aurobindo Ghosh was against the prevalent education of his times. He admitted that changes have occurred in our system of education after the attainment of independence but these are not in conformity with the mental and spiritual needs of children and demands of the nation. According to him, our education should be in accordance with the needs of our real modern life. In other words, education should create dynamic citizens so that they are able to meet the real needs of modern complex life. Shri Aurobindo thus writes: "Education to be true must not be a machine made fabric, but a true building or living evocation of the powers of the mind and spirit of human being".

The Targets

According to Aurobindo Ghosh, the aims of education are as under:

1. *Physical Development and Purity:* The first aim of education is to achieve complete physical and pure development of

a child. According to Aurobindo, it is the body which performs all religious obligations. As such, he not only emphasised mere physical development but physical purity also without which no spiritual development is possible. In this sense physical development and purification are the two bases on which the edifice of spiritual developments is built.

2. *Development of Senses:* The second aim of education is to train all the senses namely, hearing, speaking, listening, touching, smelling and taṣting. According to Aurobindo these senses can be fully trained when nerve, chitta and manas (mind) are pure. Hence, through education purity of senses is to be achieved before any other development is possible.
3. *Mental Development:* The third aim of education is to achieve mental development of the child. Mental development means the development of all mental faculties, namely, memory, thinking, reasoning, imagination and discrimination, etc. Education should develop them fully and harmoniously.
4. *Development of Morality:* Another essential aim of education is to develop the child morally. Shri Aurobindo emphasised that without moral and emotional development mental development becomes harmful to human progress. Emotions, impressions or habits and nature or temperament are the three essential factors for the moral development of a child. He yearned to educate man in the true sense of the term by the purification and sublimation of these essential factors. According to him; hearts of children should be so developed as to show extreme love, sympathy and consideration for all living beings. This is real moral development. Thus, the ideals of a teacher should be so high that the child, by mere imitation, is able to reach higher and higher stages of development by accepting the teacher as a role model.

5. *Development of Conscience:* Another important aim of education is to develop the conscience. According to him, it has four levels namely: (1) Chitta, (2) Manas, (3) Intelligence and (4) Knowledge which teacher should develop harmoniously. This will promote the development of conscience.
6. *Spiritual Development:* Aurobindo emphasised that the main aim of education is to promote spiritual development. According to him every human being has some element of divinity in him. Education should find it out and develop it to the fullest. In his own words: "The chief aim of education should be to help the growing soul to draw out of itself which is best and make it perfect for a noble use".

Study Material

Aurobindo Ghosh prescribed free environment for the child to develop all his latent faculties to the full and suggested all those subjects and activities of child's interest to be included in the curriculum. Such subjects and activities should possess elements of creativity and educational expression. He wished to infuse a new life and spirit into each subject and activity through which the development of super human being could become possible. For this, he laid down the following principles for curriculum construction:

1. Curriculum should be interesting
2. It should include all those subjects which promote mental and spiritual development.
3. Subjects of curriculum should be able to motivate children.
4. Curriculum items should involve creativity of life and constructive capacities.
5. Curriculum should motivate children toward the attainment of knowledge of the whole world.

On the basis of the above principles Aurobindo has prescribed the following subjects in the curriculum for the different stages of education:

1. *Primary Stage:* Mother-tongue, English, French, Literature, National History, Art, Painting, General Science, Social Studies and Arithmetic.
2. *Secondary Stage:* Mother-tongue, English, French, Arithmetic, Art, Chemistry, Physics, Botany, Physiology, Health education, Social Studies.
3. *University Stage:* Indian and Western Philosophy, History of Civilisation, English literature, French Literature, Sociology, Psychology, History of Science, Chemistry, Physics, Botany, International relations and integration.
4. *Vocational Education:* Arts, Painting, Photography, Sewing, Sculptural drawing, Typing, Shorthand, Cottage industries, Carpentry, Mechanical and Electrical Engineering, Nursing, Indian and European Music, Dramatisation and Dancing.

Techniques of Teaching

Aurobindo Ghosh has laid stress upon the following principles of methods of teaching:

1. *Freedom of Child:* Children should be provided with a free environment so that they are able to gain more and more knowledge by their own efforts. According to Aurobindo any restrained and imposed environment stunts growth and natural development.
2. *Love and Sympathy for the Child:* Children should be treated with utmost love, sympathy and consideration. This promotes their normal and natural development to the full.
3. *Education through Mother-Tongue:* Aurobindo emphasised that education should be imparted to the child through

his mother tongue. Thus, he will be able to grasp and understand even the most difficult subjects easily.

4. *Education According to Interests of the Child:* The teacher should first study the interests of the child and then provide education accordingly so that he feels really motivated to learn and develop.
5. *Education through Self-experience:* Aurobindo asserted that a child should be free to learn by his own efforts and experiences. This leads to permanent learning and will prove useful for his future life.
6. *Emphasis on Learning by Doing:* Aurobindo Ghosh gave much importance to the activities of a child. According to him the best method of learning is learning by doing. Hence, Aurobindo has emphasised Montessori method for infant classes and the practice of art and drawing in primary and secondary classes.
7. *Education through Co-operation:* According to Aurobindo, teaching and learning is a co-operative process. Hence, he laid great stress on such activities in the educational process.
8. *Education According to the Nature of Child:* Each child has an element of divinity as well as his own latent gifts of mind and spirit. Education should develop the child spiritually to the fullest extent by developing these elements of divinity and inherent mental capacity.

Importance of a Child

According to Aurobindo, each child had his own inherent capacities and special abilities. To fully develop these divine gifts is the chief purpose of education. In his opinion, to develop the latent faculties, capacities and abilities of the child according to some predetermined plan or scheme by force of compulsion, is to stunt the growth and do great injustice to him. Hence, according to him, education should satisfy the needs and interests of a child and develop his personality according to these powers to achieve full and complete development. In this connection Aurobindo writes:

> "The idea of hammering the child into shape desired by the parent or teacher is a barbarous and ignorant superstition. There can be no great error than for the parent to arrange before that his son shall develop particular qualities and capacities. To force the nature to abandon its own Dharam is to do permanent harm, mutilate its growth and deface its perfection".

Teacher's Position

About the teacher Aurobindo upholds, that:

> "The teacher is not an instruct or task master, he is a helper and guide. His business is to suggest and not to impose. He does not actually train the pupil's mind, he only shows him how to perfect his instruments of knowledge and helps him and encourages him in the process. He does not impart knowledge to him, he shows him how to acquire knowledge that is within, he only shows him where it lies and how it can be habituated to rise to the surface".

The Analysis

Like the Naturalists and the Pragmatists, Aurobindo Ghosh laid stress upon child-centred education. He accepted the teacher as a helper, guide and instructor only and formulated those principles of education according to which, under a free and conducive environment, the child should be made to develop in accordance with his inherent interests, aptitudes and latent capacities by receiving a loving and sympathetic behaviour from those who are engaged in developing him.

His aims of education were based upon the philosophy of Idealism. As a matter of fact, Aurobindo was an Idealist to the core. His philosophy of education was based on spiritual faith, brahmacharya and yoga. It showed the way to spiritual growth and fulfilment of a man to the fullest extent. Though he was sufficiently influenced by Western philosophy, yet he remained basically all through his life an Indian and an Idealist devoted to spiritual advancement to the optimum. He imbibed the qualities and merits of the Western thought to enrich and consolidate the Indian beliefs and culture. His philosophy is a transition from materialism to spiritualism.

Aurobindo Ghosh realised that Indians were gradually drifting from Idealism toward materialism with the result that the inherent divine light in them was gradually on the wane. He vehemently condemned the Western materialistic education as it could not sustain and develop Indian ideals, values and culture. According to Aurobindo we need an education which develops the powers of our mind and soul and achieves our fullest growth. With these ends in view, he opened an Ashram at Pondicherry and established an International University providing education suited to the ideals and values of the Indian culture and based upon Brahmacharya, Yoga, concentration and meditation through which an individual could harmoniously develop to the full his body, mind and soul.

> "Aurobindo's philosophy of education is based on the principle of evocation of potentialities of the individual in all its entirety and full development of as many sides as possible. His views on education reveal that Shri Aurobindo was one of the most eminent and distinguished educationists of our country." (R.S. Mani)

To sum up, the whole purpose of his teachings was "that man can achieve an extension of consciousness beyond the mental principle he will continue to be trapped by the dilemmas which beset him." Education, to him, must prepare the individual for this transformation. Integral Yoga was suggested by him to be the most practical and effective way of child's education for this purpose. It is only in Yoga that the psychological knowledge essential for attaining extension of consciousness and divine life exists.

Knowledge of the Past

Aurobindo hailed from Ghosh family which had come from Punjab and settled in Bengal. The name of his father was Dr. Krishna Dhan Ghosh and the name of his mother was Swaranlata Devi. Dr. Ghosh was a great admirer of English education and English way of life and hence he wanted his children to be educated in the British tradition. But the British attrocities in India turned him against them and made him a patriot. The mother of Aurobindo Ghosh was religious by nature, according to R. N. Pani. It was from such parentage that Aurobindo came.

Sri Aurobindo was born in 1872 in Calcutta. It was Janamashtami, the birthday of Lord Krishna. As already stated, the father of Aurobindo was fond of English education. As such at the age of 7 years, Aurobindo was sent to England for education. He remained there for fourteen years in order to complete his education both at London and Cambridge. In England, Aurobindo's life of fourteen years falls into four distinct periods-Manchester-from 1879 to September 1884, London-from September 1884 to October 1890. Cambridge from October 1890 to October 1892 and London-from October 1892 to January 1893.

Some notable events of the period were:

1. He acquired mastery in Greek, Latin and French languages which gave him direct access to the original classics and literature in these languages.
2. He developed abiding interest in English literature, mostly poetry and this continued till the end of his life. He spent much time in writing poetry.

3. He concentrated on the study of the classics, history and politics (but not philosophy) ancient and modern.
4. He also attempted learning Italian, something German and little.
5. The school and college studies engaged very little of his time but in one year he won all the prizes in King's College for Greek and Latin verses.

Sri Aurobindo passed the I.C.S. examination but as he did not present himself for horse riding test, he was disqualified. This happened in 1890. Sri Aurobindo left for India in 1893.

Aurobindo met Gaikwar of Baroda while in England. So on return, Aurobindo joined as a Professor of English and French in Maharaja's College at Baroda and remained in the service of Gaikwar of Baroda for 13 years from 1893 to 1906. During this period he distinguished himself as a teacher. During this period in the true spirit of a teacher, he learnt Bengali, Sanskrit, Gujarati, Marathi. He studied the Indian classics like Mahabharata. In a way during this period of 13 years, he prepared himself for future work.

Marriage: During his stay at Baroda, Aurobindo married Mrinalini Bose, eldest daughter of Bhimpal Chandra Boss at Calcutta. Aurobindo's married life was not of traditional life because he was more engaged during the period in the freedom movement of which he was one of pioneers. The married life of Sri Aurobindo did not last long and ended with Mrinalini's death in 1918. This did not have much impact on Aurobindo. The marriage was nearly a ritual.

Aurobindo resigned from Baroda in 1905 and came to Calcutta. He was Principal of Bengal National College, Calcutta which was the first of its kind. His teaching was unique. His students testified this. His political activities soon intervened in his teachership when he became an undertrial prisoner in connection unit Alipore Bomb Case.

Concept of Patriotism

Aurobindo was out and out a nationalist. And practical life of Aurobindo goes back to his days in England when he at the age of 11 had the experience that he was bound to make his motherland free. He was born with patriotism, it began manifesting in his outward life first in England by joining the Indian majors and the formation of the Lotus and Dagger Society, the members of which had taken an oath, such to work in his own way to make India free. Aurobindo lived upto his oath.

As a teacher at Baroda, during vacations, he used to visit Bengal and organise revolutionary groups with a view to rising in revolt against the alien government. The partition of Bengal in 1905 shocked him and gave Aurobindo an opportunity to inspire the people and revolutionists come out in the open revolt against the British.

The political activities of Sri Aurobindo came to a sudden stop with his arrest and detection as an under trial prisoner in Alipore Central Jail for a year from May 1908 to 1909 in connection with the murder of Kingsford. After that, the Britishers were always after him. He had to quit the scene and he left for Pondicherry where he lived till the end of his life. He died therein 1950.

Position of Literature

Of the many heights that Sri Aurobindo reached, the poet in him was most significant and interesting. He always claimed himself to be a poet, first and poet last.

Among the poems he wrote lyrics, sonnets, blank verse, heroic poems, experimental pieces. His most important poetic work is Savitri, the theme of which is the mystery of life and death and love. Sri Aurobindo translated parts of Veda, the Ramayana and the Mahabharata.

In the field of literary criticism, the future poetry is his major work. His theory of poetry is developed in this book. His writings are expressed in thirty volumes.

Human Love

Sri Aurobindo was a great lover of humanity. Though he loved motherland intently and wanted to see her great and free, it was not a narrow patriotism. Nation was a part of universal brotherhood. He granted India to be free but he never hated the British. He envisaged a world union where the entire humanity could exist in peace.

Spiritual View

Sri Aurobindo was a yogi. He was a born yogi. He had many spiritual experiences when he was a child of seven.

His practice of yogi was in the beginning confined to Pranayamma, six or more hours at a stretch in a day. He achieved many siddhis and one was in Alipore jail. He had no Guru as such but was influenced by Gita.

Concepts of Reality

There are four theories of existence or reality:

(1) We affirm absolute as the origin and support secret reality of all things. The Absolute Reality is indefinable and ineffable by mental thought and mental language.

The absolute manifests itself in two terms-a Being and a Becoming-the Being is fundamental reality, the Becoming is an effectual reality; it is a dynamic power and result of a creative energy and working out of Being, a constantly persistent yet suitable form, process, outcome of its immunitable formless essence.

(2) The second concept of the fundamental reality of the Absolute is to our spiritual perception a divine existence, consciousness and delight of being which is supercosmic

reality, self-existent but also the secret truth underlying the whole manifestation. All is a manifestation of That the one is the All it is not only an essential existence but an AP existence.

(3) *Maya:* The third concept of existence considers the manifested world as an illusion or 'maya' and views it as purely temporal and transitory constantly suitable. It believes in a supraterrestrial existence a heaven beyond the one in which man lives and where he hopes to enjoy all the delight of existence after the cessation of life on earth.

(4) The fourth is synthesis of these three views. These three views are partial is nature. They express only one aspect of truth and as such the synthesis to give us fourth aspect or concept of reality. There is material world, there is non-material world. There is sensual world. There is attraction to earth, to heaven and the supreme reality. A synthesis and integration of the three views is not only permissible but the possibility of which has been attempted by the ancient Indian culture through the different ashramas—the Brahmacharya, the Garhyastha, the Vanaprastha and the Sanyasa.

Individual's Position

Sri Aurobindo's concept of man and his evolution was based on the Indian tradition of Vedas and Upanishads as his own yogic views and spiritual realisation of the concept as contained in them.

The Individual: What is man? Sri Aurobindo has answered the question man is a transitional being. He has absolved from matter. Matter is the first stage in evolution. It proceeds through the plant and animal and it has reached the stage of man. When matter reached the stage of plant, life was gained but not wholly possessed. Life was rooted to the ground. There was no movement. When the animal appeared body, life was possessed and the first form of mind was gained but mind as such could not be possessed. This mind was confined to body and energising its movements combined with instincts and memory, according to Dr. Pant. It is only in man that mind with its reasoning found its full expression.

What is man? Sri Aurobindo answers again.

> "Man himself is little more than an ambitious nothing. He is a littleness that reaches to a wideness and a grandeur that are beyond him, a dwarf enamoured of the heights. His mind is a dark ray in the splendours of the universal Mind. His life is a striving, exaulting, suffering, an eager passion-tossed and sorrow-striken or a blindly and dumbly longing, petty moment of the universal life. His body is a labouring perishable speck in the material universe."

He is baulked of his luminous possibilities and shut off to his own divine powers. He is important to change his life beyond certain narrow and precarious limits.

Why is it so? Because man is nothing but a mind encased in a living body. He is only the third stage in the upward movement above matter and life and there are four more stages to be ascended to reach the ultimate Reality (these stages being Supermind, Bliss, Conscious-Force, and Existence). Though man is the highest of the created beings, he is not the last word in the evolutionary process. Mind is not the highest possible power of creation, for mind is not in possession of Truth, but only its ignorant seeker. It is only an ignorant, clouded and struggling power. Even when most luminous, it is possessed only of a thin, reflected and pallid light. This cannot be the end of the mysterious upward surge of Nature.

A great possibility awaits man. There is something beyond, something that mankind shall be. An immortal soul is somewhere within him and gives out some sparks of its presence, but the inner luminous soul is wrapped, stifled, oppressed in dense outer coatings. Above an eternal spirit overshadows him and upholds the soul continuity of his nature and this greater spirit is obstructed from descent by the hard lid of his constructed personality. Man's fulfilment lies in discovering his soul-consciousness, the emergence of the soul on the one hand and rising to the higher levels of consciousness with the pressure and help of the higher spirit that forebodes his destiny.

Therefore, Sri Aurobindo writes:

> "Man's greatness is not in what he is, but in what he makes it possible. His glory is that he is the closed place and secret worship of a living labour in which supermanhood is being made ready by a value Craftsman. But he is admitted to yet a greater greatness and it is this that, allowed to be unlike the lower creation, he is partly an artisan of this divine change."

In other words, this would mean that till the stage of man evolution proceeded in a blind way. Matter did not have to consent to evolve into life nor the consent of life was needed to evolve into Mind. But after the evolution of man his conscious consent and collaboration has become a necessary condition for his evolution into the higher stages, his consecrated will and participation are needed that into his body may descend the glory that will replace him.

Thus he is at once the created and the creator, though his role as the creator is nothing but the work of the Supermind to which he rises.

> "Our humanity is the Conscious meeting place of the finite and the infinite and to grow more and more towards the infinite even in this physical birth is our privilege," says Sri Aurobindo.

Elucidating the concept of man Sri Aurobindo continues:

"This Man is the Manu, the thinker, the Manomaya Purusha, mental person or soul in mind of the ancient sages. No more superior mammal is he, but a conceptive soul basing itself on the animal body in Matter. He is conscious name or Numen accepting the utilising form as a medium through which Person can deal with substance. The animal life emerging out of Matter is only the inferior term of his existence. The life of thought, feeling, will, conscious impulsion, that which we name in its totality Mind, that which strives to seize upon Matter and its vital energies and subject them to the law of its own progressive transformation, is the middle term in which he takes his effectual station. But equally there is a supreme term which Mind in man searches after so that having found he may affirm it in his mental and bodily existence. This practical affirmation of something essentially superior to his present self is the basis of the divine life in the human being."

Thus it can be seen that to fulfil God in life is man's manhood, that is his destiny:

"The appearance of a human possibility in a material and animal world was the first glint of some coming divine Light, the first far off promise of a good head to be born out of Matter. The appearance of the superman in the human world will be the fulfilment of this divine promise."

Sri Aurobindo, therefore, affirms:

"The animal is a living laboratory in which Nature has, it is said, worked out man. Man himself may well be a thinking and living laboratory in whom and with whose conscious co-operation she wills to work out the superman, the god. Or shall we not say, rather, to manifest God?"

Thus according to Sri Aurobindo:

"If it is true that Spirit is involved in Matter and apparent Nature it secret God, then the manifestation of the divine in himself and the realisation of God within and without are the highest and the most legitimate aim possible to man upon earth."

Explaining the concept of Superman Sri Aurobindo writes:

"Supermanhood is not man climbed to his own natural zenith, not a superior degree of human greatness, knowledge, power, intelligence, will, character, genius, dynamic force, saintliveness, love, purity or perfection. It is a greater consciousness than the highest consciousness proper to human nature."

In other words this means that supermanhood is not an enlarged or inflated human consciousness. Not the greatest of our poets, philosophers, scientists or artists can ever be deemed to be Superman. Supermanhood is only a possibility yet to manifest in the terrestrial nature.

In this connection Sri Aurobindo brings in the concept of the Gnostic being who is man transformed into superman. Explaining the concept Dr. Ayangar says:

"The final or culminating assault or heave of the ascending ocean of consciousness is on supramental citadel itself. Man must now grow into complete Superman, the supramental being, or the Gnostic being. The introduction of the supramental principle and power into the human being must also mean the gradual supramentalisation of man's environment, in other words the transformation of nature into supernature. The 'gnostic being' should be the consummation of the climb of the spiritual man."

Indicating the nature of the spiritual man Sri Aurobindo says:

"His whole way of being, thinking, living acting would be governed by the power of a vast universal spirituality. All the trinities of the spirit would be real to his self-awareness and realised in his inner life, all his action would originate from and obey the supreme Self and spirit's divine governance of Nature."

But supramentalisation or gnosticisation would not mean a sudden or wholesale annulment of lower order and formations of consciousness. The hierarchy from matter to overmind would continue but progressively emptied of the incursions of the ignorance. "The supplemental transformation", says Sri Aurobindo:

"The supplemental evolution must carry with it a lifting of mind, life and body out of themselves into a greater way of being in which yet their own ways and power would be, not suppressed or abolished, but perfected and fulfilled by the self-exceeding."

Finally Sri Aurobindo points out that all the developments and change that the individual has to effect are not outside, they are within himself. He says:

"What has to be developed is there in our being and not something outside it. What evolutionary Nature presses far is an awakening to the knowledge of self, the discovery of self, the manifestation of self and spirit within us and the release of self-knowledge, its self-power, its active self-instrumentation. It must lead inevitably towards an evolution in the knowledge, a self-finding and self-unfolding of the Spirit, a self-revelation of the Divinity in things in that true power of itself in Nature which is to us still a Supernatural."

In short the individual, according, to Sri Aurobindo, is a self ensheathed in body, life and mind and this self not different from universal self or the Transcendental Self. The individual shrouded in ignorance is not conscious of his triple selves. To discover his own self, the universal self and Transcendental Self and realise identity with them which are one and indivisible and manifest. It in life is the sole purpose and meaning of his existence upon earth.

Man in the Universe: Sri Aurobindo rightly prefer to think man as a part of universe and as a universal being rather than as a social being, for the universe far exceeds the society and a man, whether he identifies himself with society or not, he is always in the universe of which, the individual, the community and humanity are only diverse expressions of the one Reality.

Man the Divine Being: Aurobindo always considered man as a divine being, a self or soul with body, life and mind as its sheaths and instruments of evolutionary growth. This is the Upanishad view-point. Aurobindo writes. "India has always seen in man the individual a soul, a portion of the Divinity enumerated in mind and body, a conscious manifestation in nature of the universal self and spirit." Elsewhere he writes, "There is a soul, a self, a God in the world and in man who works concealed and all his self-concealing and gradual self-unfolding."

In other words the soul in man is the source of all light and love, his delight of existence and conscious of his unity with All Existence. It is due to this divine presence in man that he seeks delight in everything. The soul or pyschic entity which is different from life, mind and body and holds in itself the opening and flowering of essence of all to their own peculiar delight of self, to light, to love, to joy and beauty and to a refusal priority of being."

Sri Aurobindo speaks of a double soul in man-the surface or the desire soul and the subliminal or true soul. In fact man has double principles in respect of all parts of being body, life and mind and so with soul.

Describing man essentially as a soul or a psychic being. Sri Aurobindo proceeds to point out that man can attain his divinity by transforming his human nature into divine nature through the process of triple transformation-psychic, spiritual and supramental.

The Mind: Views: In man, mind is the primary means of manifestation. It is important that we have a clear concept of mind in different ways:

The scriptures expound the concept in different ways:

"He discovered that Mind was Brahman"

—Taittiriya Upanishad

"The mind is indeed endless," says Brihadranyaba.

In the first place, it has to be pointed out that mind is not a thing nor is it to be confused with the brain, it is a function or a process.

Hence we speak of 'Mental Process' rather than mind. The function express itself in higher mental processes-in feelings, emotions attention, memory, etc. This is the ordinary concept of mind.

Sri Aurobindo's concept of mind is different. He was brought it out in his writings wherein he points out the different planes of mind, namely:

The Ordinary Mind

The Higher Mind

The Illumined Mind

The Intuitive Mind

The Overmind

The Supermind.

Sri Aurobindo points out that ordinarily the world mind is used to cover the whole consciousness, for man is a mental being and mentalises everything and it is concerned with higher mental functions. Mind is not to be confused with spirit. These are two different things, "The mind is an instrumental entity or instrumental consciousness", writes Sri Aurobindo.

Ordinary mind is divided into three different parts—thinking mind, dynamic mind, externalising mind-former concerned with ideas and knowledge in their own right, the second with the putting out of mental forces for realisation of the idea, the third with the expression of them in life.

Aurobindo also writes about thinking mind and vital mind. These could be the functions of mind. Thus the action of the thinking mind is to doubt, to question, to argue and to reason, to conclude and to be certain to reject it is uncertain and respect the process again and again. We shall discuss the concept of supermind.

Man's mind is an imperfect instrument so it cannot catch the full integral truth. Sri Aurobindo believes that the errors of conceptual mind must be corrected by the supermind which is intermediary link between Sachchidananda and universe, knowledge and ignorance.

Supermind is the divine gnosis (having special knowledge) which creates, governs and uphold's the world. It is the creator. It is omnipotent, omniscient and omnipresent. It is all inclusive. It is the Lord within. In it there is no distinction of knowledge, known or known.

According to Sri Aurobindo supermind is a state of consciousness. One can acquire it gradually. After acquiring it, one must use it for transforming his entire being, his body, mind and soul. When the man attains the supermind he becomes a superman, a jnani or gnostic individual in communication with our own plane of being. Sri Aurobindo points out in the following manner the contrast between the working of the mind and that of the supermind.

"The mind acts by intellectual rule or device or by reasoned choice of will or by mental impulse or in obedience to life impulse: but supramental nature does not act by mental idea or rules or in subjection to any inferior impulse: each of its traps is dictated by an innate spiritual vision, a comprehensive exact penetration into truth of all and the truth of each thing; it acts always according to inherent reality, not by the mental idea, not according to an imposed law of conduct or a constructive thought or perceptive contrivance. Its movement is calm, self-possessed, spontaneous, plastic; it arises naturally and inevitably and, out of harmonic identity of the truth which is, felt in the very substance of the conscious being, a spiritual substance which is universal and therefore intimately one with all that is included in its cognition of existence"

Thus Sri Aurobindo finds a wide gulf between the ordinary mind and the supermind. He suggests that this gulf should be bridged by Yoga. We shall now understand his conception of Yoga.

The Information

It is through senses that one receives knowledge. Sri Aurobindo recognises six senses which help one to receive knowledge—sight, hearing, smell, touch, taste and mind. Except mind all the other five senses are dependent for their activity on the organs—eye, ear, nose, skin and palate. Sri Aurobindo attaches great importance to the training of these senses and advises that their training should be the first care of the teacher. Our senses must be accurate and sensitive and if there is any hindrance in making them so that hindrance must be rendered in order to make the senses perfect first of all the cause of their imperfection should be understood.

Sri Aurobindo believes that if the defects in the senses are not due to physical injury, these can be removed by the purification of nerve system, i.e. by breathing.

The mind as a sense organ receives throughout impression from outside and from within. The impressions are perfectly correct but they may reach intellect in a distorted manner. The full development of the sensitiveness mind is called Sukhamdristhi or subtle reception of images in Yogic discipline. Sri Aurobindo deplores that the development of the sixth sense has never been included in the system of education of man. He advises that mind should be so trained as to give a correct report to the intellect in order to enable us to start our thinking correctly. Senses, mental faculties are the gateways of knowledge.

The Values: Aurobindo believes in physical and moral values. It is a tragedy that only recently we have corrected our defect in education

Concepts of Education

Sri Aurobindo was a spiritualist. His political philosophy is based on spiritualism and as such his educational philosophy is also based on spiritualism. His educational philosophy is more spiritual and less political.

His Concept: Education thus becomes a product of his integral philosophy. The true basis of education is the study of human mind, infant, adolescent and adult. Any system of education founded on theories of academic perfection which ignore the instrument of study, is more likely to hamper, and impair intellectual growth than to produce a perfect and perfectly equipped mind. For the educationist has to do, "not with the dead material like the artist or the sculptor, but with an infinitely subtle and sensitive organism. He cannot master a piece out of human wood or stone he has to work in the elusive substance of mind and respect human body.

His Aim: The aims of education are given below:

Physical Development: Physical development of the child is the first aim of education and it should be the pure development of child. It is the body that performs all religious functions. It should be strong. Physical development is a value with Aurobindo. It is wrong to say that those who are physically strong are mentally weak. Without physical development no other development is possible. And it should be pure.

Development of Latent Powers: To Sri Aurobindo, education must develop one's latent powers and enable him to enter into right relation with life, mind and soul of his nation as well with the total life, super mind and soul of humanity. Education should aim at building the power of mind and spirit of human being, this is the central aim of education.

Development of Morality: Moral development is a must. Without moral development, the development of child's emotions is not proper. And mental development would just not be very desirable. Education must develop the intellect and moral capacities of the child to the highest limit. As such education must be based on the psychology of the child and his nature. According to Sri Aurobindo the hearts of the children should be so developed that these should be full of love and sympathy. We should be considerate to all. This is real moral development.

Realisation of Self: To Sri Aurobindo, the real meaning of life is to rise above ego and become our true self, i.e. to be conscious of our real being. To possess the self is the ultimate meaning of life on earth. Education should help one to realise his being-the self. Only that education is true which helps one to become actively conscious of supernatural and supreme being.

Spiritual Development: Spiritual development is yet another aim of education. In his own words, "The chief aim of education should be to help the growing soul to draw out that in itself which is best and make it perfect for a noble use".

Integral Curriculum: Sri Aurobindo and other researchers on him have listed the principles of integral curriculum:

(a) all life is education, i.e. curriculum is not confined to a limited syllabus and a few text books.

(b) Curriculum should be interesting.

(c) It is a means towards an end, not an end by itself, the end being the development of integrated personality.

(d) Flexibility to meet individual needs is another important aspect of good curriculum.

(e) It should provide for leisure pursuits.

(f) Adequate funds are required for curriculum development.

(g) Curriculum should involve creativity of life and constructive activities.

The preceding discussion should give us an idea about the nature of integral curriculum. It is aimed at and includes subjects and activities for the development of an integrated personality. The different curriculum subjects which contribute towards different aspects of personality development are indicated below:

1. *Physical Education:* Games, athletics, acquatics, yogis aseans, first aid.
2. *Vital Education:* (a) Sense framing, (b) General science, (c) Aesthetic education, (d) Recreational activities, (e) Moral education.
3. *Mental Education:* (a) Languages, (b) Mathematics, (c) Social sciences including history, (d) Such other subjects contributing to mental development.
4. *Psychic and Spiritual Education:* The important thing is to be noticed is that curriculum is organised according to development aspects and not subject-wise.

He has given to us three cardinal principles of teaching which tell us about his method of teaching:

(a) The first principle of teaching is that nothing can be taught. The teacher is not an instructor or task master, he is a helper and guide. He does not actually train the mind. He only suggests or shows him how to perfect his instruments of knowledge and helps and encourages him in process. He does not impart knowledge but shows him how to acquire knowledge for himself. This is the fundamental principle of ·teaching.

(b) The second principle is that the mind has to be consulted in its own growth. The idea of hammering the child into shape denied by the parent or teacher is a barbarous and ignorant superstition. It is he himself who must be induced to expand in accordance with his own nature.

A question may arise in this connection-what has this principle to do with teaching? It can be very well seen that it has something to do with selection of subjects. The job consists in exploring and identifying the potentialities in the child and helping him in making the choice.

(c) The third principle is that child is best educated in an atmosphere with which he is familiar—the atmosphere of his own culture which includes his heredity and traditions.

The three cardinal principles make it clear that in the teaching learning process, learning is more important than teaching.

What then could be methods of teaching? Some principles are:

(i) Education through mother tongue.

(ii) Education through interest of the child.

(iii) Learning by doing.

(iv) Self-experience.

Place of Teacher: We have already said about it in the first principle of teaching. We repeat.

"The teacher is not an instructor or task master, he is a helper and guide. His business is to suggest and not to impose. He does not actually train the pupil's mind, he only shows him how to perfect his instruments of knowledge and helps him and encourages him in the process."

Unity and Education

Natural Education: Education without strain-education which comes naturally and is easy and effective is called integral education. National reconstruction is to be achieved through it. Integral education is complete education.

The following points constitute integral education.

1. Mental and physical aspects have to be strengthened.
2. Education has five principal aspects—the physicals vital, mental, psychic and, spiritual. All these have to be developed together.
3. Four aspects of Truth—love, knowledge, power and beauty are to be developed.
4. Each aspect of Truth has a vehicle-four aspects have four vehicles:
   (a) Psychic for love
   (b) Mind for knowledge
   (c) Vital-power
   (d) Physical body for expression of beauty of a person-physical beauty of a person.
5. The aim, curriculum, methods of teaching are in the light of this concept of integral education.

The yogic principles of integral education are:

1. Truthfulness.
2. Right action.

3. Purity.
4. Remembrance.
5. Gratitude.
6. Humility.
7. Perseverance.
8. Faith.
9. Aspiration.
10. Devotion.
11. Sincerity.
12. Surrender.

Novel Demands

1. Aurobindo's system is child centred education.
2. Aims of education are based on idealistic philosophy of life.
3. He is a yogi. As such his philosophy is difficult to practise. It does not appeal to common man. It cannot be adopted
4. He believes in spiritualism. Whereas the world is 'full of materialism.'
5. He condemned western materialism but not of much avail.
6. He opened an ashram to practise what he preached. Overall Sri Aurobindo was one of the most eminent and distinguished educationists of our country.

The Leader

Sri Aurobindo was born in Calcutta on 15th August, 1872. His father Dr. Krishnadhan Ghosh had a fascination for western education and western life. Hence, he sent his son Aurobindo Ghosh to England for his studies when he was just seven years old. Aurobindo studied there at St. Paul School and Cambridge University. He appeared in the I.C.S. competitive examination and qualified in the written examination. But, he did not try to qualify in the horse riding test deliberately as he did not want to be a link of the foreign rule in India. He returned to India in 1893 and joined Baroda College. In 1905 emotionally stirred up by the Bengal Anti-Partition Agitation, he actively participated in the movement. He then shifted from Baroda to Calcutta as Principal of the National College. He wrote articles in the papers to motivate people to actively participate in the freedom movement of India. For one of these articles he was jailed also for one year. But, he could not continue in politics for long. In 1910 he left activism, came to Pondicherry and began to live a life of spiritualism. He founded an Ashram there known as Sri Aurobindo Ashram. He died in 1952.

Hinduism: Concept: Sri Aurobindo's philosophy was the philosophy of Vedanta and Yoga. The central point around which his thoughts were woven was attainment of Supreme Spirituality which to him, meant only realisation of the Divine. In *The Human Cycle* (1949, p. 282) he said, "For accepting the truth of man's soul as a thing entirely divine in its essence, it will accept also the possibility of his whole being becoming divine in spite of Nature's first patent contradictions of this possibility". He further said, "It (the Spiritual Aim of life) will reveal to man the divinity in himself. It will show man the way to seek for the divine in every way of his being, *Sarvabhavena,* and so find it and live in it-live and act in that, in the Divine, in the Spirit, in the eternal Reality of his being" (The Human Cycle, 1949, p. 287).

Aurobindo's concept of Reality was very much similar to that of Sankhaya philosophy. He also saw existence as the grand manifestation of the Ultimate Supreme Power. He said, "Spiritual experience tells us that there is a Reality which supports and pervades all things as the Cosmic Self and Spirit." This can be discovered by the individual even here in the terrestrial embodiment as his own self and spirit as an infinite and eternal being. Thus, the ultimates of life, to Aurobindo, were spiritual which could be achieved only in the full light of the liberated self and spirit. He said that "it is the truth that all active being is a seeking for God, a seeking for, some highest self and deepest Reality,—a seeking for the hidden Divinity."

According to Sri Aurobindo every human being has in him something divine; every one is imperfect but has a chance of perfection. The goal of life must be to find it, develop it and use it. While living in the world, one can attain to "Life Divine". To achieve this objective Aurobindo suggested "Integral Yoga" as the means for which the most needed things were (i) Calm, (ii) Peace, (iii) Equality, (iv) Faith, (v) Aspiration and (vi) Surrender. "Opening personal consciousness to a higher spiritual consciousness based on a quiet mind was the first thing needed for this purpose. Peace is still more positive a condition. Sri Aurobindo said "To be able to receive the Divine Power and let it act through you in the things of the outward life, there are three necessary, conditions: (i) Quietitude, equanimity, i.e. not to be disturbed anything, (ii) Absolute faith, and (iii) Receptivity, i.e. power to receive the divine force" (*Basis of Yoga,* p. 18). Yoga demanded, according to Sri Aurobindo "a total dedication to the spiritual life", "to surrender and to receive with joy whatever the Divine gives", "faith and reliance upon God", "opening of the being to the Mother's force and rejection of all egoism and demand and desire, all motives except the aspiration for the Divine truth," "to feel the Divine in you".

Sri Aurobindo strongly pleaded for the need of Spiritual Religion of Humanity which he thought was the hope of the future. He said, "A religion of humanity means the growing realisation that there is a secret spirit, a Divine Reality in which we are all one—It implies a growing attempt to live out this knowledge and bring about a kingdom of this divine spirit upon earth." *(The Ideal of Human Unity, 1950, p. 378).*

The fundamental aspect of his philosophy in a nutshell may be said to be (a) to attain divinity in life, (b) through integral Yoga, (perfection of inner life) and (c) Dharma (the perfection of outer life).

Shri Aurobindo said that the true education is that which helps the individual, the nation and the whole of humanity to attain spiritual development. True education is that which brings out to full advantage all that is within the individual and that helps him to enter into his right relation with the life, mind and soul of the people, with the total life, mind and soul of the whole of humanity. *(On Education)*

The principle of moral training as suggested by Sri Aurobindo is "to suggest and invite, not command or impose. The best method of suggestion is by personal example, daily converse, and the books read from day to day and good company. The books to be read should contain for the younger students the lofty examples of the past given not as moral lessons, but as things of supreme human interest: and for the elder students these books should contain the great thoughts of great souls, the passages of literature which set fire to the highest emotions and prompt the highest ideals and aspirations, the records of history and biography which exemplify the living of those great thoughts, noble emotions and aspiring ideals (On *Education*, p. 16).

Another principle that Sri Aurobindo emphasised was that the mother tongue is the proper medium of education and therefore the first energies of the child should be directed to the thorough mastering of the medium.

Sri Aurobindo said that every child is a lover of interesting narrative a hero-worshipper and a patriot. Appeal to these qualities in him and through them let him master without knowing the living and human parts of his nation's history. Every child, he said, is an inquirer, an investigator, analyser, a merciless anatomist; appeal to these qualities in him and let him acquire without knowing it the right temper and the necessary fundamental knowledge of the scientist. He further said that every child has an insatiable intellectual curiosity and turn for metaphysical enquiry; so use it to draw him on slowly to an understanding of the world and himself. Every child has a gift of imitation and a touch of imaginative power; so use it to give him the groundwork of the faculty of the artist (On *Education, p.21).*

Sri Aurobindo strongly pleaded for perfect liberty for the child. He advised teachers not to be arbitrary, despotic, impatient and ill-tempered.

Sri Aurobindo also laid great stress on physical education. Sense improvement by practice, training of the mental faculties, training logical faculty and reasoning.

The Residence

Establishing an Ashram at Pondicherry is an immense contribution of Sri Aurobindo. The Ashram provides an environment of peace and harmony which is highly conducive to spiritual development of the inmates who are *poets*, musicians, artists, physicians, surgeons from different countries of the world. Located near the seashore, the Ashram presents "Ideal of Human Unity".

There is an Ashram school for the children of Sri Aurobindo's disciples. Also, there is an international centre of education. It provides facilities for physical education, vital education, mental education, psychic and spiritual education, and international education.

Auroville: "The city of dawn" near Pondicherry was established in 1968. Representatives from 121 countries brought soils from their lands and poured into a lotus shaped urn symbolizing the unity of the human race.

9

Zakir Hussain

His Life

Zakir Hussain belonged to the family of Afridi Pathans who had migrated to India in 1719 A.D. and settled at Qaimganj town in Farrukhabad District of Uttar Pradesh where other migratory Afghans had settled down.

We begin with the grandfather of Zakir Husain. Ghulam Husain Khan had two sons—Ata Husain Khan and Fida Husain Khan. Ata Husain Khan joined the army. Fida Husain Khan was a scholarly person. He was adventurous also. From Qaimganj in U.P., he migrated to Hyderabad and opened a shop of Moradabad Brassware there. But his scholarly nature surfaced. He studied law and started practice in Hyderabad. He was married at the age of 23 and fathered seven sons. Zakir Husain was third in order.

Zakir Husain was born on 8th February, 1897 in Hyderabad. He was brought up as any upper class Muslim would have been. He was nicely dressed and was put to puritanical discipline.

In 1905, when Zakir Hussain was nine years old and a student of Sultan Bazar Govt. High School in Hyderabad, his father Fida Husain died of tuberculosis at the young age of 39.

The family had to shift to their ancestral home at Qaimganj. His mother Naznin Begum was worried about the education of her children as they could not get proper education at home.

In 1908 Zakir Husain was in a residential school at Etawah, the Islamic, started by Moulvi Bashiruddin, who hoped to impart English education as well as the Islamic way of life. The school was headed by a dedicated nationalist, Muslim Altaf Husain. Altaf Husain advised him to sacrifice the pleasures of life.

Zakir Hussain was studious. He religiously walked to the Etawah Railway Station daily to buy a copy of The Pioneer and on return would discuss contents with friends. Bright as well as respectful, Zakir Hussain won the confidence of his teachers and students alike, a peak of his Islamic phase was reached when at his persuasion, the management abandoned its practice of depriving a student of a meal for missing a prayer.

After having passed his matriculation examination in 1913 with distinction, he joined the MAO College at Aligarh from where he passed the Intermediate examination in Science with Biology. He could not become a doctor because he fell ill.

When still an undergraduate student, Zakir Hussain was married to Begum Sahjahan Bano. He was a loving father too.

Passed his B.A. in 1918 and won Iqbal Medal. At Aligarh he was popularly known as "Murshid" (Mentor). He wrote articles and was given junior lecturership.

The steel of his character was tempered when the non-cooperation call came from Gandhi in 1920. Zakir Hussain responded to the call with about 300 students, took the first 'conscious' decision of his life and left the MAO College. This strengthened the hands of Muhammad Ali who bounded Jamia Millia Islamia (National Muslim University) in 1920. Zakir Husain joined this institution as lecturer in economics but after a Ph. D. from Germany in 1926, he came back and joined

Jamia Millia Islamia as its Vice-Chancellor @ Rs. 80/-per month- Rs. 40 cash and Rs. 40 in credit..He worked selflessly for about 20 years in this institution.

In 1957, Pandit Jawaharlal Nehru offered him the governorship of Bihar.

Earlier he had contributed in the field of Basic Education.

In 1962, Zakir Hussain was elected the Vice-President of India. He attributed his success to his close involvement in education work and to the significance of education in the life of the people. From 1962 to 1967 he was chairman of Rajya Sabha in his capacity as Vice President of India.

He was elected President of India in 1967. He died in office in May 1969. He had remarkable qualities of head and heart and personality of heart. He was a true and devout Muslim. He was a sufi. He had many hobbies also. He was a passionate lover of plants, flowers a connoisseur of art, music and culture. "It was rare to find so integrated a personality as Zakir Hussain's".

Concepts of Education

Concept of Reality: This universe is real. There is reality of two worlds-material world or materialism and spiritual world or spiritualism.

(i) Material world is world of senses, and it deals with things or substances solids.

(ii) The spiritual world is soul. It is the soul which moves universe. Mind only apprehends it. Pleasures of the world are secondary. The spiritual world is to be realised by mind. Mind also catches ideas. Spiritualism is realised by ideas.

Concept of Man: An element of faith in "man" is clearly visible in Dr. Zakir Hussain's philosophy and educational ideas. He attaches the highest value to man in his educational philosophy and seeks to evolve man to the best of his potentialities.

In this sense Dr. Zakir Hussain is also a humanist. He recognises man's capacity to conquer nature. He did not consider man just a part of Nature. He deemed man not as a Progressive animal, in the words of K.R.P. Singh, but also a social impulse. Social impulse means that all members of a cosmic society, they are all brothers, children of the same father and therefore man must place universal welfare above other interests so much so that narrow national interests ought to be sacrificed at the altar of human weal. Dr. Zakir Hussain did not believe in caste, creed, colour, race and religion. He wanted a cultured man, rather than authentic man. No barriers anywhere in the interpretation of relations between human beings. He preached understanding and reconciliation. His ideas were to unite rather than to divide humanity. Truths must be applied for the good of mankind.

Dr. Zakir Hussain believed that man's destiny does not comprise of mere control over nature nor does it mean improvement in his productive efficiency just to satisfy his natural wants. Man must respect the source from which all creation springs and expands in order to deeper the meaning of man's life on earth. Therefore, Dr. Zakir Hussain exhorted the education to appreciate total human legacy—science, art, crafts, music, literature, philosophy, etc. Man has, no doubt, come to be what he is as a result of biological evolution which is an endless product. The cultural volution centres round man's creative mind and own making. He writes, "Man is a part and product of the process but a very peculiar part, capable of effecting its further course on earth and perhaps elsewhere."

Concept of Mind: Mind is source of everything. If we want peace and culture, it is mind which has got to be cultivated. Cultivated mind will bring a balance between material and spiritual world. It should have peace. Its energy should be properly utilised.

The Values: Education must cultivate-values. He wanted best values for Indians and he commended values like selfless service, secularising democracy. He stressed truths, beauty and goodness.

Education indeed refers to a set of values or ideals embodied and expressed in the purpose, for which knowledge, skills and attitudes are imparted and so directing the amounts and types of training what is given. "Almost the same view is expressed by Dr. Zakir Hussain when he writes that implies an individually organised sense of values."

Value can be defined in different ways. Ordinarily, a "value is that which satisfies human desire. All things that satisfy human desire have value or are good." In subtler form we can say "that alone is ultimately and intrinsically valuable that leads to development of self or to self-realisation." True to his conception of values Dr. Zakir Hussain laid due emphasis on self-realisation as an integral part of his value systems.

Values can be classified into eight categories-bodily, economic, creation, association, character, aesthetic, intellectual and religious. An analysis of Dr. Zakir Hussain value matrix presents almost a similar set of categories which can be classified as follows:

(a) Material.

(b) Individual-Things necessary for the development of self.

(c) Social.

(d) Cultural.

(e) Religious.

(f) Moral.

It is evident that the question of values was uppermost in the thought process of Dr. Zakir Hussain.

Concept of Awareness

Two types of knowledge were stressed upon by Dr. Zakir Hussain:

(i) Knowledge of substance.

(ii) Knowledge of essence.

Science gives knowledge of substance. Science has changed the face of the world and is doing so. Science is helping us.

Culture gives knowledge of essence. Knowledge of essence means, "Knowledge of the qualities, of the purpose, the origin, the end of the object, it involves a knowledge of its totality of the context which it makes the structural context, its 'what' and 'how'. It also talks of relational context-its 'whence' and 'whither' and 'who'. Dr. Zakir Hussain was an idealist.

Philosophy of Education

According to Dr. Zakir Hussain, "Education is the work of whole life. It begins from the time of birth and continues till the last moment of death."

This means that according to Dr. Hussain, Education is a continuous process. Every stage has its importance and significance. Education is life long activity.

Education is not merely giving information. It is leading to the maximum possible development of the mind.

Role of Learning

To quote K.R.P. Singh, a truly educated man is one who has the following five essential qualities:

Breadth of Intellectual Horizon: The educated man has a certain breadth of intellectual horizon with reference to value attached to things and persons. He has no thinker.

Open Minded: He possesses a certain degree of lively open mindedness and accessibility of new value and new ideas.

Moral Growth and Perfection: He has an inner urge towards moral growth and constantly presses towards perfection in his own person or world around him. He is not conceited and never imagines he has reached the destination.

Flexible: He has a flexible and versatile relation to value relationships amongst things as against the rigorous sufferers of the zealot or the bureaucrat.

Absolute Objective Value: His value estimations having been organised around an absolute objective value, he gives clear evidence of a central psychic focus which irritates all his action, thought and feeling. He is no internally dissipated busy body.

The Purposes

The aims of education for Dr. Zakir Hussain are neither completely unearthly nor merely mundane. They are rather a fruitful blending of the two. The aims of education should, therefore, constitute a kind of strong link between material ends and spiritual upliftment, between individual and social growth, between national and international perspective, and between man and man in every respect.

The aims of education according to Dr. Zakir Hussain are:

Fullest Development of Man: The purpose of education is to help man reach the fullest status as man. Educational programme must aim at man's creative and national values, besides inculcating in him a kind of religious faith. It is the fullest development that is important and all round development.

Stress on Creative Development: That we have already mentioned above. That leads to development of individuality.

To Enable One to Earn Livelihood: Vocational aims of education is so vital an aspect of education that no system of education would be complete unless it includes it. It is directly addressed to the breadwinning without which each man's existence would be jeopardised. Education must solve the problem of livelihood in a socially approved way. This is Zakir's vocational aim of education.

Ethical Aim: Moral development and ethical protection are most important aims of education. A truly educated man, according tc Zakir Sahib is one who has a wiser urge towards moral growth and constantly presses towards perfection.

Spiritual development is yet another aim of education.

Preservation, conservation and transmission of culture is considered one of the most significant aims of education.

The Syllabi

Regarding curriculum, Dr. Zakir Hussain observed that it must not aim at meeting individual educational needs, aspirations and attainments only but also reflect the national ethos and expectations. They, like Dewey, he was not satisfied with any cut and dry item of curriculum. He firmly believed that curriculum should not only be organic but it should also be closely related to the real life of the educands.

He agreed with Pestalozzi also and believed that, man is much more truly educated through that which he does, than through which he reads. It is with this conviction that he wanted a child to develop some reasonable skill in a basic craft. In his thought on syllabus, he laid emphasis on pupils activities rather than on teacher's activities. For him experiences constituted the heart of the knowing process. He wanted to exploit activities and crafts for pedagogical purposes and for integrating theory with practice. By curricular content he also wanted to bridge the gap between real life and schooling. Dr. Zakir Hussain wanted a happy blending of knowledge provided by mathematics, physical and natural sciences and humanities. Thus, the curricular content, as recommended by Dr. Zakir Hussain, must cater to the multi-dimensional growth of the educand.

In short, the curriculum comes down to:

1. Languages.
2. Science and technology.
3. Social sciences.
4. Art and music.

Way of Instruction

Dr. Zakir Hussain contributed a lot in the field of Basic Education and his method of teaching, thus cannot be different. It is:

(a) Learning by doing, it is manual work and useful productive work. Working with one's own hands—that the method of teaching.

(b) Principle of social orientation. Education should be socially useful.

Teachers' Responsibility

He also gave full attention to the teacher, his role and qualities, his preparation, and his professional ethics. He did not conceptualise the teacher as one who was always original or a genius but rather one who in his words and actions, repeated common-place truths not once or twice but so often and in so many ways that the educands took them for granted and they become their convictions. His main role was to transform the individual's achievement into social and moral values. The qualities which he valued most in teachers were love for humanity in general and love for children in particular and a never diminishing 'faith' in their future. His training should also attune to his role and in order to perform his professional work satisfactorily, he himself should be a morally autonomous personality. The teacher, according to Dr. Zakir Hussain, was the 'custodian' of the highest human and social values. As such, he should be ethically alive to his overall responsibilities to his students.

The Freedom: Dr. Zakir Hussain gave due consideration to this question: He created school to be true democratic society in which individuality is respected and human personality is considered as an end and not merely a means. He did not consider freedom and authority as contrary to each other. All educational theories value inner freedom and the authority is recognised voluntarily. Therefore the question of authority and freedom in schooling is resolved thus. The authority of values, freely experienced and freely accepted in the real life constitutes the test of real education. Dr. Zakir Hussain expected schools and colleges to develop students into useful citizens possessing free moral conscience personality. In a way he sought a happy blending of freedom and authority in the process of schooling at all levels and grades.

You can say that some sort of authority is required at the beginning of education for guidance.

Institutional Growth

Muslim National University is at New Delhi (near Okhla). For more than 20 years, Dr. Zakir Hussain was its Vice-Chancellor. It is a full-fledged University. Here the wisdom of East and West is pooled.

The educational views of Dr. Zakir Husain echo in a big way what other educational philosophers have said from time to time. His thought presents a synthesis of various different philosophies of education. His ideas present an essential unity between man and man, between man and nature and between man and God.

Part-III
Educational Thoughts

10

Theory of Hinduism

All schools of Vedanta claim to have their roots in the Upanishads. In fact, there was so much of contradiction and ambiguity inherent in the Upanishads that they needed systematisation. Vedanta, therefore, is an attempt to systematise the teachings of Upanishads. Differences on fundamental issues showed that the teachings of the Upanishads were, from very early times, understood in several ways by Vedantic teachers. "Bhadarayan's exposition is only one; and, in all likelihood, the most influential of them". All current schools of Vedanta, in spite of their differences, claim allegiance to what Bhadarayana himself taught yet making variety of interpretation possible, thus confusing the real teachings of Bhadarayana, as well as supporting his views in a variety of contradictory manners. Samkara's great commentary put an end to this confusion and contradiction once for all. All later commentaries were, at best, only marginal or cosmetic. His attempt at systematisation of the teachings of Upanishads is called Advaita Vedanta signifying a very particular and special type of monism as conceived and taught by Samkara.

Advaita Vedanta: a Concept

1. The particular type of monism taught by Samkara is very old, though in its final form it owes a great deal to his

contribution. Its most distinguishing feature on the theoretical side is its conception of nirguna Brahman as the 'ultimate reality with the implied belief in the Maya doctrine, the identity of the jiva and Brahman and the conception of moksa as the merging of the former in the latter'. (Hiriyanna). On the practical side, it is the advocacy of Karma-Samysa or "complete renunciation with its implication that jnana and jnana alone is the means of release.

2. The most important of Samkara's works is the bhasya on the Vedanta-sutra. The seemingly similarity of his doctrine of nirguna Brahman with the sunyavad of the Madhyamika form of Buddhistic idealism, is not only superfluous but have different roots. In fact, Samkara is far from nihilism, yet very dangerously close to it.
3. Samkara believes in the theory of representative knowledge, much the same way as Sankhya-Yoga did by ascribing knowledge to the same psychic apparatus. He is very close to Nyaya-Vaisesika when tracing the ten senses not to aham-kara as in the case of Samkhya-Yoga, but to elements as postulated by Nyaya-Vaisesika.
4. Knowledge is a blend of Saksin and vrtti. Whereas Vrtti element is contingent, saksin is eternal, and is "intrinsically Brahman itself". It leads to the concept of vrtti-jnana and saksin-jnana to distinguish the one from the other. Vrtti-jnana or empirical knowledge is experiential and is caused by the interaction between a subject and an object in the external world, and is ever present and resides in antah-karana whereas saksin is transcendent. Jiva is never without some jnana or the other except in deep sleep.
5. Samkara further distinguishes between mediate and immediate knowledge: in former only "the 'that' of an object is known, in the latter, the 'what' also is revealed".

6. Knowledge pre-supposes the existence of object before the act of perception. Perceptual knowledge arises when vrtti coincides with the object. Perception here is a sort of "communion between the knower and the known". External objects may or may not be known directly, the internal states are necessarily known immediately. The jiva, however, is always necessarily known immediately, and is never without any jnana: it is never empty. We are restricting our exposition of knowledge to cognitive and waking life.
7. Empirical knowledge is a complex "consisting of a physical factor and a psychical one, neither of which by itself is adequate to explain experience as we are familiar with it". Saksin is the psychical element: it may be jiva-saksin or Isvara-saksin (absolute consciousness). It is the root from where vrtti-jnana draws its existence, meaning and significance.
8. Advaita postulates three levels/sattas of reality. These are Pratibhasika satta, Vyvaviharika satta and Parmarthika or levels of reality each pointing toward the other for explanation, as Vyavaharik reality points to Pratibhasika indicating levels of experience and appearances. Error takes place only at these levels, because Parmarthika reality, being timeless, is beyond error. A snake in a rope, and the rope back as a rope are experiences restricted to the first two levels where appearances are relative because of each other as viewed from different levels of reality. Error, therefore, takes place within the world of experience.
9. The concept of formless (nirguna) Brahman is peculiar to the teachings of Samkara. Reality has no form, no attributes, and Samkara described it as neti, neti (not this, nor that) because the moment you say reality is 'this', it cannot be 'that'. Form and attributes set a limit on it, and it ceases to be ultimate. At experiential level, if one describes an object as it is, say, a 'chair' is a 'chair, and

therefore it cannot be a 'table'. By describing 'chair' as 'chair', we have set a limit on it. All determination sets a limit, hence 'neti, neti' Brahman is 'not this, not that,' because it is limitless and is not circumscribed by such considerations. Spinoza meant the same when he said "omnis determinatio negatio east". Determination of form and shape, attributes and qualities, restricts the meaning, significance, depth and power of the subject being described. Hence, nirguna Brahman is the logical expression of Samkara's monism: it represents the purity and honesty of thought and reason, the ultimate position where logic leads one to without any fear of contradiction.

Conclusion

1. Objects exist empirically independent of individual consciousness.
2. Whatever is not itself mind, must be for mind.
3. There is all-sustaining consciousness (unlike self and jiva), which is all comprehensive and beyond the cause-effect cycle.
4. Knowledge must be received directly and correctly, as mediate knowledge and error sets limit to this consciousness or cosmic subject "to whom the whole of existence is related as an object", and is called Isvara of Advaita.
5. Isvara is the third of the entities coeternal with time alongwith Maya and Jivas. Advaita, therefore, represents the triple factor forming the subject-matter of all philosophy and religion. Time, however, is the fourth entity which, sort of, has existence independent of the other three.
6. While all things born (except space which is in time) are in time and space, Jiva, Isvara and Maya are neither in time nor in space. They are "inter-related and together

constitute a system which, as time is included in it, may be taken to be dynamic in its character".

7. The nirguna Brahman is not the negation or the antithesis of the saguna, but is its very truth and is imminent in everything that goes to constitute it. One may say that "negation is only a preliminary to affirmation", and as such, every aspect of experience reveals it.
8. The consummation of Advaitic teaching is in becoming one with Reality.
9. Nirguna and Saguna Brahman represent "two grades" of teaching in Advaita—the higher one of the nirguna Brahman (para-vidya) that is so subtle and bright that it blinds, and the lower one of the saguna (apara-Vidya) which is more intelligible to man as it sees Reality in anthropomorphic terms.

Education of Vedas

1. Knowledge to be direct or intuitive should refer to one's own identity with Brahman. Such knowledge is the sole means of liberation, and should be the ultimate aim of education.
2. Moral purity, as it would dispel ajnana.
3. Self-realisation is possible through training and discipline.
4. Discipline is to be gone in two stages—one, preliminary which qualifies for entering upon the serious study of the Advaita; and the other, Vedantic training proper which directly aims at self-realisation.
5. Advaita lays more emphasis on jnana-yoga through sarvana, manana, and nidhidhyasana. This methodology has the following implications:
   (a) Sarvana
      (i) Ultimate philosophic truth is to be learnt through the study of a revealed text,

(ii) Need for personal interaction with a competent teacher.

(b) Manana

(i) Removal of doubt by self-discussion and contemplation

(ii) Value of analytic reflection

(iii) Secures intellectual conviction

(c) Nidhidhyasana

(i) Meditation upon the identity between the individual and Brahman to help remove 'viparita-bhavana' which may act as an obstacle to self-realisation.

(ii) Turn out jivan-muktas who have direct intuition or immediate experience of Brahman. It is the ultimate state of Advaita teaching wherein one becomes one with one: Aham Brahman Asmi.

Soul of Advaita Vedanta

1. Diversities of various things seen by the eyes of the world are not true. In fact, all these are just manifestations of the Supreme Brahma.
2. Since eternity there is a special power with Parmatma (God-Almighty) which is called Maya or Avidya. This Maya is neither true nor false. It is indescribable (Anrivachaniya). Brahma (Parmatma or God) creates the various wordly creatures (Prapanch) through this Maya (Advidya). Just as a juggler happens to create various animate and inanimate objects which are not actually true, similarly, Brahma creates through His Maya various things which are neither true (Sat) nor untrue (Asat). These various things are indescribable.
3. Therefore Brahma is the eminent cause (Upadan Karan) of this world (Jagat). Because of its relation with Maya,

Brahma is called Ishwar and all those things that are related with Maya are Jeeva.

4. The Jeeva (the animate being) forgets its relationship with God due to Maya (Ignorance) and comes under the influence of self-conceit. Mind and senses consider the body itself as the real entity. Because of this ignorance and shortsightedness the Jeeva considers himself as the agent or doer or master (Karta). Then he does various things with the desire of the outcome (Sakarma) and accumulates pieties (Punya) and sins (Pap) and gets involved in the bondage of birth and death and reaps the consequences of the same.
5. When one (Atma) realises the true relationship between himself and Parmatma (God) (after the removal of Maya-ignorance), his 'self is mitigated and gets merged into God, i.e. he becomes one with Him (God); in other words, he realises Him within himself.

The Concept of Brahma: According to Shankar Brahma is the greatest of all. That is why He is called Brahma (The meaning of the word Brahma is 'greatest'). Brahma alone is the cause of this world (Jagat). Even He is called by various names. He is attribution less (Nirgun), formless (Nirakar) and without any body (Niravayava). Therefore, he is called unique (Advitiya).

Due to Maya one unique Brahma appears to be various creatures (being Jeeva). Shankaracharya (i.e. Shankar) says that Brahma cannot be described by any name or form. Mind cannot think about its composition (structure, Rachana). Brahma is the name of origin, existence and destruction (Utpatti, Sthiti and Vinash) of this world (Jagat). Such is the nature of Almighty Brahma.

Brahma is the highest existence (Satta). His existence is beyond place and time (Desh and Kal). He is not any substance, still, He is the base (Adhishthan) of the entire world

(Sampurna Jagat), but He is invisible. According to Shankar, the existence of Brahma cannot be understood by any example. Brahma is self proved. No proof is necessary for His existence as He reveals Himself in all experience.

The Concept of Jeeva: What is Jeeva (Being)? According to Advaita Vedanta, Jeeva is the creation of Maya. Therefore Maya is the cause of Jeeva. It is due to Maya (Agyan) or (Avidya) that Jeeva appears to be the master of the body (Sharir). The work done by the sense-organs is regarded as that of the Jeeva. The senses acquire knowledge about the various wordly affairs, but it is the Jeeva which is regarded as the knower (Gyata).

The Distinction between Jeeva and Atma: From the practical viewpoint there is a distinction between Jeeva and Atma, but from the spiritual viewpoint, both are indistinguishable. Atma is eternal, formless (Nitya Nirakar and Anant) Atma is one, Atma is Brahma. By residing in a body, it is numerous (Anek). Atma is formless, therefore it is one. Since Jeeva is worldly (Sansarik), therefore it is considered as the doer, experiencer and knower. But since Atma (Soul) is unwordly, it has no relationship with attributes or characteristics.

Jeeva and Ishwar: Brahma associated with attributes is Ishwar, Ishwar is Almighty, knower of everything (Sarvagya) and omnipresent (Sarvavyapak). Jeeva is allied with Avidya or Maya. It is worldly (Sansarik). From the spiritual viewpoint there is no distinction between Jeeva and Ishwar, but from the wordly viewpoint there is a distinction between the two. Both are associated with Maya. But the Maya of Ishwar is poor. He controls this power, i.e. He controls Maya. Maya controls Jeeva. Since Maya has no control over Ishwar, He is all Blissful (Anandamaya). The Jeeva is associated with wordly sufferings, because it is controlled by Maya. Jeeva experiences happiness and miseries, but Ishwar does not experience so. Due to ignorance or Maya, the Jeeva accepts the body, as Atma (Soul), itself, experiences happiness or misery. There is no ignorance (or Maya) in Ishwar. Therefore He does not experience happiness or misery. The Jeeva is the experiencer and the Ishwar is the witness (Sakshi). Jeeva is worldly. Therefore it passes through the cycle of birth and death. Ishwar is immortal, free, enlightened and perfect.

Atma and Brahma: In the Advaita Vedanta, Atma (soul) is regarded as being of an eternal, perfect and awakened (Nitya, Sudha and Buddha) nature. Its existence is self-proved. It cannot be destroyed. It is very old but still very new. It resides in the body and it is detached with all the attributes of the same. Atma is unchangeable, because it has no place for any change. Advaita Vedanta believes that the Atma (soul) and the Brahma are the same truth. There is no distinction between the two—this is the principle of Tatvamasi'.

The Meaning of Tatvamasi: Atma and Brahma are identical. Atma is Brahma and Brahma is Atma. In the term Tatvamasi' the syllable Tat' stands for Brahma and the syllable Tva' stands for Jeeva. Thus the meaning of Tatvamasi is "both Brahma and Jeeva are indistinguishable", i.e. both are the same. There may be distinction between the two from the wordly viewpoint, but from the spiritual viewpoint the two are the same (Advaita)—not two separate truths, but the same truth. When the untruth is destroyed, knowledge of the self, i.e. Atmagyan is realised. Atmagyan is nothing but the Brahmagyan. This is exactly the status of Moksha—salvation or deliverance. In other words, Brahmagyan is Moksha.

The Concept of Moksha: In the theist tradition of Indian philosophy Moksha is considered as an ultimate objective of human existence. There are many other names for the term Moksha—they are Apavarga, Kaivalaya, Mukti, etc. All these terms mean the same thing. The freedom from the bondage of the cycle of birth and death is Moksha or Mukti. According to Shankar the position of the Atma in its original form is

Moksha. When Atma realises the real form of its nature the world and the body come to an end forever. This situation is that of Moksha or Mukti. Thus in the Advaita Vedanta knowledge of the self is Moksha.

Gyan and Karma: According to Shankar Gyan (knowledge) alone can provide Moksha. Karma cannot provide Moksha, because the outcome of Karma cannot be eternal. It (Karmaphal) is subject to destruction. So through this, one cannot obtain the eternal Moksha.

Nature of Education According to Advaita Vedanta: According to Shankar the principle of monotheism should be made the main basis of education. To realise the elements of Brahma (God) should be the principal aim of education. In order to achieve this aim ignorance (Agyan or Maya) must be dispelled. When ignorance is removed the unity between Brahma and Atma (God and Soul) will be realised. Therefore according to Shankar true education is that which helps one to realise the unity between Atma and Paramatma (Soul and God) between Nar and Narayan (Man and God). Thus, Shankar regards knowledge (Gyan) as the objective of education. To Shankar education is a tripolar process in which the teacher (Guru), the student (Shishya) and the subject matter (Pathyakram) are the three major sides. From the views of Advaita Vedanta as propounded by Shankar "education is a process which has to be continued till one attains salvation (Moksha) which will enable one to feel the inherent presence of God within himself, i.e. he will recognise no distinction between himself and God."

Aims of Education According to Advaita Vedanta: In short, we may summarise the aims of education according to Advaita Vedanta in the following manner:

Education must enable one for performing the four Purusharthas—Artha, Dharma, Kama and Moksha, i.e. valour, righteous duties, worldly pleasures and salvation. Artha stands for achievement of enough property through the other three Purusharthas. Advaita Vedanta particularly emphasises the fourth Purusharthas, i.e. the Moksha. It is for the attainment of the fourth Purushartha that the other three Purushartha have to be employed. Self-realisation or, realising one's unity with God, i.e. merging oneself into God Himself, is the ultimate end of education or all Sadhana. In other words, we may say that the ultimate aim of education is to guide the student toward attainment of spirituality (i.e. Moksha).

Techniques of Teaching

Shankar, the chief propounder of Advaita Vedanta speaks about certain methods of education which may be summarised as below:

1. *Shravan Vidhi*—i.e. listening attentively to what the Guru says.
2. *Manan Vidhi*—the method of meditating over what the Guru has taught. Meditating implies logical thinking for assimilating the essentials.
3. *Nididhyasan Vidhi*—i.e. the method of reaching the conclusion correctly. It may be noted that Shravan, Manan and Nididhyasan are not three independent methods, but they are the essentials of the one whole method.
4. *Prashnottar Vidhi*—Question-Answer Method was used by the followers of Advaita Vedanta in helping the students to get their doubts removed by the Guru. We know that this method was followed in the Upanishads. In Gita, too, Lord Krishna adopted this method for his disciple Arjun.
5. Acharya Shankar has recommended the Tark Vidhi or the method of reasoning for removing the doubts of the Shishyas (students).
6. Vyakhya Vidhi or exposition, Tika or Commentary or annotation was also used as a method of teaching the

student. Shankar thus speaks on behalf of a Guru—"Come and sit. I shall interpret for you the essentials of self-realisation."

7. *Adhyaropa*—Apavad Vidhi or the projection method—the student is guided to see the real into the unreal, i.e. to see Brahma (God) into the Jagat (world). Just as a snake (the unreal) is projected into a piece of rope (the real). Upavad comes after Adhyaropa in the process of determining and reaching a decision. Herein reasoning is employed.
8. *Drishtant Vidhi*—is used for helping the student to understand difficult subject matter through illustrations. Drishtant means illustration.
9. The Katha-Kathan is the story telling method as used in the Upanishads. The followers of Advaita Vedanta used this method of story telling for helping the students to understand the difficult things.
10. *Upadesh Vidhi*—i.e. the lecture method was also used by an Advaita Vedantist in helping Shishyas (students) to understand these matters. Shankar has used this method in his Vivek Chudanani and Upadesh Sahasri (meaning Best Wisdom and Thousand Lectures).

Responsibility of a Teacher

Advaita Vedantists believe that the relationship between the teacher and the student should be spiritual. Both the teacher and the student through their inner experience realise the existence of Brahma (God). Shankar believes that knowledge can be obtained only through a Guru. To Shankar a Guru is he who helps the Shishya (the student) to obtain deliverance. He has accepted the Guru as equivalent to God (Paramatma). The Guru is the spiritual father of his Shishya. The Guru is the knower of the Brahma (God). He should be calm and quiet as the fire without fuel. He should be compassionate by nature. He should be a friend for all his students. The Guru should not have any malice for any one. There should be no ego-consciousness in him. He should be an embodiment of all moral virtues. He should be at the height of religious and spiritual attainment.

Shankar has advised that a Guru must never discourage his students. He should attend all the students according to their needs and difficulties. But a Guru should accept one as his student only after testing his deservingness (Adhikaritva). The teacher must always respect the personality of the student.

Responsibility of a Student

To an Advaita Vedantist in the process of education the student is as important as the teacher himself. Shankar has used the term Brahmachari and Antarwasi for a student. A real student (or Shishya) must be able to exercise full control over his senses. A Brahmachari or the student is striving to realise the Brahma (God) within himself. An Antarwasi is that student (or Shishya) who resides in the Gurukul (the seat of learning). According to Shankar's Advaita Vedanta a student should have the following traits:

1. A student should be able to distinguish between the eternal and ephemeral. He should know the nature of truth and untruth. This type of student is Nitaynitya-vastu vivek (i.e. the one who has the wisdom to distinguish between the eternal and ephemeral).
2. A student should have a genuine desire for Vairagya (that is, he should believe that this world is unreal and he must be away from its Prapanch, i.e. involvements).
3. A student should strive for the realisation of Brahma.

For this realisation he should have the following qualities:

(i) Control over the mind—Sham.

(ii) Control over all senses—Dam.

(iii) Shunning external devices—Uparati.

(iv) Free from all worries and anxieties—Titiksha.

(v) To repose his intellect and be thinking only about God (Brahma).

(vi) Perfect faith in Shashtras (Great literature)—Shraddha.

(vii) A student should be desirous of deliverance—Mumukshu.

The Duties of a Student (Shishya): The student should always remain under the shelter of his Guru. As long as he is in the Gurukul, he must not make any independent research. He should have perfect faith in the Guru. He should promise to observe celibacy till he attains the deliverance. He should put questions to the Guru for getting his doubts removed. The student should always be ready to serve the Guru. Shankar has advised students to beg alms for the maintenance of the Gurukul. After completing his education the student should offer donation (Dakshina) to the Guru as the latter demands. Dakshina has to be considered as a token of gratitude to the Guru and not a repayment of debts that the student owes.

Importance of Discipline

In the philosophy of Advaita Vedanta great importance has been attached to disciplined life. Shankar has remarked that only that student can realise Brahma (God) who has perfect control over his senses and has a power of concentration. This trait in the student cannot come without hard discipline. Shankar himself has presented an ideal disciplined life by remaining a Brahmachari all through his 32 years of life. It is because of his unique disciplined life that he has succeeded in giving an immortal idea for the benefit (Kalyan) of the entire mankind.

Fixed Syllabus

According to Advaita Vedanta philosophy the ancient system of Gurukul has been accepted as the ideal place for receiving education. In this Gurukul Shankar has advised the students to study Vedas and other relevant literatures. Practical arts were also to be taught in a Gurukul. But since the main goal of education has been to attain deliverance (Moksha), the curriculum therefore abounded in religious and spiritual subjects. A fixed and unchangeable curriculum was recommended for all students. The study of Upanishads and Vedas was given the highest place in the curriculum. But suiting the different interests, abilities and aptitudes of students, the nature of the religious and spiritual subjects were to be determined. From the religious and spiritual viewpoint the curriculum has to be God-oriented (Brahma Anubhuti-oriented). With a view for Parmartha—the welfare of others, the curriculum also included certain arts for serving the people in general.

Within the co-curricular activities, worship of God, pilgrimages, practice of Yoga, Satsanga—company of righteous people, performing of Yagya, observing fasts and going out for religious preachings were included. The Advaita Vedantists prescribed this kind of curriculum with the belief that the same will help one to realise the Brahma (God).

Comments: According to Shankaracharya, reality may be divided into three categories/levels namely: (1) Reflection, (2) Practical and (3) Spiritual. The first kind of reality appears to be true for the time being, but later on it turns to be unreal as the mirage of a piece of rope appears to be a serpent in a shadow or darkness. But light clears the mirage and one realises the reality or truth. Practical reality Vyavrik satta is our normal and natural behaviour with other beings or material things. When the ultimate reality dawns, then it also becomes unreal and untrue. The spiritual reality is uncontroversial, because it is the reality of 'Brahma.' However, the types of reality are relatively real. Keeping in view all the three categories of realities, curriculum should consist of Geography, History, Economics, Sociology, Science, Commerce, Vocational and

Technical subjects. Together with these, for those children who do not evince any interest in getting spiritual knowledge, other subjects as Literature, Psychology, Physics, Biology and Philosophy should also be included in the curriculum. Those children who show eagerness about Vedanta philosophy, should be afforded full opportunities to understand and study Vedanta philosophy to the best of their capacities.

Implications of Shankar's Advaita Philosophy: Shankar's Advaita Vedanta is the highest spiritual concept ever conceived by a human mind. In the modern world of mutual rivalry, competition, exploitation, and accumulation of superfluous wealth. Shankar's philosophy provides us a breathing ground to pause and think over the futility of human endeavour for mundane gains.

For Purpose of Education:.Our students and teachers in our schools and colleges must ponder over the ultimate outcome of all their various efforts. The real purpose of education is to help an individual to attain perfection. The concept of perfection as advocated by Shankar's Advaita Vedanta may be accepted as the major objective for our education today. If we practise this ideal in actual life all our troubles will be wiped off.

If we begin to see the same soul in all creatures on earth as urged by Shankar, we shall begin to accept all human beings as our own 'selves'. Then we shall not practise any distinction between one and another. Thus the oneness of mankind will be realised resulting into peace and prosperity on earth.

For Religious Education: In giving religious education we may accept the Shankar's Vedanta ideal of Nirgun Brahma which, in a way, envelops within itself the essence of all religions of the world. The concepts of Maya, Jeeva and Brahma as explained by Shankar may be accepted as the basis of religious education in our educational centres. One may disagree with some of Shankar's views as a matter of philosophy. But with the help of the essence of Nirgun Brahma we may proceed on with the meanings of Maya (untruth), Jeeva, Jagat and Brahma for making our life sublime.

Establishment of Centres for the Education of Masses: Shankaracharya devoted all his energies to his mission of spreading the message of Vedanta all over the country. For this mission, he established four centres of learning. In the North he established Jyoti Math at Badrinath. Its gospel is Atharva Veda. It includes the territories of Punjab, Uttar Pradesh, Delhi, Kashmir and all the northern regions. In the South he established Shringeri Math. Its gospel is Yajur Veda and the territory is Karnataka, Andhra, Tamil Nadu, Kerala and other parts of South. In the East he established Goverdhan Math, its gospel being Rig Veda and it includes the territories of Assam, Bengal, Orissa, Bihar and other eastern regions. In the West was established the Shardamath, its gospel being Sam Veda and territories of Sindh, Gujarat, Maharashtra and other western regions.

The presiding heads of these maths are called Shankaracharyas and Jagat Guru or World preachers is prefixed before their names. All these Shankar Acharyas are erudite scholars, controller of senses, full of highest qualities of abstinence, renunciation, great intelligence and divine insight. These Shankaracharyas, move in their specific territories as well as throughout the land to preach Hindu philosophy of life and knowledge of scriptures for the benefit of all mankind. Evaluation of Shankar's Vedantic Philosophy.

Shankaracharya's philosophy is based upon the Upnishad's philosophy of Advaita Vedant. It may be noted that though there were many scholars before Shankaracharya who defined and explained the philosophy of Vedant in a fairly appreciable way-yet the interpretation and commentaries of Shankaracharya were singular and unique among all the other ones. By establishing the four centres of learning in all the four corners of the country, Shankaracharya provided for renaissance of the Hindu Nation imparting to the people the right sermon on religion from time to time. Shankaracharya has emphasised that Vedanta is not the renunciation cult meant for only Sanayasis but it is for all to be used as a practical guide and pattern of normal behaviour. Dr. Baldev Upadhyaya in his book 'Bhartiya Darshan' has rightly commented: "Vedanta is a practical doctrine." Those who criticise it as an unpractical doctrine are very far from truth. Vedanta as a matter of fact emphasises the existence of 'Brahma' in all the living beings of this creation. When the same 'Brahma' exists in all beings, there is no place for mutual rivalry, enmity and conflict of any sort. Vedanta subordinates material pleasures below the spiritual values and inspires all to get ahead and develop more and more toward the attainment of supreme Bliss or 'Moksha.' Vedanta despises material pleasures as short-lived and unreal in comparison with the moral and spiritual values which lead mortals toward 'Brahma' (Salvation). Further, Vedanta preaches that every being is full of inherent unlimited power and capacity to grow and develop more and more to the realisation of highest values—The Supreme Good, The Supreme Beautiful and The Supreme Truth. Finally, Vedanta raises all living beings above their narrow selfish ends towards international good, brotherhood and prosperity of the whole human family. Thus, Vedanta is the most desirable base for all educations' schemes for the whole world as it emphasises human brotherhood.

11

Buddhist Theory

Buddhist education came into existence in the 5th century B.C. Brahmans deprived the common people of their right to education, and hence the emergence of Buddhism granted the people the freedom to obtain education and to practice their religion themselves. Lord Buddha imparted to life a perfectly practicable form. Consequently, a practicable religion and a practical educational system became a variable to the common people.

It is undoubtedly true that though Buddhist education had an individual character, it was, in essence, based upon the educational system of the Vedic period. The Buddhists imparted education in Sanghas or collective groups. R.K. Mukherjee has pointed out that the Buddhist educational method is the method of Buddhist congregations (Sanghas). Just as the rituals of fire sacrifice (yajnas) were the centres of culture in the Vedic period, the congregations of the Buddhist period were the centres of education and knowledge.

In the Buddhist world, there was no opportunity for the individual to obtain education independently, away from his Sangha or congregation. Every kind of religious as well as worldly education was in the hands of Buddhist monks.

Steps in Education

During the Buddhist period, education had two levels—primary and higher levels.

Primary Level: The Jataka stories indicate that during the Buddhist period, primary education took the form of worldly or materialistic education. Fa-Hien has also mentioned the existence of a system of general education. Children of six were admitted to this level of education.

Higher Level: Altekar opines that the Buddhists raised India's international stature considerably by the high level of education in their monastries since students from as far as Korea, Tibet, Java and other distant countries were attracted to them.

Institutes for Knowledge

During this period, some prominent centres of education sprang up. Their characteristics were their collective nature and their association with Buddhist Viharas or monastries. There was no discrimination between students on any basis. Some of these centres possessed an international reputation, proved by the fact that Chinese, Japanese, Tibetan and other students came there to receive education.

As already pointed out, there were many universities in India during the Buddhist period. It was a time when democratic feelings were evolving, and hence many famous educational centres came into existence. Wherever Buddhist monastries or viharas were established, educational centres too emerged. Among the most notable universities to develop during this period were the universities at Taxila, Nalanda, Ballabhi, Vikramshila, Odantpuri, Nadia and Jagdalla.

Taxila: Taxila was an important centre of education during the Buddhist period. It was then the capital of Gandhar. It had been founded by King Bharata after the name of his son Taxa.

Being situated on the borders of this subcontinent, the kingdom was subject to frequent external aggressions. Because of this, the university in this kingdom developed on the basis of the family. Students started their education at the age of 16. The university provided education in numerous subjects, such as the three Vedas, Vedanta, Grammar, Ayurveda, the eighteen Sippas, military science, astrology, agriculture, commerce, treatment of snake-bite, (sarpa-dansha chikitsa), magical charms (Tantra Vidya), etc.

Nalanda: The Nalanda university was situated in the state of Bihar, 40 miles south west of Patna and 7 miles north of Rajgraha. It was an internationally famed Buddhist centre of education. It became famous because it was the birth place of Sariputra, the disciple of Lord Buddha. Emperor Ashok had a monastry constructed here. By the 4th century B.C. It had become a famous centre of education, and by the 7th century it became the foremost centre of education.

Kings of the Gupta dynasty took interest in the growth of the university. Buddhist monastries were constructed here by Kumar Gupta, Narsingh Gupta, Baladitya, Buddha Gupta, Vajra and Harsha. Because of these monastries, the university continued to grow and expand. Its land was surrounded by a rampart at the entrance to which lived a profound scholar who administered an entrance test to the students desirous of joining the university. The university had eight large assembly halls and 300 rooms for study. It has been stated in Epigraphic India that the highest point of Viharavali kissed the clouds. The buildings of the university are a fine example of the engineering skill existing in that age. The remains of these buildings are sufficient to prove that the art of construction had reached a peak during this period. In addition to the buildings, the university had beautiful lakes, numbering 10, according to Itsing. The university also had a massive, nine-storeyed library which was divided into three parts, called Ratna Sagar, Ratnodadhi and Ratna Ranjaka. As books of all religions were obtainable in this library, it was given the name of Dharma Ganja, or the meeting place of religions.

Thirteen of its many monastries served as hostels for the students. In each room there were stone seats, space for keeping books and other facilities. The university possessed huge kitchens. 10,000 students lived and received free education at this institution. The university fulfilled all their needs of food, clothing, medical treatment, education, etc. 200 villages had been gifted to Nalanda. Apart from the income derived from them, the university also received sizable donations from the king and the people, who thus contributed their mite to education.

It-Sing studied at Nalanda for 10 years. According to him, Nalanda was a centre of Mahayana, a branch of Buddhism, but it also provided education in Hinayana, and Vedic and Jain religions. In addition, the Vedas, Vedanga, Philosophy, the Puranas, medicine, etc. were also taught here. The method of teaching was discussion and question-answer.

In Bihar, the Buddhist monks, teachers and students led a balanced, regulated and spiritualistic life, far removed from leisure and luxury. Students of this university earned great respect in many foreign countries. Students came from Java, Sumatra, Japan, China, Ceylon and other countries to receive education here. The staff of the university consisted of 1500 teachers. Huen Tsang, in his travellogue, mentions the names of such renowned teachers as Chaṇdrapal, Dharampal, Gunamati, Sthirmati, Prabhamitra, Gyanchandra, Sheelbhadra, etc.

Nalanda continued to serve, preserve and propagate Indian culture for 800 years. It was in the 12th century that this brilliant source of light was put out by Bakhtiar Khilji.

Ballabhi: From 475 A.D. to 775 A.D., Ballabhi, in Kathiavar, was a famous centre of Buddhist education. Heun Tsang visited Ballabhi also in his travels. At that time, there were a hundred

Sangarama here. This university imparted education in politics, diplomacy, medicine and various other disciplines apart from religious education. Its students obtained senior positions in the courts of kings after completing their education. This university, too became the unfortunate victim of foreign invasion in the 12th century.

Vikramshila: Vikramshila was located on the banks of the Ganga in Magadha, Bihar. It was surrounded by a strong rampart. The teachers of this university were among the finest scholars of the day. Many important religious texts were translated into the Tibetan language at this university. Its administration was in the hands of a committee. Students were granted admission only after a test was administrated to them at the gates. Among the famous scholars of that time who administered this test were Ratankar Shanti, Baghishwara Kirti, Naroha, Pargyakamanti Ranta Vajra and Gyana Srimitra. The university provided education in grammar, logic, philosophy, tantra, etc. It, too, was destroyed in the 12th century by Bakhtiar Khilji.

Odantpuri: Odantpuri had evolved as an educational centre before the Pal dynasty came into existence. The kings of this dynasty further developed this university. Its library was internationally known. 1000 monks received education here.

Mithila: Mithila had been a centre of Brahman education in ancient time, and when the Buddhist period came, it became an important centre of Buddhist education. It was here that a scholar named Jagdwara composed his renowned commentaries on such famous compositions as the Gita, Devi Mahatamaya, Meghdoot, Gita Govinda, Malati Madhava, etc. Vidyapati was born here. Apart from other subjects, Nyaya philosophy also was taught here. A student was deemed to have passed only after he had taken a difficult examination in Nyaya and Logic.

Nadia: Nadia was established at the junction of the Bhaghirathi and Jalangi rivers in the 11th century by the Sen kings of Bengal. Jayadeva's Gita Govinda and Shoolapani's Smriti-viveka were composed here. It was a centre of teaching in Nyaya and Logic. It retained its reputation even during the middle ages.

Jagdalla: Rampal had the town of Ramvati established on the banks of the Ganges in Bengal in the 11th century. He also had a monastry named Jagdalla established here. This soon emerged as a centre of Buddhist education.

Vibhutichandra, Dansheela, Shubhkara and Mokshakara were some of the famous teachers of this university.

This period gave birth to distinctions of class and varna in the sphere of education, and it was in reaction to this that the Buddhist and Jain religions came into existence. Their system of education changed from the method of teaching by gurus to an institutional method.

Specific Traits

Buddhist education had many notable features, the most significant of which were the following:

Abilities of the Student: In the Buddhist period, every class in society, except the Chandals, had the right to receive education. It was denied only to the ill, the handicapped, the dishonoured and those punished for crimes. Education began at the age of 8. Till the age of 12, the student remained in a state of Shramana. After attaining the age of 20, he was qualified to became a monk. Education was imparted through the medium of Pali.

Pababja Ritual: Before a student could enter a monastry for receiving education, he had to perform the Pababja ritual, in which, according to the 'Vinaypitaka', the student had his head shaved of all hair, dressed himself in yellow clothes, placed his forehead at the feet of the monks living in the monastry, and then sat cross-legged on the floor to repeat the following words thrice:

I take Refuge to Buddha.

I take Refuge to Dharma

I take Refuge to Sangha.

He was then ordained to obey ten rules, which included abstaining from theft, killing of any living being, impure conduct, partaking of food at prohibited times, use of intoxicating things, use of cosmetics, taking things without being offered, accepting objects of gold and silver in alms, watching dances or listening to music, etc. After the performing of this ritual, the student was called a 'shramana'.

Upsampada Ritual: After attaining the age of twenty years, the student had to adopt 'Upsampada'. On this occasion, the presence of ten monks was essential. After this ritual, the male monks were called 'Bhikshu' and the female monks 'Bhikshuni'. Even at this stage, monks were required to observe such rules as living under a tree, eating food obtained in their begging bowls, wearing clothes begged from others, and drinking the urine of a cow as a medicine, etc.

Duration of Education: The total period of education was 22 years, composed of 12 years as pababja, and 10 years as upsampadaa.

Student-teacher Relationship: Students were required to serve their teachers, beg for alms, eat food thrice a day, wear three items of clothing, bathe themselves with pure water, and live in discipline. According to Dr. Altekar, a teacher's relations with his new students was akin to the father-son or paternal relationship. They were linked to each other in mutual respect, faith and love. During this period, equality was the foundation of this relationship in which both students and teachers fulfilled their respective obligations and duties.

Women Education: In the Buddhist period, women occupied a position inferior to men. Initially, they were prohibited from joining a Sangha or congregation. Later on, they were granted admission to such congregations and it was then that feminine education progressed. Dr. Altekar points out that the permission for women to enter congregations gave great encouragement to feminine education, particularly to the education of women belonging to the noble and trading classes. There is considerable evidence to prove that feminine education prevailed during this period. Separate monastries were established for women. Among the women who attained fame were Sheel Bhattarika, Vijayanka, Prabhudevi, etc. A lady named Sanghamitra went to Ceylon to propagate the Buddhist faith.

Vocational Education: The syllabus of education during this period was comprehensive. It comprehended education in writing, agriculture, commerce, cottage industries, animal husbandry, elephant lore, archery, magic, knowledge of reviving the dead, knowledge of animal cries and sounds, prophesy, control over sensuous activities, bodily gestures, medicine, etc. Dr. R.K. Mukherjee explains that the demand for the knowledge of Sippa or professional and scientific education was no less than the demand for general education or for religious studies.

Syllabus: During the Buddhist period education was imparted in art, handicrafts, military science, the science of taming and training animals, archery, geology, etc. alongwith education in script writing, arithmetic and religious discussion. The educational syllabus was divided into the religions and the material or worldly.

Education was conducted in this period according to two kinds of syllabus—the religious and the material. The former comprehended the teaching of Vedas and Buddhist literature, since it was a time when both these kinds of literature were studied liberally.

The material or worldly syllabus paid attention to the material or physical needs of society. It included training in such subjects as writing, arithmetic, argumentation, spinning and weaving, printing, dyeing, knitting, stitchir g, sculpture, art, music, agriculture, animal husbandry, etc.

In this period, too, as in the preceding Vedic and Brahmanic periods, the relations between students and teachers were cordial. It was the duty of the student to obey and to serve his teacher. In addition, there was provision for penance in the event of crime.

Role of Buddhism

The education imparted during the Buddhist period was, in reality, reaction to the education of the preceding post-Vedic period and the Brahman period. During this period, educational institutions for general education were established. They made provisions for imparting primary as well as higher education. An important contribution of this period is the imparting of education in various practical subjects, a tradition which has come down to the present day. It was in this period that the method of collective teaching and the presence of numerous teachers in a single institution was evolved. Educational institutions were formally organised and established in this period. The organisation of the Nalanda and the Ballabhi universities was so advanced that it continues to influence the organisation and structure of universities till the present day. The system of determining a minimum age for higher education, providing a set of rules and taking a test for admission is even today guiding the educational structure.

However, the Buddhist age too, like the Vedic age, did not remain without blemish. In the beginning, in this period too, equal respect was given to manual and intellectual skills but with the passage of time, the former came to be regarded as mean by the higher class of society. A religion which evolved as an institution led to the development of an institutional system of education, but then this itself became the cause of its downfall.

However, it is no less true that the educational method of the Buddhist period provided new standards in the sphere of morality and discipline. The accounts provided by Huen Tsang, Fa Hein and It Sing throw light on the contributions of this age to education.

Important Dimensions

As Buddha wrote no books, there is certain vagueness about his teachings which were gathered from works compiled long after his death and, therefore, admitted of distortion and even disorientation. Yet, these a the following general features that characterise Buddhistic thought which directly affected its educational precepts:

Pessimism: All life is suffering. Oldenberg described the extent of this suffering as 'All the waters of all the seas are not to be compared with the flood of tears which has flowed since the universe first was'. Evil and misery of samsara is most real and the foremost aim of man would be to escape from it. Pessimism does not mean despair: all is not lost, there is still hope whereby man may find happiness on this earth or in some promised world. Buddha points the way out of it: 'Just this have I taught and do I teach, ill and the ending of the ill'. (Rhys Davids)

Education, therefore, should be such that it helps one understand the 'ill' and then get over it highlighting the brighter side of life and action.

Positivistic: Buddha came as a reaction to anarchy of thought, and was more concerned with the hard facts of life: no speculation. His teachings excluded what could not be positively known. The positivistic character was a salient feature of ancient thought even if there were passing references to the supernatural. However, Buddha "did not recognise anything beyond the sphere of perception and reason". (Hiriyanna). He was basically a rationalist.

Education, therefore, concerned with knowledge through sense organs, but unlike a naturalist, is backed by reason. Training of senses, understanding of the environment and what all goes into its making, and a rationalist approach, were the crux of Buddhist philosophy of education. Search for the real in the midst of illusion and disillusionment, restricted education to the world here and now. Truth was what could be verified by experience.

Pragmatic: Buddha was more concerned with the alleviation of human suffering, hence his teachings touched upon only what is necessary for overcoming evil which is so very characteristic of life, as life essentially is suffering. He believed in the practical utility and raising of curiosity as essential to education." Deliverance from pain and evil was his one concern and he neither found time nor need to unravel metaphysical subtleties". (Hiriyanna) He was thus "eminently practical in his teaching". His approach to life was through and through pragmatic: whatever redeemed mankind from the affliction of suffering was dharma. Dharma, therefore, was a utilitarian concept, to be used for attaining higher ends.

While 'nirvana' is the highest goal, all forms of conduct that lead to it positively, are good. Good sects are those which lead to the conquest of passions, desires and illusion of ego. Education must help eradicate evil, both individual and social. Self-restraint, social service, welfare of others are the cardinal points of education which should be result oriented.

Ethics: Buddhism is a religion of Man and stands out for kindness, humanity and equality. It is identified with social good. Like all other Idealist schools, Buddhism also aims at self-realisation and perfection. As a matter of fact, Ethics is the strongest precept of Buddhism. Perfection in Buddhism, however, is perfection of conduct and is practical goodness, and is judged by its effect.

Based on its ethics, the Buddhist teachings emphasise on the social and mutual well being of Man. It must inculcate such values that help one to be a useful member of society. Education, therefore, should aim at self-fulfilment in the service of others, sense of well-being, benevolence, sympathy, cooperation and social goodness. It must help man regenerate himself in and through his interaction with society.

More Progress

As time passed, Buddhism gradually assumed a "more and more scholastic character", yet it remained a practical, popular creed. In contrast to teachings of Buddha who dwelt more on their practical, bearing, the new trend showed a remarkable interest in theoretic speculation unrivalled for its keenness, sophistication and refinement, adding to the richness of the Indian philosophy. This transition from the practical to the theoretic is referred to as later Buddhism which is more philosophical than religious, changing the goals, meanings, aspirations and objectives of human life, giving birth to a variety of philosophical schools varying in their origin, nature, approach, assumptions, depth and range.

These are called Later Buddhist schools which registered a shift from ethics to epistemology. The entire pattern and approach of teaching changed as education acquired new meaning and significance as these schools progressively advanced in their speculations, much in the same manner as the British Empiricists centuries later.

Different Ideologies

The four schools differed sharply from one another, especially in respect of the view they held of perception, and later of knowledge. As such, these schools have different epistemological assumptions, approaches and results, and are divided as under:

Realistic (Hinayana)	Idealistic (Mahayana)
(a) Vaibhasika	(a) Yogacara
(b) Sautrantika	(b) Madhyamika.
These schools believe in the existence of objects outside and independently of knowledge. These objects may, however, be momentary. The difference between the two is that whereas Vaibhasikas hold that objects are directly perceived, the Sautrantikas believe that the objects are perceived indirectly, i.e. they submit to some intervening agency in the process of perception.	Buddhist Idealism is of two types as mentioned above. Whereas Yogacara is pure subjectivism and reduces the whole content of knowledge as false due to lack of svalaksana, Madhyamika is the most important outcome of Buddha's teachings, and by far the most difficult to evaluate, it does not take any part of knowledge as self-evident. 'No sooner are objects thought about than they are dissipated'. The objects neither exist as parts nor as aggregate, nor as a real thing; neither existent nor non-existent. It ultimately deprives objects of having any intrinsic character, and ends up in Sunyavad.
The doctrine of momentariness, however, lands us in the field of ideas and impressions. Objects are known by their prior existence as they already perish before they are actually perceived.	
As such, the Buddhist realists, like Kant, assume a thing-in-itself and explains the actual content of perception as the result of mind imposing its own forms upon it.	As Madhyamika refuses to recognise external objects, as do the Yogacara, it admits of momentary ideas—shanikvad, to be real and directly known. The external world, therefore is the world of ideas, much in the same manner as Hume and Bradley assumed in modern time.

Educational Effects

It is clear from what has been said so far that the place which Buddhism assigns to jnana is very precarious, ending up in nihilism or sunyavada where the external world is neither existent nor non-existent. Knowledge may have value for life, and may, therefore, be considered the aim of education, it has no metaphysical validity. It is in general agreement with Buddhist positivistic and pragmatic outlook on life and education. The concept of approximate verification is considered adequate to meet the demands of practical life. Whatever its nature and extent, knowledge is at the core as it "lights up the path of action; and, so long as it successfully does so, it is regarded as true". (Hirriyanna) Truth is knowledge in action, and therefore, is the crux of all educational activities which are in and through life.

As reality is Becoming, change is not only total but also perpetual. Hence, nothing is of any permanent consequence. Life is in a flux, a continuous change creating new and peculiar situations. Education must, therefore, prepare a child to understand and deal with such fast moving situations and changes with alarcity and success. Validity is in effect and consequences. Whatever works is true and good.

Of the four schools of Buddhism, the Vaibhasika may be "described as pluralistic realism". Things are invariably accompanied by certain subjective determinations as and when perceived. "Since the Svalaksanas are supposed to be apprehended directly by the senses, they may be represented as the material of bare sensation". Perception adds subjective determination to objects and distorts/changes their form and presentation. To sum up: the external world as it is presented to us is "largely subjective though based on reality", and, therefore, has its own standing. Sautrantika position is identical with Vaibhasika with slight difference of interpretation of svalaksanas. Buddhistic realism is, therefore, far from naive, and has its own potential, depth and significance, and lends full support to the educative process.

Comments: The progressive order of the growth and development of various schools of Buddhism may remind one of the school of British Empiricism wherein Descartes, Locke, Berkeley and Hume reached similar conclusions, using almost similar examples and logic, centuries later, without any benefit of hindsight. This speaks for the universality and originality of thought, irrespective of time and tradition.

Means of Inspiration

Buddhist philosophy revolves around the happiness of man in spite of inherent misery end suffering around. For it, happiness and suffering are integrally related in the theory of Dependent Origination. The four jewels of Buddhism are as under:

Theory of Buddhism

Lord Buddha's preachings contain four Arya Satya, i.e. greatest truths. They are as follows:

1. This world is full of miseries.
2. There is a cause for a person's miseries.
3. The worldly miseries may be wiped of.
4. There is a device for removing miseries.

Concept of Buddhism

Pratitya-samutpad: Theory of Dependent Origination: The basic teachings of Lord Buddha consist of the four Arya Satya (the four Cardinal Truths). Of these four Arya Satya the second one is Dukha-Samudaya (group of miseries). This Dukha-Samudaya Arya Satya is called Pratityasamutpad which is regarded as the basis of all philosophical ideas of Lord Buddha. The cycle of birth and death has been termed as Pratityasamutpad. It was in the search of this philosophy of life that Lord Buddha had renounced his kingdom and subjected himself to rigorous penance. Man takes birth and he dies. The cycle of his birth and death is ever continued without any break. Man takes birth in order to die and he dies in order to take a new birth. The cause of birth and death is not any unknown power or unknown God. We are not born on earth because someone asks us to do so. We ourselves want to take birth, therefore we are born. There is no other cause of man. He, himself, is his cause. We shall not be born, if we, ourselves do not desire to be born. To tell the world that 'Man's desire, and craving or ambition is the principal cause of his (man's) birth is the contribution of Lord Buddha. Thus Lord Buddha considers man his own master (Swami), destiny-maker (Bhagya-Vidhata), lord and protector.

Kshanikvad-Anityavad: Kshnikvad or Anityavad is very closely related with Pratityasamutpad. Kshanikvad proves the "cause and effect" (Karana-Karya) principle of Pratityasamutpad. It is because of some cause (Karana) that some work (Karya) is done, and in the absence of cause, there can be no work (Karya). Thus all the things spring up due to some cause and they are transitory because they are born or they spring up. The deftness of birth and destruction proves that birth and death is the nature of this world, in other words, nothing is permanent and everything is destined to decay. Any thing in the world is only for a few days and then it is finished. Just as one flow creates the second flow, the second flow creates the third flow and this process ever goes on, similarly, one moment gives birth to the second one and the second one gives birth to the third one and this process goes on for ever. Because of illusion we regard this continuity of flow as eternal (Sanatana or Shashwat). In fact, nothing is eternal. Change is the nature of everything. Everything is undergoing change in some form or other. In other words, momentariness is the nature of everything, or as Hume said "you can never catch a stream twice" as for the second time, it just will not be there.

Arthkriyakaritva: Arthkriyakaritva means the power to do some work. The present is born of the past, that is, the past has an inherent power or energy to produce or generate the present. Each moment is generated from its previous moment, and each moment is the originator of its onward moment. Thus the Buddhist philosophers believe that existence of everything is momentary. The meaning of 'Artha' is 'the thing' (Vastu) or 'the existence (satta). Each thing (Vastu) is changeable and momentary. Thus each thing has the energy for affecting change. The seed sprouts out. It means that the seed has the energy for 'sprouting'. After being sprouted the seed is destroyed. This proves that the seed is momentary (Kshanik) and destructive. Thus the Arthakriyakaritva is based on momentariness (Kshanbhangvad) and Kshanbhangvad is based on Pratityasamutpad. This goes to prove that Arthakriya energy is inherent in a thing or existence (Satya). This Satta and Arthakriya Samarthya is the same thing.

Anatmavad: Buddhism does not accept the eternalness (Nityata) of soul (Atma). In the Brahmanic philosophy the soul is accepted as immortal. Lord Buddha does not accept the eternalness of soul. Lord Buddha has said that just as an individual desires woman, man, son and wealth, etc. similarly, he desires soul as well. He contends that for attainment of salvation one must shun or sacrifice the desire for soul, he cannot get salvation. Evidently, according to Lord Buddha the desire for soul (Atma-Kamana) is like the desire for any worldly thing. He believes that soul (Atma) is a group of five elements (Tatva or Skandh). These five elements (Skandh or Tatva) are form (Roop), feeling (Vedana), identification or name (giving a name-Sangya), impression (Samskar), and the knowledge of external things through the 'self.' Lord Buddha does not accept the eternal soul, but he does accept the momentary soul. The individual does exist. But he is a group of five basic elements (Skandha-Tatva). So, he is not eternal and in-destructive. The individual is not different from the five elements (Skandha). He is just an assemblage (Punja) of physical and mental states (conditions—Awasthayen).

Education under Buddhism

Educational Implications of the Four Arya Satya (Four Truths): This world is 'full of miseries' is the first truth as viewed by Lord Buddha. He has regarded the various miseries of the world as a nature of man. If one realises this truth from the very beginning he will do nothing which may cause any trouble to him. Then he will so conduct his life as to ensure his physical, mental, moral and spiritual development. Thus he will become a good citizen. If the parents and teachers are motivated by this first truth of Lord Buddha, children will be developed in a desirable manner and our educational system will be revitalised.

In the second Arya Satya (truth) Lord Buddha says that one's ignorance is the cause of misery. Due to ignorance one gets involved into various intricacies of the world. In the third truth he says that if the drives generated due to ignorance are destroyed, then a person will rise above all attachments (Rag), rivalry, lust and anger. In fact, to obtain this victory is to achieve salvation. Through the fourth truth Lord Buddha has indicated the path toward destruction of worldly miseries. In this regard he spoke of eight devices (Ashtangik Marg) which may help one in getting himself free from worldly miseries.

Lord Buddha has prescribed a middle course to be followed. He opposed the torture of body through hard penance. The middle course consists of eight devices. By following these eight devices the ultimate aim of education may be achieved. To obtain salvation (Nirvan) is the ultimate end of life. Salvation is the freedom from the cycle of birth and rebirth by right knowledge and conduct. In fact right knowledge and righteous conduct may be accepted as the ultimate purpose of education.

12

Jain Theory

Jainism is independent of Buddhism yet it resembles it in several respects, such as, in its repudiation of the authority of the Vedas, its pessimistic outlook on life, and its refusal to believe in a supreme God. But the differences it exhibits are equally noticeable, such as its recognition of permanent entities like the self (jiva) and matter. In this it resembles Brahmanism and is called 'a theological mean between Brahmanism and Buddhism. Derived from the word 'jina' with root in 'ji', it means 'victor', i.e. the one who has successfully subdued his passions and obtained mastery over himself.

Sometimes mixed up with Buddhism, it is much older than the latter, and Vardhaman or Mahavira was its last prophet. In fact, twenty three 'teerthankars' (prophets) had preceded him. However, the credit for reforming and cleaning up its creed, and to give it a shape that it has today, goes to Vardhaman.

The Basics

1. The Jains bring the whole universe under one or other of two everlasting categories: jiva and ajiva, i.e. the conscious and the unconscious, or spirit and non-spirit, "the latter" including not merely matter but also time and space.

2. Realistic and relativistic standpoint. As surely as there is a subject that knows, so surely there is an object that is known.
3. Jiva and Ajiva are properly understood only when contrasted with each other. That is why ajiva is also called 'not-jiva', or the contradictory of jiva.
4. The notion of jiva in general "corresponds to that of atman or purusa of the other schools of Indian thought. It is 'what lives or is animate'. It is self, and its number is infinite, all being "alike and eternal".
5. Jivas are classified on the basis of different levels of development of the souls.
6. Jiva is both an experient and an agent, i.e. karta and bhakta. Its intrinsic nature is one of perfection and it is "characterised by infinite intelligence, infinite peace, infinite faith and infinite power". The union with matter, however, obscures these features as well as its non-spatial character.
7. Variable size of jiva in its empirical condition.
8. Knowledge is the essence of jiva, as no self is conceivable without knowledge (jnana) or jnana without self (jiva).
9. Kevala-jnana (absolute apprehension) is the culmination of enlightenment. It is immediate knowledge and arises of itself "without the help of any external aid like the senses, etc". It is knowledge in its pristine form, is pure, is perception par excellence to contrast it with common perception.
10. Ajiva, unlike jiva, lacks life and consciousness, and are classified as Kala (time), akasa, dharma and adharma which together may be called 'space', and mudgala (matter). Of these, Time is infinite. Space also is infinite.
11. According to 'hylozoistic theory, not only animals and plants, but also the smallest particles of the elements,

earth, fire, water, and wind, are endowed with souls". (Jacobi)

12. Jiva, as Reality, always subsists in spite of various instances and conditions. 'To suffer change and yet endure is the privilege of existence'.
13. Jain form of atomic theory is probably the earliest in the Indian thought. Though the word 'anu' occurs in the Upanishads, the Vedantas pay no attention to it. Atoms, according to Jainism, are all of the "same kind, but they can yet give rise to the infinite variety of things so that matter as conceived is of quite an indefinite nature". Jainism, however, divides matter in two forms (like the Upanishads) from where the entire material world is derived, one is simple and the other is compound except that whereas in the Upanishads it is "represented by the monistic principle of Brahman, here it is taken by an infinity of atoms". Matter in its subtle form constitutes karma, which by "its flux into the jiva brings on samsara".
14. Syadvada is the conception of reality which is extremely indeterminate in its nature. This doctrine is applicable not only to matter but also to other forms of reality. Etymologically, it means the doctrine of maybe signifying that the universe can be looked at from many points of view wherein each viewpoint may yield a different conclusion and may be correct. "Absolute affirmation and absolute negation are both erroneous." The Jains support it by the famous fable of an elephant and seven blindmen, each one reporting correctly according to his perception and judgement.

Theory of Jainism

The special features of Jainism are found in its practical teaching. Its chief feature, however, is extreme severity which is applicable to a householder. Jainism insists neither on enlightenment alone or on conduct alone, but on both. As such, it has a foot in both the worlds.

1. Tri-ratna or three gems of its teaching are as under and are the three precious principles of life:
   (a) Right Faith
   (b) Right knowledge
   (c) Right conduct.
2. Five vows (vrata) of an ascetic would indicate the general character. These are:
   (a) Not to injure
   (b) Not utter falsehood
   (c) Not to steal
   (d) To lead a celibate life
   (e) To renounce the world.

   For a layman these are replaced by chastity and contentment.
3. Ahimsa (Non-violence) is the foremost virtue in Indian thought but in Jainism it acquires different meaning and depth: it is non-violence in word, thought and deed.
4. Emphasising the individualistic aspect, Jainism emphasises on the development of personality as the final aim. Jain teachings are social and tolerant, and believe in happiness of all.
5. There are two levels of discipline depending on the severity of the vows which are different for the monks and of lay life, and considers those of the monk as superior to the other kind.
6. The aim of life is to get oneself disentangled from karma. Jainism believes in the transmigration of soul. Soul united with karma is called a soul in bondage, and is to be redeemed and liberated.

7. A scheme of seven principles paves the Jaina course of practical discipline for release from bondage.
8. Karma is the link between the jiva and its body. Jiva was never free from this karmic accompaniment as karma is its essence.
9. Karma acts by itself, and hence, is the free agent and holds the individual fully responsible for what he does and is inescapable of its consequences.
10. Moksha means dissolution of partnership between soul and matter, restoring the ideal character of the jiva.
11. Adding 'punya' and 'papa' to the seven principles referred to above, make Nine-categories of Jainism.
12. Jainism rejects God as the creator of this world, as a need to create the world would be inconsistent with his necessary perfection. Jainism looks upon man himself as God when his inherent powers are fully in bloom.
13. Jaina views are both relativistic and pluralistic as it recognises jivas and the material objects.
14. The primary aim of Jainism is the perfection of the soul, rather than the interpretation of the universe, hence it fails to find ultimate solution of the metaphysical problem.

Educational Influence

1. Emphasis on self-discipline and hard work.
2. Truth is relativistic and pluralist; in a state of 'maybe', knowledge, therefore, may be viewed differently. Nothing fixed.
3. Self-realisation as jiva is divine. Education must focus on his divinity and remove the material bonds of soul.
4. Education should lead to self-enlightenment and restore the full powers of jiva.

5. Teaching of nine principles called as Nine-categories of Jainism to dissolve the partnership between soul and matter.
6. Believes in transmigration of soul, hence education may partly be the preparation for the next world.
7. Happiness and bliss through action. Man is a free moral agent, responsible for all his deliberate action.
8. Jiva is essentially karmic, therefore, education must be action-based and ideally oriented.
9. Practical discipline (of a lower order meant for ordinary householders) is essential for release from the bondage.
10. 'Punya' and 'paap' are the two principles of the Nine-categories. Hence education should develop sense of discrimination.
11. Education should include provision for attainment of Tri-ratnas, the three precious principles of life, that bring happiness, success and love, here and now.
12. Education should inculcate non-violence as a virtue, practised and not only aspired for, that would be socially desirable.
13. Development of personality as an individual. Hence, more stress on individual aims.
14. Teaching should be social and tolerant, and should bring happiness to all.
15. Teaching should give necessary jnana and penance to help jiva disentangle from Karma.
16. Cessation of Karma would disassociate jiva from it and regain its power and glory. Teaching must help train one for it.
17. Knowledge is through senses and meditation. Teaching must develop these faculties.

Jainism and Festivals

Jainas celebrate all the Hindu festivals. Mahavir Jayanti, the birthday of Lord Mahavir, is its special festival.

The Assets

According to Jainism this world is eternal and endless. Jains believe that this world is not made by anyone. The world is made of Jiva, i.e. spirit and Ajiva, i.e. matter (which is lifeless and inanimate). The Ajiva or the matter is of five types—Pudgal, Dharma, Adharma, Akash and Kal. These five elements always remain constant. Neither they decrease nor increase. Jainism does not believe in the existence of God. Neither God creates nor destroys, simply because its (i.e. God's) very concept is baseless.

Anekantvad: Jainism sees the same thing into different forms. According to this philosophy a 'truth' (Satya) may be seen with varying viewpoints. Therefore, a true Jain does not stick to a particular point of view, nor does he insist on his own views in the process of reasoning. He has a liberal outlook. He believes that a particular thing may be perceived in different ways. Because of this attitude a true Jain is able to maintain a Sambhav or poise or equilibrium in face of all circumstances. This attitude is known as Syadvad.

The Educational Implications of the Principle of Anekantvad: implies liberalism. This principle classifies that only one aspect of a thing or issue may not be acceptable. Regarding any idea or proposition there may be two or more sides. Therefore, in order to reach a right judgement on a certain issue, we have to take into consideration its various aspects.

In the democratic era of these days it is quite natural to have various points of view or a variety of opinion, regarding a certain idea. It may not be possible that the stand of a teacher or that of any student in a class will be accepted by all the students in the class. Therefore, it is necessary to effect a co-ordination between the various views expressed by students in a class.

In reaching a decision each student should have the self-satisfaction that his viewpoints have also been duly considered and the same have been accommodated in the final deliberation. This feeling on the part of the student will promote the development of his personality and help in adopting a liberal attitude about things. In the class teaching of modern days the teacher should try to co-ordinate the various views of the students for posing a consistent and acceptable whole. Evidently, the same idea can not be imposed on all students.

Non-violence: Non-violence is the main basis of Jainism. In fact, it is its main philosophy of behaviour. Non-violence has been given the highest place in the life of a follower of Jainism. Violence against any inanimate or animate being, in any form, is strictly prohibited in Jainism.

Educational Implications of Non-violence: Today the entire world is besieged with various types of violence. Each country wants to establish its supremacy over another through hurting its feelings and interests. In some part of the world battles and skirmishes are being fought between various countries. Extremists and terrorists are having their sway all over the world. Various kinds of rat races are seen in people without paying any regard to the feelings of others. Ladies feel insecure in going out on streets after the sunset because of social miscreants.

In educational centres of all types we find lack of respectful behaviour towards others. Many students do not hesitate in indulging in violence on flimsy grounds. Evidently, we have drifted away from the principle of non-violence. Jainism teaches us not to hurt anyone's feelings by speech, thought or deed. If teachers and students practise non-violence according to

Jainism many of the ills that are ailing our educational system will be eradicated and objectives of education realised in the real sense.

Penance and Righteousness: Penance has been given a very high place in Jainism. Both external and internal penance have been emphasised. No one can be righteous without restraint and non-violence. Penance is possible only with the help of righteousness. One should love all animate beings. If someone commits some mistake he should be pardoned. No feeling of animosity should be harboured against anyone. It is irreligious to show hypocrisy, anger and pride. One must not steal. Observance of continence is necessary.

Educational Implications of Penance and Righteousness: The principle advocated by Jainism through the ideal of penance and righteousness point to some basic ideals of education. Through education we want that one should become righteous. Restraint and non-violence are the central ideals of Jainism. If, through education, an individual acquires a temperament of restraint and non-violence, many of the existing ills of our society will vanish and one will have love and affection for others. Our educational ideals will be realised by this awakening in people and a person will be directed toward developing his full personality.

Special emphasis has been laid on penance in Jainism. Penance or hard efforts are necessary for achieving any objective. In our schools, colleges and universities these days students are very much afraid of hard labour. So they try to obtain good marks in examinations by unfair or foul means. This practice has led them away from real knowledge.

Therefore the standard of education is falling every day. The ideal of hard penance as prescribed for Jain Saints should be an eye-opener to modern students. They must realise that hard labour is necessary for achieving results. Righteousness should be the basis of penance as enjoined by Jainism and includes—(1) non-violence, (2) truth, (3) not stealing of the property of others, (4) continence, and (5) giving away of superfluous wealth to others (i.e. renunciation).

Jainism prescribes speaking of sweet and soft words according to justice. It enjoins the people to abstain from showing anger, pride and hypocrisy. It wants that the elders in society should be duly respected, the poor and weak should be helped. Jainism emphasises real knowledge, right character and right behaviour. Thus the various ideals of Jainism show us the path of salvation. This earth will transform into a heaven if we frame our educational goals accordingly for the practice of all in society.

Theory of Karma: In Jainism the relationship between 'being' (the animate) and the inanimate (Jad, Pudgal or the body matter) has been regarded as a bondage. In Jainism the animate, 'the being' or 'the Jiva' has been accepted as the consciousness (Chetan). The animate epitomises unlimited knowledge (Anant Gyan), unlimited vision (Anant Darshan), unlimited prowess (valour or Anant Virya), and unlimited enjoyment (bliss or Anant Anand). As a result of its deeds (Karma), ignorance (Agyana), envelops the being (Jiva) and all these powers vanish and the 'being' (Jiva) is trapped into a bondage. If the Jiva (the being) acquires knowledge, he will recapture all these powers and obtain salvation and his form will become full of lustres.

Comments: Previous deeds must be rewarded/punished based on the principle of conservation of energy, which also acts as a universally enforced system of justice. By understanding the dynamics of karmic force, we can harness that same energy for achieving a spiritually rewarding destination. You can realise your past activities by experiencing their fruits. The potential of your karma is unlimited. It all depends on what you do with it.

Educational Implications of the Theory of Karma: The foregoing accounts clarify that Jain philosophy gives all prominence to deeds in a person's life. This ideal of Jainism indicates that a person should be industrious and should be doing things in a planned manner for his culmination (i.e. optimum development).

It is, cowardice to depend upon fate. The prevailing poverty in our country is a testimony to this cowardice. Many people are seen idle cursing their fate. In-all the progressive countries of the world education is made job-oriented. If Indian education, too, is re-planned on job-orientation basis, the poverty of our people may be minimised to a great extent. Many of our youths get admission in colleges and universities thinking that at least for 4 or 5 years education will enable them to while away their time anyhow.

This attitude on their part has made them idle. Thus the prevailing education has not given them the right approach to life. Happily, now an awakening is seen in our educational fields for guiding our students for various vocations and purposes of life. If we succeed in this approach our educated youths will become believers in deeds and not in fate. Needless to add, Jainism clearly signifies to a great ideal for education.

Concept of Salvation: According to Jain philosophy the separation or disunion (Viyoga) of soul from the body (in other words, the disunion of the Jiva and Ajiva) is salvation or deliverance (Moksha). On the basis of penance a person has to rise above the fruits of his deeds. If he succeeds in this process there will be no further accumulation of worldly desires and impressions in him (i.e. he will become free of all impressions or (Samskars-Sanskarmukta) and all desires will vanish from him. As a result of this, he will attain salvation, the ultimate bliss (i.e. Parmananda). Through salvation one gets rid of all miseries and becomes bathed into real unlimited knowledge (Anant Gyan).

Educational Implications of the Concept of Salvation According to Jainism: Now it is not difficult to understand the educational ideas implied in the concept of salvation according to Jainism. In a way, it will not be an exaggeration to say that the ultimate purpose of education is attainment of salvation. In this sense, salvation (Moksha) and education become synonymous, both aiming at release. If we have no attachment with worldly things our various types of drives will vanish. Then we shall be oriented toward attainment of perfection or salvation. As a result, all our activities will be directed toward seeking welfare of others. The various tools for attainment of salvation, as prescribed by Jainism may be regarded as tools for achieving ideals of education also.

13

Islamic Theory

Islam and Christianity have common roots and history, yet there has been so much of bitterness and discord between the two that it exists even today, scattered all over the globe. In spite of these aberrations, the commonality of the ideas, originating from the same source, are obvious as both aim at the good and prosperity of mankind. According to Bertrand Russell, "the Roman Empire affected the history of culture in various more or less separate ways." Not only Rome directly affected Greek thought (which was, at that point of time, considered far superior and subtle in comparison), but also the effect of Greece and the East on the western half of the Empire where Christianity thrived. The fact that had been more pronounced and direct was "the transmission of Hellinistic civilisation to the Muhammedans, and hence ultimately to western Europe", at this point, highlighting the commonality of source. Constantine adopted Christianity as the state religion converting the western half of the Empire so prestigious that even the Germans who destroyed the western empire during the fifth century adopted the Christian religion.

The story in the Eastern part of the Empire was different as it diminished in size, yet survived till 1453, when "Constantinople was conquered by the Turks". Most of "what had been Roman province in the east, including Africa and Spain in the west, became Muhammedan. The Arabs rejected Christianity, but preserved the Greek civilisation and literature, as against that of Rome. However, the greatest cultural outcome of the Roman Empire was "the Muhammedans as vehicle of Hellenism", when in the seventh century, "the disciples of the Prophet conquered Syria, Egypt, and North Africa; in the following century, they conquered Spain", and adopted the civilisation of the Eastern Empire. They even moved westward toward India at about the same time. The Muhammedans or the Arabs not only contributed to the language such words as 'algebra', 'alcohol', 'alchemy', 'alembic', 'alkali', 'azimuth', 'zenith' in the areas of astronomy and astrology, Arabic numerals, and chemistry. But there greatest contribution to civilisation and·culture had been preservation of Greek thought which was later rediscovered by "the men of the Renaissance".

Importance of Holy Quran

Another similarity between Christianity and Islam is that both are revealed religions. The Holy Quran was revealed to Prophet Muhammad at intervals over a period of twenty-three years, partly while at Mecca, and partly while at Medina. Mecca-Medina are really the mecca of Islamic pilgrimage, undertaken by devout muslims all over the world every year, and is known as 'Hajj' and 'Ziarat'. In India, these visits are highly subsidised by the State, and are a matter of discontent and controversy. All the holy shrines of Sunni muslims are located in Saudi Arabia, and those of the Shias, in Iraq. Allah revealed the Quran to Muhammad through His angel Gabriel. Quran consists of 'Surhas' and 'Ayats', comprising 80,000 words. It gave its own calendar, Hijri, and added its words to the international vocabulary.

Quran begins with the very first words revealed to Muhammad:

"Read: In the name of the Lord who createth.

Created man from a clot.

Read: Any thy lord is the most bounteous

who teacheth by the pen.

Teacheth man that which he knew not".

The Comments: Islam considers man to be a 'clot' though with a potential to understand and act upon what the Lord ordains. CLOT literally means 'zara', so small and insignificant, nothing spiritual. It really surprises the author because Islam is virtually a religion of man, yet placed him so low in the order of existence. But it does have the potential to raise himself by following the teachings of the Lord, and have the capacity to understand and act upon His tenets. Man, as such, is an intelligent being capable of action. Unlike the Greeks whose civilisation the Muhammadens adopted and who were rather for contemplation, Islam is a religion of action and vibrance; does not abandon man, but raises him to the prescribed level; never to be equal or at par with the Lord who is his creator and sustainer. Everything happens by His will: Inshah-Allah, God willing.

Some Extracts

1. 'O men, fear your Lord who hath created you, fear God by whom you beseech one another, respect women who have borne you, for God is watching over you, if ye fear that ye cannot act equitably towards so many [four to be maximum] marry only one, or the slaves which ye shall have acquired'.

   Comments: Islam instills fear of God in man; abstain and be righteous because He is 'watching'. 'Kahre-Khudo (wrath of God) is the greatest fear in the mind of the devout. Do as ordained lest Allah takes a bleak view, and shove one in 'Aateshe Dozakh' (fire of hell). So, fear is the root, the be all of good conduct and socio-economic behaviour. Respect women not as your equal, and slave-women do not even deserve that, as they are 'acquired'. Such disparities toward women is compelling the progressive society to adopt a common civil code, which the Muslims are resisting tooth and nail. India being a secular country, such a code cannot be enforced unilaterally. The progressives amongst the community must come forward on their own accord and accept what is good for all in good measure.

2. 'O true believer, perform your contracts', as breach of faith (Vaide-shikni) is the greatest sin according to Islam. Islam ordains upon man such moral constraints of performing prescribed rites during the holy month of Ramadan—a month of fast and feasting. Abstinence during Ramadan, as by the Christians during Lent, is considered holy and mandatory. It purifies and chastises.

3. This is the scripture where there is no doubt, a guidance unto those who ward off (evil) who believe in the unseen, and establish worship, and spend of that we have bestowed upon them, and who believe in that which is revealed before thee and who have faith hereafter'.

   Comments: Islam ordains faith and worship as instruments of happiness and prosperity; on charity and distribution of a percentage of wealth amongst the poor before Eid.

4. 'They question the (O Muhammad) about strong drink and games of chance. In both is great sin.' Hence, according to Shariat, both are 'haram' to a devout, always and every time, 'and of knowledge ye have been vouchsafed but little'.

   Comments: Quran does not endow man with any spiritual and innate knowledge. All knowledge is through the Quran and its revelation. Hence, all knowledge is acquired. Further, Quran is studied through rote and repetition, its

'Surrahs', 'sunnats' and 'ayats' are to be remembered by heart. Only the scholarly may read it intelligently and write their commentaries. Quran is written in Arabic and its readings compel correct pronunciation and intonation. While reading Quran, the reader makes rhythmic movements alongwith recitation. It helps in 'hifz', memorising.

5. 'God's care for His creatures is universal, His revelation is for all—ignorant and holy as well as learned and high place.' Hence, knowledge does not add to one's claim for God's gifts: Devotion takes precedence.

6. 'Warfare is a great (transgression) but to turn (men) from the way of Allah and to expel His people thence is a greater (transgression) with Allah, for persecution is worse than killing'.

   Comments: Quran forbids warfare during the holy month of Ramadan. That is why India and Pakistan, on India's initiative, had a temporary ceasefire during 2002 during the month of Ramadan, and even beyond.

Educational Implications

1. Education is sacred as it was Allah Himself who educated the first man.
2. More emphasis on Reading.
3. Islam recommended knowledge and education. Prophet Muhammad declared:

   "To seek knowledge is a religious duty for every Muslim, man and woman'.

   "Seek knowledge from cradle to grave": Considers education as a continuous, life long process, much the same way the present day progressive educationists do. Islam had the vision of education that stood through the test of time and tribulation. There was no gender discrimination in education; women were as much entitled to education as the men were.

4. Education was not restricted to what went within the school premises alone: it had a wider meaning of education to include all kinds of experiences.
5. Islam is one of the major religions of the world, and represents a complete way of life, system of values, a code of conduct, a unique and characteristic ideology, a definite and positive socio-economic order, a progressive political outlook, and oneness of Allah, and resurrection, etc. It promises the heavenly bliss for those who follow its tenets and live in a brotherly and socially desirable manner in this world. Religion of man and equity, Islam inspires the devouts for self-realisation and dispensation of justice to all in equal measure.

Position of Muslims

Muslims leaders are much alarmed and worried about the state of education amongst the Muslims in India, reducing their contribution to the national mainstream as negligible, in spite of the fact that India had four Presidents of the Republic from that community. A survey conducted by Hamdard (Trust), later replicated, revealed Muslim contribution to barely 1 % mismatching miserably with their numerical representation. The community is seized of the crisis in their society, and a message of its awareness, alongwith suggested remedial measures, has gone around, without showing any tangible results. Recently, the Indian Prime Minister, Atal Behari Bajpai, expressed his concern in this regard, as it hampers the human resource development of a larger section of the Indian society as well as the denial of possible opportunities for self-development. He advised them to re-orientate the Maktab-Madarsa education on scientific lines so that it smoothly conjoins the national mainstream. Education, generally, is not taken seriously by the Muslims in India for whatever reasons. There are premier educational institutions of the minority status and privilege, yet the output still mis-matches, causing concern to all well-meaning social leaders and religious patrons. Absence of control on population explosion further causes socio-economic imbalance, pushing education down the drain.

Role of Madarsas

Efforts are being made to mobilise the public opinion to realign the Madarsa education to a scientifically designed syllabus.

Winds of change are soon to sweep madarsas. The new mantra for these institutions seems to impart conventional religious teachings with a modern perspective. The Anjuman Talimate-Deen is evolving it.

The organisation has introduced books of science and maths approved by the National Council of Educational Research and Training up to Class V in nearly 175 madarsas of Gorakhpur and Maharajganj districts, besides conventional religious teachings. Aiming to bring more and more students in the madarsas, the Anjuman has decided to give them a modern look.

Patron of the district unit and district president Dr. Aziz Ahmad and Muhammad Ahsan Ansari told the media here the organisation aimed to upgrade the education in 325 more madarsas.

They said a regional minority education conference would be organised by the Anjuman soon at the Islamia College of Commerce. Chairman of Muslim Personal Law Board and national president of Anjuman Talimate Deen Syed Rabe Hasni Nadvi would be the chief guest in the conference, they added.

Dr. Ahmad said the representatives of more than 500 madarsas from Gorakhpur, Basti and Azamgarh division will discuss problems before the president and office-bearers of

Anjuman Talimate Deen. During the conference, discussion will also be held on the problems in introducing the new syllabus in madarsas.

Ahmad said development of the education net work for the minorities was the need of the hour as the government had been gradually privatising the education system. Expressing his concern over saffronisation of education, Ahsan Ansari said Anjuman Talimate Deen had been emphasising to maintain the religious identity of the Muslims with modern education. Anjuman has also launched a programme of computer education in these madarsas.

Dr. Ahmad said Anjuman had launched a programme for creating awareness among the Muslims for education. He said the dropout rate has been very high among the minorities, as they had not been able to bear the cost of education.

Therefore Anjuman had launched a programme to provide modern education with religious syllabus to the Muslim masses.

He claimed that a wind of change had been blowing in the madarsas with change of the syllabus and more madarsas were in touch with Anjuman to introduce new syllabus.

Quality Education

Reacting to the dismal state of education among muslims in India, most of the national leaders have been beseeching the religious leaders of that community to encourage and spread the message of education and the promises of development, progress, prosperity and self-fulfilment that it holds. Lack of education will keep the community backward. Whereas it may suit the ends of some political parties who encash muslim-illiteracy to their advantage, keeping the community out of the national educational programmes would be derogatory and non-productive. The muslim society is aware of it, yet there is not much of follow up.

On the occasion of Sir Syed Day in Aligarh Muslim University Chief Minister of Jammu and Kashmir Mufti Muhammad Sayed said that the entire Muslim community should not be blamed for attack on Sept. 11, 2001 on World Trade Centre in New York.

It may be an act of some individual Muslims for which the Muslim community of the world can neither be defamed nor held responsible. He was speaking as the chief guest on the occasion.

He urged the Muslim community to get educated for their development and if they are adequately educated, they may easily enter into the main stream of the country.

He said that at present the Muslims have only 1 per cent share in the employment in Central services and as such, they can claim for higher proportion in job quota which is possible only if they get adequate education.

Also, they can participate in democratic system of India in the right manner if they have achieved excellence in education.

Paying tributes to AMU founder Sir Syed Ahmad Khan, Mufti said Sir Syed was a revolutionary, educationist and whose vision and message should be imbibed for the future.

Naseem Ahmad, the Vice Chancellor of AMU reaffirmed his commitments to the ideals of Sir Syed Ahmad for social reconstruction, secularism, equal opportunities and multi faith society.

Islam and Festivals

Eid, Id-ul-Fitr, Muharram, Milad-ul-Nabi, Shabe-barat.

Role of Fasting

The month of Ramadan provides an annual training course for the purification of the soul. One who completes this course in form and spirit qualifies to receive the membership of the eternal world of paradise.

Fasting is prescribed once a year during Ramadan which is the ninth month of the Islamic calendar. The fast of Ramadan lasts for the whole month beginning from sunrise and ending at sunset. God Almighty says:

> "You who believe! Fasting is prescribed for you as it was prescribed for those before you that you may learn self-restraint" (2:183)

Fasting means to refrain and abstain from food and drink and certain other things from dawn till sunset. Fasting becomes obligatory for all with the sighting of the new moon of Ramadan. With the new moon of Shawwal, the fast comes to an end. The following day, Id is celebrated.

Fasting is an exercise in self-discipline. During Ramadan, the believer abstains from food and drink in the daytime of his own free will. It is only after sunset that he satisfies his hunger and quenches his thirst. In this way he builds up his self-control. By practising restraint for one month in a year he is able to lead a life of self-discipline in all matters for the rest of the year.

It is, therefore, to condition the believer to follow the path of restraint that the rule of fasting has been laid down. It is not just a matter of temporarily enduring hunger and thirst; it is a lesson in the permanent practice of patience and tolerance throughout one's entire life.

In the hadith (the Prophet's sayings), Ramadan is called the "month of patience". This month is meant to serve as a training course to enable an individual to lead a successful life by keeping his negative feelings under control. For negative feelings are the ones that present the greatest obstacle to human progress. By observing a fast, he is brought to a life of moral restraint.

According to another tradition of the Prophet: "There is a purification for all things, and the purification of the body is fasting. There is, indeed, a way of purifying everything. Just as bathing purifies the body, so fasting purifies the soul."

Abstinence from food symbolises not only the eschewing of those forbidden things, which a believer should give up for his entire life, but also the renunciation even of lawful things for the devotion to the fast. In seeking nearness to God, the believer must cut himself from all worldliness. But to achieve this result, fasting has to be done in the correct spirit. According to a tradition of the Prophet, "the one who goes without food or drink in the wrong attitude of mind gains nothing but hunger and thirst."

In short, fasting is cutting oneself off from the world and turning to God; not in a physical sense, but in one's heart and mind to be continually directed towards God, whatever one's bodily activity. As explained in a tradition when a person has elevated himself from the world, God endows him with wisdom. He is shown the ills of the world, and their remedies. He is brought to the abode of peace, (mishkat).

Ramadan is not just about abstaining from food and drink alone. Certain things have to be kept in mind while fasting. According to a saving of the Prophet, "Whenever one of you is on a fast, he should be soft in his demeanour. In the event of being abused or provoked, he should simply say that he is on a fast." Fasting thus has a form as well as a spirit.

Two things make up a man, his body and his soul. While the material part of man, the body, is indispensable for the performance of mundane tasks, it is his soul that will take him to the higher realities. The mind or the soul must be preserved in a state of purity. That means that just as the body requires physical nourishment, the soul must be nourished spirituality. The aim of fasting is to weaken the material aspect of man and strengthen the spiritual so that he may enter the higher realms of faith.

The common goal of every religion has been to guide people how to purify their souls. Islam too, has attached great importance to it. Fasting, in fact, plays an important part in this process of purification. The aim of fasting is to raise man above the material world and bring him close to the spiritual world. This process has been called tazkia (purification) in the Quran. But Islam does not advocate with drawing from this material world for a world of seclusion that is free from the objects of temptations. The way of Islam is to live in this very world but without allowing one's heart to be attached to this world. Therefore, from Islamic point of view, one has to strive to become a spiritual person while leading one's life in this material world itself.

Likewise, the purification of the soul is not just for the sake of purification. It is in fact directly linked with the concept of reward in the life to come after our physical existence perishes. That's why it is essential from the Islamic viewpoint to strive utmost to attain this goal. Only that person is worthy of being inhabited in the heavenly world who has shown the capability of attaining spiritual heights in this material world itself.

Likewise, the purification of the soul is not just for the sake of purification. It is in fact directly linked with the concept of reward in the life to come after our physical existence perishes. That's why it is essential from the Islamic viewpoint to strive utmost to attain this goal. Only that-person is worthy of being inhabited in the heavenly world who has shown the capability of attaining spiritual heights in this material world itself.

The month of Ramadan provides an annual training course for this process of purification. One who completes this course in the real sense has qualified for receiving the membership of the eternal world of paradise. (Maulana Wahiduddin Khan)

Education among Muslims

After the defeat of Prithviraj Chauhan, Muhammad Gori laid the foundation of Muslim rule in Northern India. Many kings ruled over India during the Muslim period. The sultans of Slave dynasty were the first Muslim rulers in Northern India.

Aim of Education: The aim of education during this period was the extension of knowledge and the propagation of Islamic principles, laws and social conventions. Education was based on religion. Its aim was to make persons religious minded. The Muslim education also aimed at the-achievement of material prosperity.

Organisation of Education: Education was organised in 'Maktabs' and 'Madarsas.' Primary education was given in 'Maktabs' and higher education was given in 'Madarsas.'

***Maktabs*:** In 'Maktabs' children were made to remember the 'Ayats' of 'Quran.' They were also imparted the education of reading, writing and primary arithmetic. When the children had learnt the Arabic script, they were given the education in Persian language and script. The stories of Prophets and Muslim 'Fakirs' were also told to the children. Children were imparted the knowledge of art of writing letters and conversation.

Madarsas: After completing the primary education, the children were sent to 'madarsas' to receive higher education. Hence, there were separate teachers for different subjects. Special emphasis was given to the education of religious as well as secular subjects. The religious education included the study of 'Quran,' Muhammad Saheb and his preachings, Islamic laws and Islamic history, etc. The secular education included the study of Arabic literature, Grammar, History, Philosophy, Mathematics, Geography, Politics, Economics, Greek language, Astrology and Agriculture, etc.

State Patronage: During the Muslim period education received a great patronage of state. The Muslim rulers established many Maktabs, Madarsas, libraries, etc. and patronised many scholars. They also granted scholarships to many students.

No University: There was no university in Muslim education. Education imparted in 'Maktabs' and 'Madarsas' had the stamp of religious orthodoxy. Hence, Hindus could not get much benefit out of it. The provision of education was only for higher and middle classes. There were no means for imparting education to the children of common people.

Neglect of Vernaculars: Arabic and Persian languages had been adopted and the vernacular languages had been altogether neglected.

Teacher-Pupil Relationship: Despite the changing viewpoint towards the education, great ideal of teacher-pupil relationship which existed in the ancient India had not declined in the Muslim period.

Discipline and Punishment: In the Muslim period, the teachers did not receive that much respect. Hence, in order to ensure the maintenance of discipline, the teachers were empowered to give different types of physical punishments.

Examination: The system of examination was not prevalent in the Muslim period. It depended upon the will of the teacher to send the pupil to the higher class or not.

Degrees: There was also the system of giving degrees after the completion of education. The students, who acquired special knowledge in religion, were given the degree of 'Alim.' The students completing the education of logic were conferred the degree of Fazil.'

Education of Women: Although there was Pardah' system during the Muslim period, yet Islam did not oppose the education of women. These two contrary factors influenced the education of women in two ways. The girls were entitled to receive education equal to that of the boys upto a definite age but thereafter their education was stopped. However, the girls of higher classes used to continue their studies at home.

Military Education: In order to establish their supremacy over the Hindu kings, Muslim rulers had to wage constant wars. Keeping this situation in view provision of military education was made compulsory.

Benefits of Education for Muslims

1. *Compulsory:* Education was compulsory, specially for boys.
2. *Co-ordination:* There was proper co-ordination between religious values and material or worldly needs and well-being.
3. *Character:* Great stress was laid on character-building.
4. *Personal Touch:* There was a personal touch between the teacher and the taught.
5. *Curriculum:* Curriculum included arrangement for the teaching of various subjects.
6. *Practical:* Great stress was laid on practical utility.
7. *Incentives:* There was arrangement for rewards and scholarships for meritorious and intelligent students. This provided an incentive to learning and education.
8. *Literature:* Under Muslim rulers, through educational system, a good deal of development of literature took place.
9. *Free:* The education during the Muslim rule was mostly free.
10. *Writing of History:* During this period, the tendency to write history was developed. This tendency was different from the tendency of the ancient India. It helped preservation of record.
11. *Institutions:* During this period, great attention was paid towards establishment of educational institutions.

Prosperous people were encouraged to establish institutions.

12. *Special Centres:* There were centres of specialised education.

Education in Islam

1. *Unsuitable:* Unsuitability was characteristic of the institution of education.
2. *Disbalanced:* Education of the Hindus was neglected. This brought about a disbalanced development of education.
3. *Material:* There was predominance of material considerations.
4. *No Universal Education:* There was no provision for universal education.
5. *One-sided Curricula:* There was too much emphasis on teaching of Arabic and Persian. This led to neglect of other subjects.
6. *Lack of Co-ordination:* There was no co-ordination between reading and writing.
7. *Lack of Psychological Basis:* Muslim education lacked psychological incentives.
8. Evil Effects of Corporal Punishment.
9. *Defective Curriculum:* Curriculum was defective.
10. Indifference Towards Women Education.
11. *Low State of Teachers:* The teacher-taught relationship was not ideal. The teacher did not occupy that position that he occupied during the Vedic period.
12. *Wrong Methods of Teaching:* Oral or verbal method of teaching did not help the consolidation of the knowledge.
13. *One-sided Personality:* In Muslim education there was no place for all-round development of the personality.
14. Lack of Individual Attention.

15. *No Development of Reasoning:* No encouragement to students to develop their power of reasoning.

The Muslim prophets had urged their followers to preach and expand their religion. Education in its religious philosophy was necessary for preaching Islam. Therefore, the primary form of Muslim education was religious. For this purpose Maktabs (primary schools) were also started and attached to mosques. In these Maktabs small children were given education in Islamic religion. Gradually Muslim rulers adopted more liberal policy in education. Besides Islamic religion, other subjects began to be taught in Maktabs and Madarsas.

The Maktabs: In the Maktab children of all people were given primary education. Alongwith religious education they were also taught reading, writing and arithmetic. The children of rich people generally did not attend Maktabs. Their parents used to make private arrangement at their homes for their education.

Ceremony at the Time of Admission: The child was taken to the Maktab on the first day in new clothes. At first he was required to repeat some verses of the Koran. If he was not able to do this, his education was started by pronouncing the word 'Bismillah,' that is, his education was begun on the name of Allah (God). After this Bismillah ceremony the child was required to write something after a few days. On this occasion his close relatives were also invited. The child was required to go to a Maktab regularly for receiving education.

Maktab Curriculum: At first reading and writing were taught in the Maktab. Then the child was taught arithmetic and a certain portion of Koran. He was not expected to know the meaning of Koran, it was enough for him to memorise it. When the child was fully acquainted with the Persian script, he was taught its grammar. Then he was taught some love literature of Persian, e.g. Laila-Majanu and Yusuf-Julekha, etc. General practical education was also given in Maktabs. Letter-writing, writing applications and accountancy were taught. Hindu boys could also be admitted in Maktabs.

The children of royal families were taught in palaces under the strict control of Maulavis. The princesses were taught Arabic and Persian and Islamic religion. Besides, they were also taught political science, law, jurisprudence and military science in order that they could be able administrators. It was compulsory for princes to receive military training. Thus, the children of the higher class people were given both theoretical and practical education.

The Madarsas: After completing the education in a Maktab, one could go to a Madarsa for higher education. During the Muslim period Madarsas were centres of higher learning. Madarsas were granted Jagirs (land and villages) by the kings for their maintenance. They used to receive other financial grants as well. Some learned scholar was appointed as head of the Madarsa and he used to carry on the teaching work with the assistance of other teachers appointed for the purpose. The king never interfered in the administration of a Madarsas. The rich people also used to give financial assistance to Madarsas. There was no official person or department for supervising the work of Madarsas. Akbar himself accepted the State responsibility of promoting education. Other rulers used to take interest in it either for their personal prestige or for expansion of Islam. Some hostels were also constructed alongwith Madrasas for providing residential accommodation to students.

Significant Learning Centres

Delhi: Early Muslim rulers made Delhi their capital. Hence, it became a centre of Muslim Education. Nasiruddin established, 'Madarsa-i-Nasiria' in Delhi under the chairmanship of 'Shiraz.' Other rulers of Slave dynasty also developed Delhi as an important scat of Muslim education. Allauddin Khilji established many 'Madarsas' in Delhi and appointed renowned teachers therein. These institutions had more than 40 learned Muslim theologists and teachers of Muslim Law. Delhi had become a centre of literature and art during the days of Allauddin Khilji. During the reign of Muhammad Tughlaq and his successor Firoz Tuglaq Delhi continued to enjoy the status of an important seat of Muslim education.

During the reign of the Mughals, Delhi maintained its original status and also improved itself. It now became the most important seat of Muslim education in Northern India. Humayun established an institution for the study of Geography, Persian, Grammar, Philosophy and Astronomy. Akbar's 'Aaya' had established a big institution in Delhi in 1561, and the famous scholar Badayuni received education in this very institution. Jahangir and Shahjahan also maintained that status of Delhi and contributed to its educational importance. Aurangzeb tried to transform Delhi into a city of orthodox Muslim education. He established many new educational institutions and gave financial aid to the existing ones.

Agra: Sikandaer Lodi made Agra an important centre of Muslim education. He established many 'Maktabs' and 'Madarsas' in the city where students from foreign countries came to study. It was characterised by a rich efflorescence of learning and literature. It became a radiant centre of Islamic culture and philosophy. After Sikandaer Lodi, Babur and Humayun also established certain 'Madarsas' in Agra, Akbar made Agra a centre of learning, education and culture, craft and fine arts. During his reign, Agra became a huge university where scholars and learned men came from far and wide. In his book, Muslim Education in India' Jaffar described this situation as following: "Men of learning and erudition from Arabia, Persia, and Bokhara poured into it in ever increasing numbers at the prospect of receiving better patronage from the rulers of India, who were remarkable for their munificence. The result was that, in course of time, Agra grew into a great literary city, containing several schools and colleges where people flocked from far and wide for higher education."

Akbar built many schools at Fatehpur Sikri. After his death, Jehangir and Shahjahan added certain 'Madarsas' and educational institutions to the existing ones and also gave financial aid to them. During the reign of Aurangzeb, Agra assumed a very important place as a seat of Islamic education. With the downfall of Mughals empire Agra also declined in its reputation.

Jaunpur: During the reign of Turks, Afghans and Mughals, Jaunpur enjoyed the status of an important seat of Muslim education. Sher Shah Suri received his education in one of the schools of the city. It had institutions of various and varied types. Here students from far and wide received education and acquired knowledge of History, Political Science, Philosophy and war-crafts as well. Ibrahim Sharki established many 'Madarsas' in Jaunpur and arranged for their finance. Mughal rulers from Humayun to Shahjahan tried to maintain it as a seat of learning. During the rule of Muhammed Shah, 20 institutions were established in this city. With the downfall of the Mughal empire the importance of this city as a seat of learning started fading.

Bidar: Bidar, a city in the south under Bahmani rulers, was a famous seat of learning. Muhammad Gawan established many 'Maktabs' and a big 'Madarsa' over here. In this 'Madarsa' very learned 'Maulvis' were appointed. Attached to this 'Madarsa' there was a big library which housed about 3,000 books on Islamic theology, culture, philosophy, medical science, astronomy, history, agriculture, etc. There were 'Maktabs' in the rural areas as well. Through them Arabic and Persian were spread. There was not a single village under Bahmani rule, which did not have at least one educational institution. It was, therefore, quite natural for Bidar to be a very important seat of Islamic education in south India.

Different Programmes

Maktabs used to fulfil religious objective of education. But in the Madarsas, practical affairs of life were also attended to alongwith religious objective of education. Akbar tried to give a practical shape to education in an unprecedented manner. But education remained religious in spirit and form in spite of his efforts.

After completing Maktab education one could go for higher education in a Madarsa. Islamic religion was compulsorily taught to all the students though Akbar stopped this tradition of compulsory Islamic education to all. He provided study of Hindu religion and philosophy also in many Madarsas. He provided books for the same in some Madarsas of his days. But the Muslim students were compulsorily taught Muslim religion, Sufi philosophy and sermons ascribed to Muslim prophets. A Hindu was also free to study Muslim religion and philosophy. Akbar introduced the study of medicine, history, geography, economics, political science, philosophy, astrology, law and mathematics, etc. He made the study of Vedant, Jurisprudence and Patanjali compulsory for Sanskrit students. In his famous book 'Aine-a-Akbari" Abul Fazl has described the educational system introduced by Akbar. Aurangzeb understood the importance of practical education. He regarded as futile education purely in language. But his ideas remained confined only within the four walls of his palace and the general public was never benefited by the same.

Some persons were appointed in the Muslim courts to record historical events from time to time. Because of this tradition many Muslim rulers have themselves written their autobiographies which are still preserved as precious historical documents. Law in those days was based on religious practices. So the study of religious principles was in a way education in law. As some Muslim rulers were interested in music also, so provision was made for education in music as well.

Techniques of Teaching

Oral education and memorisation of the assigned lessons were the chief methods of teaching during the Muslim period. The Muslim students were required to memories certain portions of Holy Koran. Writing and Arithmetic were also taught in some Maktabs. There was no scientific method of teaching in the Maktabs. So most of the students used to memorise Koran and prayers for most of the time. Realising the futility of this method Akbar encouraged writing and tried to reform the scripts. He ordered that the work should be written down first before memorizing. Thus, Akbar tried to give a scientific basis to education so that the students might be trained in practical affairs of life as well. To make educational procedure systematic Akbar urged that the student should be first given the knowledge of alphabets, then word-knowledge and afterwards sentence-knowledge.

As the method of teaching was oral, the main task of the teacher was to give lectures and students used to listen to them passively. Then the students were advised to read some relevant books. They were required to prepare their lessons individually. This method made them active.

Co-operation of students was sought in maintenance of discipline during the Muslim period. Like the Buddhist system some senior students were appointed monitor for guiding and controlling junior students. In the absence of a teacher, a senior student of higher class used to teach junior ones. The students of medicine, music and crafts were given practical training also. Thus, started practical education during this period.

System of Assessment

There was no formal examination system during the Muslim period. The teacher used to decide as to when a student was competent to receive education of a higher standard. So he had his own personal method to assess the capacity of a student and to advise him for receiving education of higher standard. The purpose of education was not to prepare a person for earning his living but to develop his personality. There was no prescribed standard for declaring a student failed or passed. This does not mean that all the students were considered alike. The abler student was given recognition by awarding stipends and prizes. There was no half-yearly or annual examination fixed for students. The students were examined from time to time in practical situations of life. In courts, debates and groups of poets, the knowledge and achievement of a student was assessed at times. On such occasions kings and great scholars used to come to participate. The ability of a student was carefully evaluated on such occasions. The really deserving one was rewarded by money and praise.

Management of Education

Pupil-Teacher Relationship: The pupil-teacher relationship during the Muslim period was as cordial as during the ancient days. As the people believed that no knowledge was possible without a teacher, hence the student used to respect and serve the teacher with all devotion. The society also respected him. There were hostels attached to many Madarsas. The teachers also resided in them with their students. This situation helped the teacher and students to understand each other. The teacher loved his students and tried his best for their development. As there were no hostels with Maktabs, so no personal relationship existed there between the teacher and his students. When the students left a Maktab after completing their education they had little impact of their teacher on them. The students of Maktabs were young children, there was no problem of indiscipline in them. Consequently, there was no feeling of disrespect in the students for their teacher.

Indiscipline and Punishment: During the Vedic and Buddhist periods a student used to be expelled from the Ashram or Vihar' on a charge of indiscipline. But during the Muslim period the student was given severe corporal punishment on the charge of indiscipline. Usually most of the students were obedient. The unruly one, if located, was severely punished. The teacher was the sole judge of the indisciplined behaviour as well as the nature of punishment to be given for the same. Nobody questioned his authority. Caning, making the student to stand or run for a long time and distance or to hang him up side down were some of the types of punishments usually given. The students were usually terrified by such a severe punishment. It is difficult to say if this had a healthy effect on the child.

Rewards: Brilliant and industrious students were greatly respected. They were given praise and rewards. Sometimes they were awarded good government jobs also. In Madarsas the teacher used to reward good students. The rich people took pride in rewarding good students.

Hostels: In the Vedic days the student was to live in Ashram in a natural environment. He was required to lead a life of hardship and penance. Physical comforts were tabooed for them. During the Buddhist period the life of the student was comparatively easier in the sense that physical comforts were not tabooed for them. But during the Muslim period the student enjoyed greater physical comforts and facilities. In the hostels attached with Madarsa various types of living facilities, clothes, food and necessary books and other things were provided to the students by the State. During his travels in India Ibn Batuta has described the working of some Madarsas. Because of the good arrangements in their hostels, he preferred to live with students for some time. In his book he has written that the students were given by the State good non-vegetarian diet, good clothes, beds, fruits and milk. Perfumed oil was also given to students. Thus, the State took great care for the comforts of the students of Madarsas. However, as Ibn Batuta could not visit all the Madarsas, he has given his views about a particular Madarsa which was especially looked after by the emperor.

Some books of that period have mentioned that some hospital was also attached with some Madarsas. Some Madarsas had swimming pools also for the students.

Subjects of Education

Military Training: Muslim rulers established their empire in India because of their superior skill in warfare and higher military organisation. They were conscious of the fact that they could win because of their superior skill and organisation of the armed forces. Therefore, they paid especial attention to military education of their children. The princes were given especial military training besides education in practical affairs of life and state affairs. The young princes were also taken to battle-fields for practical experiences. The Mughal emperors paid especial attention to military education, because they knew that they could hold up their empires only through superior forces.

Fine Arts: Development of fine arts had reached its peak during the Mughal period. The Mughal emperors believed that alongwith strengthening of military powers it was also necessary to maintain pomp and show in the court. They encouraged education in fine arts so that great artists might develop their art for contributing to the glory of the court. Music and painting developed very much during this period. One of the great courtiers of Akbar Tansen, the great musician, developed many musical tunes 'Rag and Raginis.' Dancing was also developed during this period; Anarkali, the great dancer belonged to Akbar's time. Painting was also encouraged. Jahangir, himself was a great painter. Sir Thomas Row, the British Ambassador, who visited the royal court has praised Jahangir's love of painting.

Crafts: Crafts developed during the Mughal period, as it received the royal patronage. Embroidery, ivory work, exquisite ornaments were regarded as symbolic of the excellence attained by handicrafts during the Mughal period. Because at that time there was no institution for technical education training in crafts was given in the traditional manner in families.

Preparation of war goods also encouraged handicrafts. Boats, ships and chariots were manufactures on a large scale. This helped the artisans to be busy in their work and earn their livelihood. Taj Mahal of Agra, Red Fort of Delhi and Buland Darwaza of Fatehpur Sikri are excellent examples of the development of architecture during the Muslim period.

Women Education: Purdah system has been a part of Muslim culture since long. This system was observed strictly during the Muslim rule in India. Girls were not allowed to go to a Madarsa for receiving higher education. However, they were allowed to go to a Maktab for primary education. The girls could learn only reading, writing and arithmetic. But even during the Muslim period there have been some very learned women who made unique contributions to the development of literature. The empress Nurjahan was a learned woman. She very well carried on state administration. Arrangements for education of princesses were made in the palace. Similarly, rich people used to arrange for education of their girls in their own homes. Music was taught to princess in the palace by carefully selected Ustads (teachers).

Sultana Razia, Princess Gul Badan, daughter of Babur, Aurangzeb's daughter Zebunnisa are examples of learned royal ladies. Gul Badan wrote the famous 'Humayun Nama.' Zebunnisa was a scholar of Arabic and Persian. Sultana Suleema, Mumtaz Mahal, Jahan Ara were highly educated in art and literature. However, as only the royal princesses and ladies and daughters of very rich people could receive education during the Muslim period, education of common Muslim women was completely ignored.

14

Christian Theory

Catholic philosophy dominated European thought "from Augustine to the Renaissance", though there had been philosophers before and after "this period of ten centuries, who belonged to the same general school," and adhered to some "medieval system, especially that of Thomas Aquinas. The credit for perfecting the Catholic synthesis goes to the philosophers of the period between Augustine and Renaissance when the tradition lost its influence, somewhere around 1400 AD. The most notable feature of this has been the increase in the power of the Church which brought philosophic beliefs closer to social and political circumstances, and reshaped itself into an institution built on its creed, partly philosophic, partly historic, by subjugating the powerful Roman and Germanic traditions, as the intelligentsia was 'convinced of the truth of the Catholic faith". Philosophy of the period known as Middle Ages strongly based itself in Church, hence having "extensive account of the growth of ecclesiastical institutions, especially of the papacy," and is characterised by various forms of dualism found in the New Testment, Plato, and the teaching of St. Paul.

Basics of Christianity

1. The thoughts of Christian philosophers were still dominated by the Roman Empire.

2. It is a tradition of revelation wherein it is not merely theology but critical philosophy that built up a defence against criticism, especially of Muhammedans.
3. It is an outcome of popular support that combated against feudal aristocracy and anarchy wherein a new class of clergy emerged which was considered "more capable of coping up with the nobles, and more acceptable to the urban lower classes as champions of civic liberty".
4. Based on democratic social traditions and practices.
5. Catholic philosophy is essentially the philosophy of an institution, namely the Catholic Church. Most of the problems of modern philosophy especially those related to ethics and political thought, and were derived from Christian views of moral law, are still concerned with the relation of Church and State, and God and Caesar. Hence, Christianity has dual loyalty.
6. Christianity was more brutal than Muhammedans who were more civilised and humane.

Concept of Humanity

The following extracts from the New Testament which are considered education-related are quoted by the author. There is a marked transition from the earlier Catholic tendencies and attitude, and where religion stands for love of God and man.

1. "Man cannot live on bread alone, but on every word that God speaks". Education, therefore, should not restrict itself to physical development, but help one transcend into the spiritual domain where one is face to face with God. Spirituality is the essence of education.
2. Friendly to the under-privileged, sick and poor, hence humane and merciful, as "kingdom of heaven belongs to them". Let education arouse the spirit of love and service to humanity.

3. *Eternity of Truth:* "As long as heaven and earth last, the least point or the smallest detail of the Law will not be done away with—not until the end of all things". Education should emphasise and focus on what is universal, essential, rational and eternal.
4. *Forgiveness as the Ultimate Virtue:* "If you forgive others the wrongs they have done you, your father in heaven will also forgive you". Do not confuse it with bartering of wrongs. The spirit behind this is the strength of character manifested through forgiveness. Education should raise one to this level of humility, piety, compassion and charity.
5. "To have good fruit you must have a healthy tree'. Goodness brings goodness. Let education train human mind and body for the common good of all.
6. "What you prohibit on earth will be prohibited in heaven," hence no contradiction between life here and now, and the life after (if one believes in that). Education should, therefore, gear one up for life here and now, and the rest will take care of itself. It should be preparation for life, here and now.
7. *Christianity as a Religion of Promises:* "If you want to be perfect, go and sell all you have and give the money to the poor, and you will have riches in heaven". What Christ meant here was to give up lust for money and flesh, and to live a temperate life in the service of the poor. Education should help develop this richness of character and temperance.
8. *Crucification by Nailing to the Cross:* Each one is to carry one's own cross, the result of one's own deeds or misdeeds; there is no escape as the consequences would follow. Not even the supreme sacrifice for the good of humanity would be your saviour as one falls into the hands of the wicked and the ignorant. Yet, "forgive them O' Lord, as they do not know" reveals the height of one's faith in

ultimate goodness and justice. Truth shall prevail. The Christians celebrate this day as Good Friday, as whatever happened was ordained and anything that is ordained could not have been wrong. Education should develop this sense of trust and restraint; not to flare up at the slightest of provocation.

9. *Raised from Death:* Christ rose on the third day of his crucification, the day is celebrated as Return of Jesus: Easter Sunday, and speaks of hope and promise, and the ability to rise from the dumps. Education should, likewise, develop one's total faculties and abilities so that one does not feel low when in the dumps, and have the will and ability to rise.

Christianity and Festivals

(a) *Christmas:* Birth of Jesus: 25 December.

(b) *Good Friday:* Crucification of Jesus by nailing to the Cross and making him carry it on his back. It is a day of mourning and abstinence. It is observed on the third Friday of April.

(c) *Easter:* The third day from the Good Friday, Easter falls on a Sunday, and is known as Easter Sunday. It signifies hope and faith as Jesus kept his promise "I shall be back on the third day". It is a day of great rejoicing as return of good.

15

Theory of Sikhism

Basically an off shoot of Hinduism, Sikhism achieved a status of a distinctive religion. Preached by Guru Nanak and his disciples, Sikhism had ten Gurus, the last of whom, Guru Govind Singh, ordained his flock to abandon Guruism, and accept Adi Granth Sahib as their Guru. "Sab Sikhan ko hukam hai, Guru maniyoon Granth". A religion of great piety, compassion, love and sacrifice, Sikhism acquired its own 'Nishan Sahib' (symbol), Granth Sahib (scripture), and established its shrines at Amritsar, Nankana Sahib, Panja Sahib (both in Pakistan), Anandpur Sahib, Patna Sahib, Hazur Sahib, Subuki Talwandi Sahib.

These religious centres are called 'Takhts', and are held most sacred by all Sikhs as well as millions of Hindu followers who consider Sikhism as their own creed. The commonality of socio-religious tradition is a strong bond between the Sikhs and the Hindus, especially of Punjabi origin, all over the world.

Basics of Morality

Sikhism holds man as implicitly divine and capable of self-realisation and perfection. A religion of great potential, it is man-oriented and considers social service, humility and moderation as greatest of its virtues. It is progressive, positive, optimistic, chivalrous projection of man wherein women have equal rolè and responsibility. It is a very orderly and well-articulated religion which sings praises of the Lord in poetry set to classical 'ragas' of India.

The feelings of brotherhood, oneness of creation, purity of thought and action, common good of the society, bravery, love for its motherland, sacrifice, equity and justice are some of the salient features of Sikhism, now spread over the entire world, especially in the Far East, South East Asia, UK and Canada.

It has a supreme body S.G.P.C. for the management and upkeep of its Gurudwaras, their places of worship. Every devout Sikh is to do the following as externally observable measures of his faith, generally known as five 'ks'. Tradition has it that their supreme Master ordained them to do so for obvious physical identification. These 'ks' are, kes (Hair), kanga (comb) by which the males tie up their hair into a bun on top of their head. It is an essential element of hair-management and smart appearance; kara (steel braclet), kirpan (a small approximately nine inches sword which a devout Sikh is required to carry indicating his resolve to preserve and safeguard his religion); Kaccha (underwear) to indicate abstinence and self control.

Besides, Sikhism contains and follows the tenets of Hinduism and Islam with its own characteristic abundance, grace and discipline. They have their own 'panchayats' and congregations to keep a check on social order and practices. Recently, a Sikh Panchayat held at Durg in Chattisgarh ruled as under:

> The Chattisgarh Sikh Panchayat wants to prohibit bhangra dance on roads by women during marriage ceremonies. Other such 'corrective measures' are in the offing as the panchayat met here to lay out ways to make marriages simple and inexpensive.

It has prepared a blueprint for a marriage code of conduct. This includes banning the serving of non-vegetarian food at marriage feasts.

> "The poor people in our community are often compelled to spend lots of money on marriages," said Tarsem Singh Gill, president of the Durg-Bhilai Central Sikh Panchayat. "The marriage party should consist of less than 50 members to avoid unnecessary burden on the families of the bride and the groom. We have also appealed (to people) to stop bhangra dance by women in barat processions."
>
> The two-day convention assessed the role of the Sikh community in the development of culture, education, society and religion in the state. There are about 25,000 Sikh families in Durg Bhilai alone. "This convention will bind us with a common code of conduct".

The tenets and directions are mandatory as violation might have one declared as Tankhiya as it happened during 1980s and 1990s in India. Sikhism is liberal, progressive and positive, but it brooks no wilful violation and defiance of its tenets which are supremely sacred.

The Birth of the Khalsa, over 300 years ago, is a significant event in the five hundred year long and glorious history of the Sikhs. Specially designed for warfare against the Moghuls, the Khalsa was a warrior-saviour of the 'Panth' (faith).

Sikhism and Festivals

Having the common roots in Hinduism, Sikhism celebrates Diwali (Diwala), Holi (Hola), Dussehra, etc. besides the regional festivals of Lohri, Basant and Baisakhi, and their special celebrations of the birthdays of Guru Nanak Devji and Guru Gobind Singhji.

Important Dimensions

1. It is the most prominent Bhakti movement incorporating the teachings of Surdas, Kabir, Meera, etc. besides those of their Gurus and preachers.
2. Believes in life here and now, and denounces renunciation as evasive and escapist.
3. Generally consisting of agricultural class, Sikhs are powerful and affluent section of society.
4. Generosity, especially in the cause of the faith, is the crux of Sikhism.
5. Kind-hearted and socially well adjusted amongst themselves and other sections of society especially Hindus and Muslims with whom it shared the regional harmony, thought and culture for centuries.
6. God fearing: Gurus' tenets are final and respected.
7. Believes in social equality irrespective of socio-economic status.
8. The line of ten Gurus starting with Guru Nanak Dev, ended with Guru Gobind Singh. The Sikhs celebrate both the occasions with festivities and rejoicing. A large number of Hindus, especially those of Punjab, join them with equal fervour and devotion.
9. Gurmukh (Guru-oriented) person is the ideal of the Sikh society and religion.
10. Being of liberal, progressive and positive mind, Sikhism encourages social and national integration.
11. Considered as a martial race, the Sikhs take pride in joining the defence services. Two Regiments of the Indian Army, the Sikh Regiment and the Sikh Light Infantry Regiment are exclusively composed of the Sikhs.
12. Gurubani is considered holy as pronouncements of the Gurus.

13. Khalsa-panth, established, after the death of Guru Gobind Singh, consists of collective leadership.
14. God is one, eternal, absolute: sat sri akal: Nanak naam jehaz hai. God is humane.
15. Sikhism believes in most of the Hindu tenets including transmigration of soul, law of karma, cycle of birth and rebirth.
16. Faith in Humanism and the good of man.
17. Worship and chanting of the Adi Granth Sahibji, and respect and salutation to Nishan Sahibji (symbol and Flag), are the greatest virtues.
18. Professes and practices social harmony for the happiness of man.
19. Generally an extrovert, a Sikh is known for his sense of humour and robust outlook on life. It is, perhaps, the only community that could take a joke even on itself, showing their large-heartedness, simplicity of mind and good nature.
20. Sikhism combines contemplation and action.

Bibliography

Abba Sayalu, Y.B. : *Scheduled Caste Elite : a Study of Scheduled Caste Elite in Andhra Pradesh*, Booklinks Corporation, Hyderabad, 1978.

Anne, Roe : *Great Educationists*, John Wiley and Sons, New York, 1956.

Bowman, M.J. : *Education and Economic Development*, Frank Cass, London, 1971.

Brewer, J.M. : *Education as Guidance*, MacMillan Co., New York, 1962.

Charles, Jeffries : *Illiteracy : a World Problem*, Pall Mall Press, London, 1967.

Cottle, W.C. and Downie, N.M. : *Preparation for Counselling*, Englewood Cliffs Prentice Hall, New York, 1970.

Cronbach, L.I. : *Essentials of Psychological Testing*, Horper, New York, 1970.

Crow, A. : *An Introduction to Guidance Principles and Practices*, Eurasia Publishing House, New Delhi, 1962.

Desai, A.R. : *Rural Sociology in India*, Popular Prakashan, Bombay, 1978.

Dharni, P. Sinha : *Descriptive-cum-Critical Study of Education System in Andhra Pradesh*, Administrative Staff College of India, Hyderabad, 1976.

Dowing, Lester N. : *Great Educationist*, McGraw Hill, New York, 1964.

Fletcher, F.M. and Riddle, W. : *The Guidance Movement in India.* Personnel and Guidance Journal, London, 1962.

Frank, H. Krouse : *Counselling Technique with Youth*, Charles and Mervil, Ohio, 1960.

Froehlich, C.P. and Hoyt, K. : *Guidance Testing*, Science Research Associates Inc., Delhi, 1959.

Fullmer, D. W. : *Principles of Guidance: a Basic Text*, Allied Publishers Private Ltd., New Delhi, 1998.

Gandhi, M.K. : *My Views on Education*, Bharatiya Vidya Bhavan, Bombay, 1970.

Gaur, J.S. and Saraswat, R.K. : *Occupational Literature: an Annotated Bibliography*, NCERT, New Delhi, 1978.

Ginzberg, E. : *Towards a Theory of Occupational Choice*, Personnel and Guidance Journal, Culcatta, 1952.

Guilford, J.P. : *Fundamental Statistics in Psychology and Education*, McGraw Hill, New York, 1965.

Gunam Saran : *Education and Social Change a Study of Some Rural Communities in Punjab*, The Minarva Associates, Calcutta, 1972.

Hahn, M.E. and Maclean, M.S. : *Counselling Psychology*, McGraw Hill, New York, 1955.

Hansen, James C. : *Counselling: Process and Procedures*, MacMillan, New York, 1978.

Haragopal, G. : *Administrative Leadership and Rural Development in India*, Light & Life Publishers, New Delhi, 1980.

Herr, E.L. and Cramer, S.H. : *Vocational Guidance and Career Development in the Schools: Towards a Systems Approach*, Houghton Mifflin, Boston, 1972.

Hollis, Joseph William and Hollis, Lucide : *Organising for Effective Guidance*, Science Research Associates, Chicago, 1965.

Hoppock, Rebert : *Occupational Information—Where to Get It and How to Use it in Counselling and Teaching*, McGraw Hill Book Co., New York, 1957.

Inamdar, N.R. : *Educational Administration in the Zillaa P in Maharashtra*, Popular Prakashan, Bombay, 1974.

John W., Hanson and Cole S. Brem Beck : *Education and the Development of Nations*, Holt, Rinehart and Winston, New York, 1966.

Jones, A.J. : *Principles of Guidance and Pupil Personnel Work*, McGraw Hill, New York, 1963.

Julian, E., Butter Worth and Howard A. Dawson : *The Modern Rural School*, McGraw Hill, New York, 1952.

Kidd, J.R. : *Education for Perspective*, Indian Education Association, New Delhi, 1969.

Kroth, J.A. : *Counselling, Psychology and Guidance*, Springfield, Charles C. Thomas, Illinois, 1973.

Lakshmana Swamy Mudaliar A. : *Education in India*, Asia Publishing House, Bombay, 1960.

Mahler, C.A. : *Group Counselling in the Schools*, Houghton Mifflin, Boston, 1969.

McCully, C.H. : *The Counsellor—Instrument of Change*, Teachers College Record, New York, 1965.

Mehta, H.P. : *A Brief Account of Vocational Guidance Movement in India*. Journal of Vocational and Educational Guidance, New Delhi, 1955.

Miller, Carroll, H. : *Foundations of Guidance*, Harper and Brothers, New York, 1961.

Mitra, CR and Others : *Challenge and Response—Towards a New Education Policy and Beyond*, Teachers College Record, London, 1986.

Mukherjee, R.K. : *The Social Structure of Values*, S. Chand & Company, New Delhi, 1964.

Murphy, G. : *Education in the Fourth Plan : Review and Perspective*, Nachiketa Publications, Bombay, 1968.

————: *Education of the Scheduled Castes 1965-66*, Occasional Monograph, ICSSR, New Delhi, 1995.

———— : *Educational Planning in India*, Allied Publishers, Bombay, 1965.

———— : *Elementary Education in India : a Promise to Keep.* Allied Publishers, Bombay, 1975.

————: *Equality, Quality and Quantity : the Elusive Triangle in Indian Education*, Allied ·Publishers, New Delhi, 1975.

———— : *Policy and Performance in Indian Education*, Dr. K.G. Saiyidain Memorial Trust, New Delhi, 1995.

———— : *Some Perspectives on Non-Fomal Education*, Allied Publishers, New Delhi, 1977.

———— : *The Cultural Context of Guidance*, Personnel and Guidance Journal, Madras, 1955.

————: *The National Education Policy 1947-1978*, Ministry of Education and Social Welfare, Government of India. New Delhi, 1979.

————: *The Single Teacher School : Studies in Education and Psychology*, Ministry of Education, Government of India, 1953.

Niblett, W.R. : *Essential Education*, University of London, London, 1955.

Nural Hasan, S. : *Challenges in Education, Culture and Social Welfare*, Allied Publishers, Bombay, 1977.

Ohlsen, M.M. : *Group Counselling*, Holt Rinchart and Winston, New York, 1977.

Oscar, Krisen : *Second Survey of Research in Education 1972-1978*, Society for Educational Research and Development, Baroda, 1979.

———— : *The Sixth Mental Measurement Year Book*, Teachers College Record, New York, 1965.

Patterson, C.H. : *Cultural Action for Freedom*, Penguin Books, New York, 1977.

———— : *Education : the Practice of Freedom*, Writers and Readers Publishing Cooperative, London, 1976.

———— : *Theories of Counselling and Psycho-therapy*, Harper and Row, New York, 1973.

Peters, H.J. and Hanson, J.C. : *Vocational Guidance and Career Development*, MacMillan, New York, 1968.

Premi, M.K. : *Educational Planning in India : Implications of Population Trends*, Sterling Publishers, New Delhi, 1972.

Raju, V.B. : *Commentaries on the Constitution of India*, Eastern Book Company, Lucknow,. 1973.

Rao, Narayan : *Counselling Psychology*, McGraw Hill Publishing Company Limited, New Delhi, 1981.

Ratna, G. Revankar : *The Indian Constitution: a Case Study of Backward Classes*, Associate University Press, Canbury, New Jersey, 1941.

Rudolph & Rudolph : *Education and Politics in India Studies in Organisation, Society and Policy*, Harvard University Press, Cambridge, 1972.

———— : *On Education*, Unwin Books, London, 1971.

Saini, S.K. : *Development of Education in India : Socio-Economic and Political Perspective*, Cosmo Publications, New Delhi, 1980.

Saxena, Sateswari : *Education Planning in India : a Study in Approach and Methodology*, Sterling Publishers, New Delhi, 1974.

Sharma, G.S. : *Educational and Cultural Development of the Minorities—a Study in Social Effects of the Judicial Trends in India*, ICSSR, New Delhi, 1973.

Shipman, M.D. : *Education and Modernisation*, Faber and Faber, London, 1971.

Shri Prakash : *Educational System of India : an Econometric Study*, Concept Publishing Company, Delhi, 1977.

Singla, M.M. : *The Constitution of India-Studies in Perspective*, The World Press, Calcutta, 1975.

Slocum, Walter L. : *Occupational Careers: Sociological Perspective*, Aldine Publishing Co., Bombay, 1968.

Smith, H M. and Eckerson, L.O. : *Guidance Services in Elementary Schools*, Government Printing Press, Washington, 1966.

Stephen, J. Knezevich : *Administration of Public Education*, Harper and Brothers, New York, 1962.

Stewart, N.R. : *Education and Educationist*, Englewood Cliffs, Prentice Hall, New Jersey, 1978.

Super, Donald E. : *Psychology of Careers*, Harper Row, New York, 1957.

Thomas, F. Station : *Dynamics of Adjustment*, MacMillan Co., New York, 1953.

Tolber, E.L. : *Counselling for Career Development*, Houghton Miffin, Boston, 1974.

Tyler, L.E. : *The Work of the Counsellor*, Appleton Century Crafts, New York, 1969.

Vernon, P.E. : *Great Educationist India and World*, Methuen, London, 1969.

Index

C

D

E

F

S

U

V

W

Y

Z

❑❑❑

आना मेरे घर

आना मेरे घर

तुलसी देवी तिवारी

प्रतिभा प्रतिष्ठान, नई दिल्ली

प्रकाशक : प्रतिभा प्रतिष्ठान,
694-बी, (नियर अजय मार्केट) चावड़ी बाजार, दिल्ली-110006
 / संस्करण : प्रथम, 2019 / मूल्य : तीन सौ पचास रुपए
मुद्रक : आर-टेक ऑफसेट प्रिंटर्स, दिल्ली ISBN 978-93-87980-57-0

AANA MERE GHAR *stories* by Smt. Tulsi Devi Tiwari ₹ 350.00
Published by Pratibha Pratishthan, 694-B, (Near Ajay Market)
Chawri Bazar, Delhi-110006

प्राण-प्रिय

अनुज स्व. अनंग मिश्र को,
जिनके मोती जैसे अक्षरों ने मेरे अनपढ़ शब्दों को
काव्य बना दिया।

पुरोवाक्

प्रत्येक कला मूलत: एक आख्यान होती है, जिसकी अपनी भाषा और रंग रेखाएँ होती हैं। काव्य-कला में कहानी एक ऐसी विधा है, जो अभिनीत नाटक की तरह होती है, अर्थात् नाटक में जो काम रंग-निर्देशों के अनुरूप अभिनेता करते हैं, वह कहानी में वर्णन से संपन्न होता है, जो अनेक खतरों से भरा होता है, यदि सपाट हुआ तो ऊब पैदा करेगा और यदि लंबा हुआ तो कहानी की सुघड़ता नष्ट हो जाएगी। कहानी में शब्द ही रूप, रस, गंध और स्पर्श की अनुभूति कराते हैं और एक ऐसा संसार रचते हैं, जो प्रत्यक्ष गोचर होता है।

कथा-साहित्य यथार्थ (यथा अर्थ) जीवी होता है। यथार्थ प्रत्येक व्यक्ति की दृष्टि की सृष्टि है, जिसमें सच कल्पना के आवरण-आभरण में कलात्मक ही नहीं और भी अधिक विश्वसनीय, रोचक और आत्मीय हो जाता है। जिस चरित्र, घटना अथवा परिस्थिति से संवेदित होकर कहानीकार कहानी रचता है, वही अथवा वैसी ही संवेदना पाठक/श्रोता में जगाने का प्रयास करता है। इसी दृष्टि से तुलसी तिवारी की कहानियों का पाठ न्यायसंगत है।

तुलसी दूर की कौड़ी लाने के फेर में अपनी आँखों पर कोई चश्मा नहीं लगातीं, क्योंकि यथार्थ उपजता है दिक्-काल से मनुष्य की अंतरक्रिया में। 'आना मेरे घर' की कहानियाँ उस शाश्वत मानव प्रकृति को उकेरतीं हैं, जो गत-आगत-अनागत के त्रिधा विभाजन के आवर्त में नहीं घिरतीं, वरन् समकालीनता को उजागर करती हैं। पर्वत, पहाड़, वन, नदियाँ, सूर्य, चंद्र, तारे इत्यादि कब नहीं रहे ? केवल हमारी सोच या दृष्टि बदली है। इन कहानियों

में गाँव से शहर तक कथा के केंद्र में हैं, जिसमें एक परिवार है, परिवार में संबंधों का जालतंत्र है, जिसके ताने-बाने बुनती है नारी—कहीं पत्नी, कहीं बेटी, कहीं बहन और कहीं दादी। इन संबंधों का विकास तथाकथित समाज में भी देखा जा सकता है। परिवार या समाज संश्लिष्ट है, जिसमें तीन पीढ़ियाँ एक साथ चलती हैं, अर्थात् प्रत्येक पीढ़ी एक ही समय को अपने ढंग से समझती ही नहीं, रचती भी है। 'पहला दिन' कहानी में तो शिक्षिका सेवा प्रारंभ के दिन और सेवा-निवृत्ति के बाद के पहले दिन में पर्याप्त अंतर पाती है।

'आना मेरे घर' में मालती रोहन के सारे पाशविक कृत्यों को बरदाश्त करने की कोशिश करती है, किंतु जब उसे उसकी मनोवृत्ति का पता चलता है, तब 'जैसे को तैसा' सबक देकर उसे उसकी गलती का अनुभव कराती है। मानवीय संवेदना ही सारे संबंधों का स्थायी भाव है, जिससे प्रेम, करुणा, दया, सहानुभूति जैसे भाव उत्पन्न होते हैं। इन्हीं भावों से प्रेरित 'अकेला' का देव मन पसंद लड़की से भी विवाह करने से इनकार कर देता है, ताकि वह पूरे मन से कुंजू की सही परवरिश कर सके। संवेदना जब पिघलती है, तब वह आँसू बन जाती है—अनाथ रघुबर जीवन के सुख-दुःख सदा हँसकर सहता है, पत्नी के निधन के बाद तो जैसे पाषाणवत् हो जाता है, परंतु जब उसके बेटे-बहू विदेश से घर लौटकर आगे से हमेशा साथ रहने की बात कहते हैं, तब रघुबर रो पड़ता है। विदेश में बसने का मोह पालनेवालों के लिए 'और वह रो पड़ा' कहानी एक नसीहत है। जीवन केवल रोटी-कपड़ा-मकान से नहीं, परिवार में एक-दूसरे की इज्जत और सहभाव के साथ ही सामंजस्य से कृतकार्य होता है, जो सुनैना कभी शेखर की रानी थी, वही वृद्धावस्था में मथुरा के कृष्ण जन्मभूमि मंदिर में पनाह पाती है। 'कहाँ गई सुनैना' मोहभंग की तथाकथा है।

'बड़ी दीदी' कहानी में शांता के समक्ष ऐसी परिस्थितियाँ उत्पन्न हो जाती हैं कि उसे घर से ज्यादा सुविधाजनक वृद्धाश्रम जान पड़ता है। बाद में उसका भाई रतन सारी विषमताओं का परिष्कार कर उसे घर ले जाता है। 'खोज सको तो' कहानी बच्चों के जीवन में बुजुर्गों के स्थान की खोज है। 'कहाँ जाऊँ' की लाची सुमता की बेटी दसमत को पाल-पोसकर बड़ा करती है, ब्याह भी कर

देती है, परंतु अंत में वह बेघर हो जाती है। 'छींटे गुलाल के' का सीताराम वृद्धावस्था में दर-दर भटकता है। 'चूहेदानी' रिया के उस मुकाम पर पहुँचने की दु:खद स्थिति को आरेखित करती है, जिसमें वह अपनी सास से घृणा के चलते अपना पति-पुत्र भी खो देती है, किंतु जब राजेश से दूसरा विवाह करती है, वहाँ भी उसे राजेश की मुँह बोली माँ सास के पद पर आसीन मिल जाती है।

'दान-दहेज' की दादी अपना सारा अपमान भूलकर पोती के भले का विचार रखती है। अत्याधुनिक कहे जानेवाले युग में भी बेटी-बेटा में फर्क करनेवाली स्नेहा गर्भपात कराकर किस दशा में पहुँच जाती है, 'माटी कहे कुम्हार से' कहानी कहती है। उसकी सास राजेश्वरी जब उसे बचाने के लिए अपना एकमात्र घर बेच देती है, तब उसे समझ में आता है, उसने क्या गँवा दिया।

'राख के नीचे' बाहर से शुष्क, लेकिन अंदर से स्नेहिल और जिम्मेदार पिता को मिती तब पहचानती है, जब कल्पना मैडम उसकी शादी अधेड़ उम्र के पागल से करने की राय देती हैं और ठाकुर साहब उन्हें डाँटकर घर से भगा देते हैं, मिती का 'पापा' कहना चौंका देता है, क्योंकि वह उनके प्रति घृणा से भरी रहती है।

'आना मेरे घर' कहानी-संग्रह में और भी कहानियाँ हैं, जिनका दायरा गाँव नगर और महानगर तक फैला हुआ है। ये कहानियाँ विभिन्न परिवेशों में पल रहे जन-जीवन, उनके सुख-दु:ख, आशा-निराशा, बार-बार गिरकर सँभलने के जीवंत चित्र उकेरती हैं।

'आएँगे फिर लौटकर' में जीविका के लिए गाँव से शहर गए जयंत और शीला जीवन की सांध्य वेला में पुन: गाँव लौटते हैं। स्वास्थ्यगत समस्या के कारण खड़ी फसल का मोह त्यागकर शहर की ओर भागते हैं। 'वसूली' में धजाराम और ज्ञानदास—जैसे धोखेबाज चरित्रहीन सरपंच-महासरपंच के चलते गाँव के स्कूल की दुर्दशा, 'चार रुपए बीस पैसे' में उदय और सूरज पासवान परिवार के बीच जातीय वैमनस्य, 'सुबह से शाम' में होली की हुड़दंग, 'तुम मुझ में रहते हो' में नेकदिल पूजा की बेबसी, आदि-आदि।

जीवन के विभिन्न पहलुओं को तुलसी ने अपनी लेखनी से सँवारा है—संवादों के जरिए, बोल-चाल की सहज-सरल भाषा में, सुगठित शिल्प में, अपनी शैली में।

मैं आश्वस्त हूँ कि 'आना मेरे घर' कहानी-संग्रह को पाठकों का असीम स्नेह मिलेगा।

—डॉ. चित्त रंजन कर

पूर्व प्रोफेसर, साहित्य एवं भाषा-अध्ययनशाला
पंडित रविशंकर शुक्ल विश्वविद्यालय, रायपुर (छ.ग.)

आत्मनिवेदन

किसी नई कहानी को भाषाई कलेवर दिए जब कुछ समय गुजर जाता है, तब मन में एक अनजानी सी हूक उठने लगती है; लगता है, जैसे मैं अपने आपसे बहुत दूर होती जा रही हूँ, कुछ छूटता जा रहा है, जो नितांत मेरा अपना है, जिसके साथ रहना मुझे बहुत-बहुत भाता है। मन एकांत की खोज में बौराया सा होकर छोटी-बड़ी व्यावहारिक त्रुटियाँ करवाता है, जिसके फलस्वरूप शर्मिंदगी उठानी पड़ती है। भटकती चेतना कभी अतीत की अतल गहराइयों से किसी ऐसी घटना के मोती चुन लाती है, जिसके चारों ओर किसी दिलकश कहानी की काया का सृजन होने लगता है। हर कहानी यह विश्वास दिलाती चलती है कि वह मेरी सर्वश्रेष्ठ कहानी होगी, किंतु अंत में लगता है, यह वह नहीं, जिसे मैं लिखना चाहती थी, इसमें कहीं-न-कहीं कमी रह गई है, जिसका परिहार किए बिना यह मेरी सर्वश्रेष्ठ रचना नहीं हो सकती। कुछ दिन मन उसी रचना में रमा रहता है। उसके पात्र, घटनाएँ, पात्रों की विवशताएँ, उनकी खुशी, उनके गम मुझे अपने से बाहर निकलने नहीं देते, फिर आस-पास घटनेवाली विस्मयकारी, लज्जाजनक, विसंगतिपूर्ण घटनाएँ आकर्षित कर लेती हैं, जिनमें से कुछ नई कहानियों की पीठिका बनती है।

इसी तारतम्य में वर्षों पूर्व पड़ोस में रहनेवाली एक बहू के अग्निस्नान और उसके स्थान पर ब्याहकर आई नई बहू की शारीरिक-मानसिक प्रताड़ना मुझे अकसर कुरेदा करती। नई बहू के शरीर पर पड़े फफोले जलते, जैसे मेरे शरीर पर ही बर्बरतापूर्वक रगड़कर उन्हें फोड़ा गया हो। मैंने अवसर देखकर उसे मुक्तिमार्ग अवश्य दिखा दिया था, किंतु इतने से मुझे संतुष्टि नहीं थी,

अत: मैंने अत्याचारी को भुलावे में डालकर पीड़िता के घर भेजा, तब जाकर कहानी बनी 'आना मेरे घर'।

इसी प्रकार दो साल पहले मैं अपने गृहग्राम मुंगारी में गरमी की छुट्टियाँ बिताने गई थी। हमारे गाँव की चक्की पर ही चार रुपए बीस पैसे के लिए नृशंस हत्याकांड हुआ, जिसमें देश के तीन होनहार बेटे काल-कवलित हो गए। मैं अंदर तक सिहर गई। सबकुछ तो महँगा है अपने देश में, फिर आदमी की जान इतनी सस्ती क्यों है? मानती हूँ कि मुगलों के आधिपत्य से लेकर स्वतंत्रता-प्राप्ति तक के काल में तथाकथित निम्न कहे जानेवाले वर्ण पर बड़ी ज्यादतियाँ हुईं। तत्कालीन सामाजिक, आर्थिक, सांस्कृतिक परिवेश ही इसके लिए जिम्मेदार हो सकते हैं। इसके दुष्परिणामों के मद्देनजर सवर्ण विद्वानों, समाज-सुधारकों, संत-महात्माओं ने ही उन्हें जाग्रत् किया कि तुममें भी वही परमात्म ज्योति जल रही है, जो सवर्णों में है। तुम भी उसी परमात्मा की संतान हो, जिसके और लोग। पंडित जवाहर लाल नेहरू ने आरक्षण लागू किया, महात्मा गांधी ने अछूतों को हरिजन नाम दिया, फलत: आज उनकी स्थिति बेहतर है। आरक्षण के बढ़ते दायरे के कारण आज योग्य सवर्ण बेरोजगार घूम रहे हैं, विवशता में मेहनत-मजदूरी करने लगे हैं तो अब उनकी मजदूरी न देना भी कुछ लोग अपना हक समझने लगे हैं। उनके अंदर अपने विकास से अधिक बदले की आग जल रही है। समाजरूपी समुद्र के मंथन से यह कैसा हलाहल निकला, जो देश की समरसता का नाश करने पर उतारू है? उदारतारूपी शिव का अवतरण कब होगा? मेहनतकश की मजदूरी सम्मान सहित कब दी जाएगी? इन्हीं प्रश्नों को लेकर 'चार रुपए बीस पैसे' कहानी लिखी गई।

वर्ण-व्यवस्था के विघटन से उपजी विकट विसंगतियों ने मनुष्य को इस कदर तोड़ दिया है कि कभी समाज के शीर्ष पर रहे लोग आज कल-कारखानों, खदानों, या अन्य जहाँ भी दो पैसे का काम मिला, करने लगे हैं, अतीत की मान-प्रतिष्ठा उन्हें निराशा के गहरे गर्त में गिरा रही है। अपने खेत-खलिहान उन्हें सदैव पुकारते रहते हैं। एक समय हमारे पड़ोस में एक ऐसा

ही परिवार रहता था। सेवानिवृत्ति के पश्चात् प्राप्त राशि से उन्होंने भूमि क्रय करके उसे खेत बनाया, किंतु देह में इतना बल शेष न रह गया कि उसे अधिक दिन सँभाल सकें। कथानायक की गंभीर बीमारी के कारण अपनी खड़ी फसल का मोह छोड़ पति-पत्नी जीवन रक्षा का उपक्रम करते हैं। अपनी मृगतृष्णा में आकंठ डूबे अभी कुछ दिन पूर्व ही उनका परलोक गमन हुआ। उनकी आँखों में बसे सपने मुझे पुकार रहे थे, शायद कह रहे थे हम 'आएँगे फिर लौटकर'। समाज समय-समय पर अपने सामाजिक मूल्यों में संशोधन करता रहता है। वे दिन अभी गुजरे नहीं हैं, जब लोग अपने बेटे की परवरिश और शिक्षा-दीक्षा में आया संपूर्ण खर्च अपने समधी से दहेज के रूप में वसूल करते हैं। इच्छा पूरी न होने पर अनेक शादियाँ टूटती हैं, बहुएँ दग्ध होती हैं। कई जगह घर के सभी लोग जेल में सड़ते हुए, जहाँ से कूच कर जाते हैं। दहेज लेकर आई बहुओं की दया-ममता से असंख्य बुजुर्ग या तो अकेले अपने गाँव के घर में रहते हुए दाने-दाने को तरसते हैं या असामाजिक तत्त्वों की हिंसा का शिकार हो जाते हैं। वृद्धाश्रमों की संख्या लगातार बढ़ती जा रही है। शिशु पालन में दादा-दादी के अभाव के कारण नई पीढ़ी असुरक्षा के घेरे में है। अपराधों के ग्राफ ऊपर उठते जा रहे हैं। इन्हीं दुष्परिणामों ने समाज को नई सोच दी है। अब कुछ लोग दान-दहेज नहीं, ऐसी लड़की माँगने लगे हैं, जो अपने बुजुर्गों की छत्रच्छाया में पली-बढ़ी हो, ताकि वह घर के वरिष्ठजन की उपस्थिति को सहज ढंग से ले सके। 'दान-दहेज' कहानी चुपचाप बदल रहे मूल्यों की मुखर साक्षी है।

हम जिनके बूते अपने घर में सुरक्षित अनुभव करते सहज जीवन जीते हैं, उन पुलिसवालों से एक प्रकार की दूरी बनाकर रखते हैं, उनके घर (पुलिस लाइन या पुलिस कॉलोनी) भी अलग होते हैं, जिससे उनका परिवार आम जन से घुलमिल नहीं पाता। उनके त्योहार कैसे गुजरते हैं, उनके जीवन में कितनी परेशानियाँ हैं और उन्हें निरंतर ऊर्जा कहाँ से मिलती है। 'सुबह से शाम' कैसे होती है ? सबकुछ जानने के लिए इस विभाग की लंबी संगति की है मैंने। ऐसे ही कभी वृद्धाश्रम में समय दान करते समय बुरी तरह जली सिर पर सफेद बालों की टोकरी औंधाए अपने घर से वृद्धाश्रम को अधिक अनुकूल

माननेवाली 'बड़ी दीदी' मिल गई तो कभी असंख्य भवनों का निर्माता बटुक मिस्त्री दरवाजे पर एक मुट्ठी अन्न के लिए टेर लगाता मिल गया। मैं उन शिक्षिकाओं से भी मिली हूँ, जिनके वेतन से हिस्सा माँगने वाले सरपंच के चमचे ने सब्जबाग दिखाकर उनकी मेहनत की कमाई ठग ली।

इन्हीं लोगों ने बलात् मुझसे 'आना मेरे घर' का सृजन कराया, ये सभी अपना नवीन कलेवर पाने के लिए व्यग्र थे। इन्होंने मुझे बार-बार उकसाया कुछ लिखने के लिए।

जब मैंने सारी कहानियों को पुस्तक के रूप में (प्रूफ देखने के उद्देश्य से) पढ़ना प्रारंभ किया, तब पीड़ा के इस समुच्चय ने मेरी आँखों को सूखने न दिया।

मेरा ग्यारहवाँ कहानी-संग्रह 'आना मेरे घर' स्वनामधन्य साहित्यिक पत्रिका 'साहित्य अमृत' में छपी और पाठकों द्वारा सराही गई कहानियों का संग्रह है। इसे पुस्तक का रूप देने में सारस्वत सहयोग हेतु सर्वश्री बद्रीधर दीवानजी, भूतपूर्व विधानसभा अध्यक्ष, छत्तीसगढ़, श्री नंदकिशोर तिवारीजी, निवर्तमान रजिस्टार गुरुघासी दास विश्वविद्यालय, बिलासपुर (छत्तीसगढ़), यशस्वी संपादक छत्तीसगढ़ी पत्रिका 'लोकाक्षर', डॉक्टर विनय कुमार पाठक, पूर्व अध्यक्ष, छत्तीसगढ़ राजभाषा आयोग, प्रख्यात् भाषाविद्, समीक्षक, साहित्यकार श्री कृष्णकुमार भट्ट 'पथिक' सेवानिवृत्त प्राचार्य, अध्यक्ष 'संदर्भ' साहित्यिक संस्था बिलासपुर (छत्तीसगढ़) की हृदय से अभ्यर्थना करती हूँ। इन्होंने हर कदम मेरा उत्साहवर्धन किया। इनके आशीर्वाद की मंद बयार ने मुझे हर प्रकार की नकारात्मकता से दूर रखा। पतिदेव श्री अक्षयवरनाथ तिवारी, जिनके अथक प्रयासों ने सुधी पाठकों की नजर में एक साहित्यकार का दर्जा दिलाया, मुझे हर पल उनके आशीर्वाद की आवश्यकता है।

परम श्रद्धेय भइया डॉ. चितरंजनकर, सेवानिवृत्त प्रोफेसर, रविशंकर शुक्ल विश्वविद्यालय (कई भाषाओं के सुविख्यात रचनाकार) के श्रीचरणों में प्रणाम निवेदन करती हूँ। इन्होंने अतिव्यस्तता के मध्य 'आना मेरे घर' की भूमिका लिखकर इसे श्रेष्ठ साहित्य होने का गौरव प्रदान किया। मैं उस अदृश्य

सूत्रधार के प्रति अपने भावसुमन अर्पित करती हूँ, जो अहेतुक प्रेमवश मेरे सारे योगक्षेम का वहन करता रहता है।

अपने कनिष्ठ पुत्र विवेक तिवारी (मेधावी पत्रकार, इंडिया टी.वी. एवं दूरदर्शन के संभागीय ब्यूरो चीफ, प्रोपराइटर माँ अंबिका ज्वेलर्स बिलासपुर), छोटी बहू आरती तिवारी के सकारात्मक सहयोग के लिए सदा उनकी कल्याणकामी रहूँगी।

देश-विदेश में फैले अपने पाठकों के प्रति मैं हार्दिक आभार व्यक्त करती हूँ, जिनके फोनकॉल्स सदा मुझे कुछ नया लिखने की प्रेरणा देते हैं। उनके पत्र ही मुझे हजार व्यस्तताओं में से कुछ पल चुराकर कुछ लिख लेने की जुगत सुझाते हैं। आशा और विश्वास है कि मेरे पहले दस कहानी-संग्रहों के समान ही इसे भी आप सुधी पाठकों की व्यापक स्वीकारोक्ति और स्नेह प्राप्त होगा।

—तुलसी देवी तिवारी

बी/28 हरसिंगार राजकिशोर नगर,
बिलासपुर (छ.ग.),
मो. : 9907176361

अनुक्रम

आना मेरे घर

पहली रात तो उसकी गोद में सिर रखकर वह फूट-फूटकर रोया था, उसके आँसू गले तक बह आए थे। इस तगड़े से रोबदार नौजवान को इस प्रकार रोते देख वह सहम गई थी। उसने सुना अवश्य था कि यह उसकी दूसरी शादी है, पहली जलकर मर गई थी, दुनिया में लोग दूसरी शादी करते हैं। जो जल-भुन गया, उसके बारे में सोचने की जहमत उसने नहीं उठाई थी। पुलिस की नौकरी है लड़के की, ससुर भी पुलिस विभाग से रिटायर हैं, अच्छी-खासी पेंशन पा रहे हैं। माना कि एक चार वर्ष का बच्चा है, कोई बात नहीं! खाता-पीता पड़ा रहेगा, उसे सँभालने के लिए तो सास-ससुर ही पर्याप्त हैं।

वैसे भी उसकी तीस की पक्की उम्र हो रही थी, एक तो बाप की गरीबी, दूसरे गाँव की बदनामी, जीवन चुटकी भर सिंदूर के लिए तरस गया था। उसके माता-पिता और स्वयं उसने भी मान लिया था कि अब उसे समझौते वाली शादी करनी पड़ेगी। उसने पूरे मन से अपनी स्थिति स्वीकार की थी। रह गई बात दूसरी औरत के जूठन की, तो कौन जानता है कि कौन निजूठ है? वही कौन सा इसके लिए अपने को बचाकर रख सकी है? जीवन जीने के लिए समझौता तो करना ही पड़ता है।

“मैंने उसे जी-जान से प्यार किया था, न जाने क्या हुआ, जो इस प्रकार मुझे छोड़कर चली गई?” वह सिसक रहा था।

“शांत हो जाइए! तकदीर पर किसका वश चला है? जितने दिन का संग-साथ लिखाकर लाई थीं, उतने दिन निभाकर चली गईं, यह तो लगता है, मुझे आपकी सेवा का मौका मिलना बदा था। यदि वे होतीं तो मैं भला क्यों

आती आपके जीवन में?" उसने अपनी कामदार साड़ी के आँचल से उसके आँसू पोंछे। उसकी आँखें भी भरी गागर सी छलक आई थीं।

नादान बच्चे की तरह वह उसकी बातें स्वीकारता रहा।

"आप पुराना सबकुछ भूल जाइए, जैसे वह आपका पिछला जन्म हो! मुझसे जितना बन पड़ेगा, आपकी सेवा करूँगी, समय सबकुछ भुला देता है।" उसने दार्शनिक मुद्रा में समझाया था।

"मेरा एक नन्हा सा बच्चा है, देखा नहीं तुमने उसे?" उसने उम्मीद भरी निगाहों से उसे देखा।

"देखा है, वह तो पहले ही मेरी गोद में आकर बैठ गया था।" उसने बात समाप्त की थी।

वह सुबह देर तक सोता रहा, उठा तो बेहद झुँझलाया हुआ, इसे डाँटा, उसे डाँटा, यह तोड़ा वह पटका। माँ दौड़-दौड़कर उसके काम करती रही। ले-देकर वह ड्यूटी गया, बार-बार अंदर-बाहर होते-होते।

दूसरी रात उसने पी रखी थी, पहले घर में घनघोर तमाशा मचाया, माणिक डरकर कहीं छिप गया था, माँ थर-थर काँप रही थी। बाप से कुछ कहते नहीं बन रहा था। उसे काटो तो खून नहीं।

"शराब पीता है! चलो कोई बात नहीं, हमारे सैदा में तो लगभग सभी पीते-खाते हैं, पापा भी पीते हैं, वे तो ड्राइवर हैं, उनका पिए बिना कहाँ चलनेवाला है? यह भी तो पुलिस में है, बहुत तनाव रहता है इनके जीवन में। सब चलेगा।" उसने स्वयं को हर प्रकार के सदमे से मुक्त किया।

"मैं पीता नहीं, शादी की खुशी में दोस्तों ने पिला दी, तुम नाराज तो नहीं?" कमरे में वह एक अच्छे आदमी की तरह शांत था।

"कोई बात नहीं, हो जाता है कभी-कभी।" ऊपर से वह भी सामान्य लग रही थी। उसकी आँखों में वासना के डोरे उभर रहे थे। सिगरेट की कश के साथ-साथ वह उसके एक-एक अंग की माप-तौल कर रहा था, उसने अनायास उसकी साड़ी खींच दी, उसका आशय समझकर वह गहरे से मुसकराई।

"बड़ी गरमी है!" कहते हुए उसने अपने कपड़े उतारकर कुरसी पर रख

दिए। उसने शर्म से अपनी आँखें बंद कर ली थीं।

बाहर एकदम शांति थी। ऐसा लग रहा था, जैसे सब सो गए हों। गरमी की रात थी, दो कमरे का क्वार्टर, सामने घेरकर आँगन बना लिया गया था, उसी में सब लोग गरमी की रातों में सोते थे। वैसे तो कमरे में सीलिंग फैन चल रहा था, किंतु लग रहा था, जैसे हवा सूरज से मिलकर आ रही हो। उसके शरीर पर जैसे चींटियाँ रेंगने लगी थीं। वह पास आ गया था, उसकी बाँहों का घेरा सख्त हुआ। वह पलंग पर गिरा दी गई।

"अरे! यह क्या करते हो?" वह पीड़ा से चीख उठी थी। कुछ समझे, इसके पहले ही छाती तथा जाँघों के बीच कई जगह सिगरेट से जल चुकी थी। जलन और अपमान की स्वाभाविक प्रतिक्रिया! उसने उसे परे धकेल दिया।

"मुझे धकेलती है ऽ…ऽ… ? मादर…! कहाँ-कहाँ भाड़े पर चली है। मैं नहीं जानता क्या?" उसने एकदम से अपना रंग बदल दिया।

"जलाते क्यों हो मुझे?" उसने कातर दृष्टि से उसे देखा।

"अरे! क्या करूँ, यह शरीर है तेरा! खुरपी से छीलो, तब भी कुछ हाथ न आए, तू तो पूरी खोजा है, हाय रे मेरी बड़ी ऽ…ऽ…!" उसने उसाँस भरी। कमर का सारा मांस गोल-गोल होकर जैसे छाती पर सज गया था। नशे के कारण मन की कुंठा जबान पर आ गई।

"अरे! तो इसमें मेरी क्या गलती है? सबके शरीर की बनावट एक जैसी होती है क्या?" वह तिलमिला उठी थी।

"जाओ कमरे से बाहर! मुझे तुम्हारी कोई जरूरत नहीं है।" वह भयानक ढंग से चीख रहा था, उसकी आँखें सूर्ख अंगारे की तरह दहक रही थीं। मुँह से लार निकलकर चेहरे पर इधर-उधर फैल रही थी।

उसे तो जैसे जीवनदान मिल गया। वह तेजी से दरवाजे की ओर भागी थी कि उसने बाँह पकड़कर खींच लिया।

"खबरदार! बाहर निकली तो हमेशा के लिए बाहर!"

"ठीक है, हमेशा के लिए जा रही हूँ।" उसका गला रुँध गया था।

खींचकर बाँहों में जकड़ लिया था उसने। चूम-चूमकर उसे बेहाल कर दिया, न जाने कहाँ से इतना प्यार का सागर उमड़ आया उसके व्यवहार में?

"माफ कर देना मालती, मैंने मजाक किया था। मैं देख रहा था कि तुम कितना सह सकती हो। तुम तो मेरा उजड़ा घर बसाने आई हो, कभी मुझसे दूर मत जाना, वरना मैं तो बिना मारे मर जाऊँगा।" वह जार-जार रोने लगा था।

"मुझे माफ कर दो, वरना अपनी जान दे दूँगा।" वह इधर-उधर कुछ खोज रहा था, जिससे अपना जीवन खत्म कर सके।

"यह रहा बिजली का बटन! इसे उखाड़कर तार छू लेता हूँ।" वह बोर्ड की ओर बढ़ा।

"नहीं-नहीं ऐसा मत कीजिए! मैं भला आपसे नाराज होकर कहाँ जाऊँगी? अब तो जीवन-मरण आपके ही साथ है।" उसने बलपूर्वक उसे अपनी तरफ खींचा। वह चीखती रही, सारे फोड़े फूट गए, देह जैसे कोल्हू में पेरी गई हो, अंग-अंग टूट रहा था उसका। अंतर्मन में घृणा का सैलाब उमड़ रहा था।

सुबह उस दिन वह बड़ा प्रसन्न था। सबसे हँस-हँसकर बातें कर रहा था।

वह दर्द और जलन की मारी कमरे में ही लेटी थी। किसे बताए? चेहरा किसी को दिखाने लायक नहीं बचा। चाल में लँगड़ाहट, चेहरे पर मुर्दनी, वह सुबह जल्दी उठ नहीं पाई, सास ने बुरा सा मुँह बनाए सारा काम निबटाया। वह उसे एक प्याला चाय दे गया था।

"आराम करो। अम्मा सब सँभाल लेगी!" कहता हुआ ड्यूटी पर चला गया था।

हर रात उसके लिए कालरात्रि थी, सिर पर सिंदूर जलता रहता था आग की तरह।

"मेरी तकदीर ही फूटी है, पहली ने इतने कलंक लगाए, लोगों ने जलाकर मार डालने तक का आरोप लगाया। दस साल के बाद उसे न जाने क्या सूझी, जो एक बच्चा छोड़कर जल मरी, दूसरी लाए तो यह अपने आपको न जाने क्या समझती है? औरत जात का धरम क्या होता है किसी ने बताया नहीं इसे, ऐसा लगता है। अरे! मुँह अँधेरे उठो, घर-बाहर साफ-सुथरा करो, सबका भोजन बनाओ, समय बचे तो कुछ सिलाई-बुनाई करो।" महीना भर

सहने के बाद सास ने एक दिन सुना ही दिया था।

"माँ, मैं करना चाहती हूँ, परंतु कर नहीं पाती, जरा देखो! ये दाग किसके हैं? गोल-गोल जले हुए, कुछ ठीक होते हैं तो कुछ नए बन जाते हैं। ये पूरे शरीर पर हैं, इनके दर्द से मैं बेहाल रहती हूँ।" नजरें झुकाए-झुकाए उसने आँचल हटाकर सीने की गोलाइयों पर पड़े घाव दिखा दिए।

"हाय राम! यह किसके दाग हैं? लगता है कोई चर्म रोग है, परंतु ऐसे दाग तो बड़ी के शरीर पर भी दिखते थे!" उसकी आँखें कुछ सोचनेवाले अंदाज में सिकुड़ गईं।

"यह सिगरेट से जलने के घावों से बने दाग हैं।" उसके स्वर से पीड़ा की गागर छलक रही थी।

"कैसे जल जाती हो तुम लोग? रुको! आज रोहन से कहती हूँ कि कमरे में सिगरेट न पिया करे!" उसने सबकुछ समझकर भी अनजान बनते हुए कहा था।

उस रात उसने जरा सा संकेत भर किया था, "मुझे घर के काम में माँ की मदद करनी चाहिए। ऐसे अच्छा नहीं लगता।"

"माँ ने कुछ कहा, कुछ कह रही थी क्या?" उसकी त्योरियाँ चढ़ गईं।

"कह रही थीं तो क्या गलत कर रही थीं? शादी एक ही काम का नाम नहीं, मुझे भी थोड़ी राहत चाहिए। आप आज बाहर सो जाइए!" उसके स्वर में निवेदन था।

वह इस प्रकार उछलकर बाहर निकला, जैसे बिच्छू ने डंक मार दिया हो।

"मेरा जरा सा सुख तुझसे देखा नहीं जाता? तू तो साँपिन से भी ज्यादा जहरीली है! कितने दिन उसे आए हुए, जो उसने तेरा पानी पिंडा नहीं किया? बक-बककर तेरा मुँह खुल गया है। इसी मुँह के कारण बड़ी जल मरी। अब फिर वही शुरू कर रही है?" वह बिफरे साँड़ की तरह आँगन में फेरा दे रहा था।

वह संकोच से मरी जा रही थी, "क्या सोचेगी सास? आते ही चुगली करके माँ-बेटे को लड़वाने लगी!"

"मैंने ऐसा क्या कह दिया, जो इतना बिगड़ रहा है? मुझसे पूरा काम हो नहीं पाता, इसलिए थोड़ा मदद करने को कहा है।" सास की आवाज एकदम धीमी थी। अपराध-बोध से दबी-दबी सी।

ससुर की बोलती बंद, जाकर दरवाजे के बाहर बैठ जाते हैं। "तूने जनमाया तू ही भोग अब।"

वह निकलकर माता चौरावाले पेड़ के नीचे जाकर अँधेरे में छिप गई थी। इसके बाद तो उसने रोज उसे गाली-मार खाते देखा। एक दिन उसने ऐसा धकेला कि जाकर नहानी के पत्थर से टकराई। सिर फूट गया। बाप बीच में आया तो वह भी धक्का खाकर गिरा। रोहन उससे लिपट गया था, उसे भी चोट लगी थी।

उससे रहा न गया, उसने उसकी मरहम-पट्टी करके खून बहने से रोका। दूसरे दिन ननद आकर उन्हें अपने घर ले गई।

अब तो रोहन की पाँचों उँगलियाँ घी में, मारे तो सहो, जलाए तो जलो, जब जो कहे पकाकर दो, अब तो मालती के लिए 'मरे बिहान' हो गया। बहुत रोई-गाई तब कहीं एक दिन के लिए मायके ले गया तो पूरे समय साथ-साथ लगा रहा, न माँ-बाप को कुछ पूछने का अवसर मिला, न उसे कुछ बताने का।

"चलो सास-ससुर का टंटा भी छूट गया। अपने आप घर छोड़कर चले गए। बड़ी की जमी-जमाई गृहस्थी, उसके सारे गहने सबकुछ तो अपनी मालती को अनायास ही मिल गया, बहुत है भगवान् का दिया, परंतु इसके शरीर पर ये गोल-गोल दाग कैसे पड़ गए? वह इतनी भकुआई हुई क्यों है?" उनके मन में कुछ प्रश्न थे, जिनका उत्तर देनेवाला कोई नहीं था।

❑

ड्यूटी के दौरान शराब पीकर हुल्लड़ करने के कारण उसे सस्पेंड कर दिया गया था। अब तो बस हाजिरी देकर आओ और घर-बाहर बखेड़ा करो!

"मेरे दिन चढ़े हैं जी, अब जरा सँभल जाएँ।" उसने उस रात पहली बार हुलसकर उससे कुछ कहा था।

"दिन चढ़कर क्या होगा? हाँ ऽ…ऽ…ऽ…ऽ…? एक है, उसे ही

सँभालते नहीं बनता, कभी उसे गोद में लेकर प्यार किया? बिचारा टूअर-टापर जैसे घूम रहा है!"

"अरे! यह कौन बोल रहा है? क्या यह भी अपने बच्चे के बारे में सोचता है?" उसे जोरदार झटका लगा था।

"अभी तो आप से ही फुरसत नहीं है, क्या करूँ, क्या न करूँ।" उसके मुँह से निकला ही था कि उसने खींचकर थप्पड़ जड़ दिया उसके गाल पर। वह दर्द से बिलबिला उठी थी। उसके दुबारा उठे हाथ को उसने कसकर पकड़ लिया था।

"हाथ पकड़ती है हरहट!" और इसके साथ ही कसकर लात पड़ी कोख पर, जहाँ कोई बसेरा करने लगा था। वह दूर जाकर गिरी थी।

"अरे, कोई बचाओ! यह शैतान मुझे मार डालेगा।" वह बेतहाशा चिल्लाने लगी थी। उसकी आवाज सुनकर कोई आता, इसके पहले ही उसने उसके मुँह पर हाथ रखकर उसे बंद कर दिया।

"अरे, यह क्या करती है? आपस की बात है, थानेवाले आ गए तो मुझे अंदर कर देंगे, फिर क्या खाएगी? क्वार्टर से निकाल देंगे, कहाँ रहेगी? बेवकूफ!" वह उसकी बाँहों में कसमसाई। पूरी रात वह उसे भाँति-भाँति से मनाता रहा।

सवेरे वह संतुष्ट था और वह बार-बार बाथरूम जाकर कपड़े बदल रही थी। उसकी कमर और पेड़ू में दर्द उठ रहा था। थोड़ी-थोड़ी देर में मरणांतक पीड़ा की लहर उसके उदर में दौड़ रही थी। वह स्वयं उसके लिए एक कप चाय बनाकर ले आया।

"मुझे अस्पताल ले चलिए। मेरी तबीयत बहुत खराब है।" वह कराह रही थी।

"मैं ठीक कर दूँ?" उसकी आँखों में खेल रही शरारत का आशय समझकर वह काँप उठी।

"रहने दो, ठीक हो जाऊँगी!"

"कुछ रुपए हों तो दे दो!" वह नरमी से बोला।

"सारे तो ले गए, अब कहाँ बचे!"

"क्या मैं ही खा गया? जो कुछ करता हूँ तुम्हारे लिए ही तो! क्या सारा सुख मुझे ही मिलता है? तुम्हें कुछ नहीं मिलता मुझसे?" वह सुबह-सुबह फिर लड़ने पर आमादा था।

"वेतन आधा मिलता है तो खर्चे भी कम करो न···ऽ···ऽ··· !"

"अरे! अब तू मुझे सिखाएगी? चल, यह टॉप्स दे दे, गिरवी रखूँगा, वेतन मिलने पर छुड़ा लेंगे!" वह उसका सिर अपने आगे करके टॉप्स उतारने लगा।

"एक बात बोलूँ?" उसने स्वयं को संयत रखकर पूछा।

"हाँ बोल!"

"शराब खरीदकर पीने से बहुत महँगी मिलती है। आप सामान ला दीजिए, मैं बना दिया करूँगी। घर की बनी में नशा भी ज्यादा रहेगा और चौथाई दाम लगेगा।" सारा दुःख भूलकर उसने यह सुझाव दिया।

"तुम्हें बनाना आता है?" उसने आश्चर्य से उसे देखा।

"हाँ! हमारे गाँव में तो सभी अपने-अपने पीने के लिए बना लेते हैं। महुए के फूल सीजन में ही इकट्ठा करके रख दिए जाते हैं। लकड़ी फाटे की कमी नहीं, बस थोड़ी सी मेहनत लगती है।"

"बाप रे! यह तो छुपी रुस्तम निकली।" उसने मन-ही-मन कहा।

"तुम्हें पता नहीं शायद, बिना लाइसेंस के शराब बनाना कानूनन जुर्म है।" वह बेहद गंभीर था।

"मैं यह सब नहीं जानती। जब खरीदकर पीना मना नहीं है तो बनाना क्यों मना है? जैसे अपने लिए खाना बनाते हैं, वैसे ही शराब बना सकते हैं।"

"बेवकूफी भरी बातें मत किया कर! यदि सभी अपने लिए बनाने लगें तो सरकार को टैक्स कहाँ से मिलेगा? हम पुलिसवाले हैं। ऐसे लोगों को पकड़कर सजा दिलवाना हमारी ड्यूटी है और फिर यह पुलिस क्वार्टर है। बात फैलते देर नहीं लगती। दुबारा ऐसी बात मत करना। अच्छा! मैं आता हूँ, तुम कुछ बना लो खाने के लिए।" वह कपड़े पहनकर बाहर निकल गया, जाते-जाते बाहर से दरवाजा बंद करता गया।

"तो क्या सरकार को पैसा देकर आदमी जहर भी पी सकता

है···ऽ···ऽ··· ?" वह जोर से चिल्ला पड़ी। उसके कंठ से रुदन के स्वर फूट पड़े, "हाय राम! कहाँ फँसा दिया? यहाँ तो अड़ोसी-पड़ोसी बोलते भी नहीं, हमारे गाँव में एक आवाज पर सारा गाँव उमड़ पड़ता है।" वह इतने जोर-जोर से इसलिए बोल रही थी कि दीवार के उस पार से पड़ोसन को सुनाई पड़ जाए।

थोड़ी देर बाद बाहर से साँकल खोली गई, एक अधेड़ औरत ने घर में प्रवेश किया। उसने हठात् मालती को अँकवार में भर लिया।

"मैं तेरी सारी तकलीफें जानती हूँ मेरी बच्ची, परंतु रोहन की दुष्टता के कारण चुप रहती हूँ, यह ले मोबाइल, तुरंत फोन लगाकर अपने पापा को बुला और निकल जा यहाँ से! तू क्या जानेगी कि बड़ी ने दस साल कैसे बरदाश्त किया। अंत में उसे अग्नि-स्नान करना ही पड़ा। स्त्री को पीड़ा देकर ही रोहन को संतुष्टि मिलती है। लगता है, पी-पीकर इसका दिमाग फिर गया है।"

उसने जल्दी से मोबाइल ऑन करके अपने पापा से बात की। माँ की बीमारी के बहाने विदा कराने की बात समझाकर उन्हें तुरंत बुलाया।

पड़ोसन जैसे आँधी की तरह आई थी, वैसे ही तूफान की तरह चली गई। रोहन दर्जन भर अंडे और शराब की बोतल लेकर जल्दी ही वापस आ गया।

"अब तो मेरे नाटक करने की बारी है मिस्टर रोहन! मुझे पता नहीं था आपके बारे में, इसलिए इतना सह लिया।" मालती ने सारे दर्द पर विजय पाकर उसके लिए अंडा-करी, आलू की भुजिया और भात बनाया। गरम-गरम दो पराँठे भी सेंक दिए।

वह अपनी पसंद का खाना देखकर प्रसन्न था।

"मैंने ठीक नहीं कहा जी? रही बात लोगों की तो उन्हें पता नहीं चलेगा। यह मेरा दावा है या फिर मायके जाने दिया करो हफ्ते में एक बार, वहाँ से आठ-दस बोतलें ले आया करूँगी, आपको किसी चीज की कमी नहीं होगी।" वह उससे घुल-मिलकर बातें कर रही थी।

"अस्पताल चलोगी क्या?" वह जरा द्रवित हुआ।

"रहने दीजिए! वैसे ही आपके पास पैसे नहीं हैं, अच्छा लगे तो दो दिन के लिए मुझे सैदा भेज दीजिए!"

"मैं कैसे रहूँगा तुम्हारे बिना?" वह मुँह का कौर चबाते हुए बोला।

"आप भी छुट्टी लेकर आ जाना, फिर दोनों वापस आ जाएँगे।" उसने पटाक्षेप किया।

दूसरे दिन ससुर को आया देख वह हड़बड़ा गया। उसे दाल में कुछ काला प्रतीत हुआ, "वह कल से ही जाने की रट लगाए हुए है और आज यह आ गया बिना किसी सूचना के!"

"कैसे आना हुआ पापाजी का?" उसने मालती से पूछा था।

"माँ की तबीयत खराब है, उन्होंने मुझे बुलाया है, प्लीज न मत करिएगा। पता नहीं कैसी हालत है उनकी।" वह रोहन के आगे गिड़गिड़ा रही थी।

पापा को उसने पहले ही समझा दिया था, फोन की चर्चा न करने के लिए। वह टालमटोल करता रहा, किंतु उसे रोक न सका।

"आपको मेरी कसम है, जल्दी-से-जल्दी आ जाना मेरे घर! मैं आपका इंतजार करूँगी।" मालती ने विधिवत् विदाई ली।

❑

"ऐसी क्या बात हो गई बेटी! हम लोग एक़दम से हड़बड़ा गए थे। कहीं इस प्रकार फोन किया जाता है?" माँ ने स्नेह भरी झिड़की दी। उत्तर में उसने ब्लाउज उतारकर माँ के हाथ में दे दिया। सीना, कमर, पीठ, पेट सब जगह ढेरों चवन्नी के बराबर जले के घाव, ढेरों दाग, साया उतारकर जाँघों के घाव दिखाए, पेट की चोट से उसका गर्भस्राव हो गया था। रक्तस्राव अब भी जारी था। माँ उसे हृदय से लगाए देर तक रोती रही। पापा ने अस्पताल ले जाकर इलाज करवाया। चार माह में उसका वजन दस किलो कम हो गया था। चेहरा श्रीहीन, गाल पिचके और सामने के दाँत बड़े दिखने लगे थे, वह तो माँ से भी बड़ी नजर आ रही थी।

"कुछ खातिरदारी करनी चाहिए पतिदेव की! आना तो पक्का है।" क्योंकि उसे पूरा विश्वास था कि वह उसके मनोभावों से अपरिचित था।

उसके सारे गोल धब्बे एक साथ जल उठे, वह ऐसे छटपटाई जैसे ताजे फोड़े रगड़ खाकर अभी फूट रहे हों।

वादे के अनुसार घर के पिछवाड़े मटकी चढ़ाकर एक नंबर की दारू

उतरवाई। इसके तेज को सहना सबके बस की बात नहीं।

तीसरे दिन एक जिम्मेदार पति की तरह वह आ पहुँचा। सास का हाल-चाल पूछा, सबने पहले जैसे ही मान-सम्मान किया, वह पूरी तरह आश्वस्त था। तालाब से मारकर लाई गई रोहू मछली और हाथ की उतारी शराब! "मजा आ गया भई ससुराल का।" उसके लिए अलग कमरे की व्यवस्था थी।

"बड़े गुरु हैं। जानते हैं बेटी-दामाद मिलना-जुलना चाहेंगे या हो सकता है मालती ने ही होशियारी से यह व्यवस्था करवाई हो।" नशा गहराता जा रहा था। वह मालती के दबे पाँव आकर बगल में सो जाने का इंतजार कर रहा था। नंबर एक अपना असर दिखा रही थी, आँखें मुँदी जा रही थीं।

नींद और नशे के प्रभाव से वह बेसुध हुआ जा रहा था कि कमरे में कुछ हलचल हुई, कुछ परछाइयाँ झिलमिलाईं। हाथ-पैरों में कुछ तनाव का अनुभव हुआ। लगा जैसे उसे कसकर बाँधा जा रहा है। चढ़ने से पहले ही उसका सारा नशा हिरन हो गया। हाथ में डंडे लिये चार युवक और चप्पल लिये चार युवतियाँ धीरे-धीरे उसकी ओर बढ़ रही थीं। आसन्न संकट देख उसकी सारी हेकड़ी निकल गई। वह घिघियाने लगा।

पहला डंडा पड़ने से पहले ही वह चीखने लगा।

"अरे! मुझे क्यों मारते हो? दामाद की ऐसी खातिर की जाती है तुम्हारे गाँव में⋯ऽ⋯ऽ?"

तड़ातड़!⋯तड़ातड़! चारों ओर से डंडे बरसने लगे। उसकी चीख कमरे में गूँजती रही। लड़कियाँ उसके सिर पर चप्पल बरसा रही थीं।

"जिसने तेरे साथ जीने-मरने की कसमें खाईं, उसे अकेली पाकर मारता है? ये ऽ⋯ऽ ले ऽ⋯ऽ जरा ढंग से दो तो दो-चार हाथ!" यह पड़ोस में रहनेवाली लड़की थी, शादी में बहुत लाड़ लड़ा रही थी। उसकी कीलदार चप्पल उसके चेहरे पर पड़ी थी।

"इसके कपड़े फाड़ दो!" एक महिला ने आदेश दिया। किसी ने इधर से खींचा, किसी ने उधर से, कपड़े फट गए, वह नंग-धड़ंग पड़ा था इतने लोगों के बीच।

"इसे जले का दर्द बहुत आनंद देता है, बेचारा दामाद है, खातिर करो

इसकी!" वही औरत फिर बोली। चारों युवकों के हाथों में सिगरेटें नाच उठीं।

"अरे! अरे ऽ···ऽ···ऽ···ऽ रे! मुझे मत जलाओ मेरे बाप! छोड़ दो, तुम्हारे पाँव पड़ता हूँ ऊ···ऊ···अरे बाप रे, जला डाला हैवानों ने।" वह चिल्ला-चिल्लाकर रो रहा था।

"पेट, पीठ, बाँहें, चेहरा सब हो गया?"

"अभी जाँघों के बीच बाकी है।" एक ने निर्लिप्त भाव से कहा। "नहीं बाप! मुझे छोड़ दो। मालती! ओ मालती! कहाँ हो तुम? बचाओ मुझे इनसे!"

"मैं पुलिस का जवान हूँ, बाद की भी सोचो जरा! दूर हटो मुझसे!" वह पलंग पर बँधे-बँधे कसमसा रहा था।

"हाँ ऽ···ऽ!" उसने निःश्वास छोड़ी

"अच्छा लगा न ऽ···ऽ जीजाजी?" उसने जैसे उसकी बात सुनी ही न हो।

"अब थोड़ा रगड़कर नमक-मिर्च डाल देते हैं, पूरा आनंद ले लीजिए।" वह युवक पूरी तरह संजीदगी से बोल रहा था।

"भगवान् के लिए मुझे माफ कर दो! मैं कान पकड़ता हूँ, किसी को नहीं जलाऊँगा।" वह पूरी ताकत से छटपटाया।

"भैया! बहुत हुआ, अब इसे छोड़ दो! अपनी करनी का फल भोगे जाकर!" मालती दरवाजे पर हाथ जोड़े खड़ी थी।

□

अकेला

साल भर से घर में छाई हुई मुर्दनी को भंग हुआ पा रहा था वह। दादी रसोई में कुछ तल रही थीं, जिसकी मीठी सुगंध से घर भरा जा रहा था। लगा जैसे शुद्ध देशी घी के पुए बना रही हैं।

"दादी···! दादी···!···!! जरा एक कप चाय के लिए कह देना विन्नी से!"

"आ रही हूँ देव, मैं ही आ रही हूँ चाय के साथ कुछ और भी लेकर, बैठो जरा सा!" दादी के स्वर में इतने दिनों से एकाकार हुई उदासी का कहीं कोई अंश भी उसकी पकड़ में नहीं आया।

"कुंजू अभी स्कूल से नहीं आया दादी?" उसने जूते-मोजे उतारते हुए पूछा। बाथरूम जाते हुए उसने सुना।

"आ रहा होगा बेटा, उनके स्कूल में कोई प्रोग्राम होनेवाला है, कुंजू नाटक में भाग ले रहा है। इसीलिए एक घंटे बाद में छोड़ते हैं।"

"अच्छा अभिनय करता है कुंजू, चलो ठीक है, जैसे खुश रहे, वैसे ही सही।" वह सोच रहा था।

हाथ-पैर धोकर तौलिए से मुँह पोंछता वह सिद्धेश्वरी के पास आ गया। इस समय प्याज के पकौड़े छन्न-मन्न करते सिंक रहे थे। अच्छा लगा उसे, चाहे जिस कारण से हो, दादी सामान्य जीवन में वापस तो आ रही हैं। साल-भर से ऊपर हो गया था उन्हें हँसते हुए देखे। देव जब भी घर आता, उससे अपने हजार दुखड़े रोतीं और हर बार अपनी किस्मत को दोष देतीं, जैसे देव उनका कोई बड़ा हो।

"बस अब कुंजू आता ही होगा, ले तब तक तू अपनी पसंद के पकौड़े खा! मैं चाय ले आती हूँ।"

"अरे दादी! यह आप की बाँह पर क्या हुआ?" देव ने उनकी बाँह पकड़कर दाहिनी हथेली पलट दी। कलाई के पास की त्वचा जली हुई थी।

"कैसे जल गई दादी, कुछ लगाया भी नहीं अब तक?" वह हाथ में रखी प्लेट टेबल पर रख बरनॉल लेने दूसरे कमरे में तेजी से चला गया।

"अरे कुछ नहीं रे! तू परेशान न हो। मुझे कुछ याद तो रहता नहीं, गरम झारा उठाया और भूल गई कि अभी-अभी इससे भजिये तल रही थी, बस छू गया जरा-सा।" सिद्धेश्वरी ने लापरवाही से कह दिया।

"अरे दादी! ऐसा काम मत किया करो तो, मैं अपनी पसंद की चीजें खाए बिना ही रह जाऊँगा, जब नहीं होता तो क्यों करती हो?" बरनाल लगाते-लगाते वह क्षुब्ध स्वर में बोला।

जिम्मेदारियाँ बढ़ाकर परिस्थितियों ने जैसे अड़ंगी मारकर गिरा दिया हो। उसकी जिम्मेदारी तो थी ही, कुंजू की भी आ पड़ी। छोड़ कैसे दे, अपना रक्त है। न उन्हें सुबह चैन, न रात को। महरी ऊपरी काम कर देती है, वह स्वयं तैयार होते-होते कुंजू की तैयारी कराता है, दादी सभी का नाश्ता, टिफिन बनाती हैं। दादाजी की पूरी सेवा-टहल बजाती हैं, घर का रख-रखाव, आना-जाना, सारा कुछ तो उन्हीं के सिर पर है।

"ले चिंता मत कर बेटा! रसोई करनेवाले को इतना-उतना लगता ही रहता है। ठीक हो जाएगा, तू पकौड़े खा ले।" उन्होंने उसे बहला दिया।

"लो फिर तुम भी खाओ!" देव ने एक पकौड़ा सिद्धेश्वरी के मुँह में डाल दिया, फिर एक-एक पकौड़ा उठा-उठाकर खाने लगा। इतने में कुंजू भी आ गया, मुँह सूखा, बाल बिखरे, कपड़े मैले, सोफे पर बस्ता फेंका और वैसे ही देव से लिपट गया। "भइया! आज मुझे एक लड़के ने मारा, मैं गिर पड़ा, देखो मेरे कपड़े गंदे हो गए।" वह रोने लगा। उसे देव ने अपनी गोद में बैठा लिया।

"मैं कल स्कूल जाकर उसे डाँटूँगा, तुम परेशान न हो कुंजू, जाओ कपड़े बदलकर मुँह हाथ धो लो!" उसने कुंजू के बाल सँवारे।

"अरे, मेरे बच्चे को किस शरारती ने मारा?" सिद्धेश्वरी दौड़ी आईं।

"कुछ नहीं दादी, वह दोस्त ही है मेरा। छोड़ो! अब मार दिया तो मार दिया।" कुंजू ने सयाने की तरह बात सँभालने की कोशिश की और अंदर के कमरे में जाकर कपड़े बदलने लगा। बड़ा भावुक है कुंजू, नौवें वर्ष में लगा है, परंतु छोटे बच्चे जैसे बार-बार देव के सीने से चिपकता रहता है, झट आँखों में आँसू भर आएँगे, झट होंठ मुसकराने लगेंगे, इतनी-सी उम्र में सहा भी तो बहुत है न उसने, अभी इसी इतवार को तो दिव्या की बरसी थी, लंबी, छरहरी, गोरी नारी तीखे नैन-नक्शवाली दिव्या से जब दादी ने पापा की शादी तय की, तब उससे पूछा था एक बार "बेटा, अकेले कब तक जीवन की गाड़ी चलेगी? अच्छी लड़की मिल रही है, उसकी भी माँ नहीं है, वह तेरा दर्द समझेगी, फिर बेटा, माँ कहे बिना तू इतनी बड़ी जिंदगी कैसे गुजारेगा।" वह उनकी गोद में सिर छिपाकर बहुत रोया था।

"नहीं दादी, मुझे दूसरी माँ नहीं चाहिए, मैं ऐसे ही ठीक हूँ। दादी ने पापा के पक्ष में दलीलें दी थीं, अपनी उम्र का हवाला दिया और एक दिन दिव्या आ गई, उसकी माँ के स्थान पर। दादी को उसने देखा था, कमरे में जाकर रोती और आँगन में आकर औरतों के बीच नाचती हुई।

"मेरा उजड़ा घर बस रहा है, मैं नई बहू को पूरे मन से अपनाऊँगी, ताकि उसे लगे कि उसकी माँ अभी मरी नहीं है।" अंदर-ही-अंदर बुदबुदातीं—

'यदि तूने हमें छोड़ा न होता तो ये दिन देखने को क्यों मिलते? वे आँसुओं से आँचल भिगातीं!'

उसे सिखाया गया, 'माँ' कहो दिव्या को। उसने कहा भी, लेकिन इसके अवसर बहुत कम आए, कहाँ वह नई-नवेली दुलहन और कहाँ वह दस वर्ष का बालक! मातृभाव जागा ही नहीं दिव्या के हृदय में। खैर, दादी के कारण उसे कहीं कोई कमी का एहसास नहीं होने पाया। हाँ! पापा 125 प्रतिशत दिव्या के हो गए। शायद वे अपने अतीत से बेहद भयभीत थे अंदर-ही-अंदर।

"चलो जैसी भी हो, घर में एक औरत तो है, कुछ करे या न करे, चलेगा।" दिव्या को सबसे अधिक दादी और देव से समस्या थी।

"मैं इतने बड़े बच्चे की माँ लगती हूँ? कह दो इससे! सबके सामने माँ

न कहा करे!" कैसी निर्दयता से मारा था पापा ने उसे।

"न कपड़े का रंग-ढंग न चेहरे का, सब के बीच चला आया माँ-माँ कहते पार्टी में, समझ नाम की तो कोई चीज ही नहीं है इसके दिमाग में।"

"यह क्या कर रहे हो अभय? इतना ही था तो अपने साथ उसे भी तैयार करके ले गए होते।" दादी आई थीं बीच में, उन्हें पूरी ताकत से ढकेल दिया था उन्होंने, धड़ाम से गिरी थीं वे। वह तो डर के मारे रोना भी भूल गया था।

"देव! घर साफ कर ले, बगीचे में पानी डाल दे, सीढ़ियाँ धो डाल। टॉयलेट की दीवारें गंदी हो गईं हैं, कपड़े से रगड़कर धो डाल, तेरे पापा को अच्छा लगेगा। सी.एम.ओ. हैं आखिर वे। गंदगी से बहुत चिढ़ते हैं। अरे!! अभी तक नहीं हुआ? यह लड़का तो किसी काम का नहीं है। इतनी देर में जरा सा काम नहीं कर पाया।"

"कर तो रहा हूँ।" उसने बेचारगी से उसकी ओर देखा था उस दिन।

"जबान चलाता है? ले चला जबान!" उसके सिर पर चप्पल की भरपूर चोट पड़ी थी। फिर तो कोई जगह खाली नहीं बची। वह रोने लगा।

"रोएगा तो और दूँगी खाने भर को, ठूँसने के लिए है किलो भर, जरा सा काम कहो तो दस ठो नाटक! चल जल्दी नाली साफ कर ले! आज स्वीपर नहीं आया है।" वह बहते आँसुओं की अनदेखी कर जल्दी-जल्दी झाड़ू चलाने लगा था।

"अच्छा हो गया? जा दुकान से सामान ले आ!"

"भूख लगी है माँ!"

"जा फ्रिज में रोटी रखी है, नमक के साथ खा ले! और हाँ, आज स्कूल मत जाना, मेरे दोनो भाई आनेवाले हैं, उनकी सेवा करनी होगी। तेरे पापा ने कहा है, देव सब सँभाल लेगा।"

पसीने से लथपथ वह दादी के पास आया था।

"कुछ खाया सुबह से?" चेहरे की रंगत देखते ही उनकी आँखों में पीड़ा उतर आई थी।

"खाऊँगा दादी।"

"अरे! दोपहर ढल रही है, तू कर क्या रहा था अब तक?" वे जल्दी से

कुछ खाने के लिए ले आई थीं। "आज जरा काम था दादी!"

"यह तो रोज ही देख रही हूँ।" दादी की पीड़ा का अनुभव करके वह सामान्य होने की कोशिश करने लगा था।

"उसके लिए बनाती हो तो सबके लिए बनाओ! हम क्या आपके बच्चे नहीं हैं?" उसने रसोई की तरफ झाँकना भी छोड़ दिया था। उसके दोनों भाइयों की खातिर करते-करते दादी को दाँतों पसीना आ रहा था। दिव्या के स्वभाव के कारण वर्षों पुरानी महरी और रसोइया काम छोड़कर चले गए थे। पापा के सिर पर उन दिनों न जाने कौन सा भूत सवार रहता था, घर आते ही खोज-खोज कर दादी और उसकी खबर लेते रहते।

"तुम ही बिगाड़ रही हो लड़के को, तुम्हारे कारण ही मेरा घर उजड़ा था, अब क्या चाहती हो, मैं फिर से रँडुआ हो जाऊँ? तो सुन लो, अब ऐसा नहीं होगा। तुम्हारी एक न चलेगी।" दादी के आँसू अपनी व्यथा-कथा कहते। वह घुटकर रह जाता। कभी-कभी तो दरवाजा बंद करके फूट-फूट कर रोता।

"भगवान्! तूने मुझे जन्म ही क्यों दिया? मेरे कारण परिवार में हमेशा कलह मचा रहता है।" बहुत जल्दी ही दिव्या ने अपना चूल्हा अलग कर लिया। अब तो बस, जब लानत-मलानत करना हो या लड़ना हो, तभी बातचीत होती।

साल के अंदर ही सर्वसुविधायुक्त दो मंजिला मकान बनकर तैयार हो गया। देव के लिए स्पष्ट हो गया कि वह दादा-दादी के साथ रहे या नाना-नानी के साथ, नए घर में उसके लिए कोई स्थान नहीं था। दादा-दादी ने उसे अपनी गोद में स्थान दिया। एक बार पुनः बच्चेवाले बन गए। इसी बीच इस कुंजू का जन्म हुआ। उसे तो अच्छा लगा था, माँ की गोद में छोटा सा भाई, हाँ! उसने तो सदा माँ ही समझा था। भले ही ममता भरा हाथ उसके सिर पर कभी न फिरा हो। थी तो आखिर माँ ही।

"देव! आज मेरी सहेली आ रही है दिल्ली से अपनी पोती के साथ, देखना यदि तुझे अच्छी लगे तो⋯!?

"क्या दादी तुम्हें तो बस यही एक काम रह गया है। अभी-अभी नौकरी लगी है, थोड़ा धीरज रखो, फिर हमें इतने भयानक हादसे से गुजरे दिन ही

कितने हुए हैं ? थोड़ा तो वक्त लगेगा न सँभलने में। कुंजू को भी जरा सामान्य होने दो।" उसकी निगाहें झुकी हुई थीं।

दुःख भुलाने से भूलता है बेटा, इस सीने पर जवान बेटे और दो-दो बहुओं की मौत का बोझ है। सामने तुम न होते तो हमारे जीने का बहाना ही क्या था ? सोचती हूँ अपनी आँखों के सामने तुम्हारा घर बसता देख लूँ, जब तुम्हारी ही रोटी का ठिकाना न रहेगा तो कुंजू को कैसे पालोगे ?" उनका स्वर आर्द्र हो उठा, आँखों से आँसू बह चले।

"दादी ! आप ही समझाती हो, आप ही रोती हो, हम हैं न ! एक-दूसरे के लिए ?" उसने दादी को कंधे से लगाकर सांत्वाना दी।

दरवाजे पर दस्तक हो रही थी, उसने आगे बढ़कर दरवाजा खोला। ऑटोवाला सामान उतारकर रख चुका था। दादी की हम उम्र एक महिला एक सुंदर सी युवती के साथ दरवाजे पर खड़ी थी। संस्कारवश उसने महिला के पैर छू लिये। युवती ने 'हाय !' कहकर उसका अभिवादन किया। वह उनका सामान अंदर ले आया। दादी अपनी गीली आँखें पोंछकर उस महिला के गले मिलीं और बड़े अपनेपन के साथ ड्राइंगरूम में ले आईं। वे उनके आगत-स्वागत में ऐसी लगीं कि अपने सारे दुःख जैसे भूल ही गईं। वह अपनी पकौड़े की प्लेट पकड़े अपने कमरे में चला गया। अनायास उसकी नजर सामने की दीवार पर जाकर ठहर गई। वहाँ पापा की फोटो फूलों के हार पहने दीवार पर टँगी थी। छह फुटे जवान, पापा का रंग अंगारे की तरह दहकता था, थके होने पर चिड़चिड़ाते थे। अस्पताल की हजारों समस्याएँ घर में भी उनका पीछा नहीं छोड़ती थीं। कभी प्रसन्न होते तो अत्यंत मीठी मुसकान छा जाती चेहरे पर। कभी-कभी ठहाके भी सुने थे उसने।

उन्होंने सोचा था, अलग रहकर वे अपने नए परिवार के साथ खुश होंगे, दादी और देव नाम के दोनों काँटे अपने जीवन से निकालकर फेंक दिए थे उन्होंने। अकसर घर पर बड़ी-बड़ी पार्टियाँ होतीं, दिव्या भाँति-भाँति के श्रृंगार करती, कभी-कभी पापा उसे भी बुला लेते, उसने कभी उनकी आज्ञा का उल्लंघन नहीं किया। शायद कभी ममता की खोई हुई छाँव मिल जाए।

एक दिन सुबह-सुबह कोहराम मचा मोहल्ले में, सभी दौड़े, पापा का

जिस्म उनके कमरे में पंखे से लटक रहा था। दिव्या पछाड़ खा-खा-कर रो रही थी। दादी-दादा रोते-रोते बेहोश होकर गिर पड़े थे। उसकी आशा पर तुषारापात हो चुका था, अब जब पापा ही न रहे तो वह किसे मनाएगा? किसे समझाएगा कि उनके अंश से जन्म लेकर उसने कोई अपराध नहीं किया।

माँ के समय तो वह अबोध था। पापा के समय उसने जीवन के इस कटु सत्य का गहराई से अनुभव किया। आनन-फानन में दिव्या के मायकेवालों ने सबकुछ अपने हाथ में ले लिया। अंत्येष्टि में भी दादा-दादी परायों की तरह दूर-दूर रखे गए।

थोड़ी भाग-दौड़ के बाद दिव्या को स्वास्थ्य विभाग में नौकरी मिल गई (अनुकंपा नियुक्ति)। वह कुंजू के साथ मायके चली गई और वहीं से ड्यूटी करने लगी। महराजपुर के घर में ताला बंद हो गया। लुटे-पिटे से दादा-दादी और हतप्रभ-सा देव, आते-जाते घर में लगे ताले को देख-देखकर रोया करते।

"तबाह हो गया परिवार, बेटा गया अपना, अब क्या रह गया? जहाँ रहे, बहू अपने बच्चे के साथ खुश रहे। हाँ, पड़ोसियों के मुँह से सुना अवश्य गया कि देव और सिद्धेश्वरी का नाम लेकर दिव्या हमेशा लड़ती रहती थी कि तुम अपनी माँ और बेटे से मिलते-जुलते हो। बड़ी की तरह मैं भी मर जाऊँगी, परंतु यूँ ही नहीं मरूँगी, तुम लोगों को फँसा कर मरूँगी। संभवतः इसी दिन-रात के कलह ने पहाड़ जैसे—आदमी से कायराना फैसला करवाया था। अब तो देव के लिए ही जीना है, मना लिया था दोनों ने खुद को।

अकाल मृत्यु की यह पहली घटना नहीं थी इस घर में, पापा के पहले माँ ने भी तो स्वयं को आग के हवाले कर दिया सात साल के देव का मोह त्यागकर। सी.एम.ओ. होने के कारण पापा ज्यादा समय घर पर नहीं दे पाते थे। कहते हैं, माँ निराशा और संदेह के गहरे गर्त में गिर पड़ी थीं। उन्हें लगता कि उनका पति तो सैकड़ों सुंदर स्त्रियों से घिरा रहता है, अवश्य उनसे उसके संबंध होंगे, तभी तो वह 'सूप के कोने' जैसी पड़ी घर में मक्खियाँ हाँका करती है। दादी के समझाने पर भी कोई असर नहीं हुआ था उन पर। ऐसा ही तो सुना है देव ने दादी से।

परमेश्वरी और सपना को आए लगभग महीना भर हो चुका था। गरीब परिवार की पढ़ी-लिखी लड़की दादी को तो सोलह आने जँच गई थी। वह घर के सारे काम करती, दोनों सहेलियाँ बैठी बातें करती रहतीं अपने जमाने की। वह रोज-रोज नए-नए व्यंजन बनाती, दादाजी से दोस्ती गाँठ ली थी उसने।

कुंजू से गहरी छन रही थी सपना की। देव वैसे तो लड़कियों से कम ही बोलता है, किंतु सपना से बोलने लगा था।

"सिद्धू देख! तुझे यदि पैसे का लालच हो तो जाने दे, नहीं तो सपना जैसी लड़की आज के जमाने में दीया लेकर खोजने से भी नहीं मिलेगी तुझे। तेरा घर सँभाल लेगी। तू देखती रहना केवल।" परमेश्वरी दादी को विश्वास दिला रही थी। देव की कनपटियों पर हथौड़े की चोट पड़ी, उसे गोद में लेकर दिव्या ने क्या कहा था—

"मैं देव को अपनी जान से ज्यादा प्यार करूँगी!" खूब भोगा था देव ने उसके प्यार को।

"देव! परमेश्वरी दादी पूछ रही हैं, बता दे तुझे सपना पसंद है या नहीं?" साफ-साफ पूछा था दादी ने उससे। अच्छी है दादी, परंतु शादी का विचार अभी नहीं है मेरा। उसने कहा तो था, किंतु लगता है किसी ने सुना नहीं था। सपना उसका विशेष खयाल रख रही थी।

उस दिन वह कुंजू को लेकर अस्पताल गया था, जब ड्यूटी से आया तो उसकी लाल आँखें देखते ही समझ गया था कि उसकी तबीयत ठीक नहीं है। दादी ने कहा था कि यह कल से ही अनमना है, दिखा दो जरा डॉक्टर को। अस्पताल में बड़ी भीड़ थी, शायद कोई दुर्घटना घटी थी। लोग रोनी सूरत बनाए खड़े थे। यही हाल तो उनका भी हुआ था न वर्ष भर पहले, दिव्या मीटिंग में जा रही थी हेड ऑफिस, ट्रेन पर चढ़ते समय हाथ छूट गया और ट्रेन चल पड़ी, वह पटरी पर गिरी और अनेक टुकड़ों में विभक्त हो गई। बोरे में भर कर लाना पड़ा था पोस्टमार्टम के लिए। इस बार भी मायकेवाले झूम गए थे, सबकुछ किया उन्होंने, सारा घर साफ कर गए, बैंक में कहाँ क्या था, ये तो वे ही जानें, घर की वसीयत थी दिव्या के भाई के नाम। बस कुंजू को पहुँचा गए तेरहवीं के दो दिन बाद।

"माँजी! कुंजू आपकी अमानत है, आपका खून है। यह आप के पास ही शोभा देता है, जैसे देव को बड़ा किया, वैसे ही इसे भी पाल लेंगी आप, हमें विश्वास है," फिर तो साल भर हो गए कोई खोज-खबर नहीं ली किसी ने।

सपना का रंग चढ़कर रहेगा मुझ पर, कैसे मना करूँ? मुझ जन्म के अभागे, प्यार के भूखे को इतना चाहने लगी है वह। कैसे बचाए स्वयं को देव? उसे वायदों की सच्चाई का ज्ञान है, जो कुछ सिखाया है समय ने, उसे वह भूल नहीं सका है।

रात जब दादी-दादा सो गए, तब सपना आई थी उसके कमरे में। उसकी आँखें प्रश्न पूछ रही थीं। "मुझमें क्या कमी है, जो मुझे ठुकरा रहे हो?"

"सपना, कल सुबह बात करते हैं, मैं कुंजू को सुला रहा हूँ, तुम्हें पता है न इसकी तबीयत खराब है?" उसने सहजता से कहा था।

"आप के जीवन में कुंजू के सिवा किसी और का कोई महत्त्व है भी या नहीं।" वह झुँझला गई थी।

"मैंने कहा न, कल बात करेंगे।"

वह पैर पटकती चली गई थी। दादी के सामने पेशी हुई थी उसकी, "बोलो देव क्यों उलझाकर रखा है?"

"क्या बोलूँ दादी?"

"सपना से तुम्हारी शादी पक्की कर दूँ न?"

"नहीं दादी! अभी मैं इस चक्कर में नहीं पड़ना चाहता, मुझे क्षमा कर दीजिए।" उसकी निगाहें धरती पर जमी हुई थीं।

"कारण बताने की कृपा करोगे?" दादी का चेहरा अपमान से पीला पड़ गया था। उन्हें अपने देव से ऐसी उम्मीद नहीं थी।

"जब तक कुंजू बड़ा नहीं हो जाता, मैं सिर्फ इसी के लिए जिऊँगा।" उसके स्वर में दृढता थी।

"अरे बेटा! कुंजू की भली लगाई, बहू रहेगी तो तुझे कुंजू की क्या चिंता करनी पड़ेगी?" दादी के चेहरे की बुझी हुई रौनक वापस लौटी।

"दादी जिस भैंसे के सींग होती है, वही उन्हें सँभालता है, किसी अन्य पर जिम्मेदारी डालना मैं उचित नहीं समझता, बस्स और यह समझ मेरे

अनुभव से आई है।" वह सामान्य था।

"तो क्या तुम्हें मेरी पोती पर विश्वास नहीं है?" परमेश्वरी ने रोते हुए पूछा था।

"दादीजी, मुझे स्वयं पर भरोसा नहीं है। अकेलेपन की पीड़ा मेरे मन में हद से ज्यादा है, कहीं मैं इतना स्वार्थी न हो जाऊँ कि कुंजू एकदम अकेला रह जाए मेरी तरह।"

□

और वह रो पड़ा!

रोना कौन कहे, आज तक उसे उदास भी किसी ने नहीं देखा। जब उसकी माँ का देहांत हुआ था, तब वह मात्र ग्यारह वर्ष का था। मोहल्ले की औरतें उसे छाती से चिपका-चिपकाकर रो रही थीं, किंतु उसकी आँख से एक बूँद भी न टपकी। होंठ फैले रहे, जैसे आँसू रोकने के लिए हँस रहा हो।

"अभी लइकाई बा, का जानसू जे का भ गईल।" औरतें उसके भोलेपन पर तरस खाती रो रही थीं, वह फैले होंठों से माँ का दाह कर्म कर आया था। उसने कभी किसी की बात नहीं काटी। बाप के बारे में वह कुछ नहीं जानता। माँ ने कभी बताया नहीं। कुछ लोग कहते हैं कि वह किसी साधु की औलाद है, जिसने लोकापवाद के भय से कभी अपना नाम नहीं दिया उसे। चूँकि उसकी माँ इस गाँव की बेटी थी, इसलिए सारे लोग उसके नाना-नानी, मामा-मामी या मौसा-मौसी, दीदी-भइया लगते थे। जहाँ चार काम करता, वहीं खाकर सो जाता। उसे आया देखकर मामियों की गगरी खाली हो जाती, आटा खतम हो जाता या नाली जाम हो जाती।

"जा त बबुआ दूगो लकड़ी फारि द! हम तहरा के चाह बना दीं।" बहुत दिनों से पड़ी पेड़ की जड़ फाड़ते-फाड़ते कब बेरा उतर जाता, पता ही न चलता। सबके खाने के बाद कुछ ताजा, कुछ बासी करके मिल ही जाता पेट भरने लायक। भइया लोगों को स्कूल पहुँचाने जाना उसे बहुत अच्छा लगता।

"कोई मारे तो भइया को बचाना रघुबर! यह तुम्हारा छोटा भाई है। गुरुजी मारें तो अपना हाथ रोक देना। रात में तुम को कढ़ी-भात खिलाऊँगी।" लड़के कूट-कूटकर मारते, गालियों की तो कोई बात ही न थी। वह अपनी देह

के लाल-नीले दाग हँसते हुए दिखाता, जैसे प्रसाद पाया हो। पूरे समय स्कूल में बैठता, उसे पाठ अपने आप याद हो जाता। भाइयों से पूछे गए प्रश्नों के उत्तर वह दरवाजे के बाहर से तुरंत दे देता। गुरुजी कई डंडे लगाते।

"क्यों बे भाड़े के टट्टू, तुझसे पूछा क्या किसी ने?" वह दाँत निकाले मार खाता। मास्टर लोगों की मार के डर से बच्चे पढ़ने आने से डरते थे, यहाँ तक कि घर छोड़कर भाग जाते थे। उस समय स्कूल में दर्ज संख्या इतनी कम हो गई थी कि तीन मास्टर अन्यत्र भेजे जाने की बात चल रही थी। उसके हँसते-हँसते ना-ना करते-करते भी बहिनजी ने उसका नाम न जाने क्या गुनताड़ा करके कक्षा चार में लिख लिया।

"न कपड़ा न लत्ता, न किताब न कॉपी, न कलम, न दवात, का पढ़ूँगा और पढ़कर कौन सा लिखनी करूँगा?" वह शरमा-शरमाकर अपने में सिमटा जा रहा था। उसके गुलाबी चेहरे पर हँसी लगातार नृत्य कर रही थी।

"अपने बेटे का कपड़ा-किताब-कॉपी सब हम तुमको देंगे, और हाँ, पढ़ना भी जरूरी नहीं है, नाम चलने दो! रहो तो हाजिरी बोल दिया करो बस! हमको अपने गाँव में रखना चाहते हो तो।" वह जी भरकर हँसा था। 'आप मिया मँगते द्वार खड़े दरवेश', वह कैसे बहिनजी को गाँव में रख सकता है? हाँ, गुरुजी की जितनी ताकत मारने की है, उतनी मार अवश्य खा सकता है। दो-चार दिन गाँव में बड़ी हँसाई हुई। मामियाँ उसे बुलाकर बार-बार पूछतीं, "कइसे बोलीं बहिनजी रघुबर?" वह हू-ब-हू नकल उतारता। न जाने क्या हुआ कि गुरुजी ने रघुबर को मारना-पीटना बंद कर दिया। अपने घर का काम कराते और खाना दे दिया करते, उन्हीं के ओसारे के एक कोने में वह बिजली की रोशनी में पढ़ भी लेता। आठवीं में जब बोर्ड परीक्षा का परिणाम निकला तो पूरे स्कूल में वही एक पास हुआ।

"आरे रघुबरवा ने नाक रख ली, वरना यही होता कि मास्टर लोग मुफ्त की तनख्वाह लेते हैं।" बड़े गुरुजी ने आँखों में स्नेह भरकर देखा था उसे। वह मंद-मंद मुसकराता रहा।

"ई रघुबरवा के देखीं जा मजाल कि हमनी के लइकन के फेल करवा के अपने पास हो गइल। बड़ा नू सुरतवल्ला है, अइसा निमकहरामी किया

कि पूछो मत, मास्टर के···धो-धो के बड़ा हुसियार बन गया है जुठखोर कुत्ता, एकर माटी लागो, एकर खटिया कटाउ।" वह हँसता ही रहा। रात में सब फेलवरों ने मिलकर बहुत मारा। वह सब सह गया। उसी रात कलकत्ता जानेवाले जमुना अहीर के पैर पर गिर गया था जाकर, "ए मामा! हमको भी लेते चलो अपने साथ। आपकी सेवा करूँगा! अब यहाँ रहा नहीं जाता। देखो न, बिना मतलब सब लोग परेशान हो रहे हैं, जो पूछा था सो लिख दिए, उतने में समय खत्म हो गया, अब आप ही बताइए, हर एक से कॉपी कैसे बदल सकता था? न हमको पढ़ने की चाहत है, न पास होने की। ये लोग ही अपने बच्चों को बचाने के लिए मुझे स्कूल भेजते थे। वहाँ बहिनजी ने नाम लिख लिया।" उसने मुसकराते हुए विनय की थी। उस रात वह गंगा किनारेवाली अपनी छोटी सी कुटिया छोड़कर निकल गया था। आज वह लॉन में कुरसी डाले अपनी पत्नी के साथ बैठा गंगाजी की ओर से आने वाली ठंडी-ठंडी हवा खाता रहा और अतीत उसके दिमाग में किसी चलचित्र की भाँति कई जीवंत चित्र दिखा रहा था।

"वे दोनों कौन हैं? लगता है, उसी से मिलने आ रहे हैं। कोट का ऐसा बिरला ही कोई होगा, जो उससे मिलकर न गया हो। होंगे कोई संगी-साथी बचपन के।" वह उसी ओर देख रहा था।

"लोग कह रहे थे कि रघुबरवा है। अब तो रघुनाथ राय हो गया है। हमारे ही साथ तो पढ़ता था, बाहर निकलकर देखो, कैसे ठाट-बाट बन गए हैं इसके। यहाँ तो आँख पर घुनघुटी झूमती रहती थी। अच्छा रामजी भइया, चलो मिल लेते हैं, कुछ भी हो, आखिर हमारा संगी है!" वे आपस में धीमे स्वर में बातें कर रहे थे, जिसे वह सुन नहीं पाया।

"अरे भइया, आज तक समझ में नहीं आ रहा था कि इतना सुंदर घर कौन बनवा रहा है, बाहरे-बाहर यही बनवा रहा था, एक बड़ी गाड़ी में सामान आया है, कल से ही लोग जा रहे हैं मिलने, हम तो सोचते ही रह गए, गोरुआरी से फुरसत मिले तब तो, बेटा-बहू को दूध चाहिए, अपना तो उन्हें टी.वी. मोबाइल से फुरसत नहीं है, हम ही जवान हुए हैं।" रामजी के मुँह से अंतर की पीड़ा बोल उठी।

जब ये उसके नए बने घर के सामने पहुँचे, तब अँधेरा हो चुका था। वह उन्हें देखते ही उठकर खड़ा हो गया। उसकी आँखों में अपरिचय के भाव देख ये स्वयं बोल पड़े, "नहीं पहचाने न रघुबर भाई ? हम तहार रामजी आऽई तहार लालजी!" उनकी आँखें खुशी से छलक आई थीं।

"तहरा लोग के कइसे नहीं पहचानूँगा। तहरा लोग के बस्ता ढोवत-ढोवत आठ पास हो गए थे हम।" वह गर्मजोशी से मिला उनसे।

"इतने दिन कहाँ रहे भाई, कभी गाँव की याद भी नहीं आई क्या ?"

रामजी की बात सुनकर वह अपनी विशिष्ट हँसी हँस पड़ा। "भाई! न गाँव कभी भूला, न तुम लोग ध्यान से उतरे। मैं तो गंगा मइया का बच्चा हूँ। अपने माँ-बाप नहीं थे तो क्या हुआ, गाँव भर के प्यार-दुलार से जी गया। अब जा के संसार के प्रपंच से छुटकारा मिला है। दोनों लड़के अपने पैर पर खड़े हो गए हैं, शादी-बियाह करिये दिया। बस अब गंगाजी के कोरा में अराम करेंगे। तोहार भउजी एही गाँव के बेटी हैं। आप को याद होगा, हम जमुना यादव के संग यहाँ से गए थे, तब ये छोटी थीं। हम यादवजी के साथ काम करते-करते अपना व्यापार बढ़ाते गए। पहिले कपड़े की फेरी लगाई, फिर छोटा सा होटल खोल लिया। गंगा बराबर साथ देती रही। कारोबार साझे में ही था। समय आने पर यादवजी ने हमारी शादी कर दी। उनके स्वर्गवास के बाद गंगा हिस्सेदार बनी। भगवान् ने हमारी मदद की भइया, दोनों बेटे पढ़-लिखकर कमाने दुबई चले गए। तब हम लोग अपने गाँव लौट आए।" वह मुसकराता जा रहा था और बोलता जा रहा था। अभी बातें चल ही रही थीं कि गंगा गरम-गरम पकौड़ियाँ ले आई।

"गंगा बहिन तोहार नांव त लछिमी होना चाहिए। हमरा भइया के कहाँ-से-कहाँ पहुँचाई दिए।" वे दोनों बेहद प्रसन्न थे। थाली भर पकौड़ियाँ पलक झपकते पार कर दीं। उनके पास बताने को क्या था, तीन साल आठ फेल जो हुए तो बस माई-बाबू ने बियाह करके खेती-बारी में लगा दिया। बाल-बच्चे पल-पला गए, चल रही है जिंदगी।

जब से वे वापस आए थे गाँव में, नई रौनक सी आ गई थी। बूढ़े-बूढ़ियों की तो जैसे बन ही आई थी। बड़ा जमघट लगता सुबह-शाम, न जाने

कितना रुपया कमाकर लाया था रघुबर? रोज सुबह-शाम बेटे-बहू का फोन आता—"पैसे की चिंता मत करना पापा। हम और भेज देंगे। जैसे आप लोगों को अच्छा लगे, वैसे ही रहिए।" वाह रे तकदीर रघुबरवा की। लोग सिहाते।

"कवन सुख ये भइया? जाँगर न चले तो बैठे रहो बिना खाए-पिए। पइसा पेट भरेगा क्या? ये समय तो बेटा बहू के साथ चाहिए।" लोग जोड़-घटाना करते रहते। वह हमेशा हँसता रहता। जब बोलता, हँसी की ही बात बोलता, न जाने कितने लोट-पोट करनेवाले किस्से, संस्मरण याद थे उसे। बच्चे-बूढ़े सभी के लिए कुछ-न-कुछ था उसके अनुभव के पिटारे में। गंगा पढ़नेवाली लड़कियों को खाना बनाना सिखाती, होटलवाली होने के कारण उसे पता था कि कौन से व्यंजन को और स्वादिष्ट कैसे बनाया जा सकता है। नई बहुएँ आतीं उससे कलकत्ते के जनजीवन के बारे में पूछने, खास करके बंगाल के काला जादू के बारे में उनके बहुत से प्रश्न होते। गाँववालों की संगति में जाड़े में रामायण होता तो बरसात में महाभारत। आराम से दिन गुजर रहे थे उनके। लोग जब पूछते कि भउजी, आपके बेटे-बहू कब आएँगे? गंगा उदास हो जाती। रघुबर ठठाकर हँसने लगता।

"आएँगे जब खूब रुपया कमा लेंगे, चिंता क्या है? तुम भी तो हमारे बेटे-बहू ही हो! हम दूसरा नहीं मानते, तुम हमें अपना न मानते हो तो बताना।" पूछनेवाला लजाकर चुप हो जाता।

तीन साल तो बीत ही गए होंगे उन्हें वापस आए। गाँव में होनेवाला जुआ बंद हो गया था। लोग काम-धंधे में लगे रहने लगे थे। गाँव से शराब की दुकान उठवाने के लिए उसने गाँववालों को तैयार किया था। धरना-प्रदर्शन, शोर-शराबे के बाद बस्ती के बीच से दुकान उठकर गाँव के बाहर चली गई थी। अब रघुबर की सीख थी कि कोई भी शराब न खरीदे, ताकि दुकान खुद ही बंद हो जाए। इसके लिए दुकान पर कुछ लोग नजर रखे रहते थे। गंगा ने शायद कुछ देखा था, वह तेजी से घर की ओर आ रही थी कि ईंट से भरे ट्रक ने उसे ठोकर मार दी। कोई कुछ कहता या करता, उसके पहले ही वह ट्रक नजरों से ओझल हो गया। गाँव में कोहराम मच गया। औरतें छाती पीट-पीटकर रोने लगीं। रघुबर को एक पल के लिए ऐसा लगा जैसे उसकी आँखों

की ज्योति बुझ गई हो, उसने दाँतों पर दाँत चढ़ाकर सारा आत्मविश्वास समेटा और थोड़ी ही देर में सामान्य जैसा दिखने लगा। बच्चों को फोन लगाने लगा तो लगा ही नहीं। इस समय शायद वे अपने काम पर होंगे। काम के समय मोबाइल बंद रखना पड़ता है, उन्होंने ही बताया था, अतः उनके आने की उम्मीद करना व्यर्थ था। रामजी और लालजी के बेटों ने सारा इंतजाम किया। बहुएँ काका को घेरकर बैठी आठ-आठ आँसू बहाती रहीं। गंगा के शव को पोस्टमार्टम के बाद जब पुलिसवालों ने दिया, तब तक रात हो चुकी थी। रात में तो दाह-संस्कार होता नहीं, इसलिए बर्फ की सिल्ली पर सुलाकर शव को रखा गया।

"हमारी सीता जैसी भउजी हमें छोड़ गईं। गंगामाई उस पापी का नाश करें, जिसने देवी समान भउजी को कुचला।" रामजी रह-रहकर रो पड़ता। रघुबर जैसे काठ हो गया हो। न एक शब्द मुँह से बोल रहा था न उसकी आँखों में जरा भी नमी आई थी।

"ई मरदा पागल-वागल ह का ए दादा? पूरा गाँव गंगा खातिर छछनि-छछनि के रोवता ऽ···आ एकरा आँखि ले पसेइवो नइखे फूटत।" कई महिलाएँ उसे कोस रही थीं।

"अरे, तुम लोग बड़े नीक हो, जरा सा कुछ हुआ कि फें···फें करने लगते हो। रघुबर भइया मर्द हैं मर्द! कितनी भी विपत्ति आए, धीर-गंभीर बने रहते हैं। आखिर कार ओह जमाने के आठ पास हैं, जब पाँच-दस गाँव में सब लिख लोढ़ा-पढ़ पथरा हुआ करते थे। देश-विदेश घूम आए हैं, रोएँगे तब भी तुम्हीं लोग हँसोगे कि देखो, मेहरारू खातिर कइसे रो रहा है, एकरा लाजो नहीं है।" लालजी ने फटकारकर महिलाओं को चुप कराया।

"ए भइया आँसू मत रोको, बह जाने दो, इतना कड़ाई से का हासिल होगा?" रात के अँधेरे में जब अधिकांश लोग सो गए, तब रामजी ने उसके दुःख को पिघलाने की कोशिश की।

"का बोलें भइया? रामजी ने दुःख सहने के लिए ही संसार में भेजा है। अब जब लगा कि सारे दुःख कट गए, तब देह में से जान ही निकाल लिये, उनके बिना अब क्या रह गया रोने-हँसने के लिए?" उसके होंठ ऐसे फैले थे,

जैसे उसकी तकदीर पर हँस रहे हों।

दूसरे दिन सुबह सात बजे नियमानुसार उसने अपने बेटों से फोन पर बातें कीं। उसने गंगा के साथ घटी दुर्घटना की बात छिपा ली, बस इतना कहा, "तुम्हारी माँ बहुत बीमार है, अस्पताल में भरती है, जल्दी-से-जल्दी आने की पूरी कोशिश करना, बेटा।" उसकी आवाज में जरा भी कंपन नहीं था।

"क्या करूँगा बता के? इतनी जल्दी वे कैसे पहुँच पाएँगे?" घबराहट में कहीं और कोई अनवाद न हो जाए, इसलिए वह सच्चाई छिपा ले गया।

दूसरे दिन वह गाँववालों के साथ गंगा को गंगाजी में तिरोहित कर आया। रामजी ने सारे कर्मकांड संपन्न कराने का जिम्मा ले लिया। लालजी ने तेरहीं की जिम्मेदारी ली। गंगा की लगाई नीम के नीचे कुश गाड़कर गाँव भर के नर-नारी उसकी आत्म-शांति के लिए तर्पण करते। पंडित जैसा-जैसा कहते, रघुबर यंत्र की भाँति करता जाता। तेरहीं बीत गई, बेटे नहीं पहुँचे। सब लोग पीठ पीछे अपने मन की भड़ास निकालने लगे थे।

"भगवान् की करनी भी जानी नहीं जाती, गंगा दीदी की कोख से ऐसी औलाद ने जन्म लिया, सोचकर मन कसेला हो जाता है। बीमारी का समाचार सुनकर एक लाख रुपया भेज दिए, जैसे सबकुछ पैसा ही है। आज अगर होते तो बाप को सँभालते, उन्हें देखकर रघुबर भइया को भी थोड़ा अच्छा लगता, मैं तो ऐसी औलाद का कभी मुँह न देखूँ, उनके रहने न रहने से क्या घाटा-नफा है?"

समय के साथ-साथ रघुबर के घर की भीड़ कम होने लगी। वह तो अब भी हर मिलनेवाले से हँसकर ही मिलता, परंतु मिलनेवाले उसकी हँसी में से न जाने कैसे गम के रेशे तलाश लेते।

रामलाल और लालजी ज्यादातर रघुबर के साथ छाया की तरह लगे रहते। अपने घर से खाना बनवाकर लाते और एक साथ तीनों बैठकर खाते। इधर दो-चार दिन से बच्चों के फोन नहीं आ रहे थे। वह चिंतित था।

एक दिन सुबह-सुबह नहा-धोकर तुलसी में जल दे रहा था कि उसकी नजर अपने घर की ओर आतीं दो कारों पर पड़ी, गाड़ी रोककर कार पर सवार व्यक्ति कुछ पूछ रहा था, शायद किसी का पता! या कहीं का रास्ता!

उसका दिल जोर-जोर से धड़कने लगा। कहीं मेरे मोहन-मिलन तो नहीं आ गए? उसने आँखों पर हथेली लगाकर ध्यान से देखा, चरवाहा उसकी ओर उँगली से संकेत कर रहा था।

"अरे, यह तो मेरी ओर ही उँगली दिखा रहा है। देखता हूँ, क्या पता मेरा मन सच कह रहा हो, मेरे बेटे आ रहे हों।"

"आएँगे भी तो क्या कर लेंगे, चार दिन मोह-ममता बढ़ा कर फिर चले जाएँगे।"

परंतु इसमें बच्चों का क्या दोष है भला? रोजी-रोटी के लिए वह भी गया था इतने दिनों तक! वही तो चाहता था कि बच्चे कभी गरीबी से दो-चार न हों। उसके जैसा बचपन भगवान् करे किसी को न मिले। वह तो पेट भर खाने के लिए दिनभर गोबर ढोता रह जाता था। जब तक गाँव में रहा, सबके तलवे चाटता रहा। वह तो भला हो जमुना यादव का, जिन्होंने उसे कुत्ते से इनसान बना दिया। अपनी हीरा जैसी बेटी ब्याह दी। नहीं तो वह कुँआरा मर जाता, अरे जिसके न रहने का ठिकाना, न खाने का, यहाँ तक कि जिसके बाप का भी पता नहीं, कौन उससे अपनी बेटी का ब्याह करता? देनेवाले ने तो भरपूर दिया, उसी की झोली छोटी पड़ गई तो कोई क्या करे? गंगा की दिव्य छवि उसकी आँखों में डोल गई। 'चाहे सबकुछ चला जाता, गंगा न जाती।' उसने एक निःश्वास छोड़ी। और बच्चों की ओर से अपना मन साफ कर लिया।

आज इतना है तो सब आछो-आछो करते हैं, जब नहीं था, तब का अनुभव भी है उसके पास।

दोनों गाड़ियाँ आकर उसी के दरवाजे पर रुकीं। ड्राइवर ने दरवाजा खोला। आगेवाली गाड़ी से मोहन निकला, साथ ही बहू और दोनों बच्चे भी। दूसरी गाड़ी से मिलन उतरा, साथ में बहू भी। रघुबर अपने सूटेड-बूटेड बच्चों को देख रहा था टुकुर-टुकुर। उसके दरवाजे पर गाड़ी रुकती देखकर जिसने देखा, स्वयं तो दौड़ा ही दूसरे को भी खबर देता आया—

"अरे! रघुबर के लड़के आ गए। अब आ रहे हैं पद जियाने। वह तो शायद इन लोगों से बात भी नहीं करेगा। चलो देखते हैं, क्या कहता है? कुछ तो लाए होंगे। अपन ऽ···ऽ को किसी के घरेलू मामले में दखल देने की क्या

जरूरत, खाए-पिए खिसके, बबलू भाई किसके?"

"अब आ रहे हैं? महतारी का मुँह देखने भी नहीं आ सके?" भीड़ में से किसी ने बात उछाली।

"तो क्या माँ... ?"

"ऊ···ऽ तो कब्बे···!"

"माँ···ऽ···ऽ···ऽ···ऽ···!"

"नहीं भइया, माँ है, ऐसा किसने कहा कि हमारी माँ नहीं है?"

भीड़ में चुप्पी छा गई। बहुएँ रोने-पीटने लगीं। बच्चे हक्के-बक्के से इधर-उधर देख रहे थे। रघुबर कठुआया सा खड़ा था, "ये किसने आते ही बच्चों को रुला दिया?"

"मोहन-मिलन, सुनो तो, पहले बैठो, पानी-वानी पीओ, फिर बातें करेंगे!" उसने बच्चों को सँभालना चाहा। दोनों बेटे उससे लिपट गए।

"पापा! हम सदा के लिए आप के पास आ गए हैं, अब हम अपने देश में ही मेहनत कर लेंगे। आपको छोड़कर अब कहीं नहीं जाएँगे, आपके आशीर्वाद से इतने लाचार नहीं रह गए कि परदेश में कमाना मजबूरी हो, आपने बड़ी पीड़ा झेली है पापा! अब हम आपके साथ हैं।" मोहन किसी बच्चे की तरह उसे सँभाले था। उसके कंधे पर सिर रखे रघुबर अपने आप को नियंत्रित करने का प्रयास करता रहा। कुछ पल बाद न जाने कैसे धैर्य का बाँध टूट गया और वह फफक-फफककर रो पड़ा।

□

बड़ी दीदी

सबकुछ तो है यहाँ—पक्की दीवारें, विस्तृत छत, सामने सुंदर सा गार्डन, दरवाजे की बगल में तुलसी चौरा, लाइन से बिछे पलंग, दो पलंग के बीच एक सीलिंग फैन, सफाईवाली नियमित आती है। भोजन बनानेवाली भोजन बनाती है। अकसर दानदाता आते रहते हैं, हमदर्दी जताते हैं। मन के अंदर कहीं कुछ खटकता है, निगाहें अपने आप झुक जाती हैं। जिंदगी भर मेहनत-मजदूरी करके परिवार पालनेवाले लोग आज दया के पात्र बन गए हैं, यही तो वह बात है, जो इस सुंदर से भवन को घर नहीं बनने देती। घर में कौन सा फल-फलहरी धरा रहता था? यहाँ तो फिर भी लोग अपने दिवंगत रिश्तेदारों के नाम पर उनकी पुण्य तिथि, जन्मदिन आदि के अवसर पर फल-मिठाइयाँ लाते ही रहते हैं, भले ही आधा-तिहा बँटे, बँटती जरूर हैं। वह तो प्लास्टिक की टोकरी में कपड़ा बिछाकर पंखे के नीचे रख देती है, दूसरे दिन भगवान् को भोग लगाकर सभी में बाँट देती हैं। ''प्रभु अपना इंतजाम स्वयं करते हैं, उसने तो अपना सबकुछ उन्हें ही सौंप दिया है, आज से नहीं, बहुत पहले से, जब से सुना कि पूर्णत: जो उन पर आश्रित रहता है, उसके योग-क्षेम की चिंता वे स्वयं करते हैं। तब से अब तक जैसे लाज रखी, वैसे ही सदा रखना हे गोविंद!" उसने अपने टेढ़े-मेढ़े दोनों हाथ जोड़कर प्रार्थना की।

"शांता दीदी! स्कूलवाले बच्चे आए हैं राखी बाँधने, जल्दी पूजा खत्म करो!" यह कांता तो और है! बूढ़ी हो गई, बचपन नहीं गया। राखी बँधवाने के लिए मरी जा रही है। उसे कुछ अच्छा नहीं लगता। सब त्योहार खानापूर्ति जैसे लगते हैं, देखते-देखते दस साल बीत गए, रतन को देखे हुए। जब गोद

में था, तब भी माँ से ज्यादा उसी के पास रहता था। वह अगर दिनभर बच्चा ही पकड़े रहती तो बाकी का काम कब करती? शांता ने कभी कोई खेल नहीं खेला। रतन ही उसका खिलौना था। बड़ा भाई रतन से बीस साल बड़ा था, खेती-खार के काम में जितने आदमी हों, उतने ही कम हैं। बाईस का भी नहीं था भइया, जब पिताजी ने उसकी शादी कर दी। शायद महाप्रयाण से पहले बेटे को सारी जिम्मेदारियाँ सौंप देना चाहते थे। उसने सँभाल भी लिया सबकुछ, ससुराल बड़ी होशियार मिली थी उसे। साल के भीतर ही सारा खेत, घर-द्वार अपने नाम करा लिया। दाने-दाने को मोहताज हो गए थे तीनों। कुछ कहो तो सारा दोष माँ का ही निकले। जमीन अपने नाम न कराऊँ तो क्या करूँ? पागल तो है तू! कोई भी बहला-फुसलाकर अपने नाम करा लेगा, फिर क्या करेंगे? बाहर-भीतर सँभालना तो मुझे है, कहाँ-जाएगी नाक कटाने, मन आएगा, सो करेगी तो कौन सहेगा, भुगतना तो मुझे है न! पंद्रह की थी शांता, माँ कहती थी ब्याह हो चुका उसका, उसे क्या पता, कब क्या हुआ? न उधर से कोई आया, न इधर कोई गया। सुना गया कि लड़के ने अपनी पसंद से दूसरी शादी कर ली। अब तो बस दिन भर गोबर-कचरा, बरतन-भाँडा। माँ दिनभर अनाज कूटने-पीसने में लगी रहती, रतन धूल मिट्टी में सना बिना खाए-पिए रिरियाता रहता।

"बासी ही सही, दो रोटी दे दिया करो बहू रानी अपने देवर को, बड़ा होकर यह भी तुम्हारी सेवा करेगा।" माँ ने दाँत चियारकर विनय की। बहू ने न जाने पति से क्या कहा वह तो टँगिया लेकर पिल पड़ा।

"हाँ, तो तुम लोगों को पेट भर खाना नहीं मिलता न? आज खत्म ही कर देता हूँ सारा किस्सा! उसने रतन को उठाकर पटक दिया। संयोग की बात थी कि वह झउहे में गोबर लेकर आँगन से गुजर रही थी, उसी में धप्प से गिरा। अचानक लगे धक्के से वह भी गिर पड़ी, दोनों गोबर में बुरी तरह सन चुके थे। माँ को काटो तो खून नहीं, वह समझ ही न पाई कि बड़का यह क्या कर रहा है। जब समझी तो राग धर के रोने लगी। बड़के ने उसे भी धकेला, गंदी-से-गंदी गालियाँ दीं, "सब तेरा ही किया-धरा है बुढ़िया, जा न खिला अपने बाप के यहाँ से। कोई ठेका है दोजख भरने का? मर रहा हूँ अकेले खट-खट के

और इनका है तो पेट ही नहीं भरता, अब क्या करूँ अपना मांस खिलाऊँ?" वह चीख रहा था।

"मैंने कब कहा कि मेरा पेट नहीं भरता?" माँ ने हिम्मत करके कुछ कहने की कोशिश की।

अड़ोसी-पड़ोसी जुट गए। बड़के का तेवर देखकर माँ को ही समझाने लगे, "जैसा कहता है, वैसा करती क्यों नहीं बड़के की अम्मा? तेरा और तेरे दोनों बच्चों का पालनहार यही तो है, तुझे तो सब को मिलाकर चलना चाहिए।"

उसी रात भागी थी माँ शांता और रतन को लेकर गाँव से। पहले मामा के यहाँ गए, वहाँ शरण नहीं मिली। पैदल चलते, माँगते-खाते महीनों में जाकर शिवरीनारायण पहुँचे। यहाँ भगवान् की शरण में जीने के नए रास्ते मिलने लगे। माँ मंदिर की सफाई का काम करने लगी। रहने के लिए मंदिर के पास ही एक छोटा कमरा मिल गया। शांता ने भोजन बनाने का काम शुरू किया। वह सौ-पचास आदमी का भोजन अकेले ही बना लेती थी। मंदिर में कभी ब्राह्मण-भोजन तो कभी कन्या-भोजन, कभी किसी की शादी तो कभी मुंडन, जनेऊ, ढेरों त्योहार, जिनमें भोग-प्रसाद बनता, वह पहले से काम करनेवालों के साथ चाचा-भइया करके लगी रहती। जीवन चलने लगा, उनके कपड़े साफ रहने लगे। पेट भरने लगा। इसके साथ ही नारायण प्रभु की भक्ति रग-रग में समाती चली गई।

"दीदी परसाद दे तो मय जात हों अपन भाई ला राखी बाँध के आहूँ!" जमुना अपनी धराऊँ साड़ी पहनकर आ गई थी। अपना कहने को कोई नहीं है उसका, एक राखी भाई है, उसी को हर साल राखी बाँधती है।

"जिसका कोई नहीं है, वह तो रिश्ते की एक पतली-सी डोर बाँधकर अपने लिए खुशी के पल तलाश ले रही है, उसका तो भाई है 'रतन', जिसे छोड़कर वह यहाँ लोगों की दया के भरोसे जीने आ गई है, वह भी ऐसे समय, जब उसे उसकी सबसे ज्यादा जरूरत थी, भाभी के मरने के बाद वह कितना अकेला हो गया था, भले ही दोनों बहुएँ उसका ध्यान रखती थीं। छोटे-छोटे नाती-पोते थे, जिनके साथ समय कट जाता था। मंदिर के सामने नारियल फूल

की दुकान लगाते–लगाते उसने अपनी किताबों की दुकान खोल ली थी। समय पर सबकुछ दिया नारायण प्रभु ने, उसने अपने रतन की शादी की, वह बाल–बच्चेदार हुआ। उसने पैसा–पैसा बचाया अपने घर के लिए। जहाँ खाना बनाती, वहीं खा लेती, मजदूरी के सारे रुपए लाकर माँ के हाथ पर रखती। खुशी के मौकों पर वह अपने मालिकों से अपने लिए कपड़े माँग लेती। एक छोटी सी जमीन खरीदकर उन्होंने अपने लिए घर बनाया। वह देर रात तक ईंटें ढोती, उन्हें भिगाती, माँ और भाभी रेत चालतीं, रतन सारा सामान खरीदकर लाता, साथ ही दुकान भी सँभालता। उसी समय तो मरते–मरते बची थी शांता, वैसे मर जाती तो ज्यादा अच्छा हुआ होता, शादी का खाना बनाने गई थी वह अपनी टीम के साथ। मैदान में टेंट लगाकर आड़ कर लिया गया था। उस दिन हवा तेज चल रही थी, उनींदी तो वह थी ही, उसकी आँखें झपकी थीं जरा सी, न जाने कैसे कपड़े में आग लग गई! कोहराम मच गया वहाँ। बचाते–बचाते भी वह काफी जल गई थी। वह तो जिनके यहाँ वह खाना बना रही थी, वे बड़े भले लोग थे, इलाज का सारा खर्च दिया था, किंतु जले हुए अंग देना उनके वश में कहाँ था? रतन ने जी–जान से सेवा की थी उस समय। चेहरा विद्रूप हो गया। होंठ मोटे होकर लटक गए। माथे का सफेद दाग आज तक वैसा ही है। सिर के बाल जो जले तो दुबारा नहीं उगे। बाँहों में बल आ गए, जैसे मोटी रस्सी बँटी गई हो। साल भर लग गया था उसे सँभलने में, आग की आँच बरदाश्त करना मुश्किल हो गया। फिर भी वह टोली के साथ जाती थी, कुछ–न–कुछ काम मिल ही जाता था। रतन ने बहुत मना किया, तब उसने घर में रहने का फैसला किया। जीवन और प्राण दोनों का काम बहुत अच्छा चल निकला था। दोनों बहुएँ भी चाहती थीं कि बुआ अब घर का मालिकाना सँभालें। भाभी के स्वर्गवास के बाद अब कोई सयानी स्त्री घर में रह भी नहीं गई थी।

ऐसे मकड़जाल में फँसी कि भागे बिना मुक्ति संभव नहीं लगी उसे। एक बार पहले भी वे इसी बात पर घर से भागी थीं, जब बचपन में सहन न हो सका तो बुढ़ापे में कहाँ से होता?

"जब हम तुम्हारा पालन कर रहे हैं तो जैसा हम कहें, वह करना पड़ेगा।"

"ऐं··· ! पालन···, उस नारायण के सिवा ये कौन हैं पालनेवाली? अपने को बंधन नहीं चाहिए। घर से अच्छा है यहाँ। भजन करो, सत्संग में जाओ, किसी से मिलने-जुलने चले जाओ, माघ में कल्पवास कर लो, तीर्थ यात्रा पर चले जाओ। यह क्या जीवन है? पूरी जिंदगी चूल्हा-चौका, कपड़ा-लत्ता, झाड़ू-पोंछा, ऊपर से पालने का ताव।" आरती गाते-गाते वह मन ही मन फनफना रही थी।

स्कूलवाले बच्चे ऊपर आकर आपस में चुहल करते हुए दादियों को राखी बाँध रहे थे। वह भी तो अपने रतन को नहला-धुलाकर नए कपड़े पहनाकर हर साल राखी बाँधती थी, कैसे चमक उठता था उसका चेहरा राखी बँधवाकर? सारे रिश्ते-नातों से बड़ा उसका स्वाभिमान ही हो गया। यहाँ की सभी औरतें राखी बाँधने घर जाती हैं, जिनके भाई जिंदा हैं या फिर उनके भाई आकर राखी बँधवा जाते हैं, वही एक ऐसी पत्थर-दिल है, जिसने अपने भाई को अपना पता भी नहीं बताया। रतन! उसके दिल से एक आह निकली। जब भी उसे लगा कि उसे भी एक बच्चा चाहिए, जिसे वह चूम सके, हृदय से लगा सके, तब रतन को ही गले लगाया था उसने। पता नहीं वह कैसा है, अकेला पाकर 'पालक' लोग कहीं उसे सता तो नहीं रहे हैं? उसकी आँखों से निकले मोती कलाई पर बँधी राखी में समा रहे थे।

"दादी, रो मत! हम आए हैं न तेरे पास?" वह लगभग दस साल का होगा, उसने शांता के आँसू पोंछें।

"शांताबाई···! ओ शांताबाई···! ऐ देखो कौन आया तुमसे मिलने।" वृद्धाश्रम का चौकीदार था।

"मुझसे मिलने कौन आएगा?" निःश्वास छोड़ते हुए वह बुदबुदाई। नजरें उठाकर देखा तो उसके सामने उसका रतन था। जैसे ही वह दीदी कहकर उसके पैरों में झुका, शांता खुशी के मारे रो पड़ी, "मेरा रतन! आ गया, अपनी दीदी को ढूँढ़ते हुए। आज नारायण ने मेरी पुकार सुन ली।

"क्यों चली आई दीदी अपने रतन को छोड़कर? एक बार मुझे बताया तो होता कि परम सुंदरी बहुओं को तुम्हारा चेहरा पसंद नहीं आ रहा था या दो जली-भुनी बासी-कुसी रोटी के लिए तुम्हें गुलाम की तरह खटना पड़ रहा

था या तुम घर से बाहर उनकी इच्छा के बिना नहीं जा सकती थी या मेहमानों के सामने पड़ जाने पर तुम्हें जलील किया जाता था। इतना कुछ सहा दीदी और मुझे हवा तक न लगने दी। सब को सुधार देता मैं।" रतन की आँखें बरस रही थीं।

"तुमने गलत सुना भाई, ऐसा कुछ नहीं हुआ मेरे साथ, सदा दिन स्वतंत्र रही, किसी का दबाव सहने की आदत जो नहीं पड़ी। यहाँ मुझे कोई तकलीफ नहीं है, बस एक बार तुम्हें देखना चाहती थी, यह इच्छा भी पूरी कर दी नारायण ने। आओ बैठो! मैं हर साल तुम्हारी राखी भगवान् को पहनाती रही हूँ। आओ उनका प्रसाद तुम्हें पहनाती हूँ!" वह रतन को अपने पलंग पर बैठाकर भगवान् पर चढ़ाई राखी ले आई।

"दीदी! राखी तो हम अपने घर पर ही मनाएँगे, चलो मेरे साथ, गाड़ी लेकर आया हूँ। रतन ने अधिकारपूर्वक कहा और उसके नारायण का सिंहासन उठाकर आगे-आगे चल पड़ा। सम्मोहित-सी शांता अपने थैले में जल्दी-जल्दी अपने सूखे-गीले कपड़े रखने लगी। नारायण के पीछे तो चलना ही होगा न उसे।

□

चार रुपए बीस पैसे

पूरी रात डी.जे. पर गाने बजते रहे थे। भंडारा था सुराज पासवान के घर। उसके लड़के राजेश का सलेक्शन उ.प्र. पुलिस में हो गया था। नया-नया आया था पुलिस की वरदी पहनकर। गर्व से भर उठा था सुराज। वह तो जेल में वार्डन ही रह गया, बेटे ने मान बढ़ाया। सभी रिश्तेदारों को बुला लिया था उसने। चार बहन-बेटियाँ, नई-पुरानी सब आई थीं। पहले दिन सत्यनारायण भगवान् की कथा हुई। देर रात तक भजन होता रहा, फिर नाच प्रारंभ हो गया। सुराज का इकलौता भानजा दीपक भी पुलिस में भरती हो गया था। दोहरी खुशी थी।

जेठ की जान लेवा गरमी। दिन भर जैसे आग बरसाता हो आसमान, खेतों में दूर तक हरियाली का नामोनिशान तक नहीं। अहीरों के जानवर न जाने कैसे खेतों की सूखी मेंड़ों पर हरित तृण ढूँढ़ लेते हैं, दिन भर डोलते रहते हैं इधर से उधर। गाँव के उत्तर की ओर आम-महुए की बारी है, चरवाहे वहीं लाठी टेके बैठे रहते हैं। कभी बिरहा की तान, कभी ताश की बिसात। नई-पुरानी बतकही। इन्हें तो जैसे एहसास ही नहीं होता इस भीषण गरमी का। घरों-घर काज-परोजन पड़े हैं। किसी के यहाँ ब्याह-गवन तो किसी के यहाँ भागवत-भंडारा। पलक मारने की फुरसत नहीं उदय को। लगातार चक्की का धड़-धड़ बजता शोर, तपती छत। पड़ोस में बजता डी.जे. कब तक अच्छा लगे किसी को। दस बोरे पीसकर खाली नहीं हुआ कि दस और गँज गए।

"भइया, तोहरे बिटिया के बिआह बा। परसों बारात होये। पिसान पीस देह रचि क।" दाँत निकालकर विनय करते लोग।

"ठीक है, पीसने के लिए तो बैठे ही हैं। पीसेंगे नहीं तो बिजली का बिल, पूरे घर का खर्च कैसे चलेगा?" वैसे तो दोनों भाई सिक्यूरिटी गार्ड की नौकरी में हैं। दस-दस हजार लेकर आते हैं महीने में। उसे भी तो निकालना चाहिए कुछ-न-कुछ। उसने एक लंबी साँस ली। कब सुबह का धुँधलका फैलने लगा, उसे पता भी नहीं चला। बार-बार चक्की में गेहूँ डालते, कपड़े की थैली सीधी करते, आटा देखते रात गुजर गई। वह तो हवा में आई सुहानी सी ठंडक ने पसीने में डूबे जिस्म का जब हौले से स्पर्श किया, तब उसने नजरें उठाईं। लोग लोटा ले-लेकर खेतों की ओर जा रहे थे। वह सुराज पासवान के घर का गेहूँ पीसकर आटे की बोरियों को चबूतरे पर रख रहा था। कमर घाव-जैसे दुख रही थी। यों तो पूरा बदन ही टूट रहा था, मन हो रहा था, कोई चढ़कर जरा कचर दे! चक्की बंद कर वह घड़ी भर के लिए चक्कीवाले कमरे के बाहर रखे बोरों पर लेट गया। आह! इस सुख का वर्णन करने के लिए शब्द कहाँ से लाए उदय।

उनका दो मंजिला पक्का घर अभी नया ही बना था। यही कोई दस वर्ष हुए होंगे। इसके पहले तो उनका घर यहाँ से पचास किलोमीटर दूर के गाँव सीतापुर में था। पुरखौती घर-द्वार, खेती-बाड़ी, इज्जत-आबरू सबकुछ जमा-जमाया था। गाँव में अनायास बढ़ गई दुश्मनी के कारण पिताजी सबकुछ बेच-बाचकर कमालपुर में आ बसे। यहाँ थोड़ी सी अपनी जमीन थी, उसी पर दो मंजिला घर बनाया। सामने यह चक्की लगा ली और मेहनत करके अपने तीनों बच्चों को पढ़ाने-लिखाने लगे। वह स्वयं मेकैनिकल इंजीनियर की डिग्री रखता है। बड़े भइया ने एम.एस-सी. किया, मझले ने एम.ए., एल-एल.बी. किंतु नौकरी के नाम पर यही प्राइवेट सिक्यूरिटी गार्ड की नौकरी पा सके। दो बंदूकों के लाइसेंस लेते-लेते सारी जमा-पूँजी चुक गई। पर हाँ, रोजी-रोटी का ठिकाना तो हो गया। आँखें बंद होने के पहले माँ-पिताजी को संतोष हो चुका था कि बच्चे जी-खा लेंगे।

आह! जरा कमर सीधी कर लूँ, फिर खेत की तरफ जाऊँ। एक तरह से देखा जाए तो कमालपुर है कमाल का, सभी श्रेणी के लोग हैं। धनी से धनी और गरीब से गरीब। गेहूँ ज्यादा होता है। इसलिए लोग रोटी ही ज्यादा

खाते हैं। चक्की खाली नहीं रहती, लगन के दिनों में तो लगता है, दो-तीन चक्की और लगा लेते तो काम चलता। सभी से प्रेम का रिश्ता। ज्यादातर लोग नाना-नानी या मामा-मामी, भइया-बहन होते हैं। उसका ननिहाल जो है कमालपुर। उसकी चक्की के दक्षिण में अनुसूचित जातिवालों का टोला था। सामान्य जनों से लेकर गरीब-गुरबा तक अधिकांश की एक ही प्रवृत्ति, पिसाई देते नानी मर जाती है—"काल्हि नई लेह बेटवा, तू त हमार भयने हयय हमसे का पिसाई? आधा ले लो, आधा दूसरी बार ले लेना।" फुटकर तो किसी के पास रहता ही नहीं।

पासवानों की तो इस समय चाँदी है। पढ़े-लिखे सरकारी नौकरी में लग गए हैं। धड़ाधड़ पक्के घर, पक्की सड़कें, शौचालय, चकाचक है पूरा मोहल्ला, लेकिन दाँत निपोरने की आदत कहाँ जाएगी? पिसाई देते फटती है, "दई जाब महाराज, का लई के भागि जाब? होत बिहाने पहुँचाई देब, फुटकर नहीं आय, का गाँव छोड़ के भागि जाब?" पिसवाए और लेकर चलते बने, फिर जब गेहूँ लेकर आएँगे तभी भेंट होगी, जब नए बहाने रहेंगे। वह रात-दिन खड़े-खड़े आटा पीसता है, दुनिया भर का बिजली बिल आता है। ससुर पिसाई नहीं देंगे तो कहाँ से होगा सब? अभी आते होंगे महाराजा सरीखे पिसान लेने, बुला लिये हैं गाँव भर को। उसका ध्यान सुराज पासवान के तीन बोरी आटे की ओर था, कितनी मुश्किल से पीसा था, तीन बजे रात से, इसी समय तो जरा सी ठंडी होती है धरती हवा के शीतल संपर्क में आकर, सो लो या कोई जरूरी काम कर लो।

उसे झपकी आ गई, बंद आँखों के आगे तरह-तरह के दृश्य नाचने लगे, आराम का यह प्यारा सुख तो आज जैसी मेहनत के बाद ही मिल सकता है। "ए-इ-ऽ-ऽ उठो! अब तक सो रहे हो।" किसी की आवाज सुन उसे लगा, वह सपना देख रहा है। नींद नहीं खुली उसकी।

"ए-ई-ऽ-ऽ चक्कीवाले! उठो न, उठो! हमें जल्दी पीसना चाहिए।" रात भर सोए तो पेट नहीं भरा। आगंतुक सुराज पासवान का भानजा दीपक था। उदय ने लाल-लाल आँखें खोलकर एक पल उसे देखा, "अरे यार! पाँच मिनट रुक जाओ!" विवश आँखें फिर मुँद गईं।

"नहीं एक मिनट भी नहीं! हलवाई आकर बैठ गए हैं, अभी घंटे भर में गरमी बढ़ जाएगी, तब क्या तुम भुगतोगे?" वह जोर-जोर से चिल्लाने लगा।

"काहे चिल्लाता है यार? दे पिसाई। वह देख, बोरियाँ उठा ले।"

"तौल दो।" उसने आँखें लड़ेरते हुए कहा।

"लाओ उठाकर।" उदय ने जम्हाई लेते हुए कहा।

वह खड़ा रह गया।

उदय उसका आशय भाँपकर बोरियाँ तौल-तौलकर रखने लगा। सभी में थोड़े-बहुत अंतर से बराबर आटा था। टीपे में रखे आटे से उसने ठीक कर दिया। वह बोरी साइकिल की कॅरियर पर लादने लगा।

"पहले पिसाई दे दो भाई।"

"एक बोरी रखकर आऊँ, फिर देता हूँ।"

"लेकर आना चाहिए न, मुझे भी इधर-उधर जाना है।" उदय को झुँझलाहट हुई।

"अरे, खा नहीं जाएँगे भाई। जरा सब्र करो।" वह भी झल्लाता हुआ साइकिल पर बोरी लेकर चला गया।

"साले रहेंगे वहीं के वहीं, दाँत निपोरकर माँगने-खाने की आदत नहीं जाएगी। धन-पद चाहे जितना मिल जाए। ले लेना आवश्यक है, वरना यह अपने गाँव चला आएगा। फिर कौन देता है पिसाई!" उदय को उस लड़के के बात करने का ढंग शुरू से ही अच्छा नहीं लगा था।

थोड़ी देर बाद फिर आया। बोरी उठाकर चलता बना।

"अरे भाई, पिसाई?" उदय आवाज देता रह गया।

"मामा खेत गए हैं, आते ही होंगे। ले आता हूँ पिसाई।" कहते-कहते वह साइकिल की सीट पर बैठकर दूर निकल गया था।

"अरे भाई, 304 रुपए 20 पैसे लाना, 4 रुपए 20 पैसे पहले के पड़े हैं।" उदय जान नहीं सका कि उसने सुना या नहीं।

"एक बार उधार छूटा कि भूल ही जाते हैं, कौन लाठी चलाए इनसे रोज-रोज। आज मौका है, दे देगा तो दे ही देगा।" वह जैसे स्वयं से बातें कर रहा था। तब तक उदय न सो सका, न कहीं बाहर-भीतर जा सका। अधूरी

नींद के कारण सिर दर्द से फटा जा रहा था। शरीर में जैसे कुछ ताकत ही न रही हो। "यह दस बोरी धान है भइया। दरि दिहौ।" ठकुराने से एक आदमी आया था। विनय से बातें कर रहा था। "गेहूँ के बाद दर देंगे दद्दा, रखकर चले जाओ। शाम को आकर देख लेना।" उदय को वह आदमी अच्छा लगा।

छह नहीं बजे कि सूर्य की किरणें प्रखर हो गईं। शरीर से पसीना बहने लगा। हाँ, अभी चौक पर लोगों की भीड़ थी। चाय-समोसेवाले के यहाँ लोग खड़े-बैठे खा-पी रहे थे। दूध के ठेले से लोग दूध के पैकेट ले जा रहे थे। गँजेड़ी लोग गाँजे की चिलम सुड़क रहे थे और देशी शराब की दुकान पर कई नए-नए लड़के सुबह-सुबह मुँह जूठा करने के लिए खड़े थे। उदय की सुबह बिगाड़ दी साले दीपकवा ने। "बहुत शान बढ़ गई है इनकी। कोई सुधारने वाला नहीं है न इसीलिए। ये लोग आज से 40-50 वर्ष पहले हमारे घरों में चाकरी करते थे। और मजूरी के लिए रिरियाया करते थे। अब देखो, समय ने ऐसा पलटा खाया कि ये हमारी मजदूरी देने में मरने लगे हैं।" उदय उबाल खा रहा था कि दीपक फिर साइकिल लेकर आ गया।

"ये लो तीन सौ रुपए। ऐसे जान खा रहे थे, जैसे हम कोई चोर-बदमाश हैं। अरे काम कराए हैं तो पइसा तो देंगे ही।" उसने बड़ी हिकारत से उदय की ओर देखा और उसके हाथ पर तीन सौ रुपए पटक दिए।

"अरे भले मनई, 4 रुपए 20 पैसे पहले के बाकी हैं तुम्हारे मामा के हाथ के। वह भी दे दो न।" उदय हिसाब साफ करना चाहता था।

"अभी इतना ही लाया हूँ, उनके हाथ का उन्हीं से लेना।" उसने लापरवाही से कहा और अपनी बोरी उठाने लगा।

"जब तक बाकी न दे दो, आटा नहीं ले जा सकते।" उदय अड़ गया। उसने बोरी उसके हाथ से लेकर अलग रख दी।

"ठीक है, जा रहा हूँ। लेकर आता हूँ, जब तुम्हें सब्र नहीं है तो।" वह ताव खा गया। क्रोध के लक्षण उसके चेहरे पर स्पष्ट झलक रहे थे। वह साइकिल पर चढ़कर फनफनाता पैडल मारता चला गया। "नीच कहीं के, पिसाई देने में फटती है। बिजलीवाले बाप होते हैं न।" उदय भी बड़बड़ा रहा था।

थोड़ी ही देर मैं दीपक वापस आ गया। उसने 4 रुपए 20 पैसे उदय के सामने फेंक दिए। "ले भिखारी बाम्हन, भर ले अपनी बेटी के··· में।" सुनते ही उदय के तन-बदन में आग लग गई। उसने पास पड़ा हँसिया फेंककर मार दिया। वह आटा लेकर जाते दीपक के पैर में लगा। वहाँ से खून निकलने लगा। वह रुका नहीं, गाली देता, रोता-चिल्लाता घर की ओर तेजी से चला गया।

"मार दिया रे! जान से मार दिया!"

"मादर···! मामा हो मामा।" वह रो रहा था।

"रुक साले, जान न ले लिया तो असल बाम्हन की बूँद का नहीं।" उदय आपा खो चुका था।

अभी वह घर के अंदर जाने के बारे में सोच ही रहा था कि उसकी नजर सामने से आती भीड़ पर पड़ी। पचास के लगभग स्त्री-पुरुष हाथों में लाठी, भाले, टँगिया लिये हल्ला करते, गालियाँ बकते, ललकारते चले आ रहे हैं।

"कहाँ है, वह कमीना, जिसने हमारे बच्चे को चोट पहुँचाने का साहस किया?"

"वह बच नहीं सकता।"

"आज मजा चखा देंगे बम्हनौटी का।" अगले पल ही वह घिर चुका था। लोग उस पर लाठियाँ बरसाते, उससे पहले ही छत से आवाज गूँजी, "हाथ मत छोड़ना कोई भी। वरना सबको भून के रख दूँगा।" वह भय से काँप रहा था। उसने मझले भइया विजय की दहाड़ सुनी, रात की ड्यूटी कर अभी-अभी आए थे। उसने तो उन्हें घर में घुसते भी नहीं देखा। मेन गेट से गए होंगे शायद।

"चला के देख दोगला गोली। आन गाँव से आकर गुंडई कर रहा है? आज दिखा देंगे कि हम भी किसी से कम नहीं।" लोग चिल्ला रहे थे। वह उन्हें रोकना चाहता था, गुस्से में उससे पहले ही गलती हो चुकी थी। परंतु अब तो माफी माँगने का भी अवसर नहीं था। विजय की चेतावनी के पश्चात् भी उनका क्रोध शांत न हुआ। लोगों ने उसे डंडे से पीटना शुरू कर दिया।

बस फिर क्या था, ऊपर से फायरिंग शुरू हो गई, और लोग तो भाग

गए, किंतु दीपक और राकेश लहूलुहान होकर पड़े रह गए। विजय भी सकते में आ गया। किसी की हत्या करना उसका उद्देश्य नहीं था। बहरहाल अब तो परिस्थिति से दो-चार होना ही था। वह बंदूक लिये नीचे आया और चक्की के कमरे का शटर गिराकर ताला बंद कर उदय को सहारा देकर उठाया तथा घर के अंदर ले जाकर दरवाजा अंदर से बंद कर लिया।

उदय के माथे से खून बह रहा था। उसकी मरहम-पट्टी की गई। घर की औरतें राग धर के रोने-पीटने लगीं, कुत्ता भी रोने लगा। विजय ने थाने फोन करके घटना की सूचना दी। उसे पता था, यह अंत नहीं, प्रारंभ है। थोड़ी ही देर में सैकड़ों लोगों ने आकर उनका घर घेर लिया। सबके हाथ में हथियार थे। मिट्टी-तेल के पीपे भी दिखा रहे थे, लड़कों के हाथ में बम के गोले भी दिखाई दे रहे थे। यों तो सारे कमालपुर में खबर आग की तरह फैल चुकी थी, किंतु इस आग में जलने के लिए कोई तैयार नहीं हुआ था।

पहले तो उन्होंने गंदी से गंदी गालियाँ दीं, ललकारा। माँ के दूध को धिक्कारा, जब अंदर से दरवाजा नहीं खुला तो सबने मिलकर लोहे का दरवाजा तोड़ दिया। भीड़ अंदर घुस चुकी थी, जब बाहर से पुलिस का सायरन बजा। जल्दी-जल्दी में भीड़ ने घर में आग लगा दी। पुलिस ने भीड़ को तितर-बितर किया। पांडे परिवार के साथ ही पासवान परिवार को भी पुलिस ने वैन में बैठा लिया। शवों को अपने कब्जे में ले लिया। अभय ड्यूटी जा चुका था, खबर पाकर पहुँचा तो विरोधी की रिपोर्ट पर उसे भी अंदर कर दिया गया। पूरा परिवार दिखा, किंतु अभय का ग्यारह वर्षीय बेटा मिंटू वहाँ नहीं था, पुलिस ने खोज की। परंतु वह कहीं नहीं मिला। दमकल मँगाकर घर की आग बुझाई गई। किंतु तब तक सबकुछ जलकर राख हो चुका था। चक्की पर रखा अनाज और इंजन गाँववाले लूट ले गए। दूसरे दिन मिंटू की लाश मिली थी नाले में क्षत-विक्षत फूली हुई।

घर की औरतें बार-बार बेहोश हो रही थीं, बयान लेकर उन्हें उनके रिश्तेदारों के यहाँ भेज दिया गया। दूसरी पार्टी अपने बच्चे गँवाकर खून की प्यासी हो रही थी। मिंटू को मारकर अब शांत हो गई थी। उधर से पचास आदमी आरोपी बने, इधर से तीनों भाई। उदय के ऊपर उकसाने वाला व्यवहार

करने की धारा लगी, विजय हत्या का आरोपी बना और अभय साथ देने का।

सुराज तो नैनी जेल में वार्डन रह चुका था। उसे इसका लाभ मिल रहा था। उसने तीनों भाइयों की खूब खातिरदारी करवाई जेल के अंदर। "और लेगा 4 रुपए 20 पैसा?" उदय पर लात से प्रहार करते, दाँत किटकिटाकर उसने पूछा था। आँखों में आँसू भरकर मुँह से बहते हुए खून को पोंछते हुए उदय ने कहा था, "मेरी मजदूरी के थे, माँगकर कोई गुनाह तो नहीं किया मैंने?"

□

छींटे गुलाल के

"जवाँ है मोहब्बत, हसीं है जमाना, लुटाया है दिल ने, खुशी का खजाना।" मोबाइल की रिंगटोन सुनकर सुधा ने झपटकर उसे उठाया और कान से लगा लिया। "हैलो! कौन बोल रहा है?"

"हैलो सुधा! मैं बोल रहा हूँ"।

"हाँ… हाँ, कहो कब पहुँच रहे हो, आज रात या कल सुबह?"

"सॉरी सुधा! मैं शनिवार को ही चल पाऊँगा, बैंक से नकद न मिल पाने के कारण मजदूरों का पेमेंट नहीं हो सका, तुम तो जानती ही हो कि उनकी मजदूरी देना मेरी जिम्मेदारी है। कल तो होली के कारण बैंक बंद रहेंगे, देखो इधर-उधर से कोशिश करके कुछ व्यवस्था करता हूँ।"

"साल भर का त्योहार है और आप घर से इतनी दूर हैं!" उसकी आवाज भर्रा गई।

"भावुक मत बनो सुधा! सोचो जरा, जब हमारे मजदूर होली नहीं मनाएँगे तो हमीं मनाकर क्या करेंगे? उन्हीं से तो हमारी सारी खुशियाँ हैं। तुम्हें मेरी कसम! जरा भी उदास मत होना! भगवान् ने चाहा तो इसी संडे हम अपनी होली मना रहे होंगे।"

"ठीक, है आप अपना खयाल रखना।" उसने फोन काट दिया। उसके मुँह से सिसकी निकल गई। शादी के बाद यह कोई पहला अवसर नहीं, जब निलेश त्योहार के दिन घर से बाहर है, प्रायः उसे कोई-न-कोई आवश्यक काम निकल ही आता है, एकाकीपन सहना तो जैसे उसकी नियति बन चुकी है।

रक्षा जब तक थी, उसकी हमउम्र लड़कियों का आना-जाना लगा रहता था, भले ही उसने कभी उसे अपना नहीं माना, फिर भी कुछ काम तो मिलता था उसे। कभी उसकी सहेलियों की फरमाइश पर पकौड़ियाँ तलनी पड़तीं, कभी सौंफ का शरबत बनाना पड़ता। इतनी समझ तो उसे थी ही कि घर का मतभेद घर में ही रखना चाहिए। अपनी कोख तो बंजर भूमि ही रह गई, निलेश को रक्षा के बाद किसी और संतान की अभिलाषा नहीं थी। अपनी तरफ से उससे जो हो सका, उसने किया। जिस समय वह इस घर में आई थी, रक्षा मुश्किल से आठ वर्ष की थी। निलेश की पहली पत्नी सीमा एक लंबी बीमारी के बाद इस दुनिया से जा चुकी थी। चारों तरफ फैला कारोबार, जमी-जमाई गृहस्थी, निलेश का व्यवहार, अपनी गरीबी, चार-चार बेटियों के भार तले दबे मम्मी-पापा को सुधा और निलेश की उम्र का लंबा अंतराल महत्त्वहीन लगा।

"औरत की उम्र का क्या? दो-चार साल बाद यही बड़ी लगने लगेगी। धन बड़े-बड़े अभाव ढँक देता है, हमारी बेटी लाखों में खेलेगी, रही बात सुहाग की, वह तो तकदीर की बात है, जो जितने दिन लिखाकर लाया होगा, उतने दिन टिकाएगा।" पता नहीं माँ ने उसे समझाया था या स्वयं को। वह क्या जाने दुहाजू क्या होता है, या उम्र का इतना अंतर उसके भविष्य पर क्या प्रभाव डालेगा? वह तो अपने गहने, अपना घर, अपने पति का प्यार पाकर ही अपने भाग्य पर इठला रही थी। मायके में तो दो वक्त की रोटी के लिए दिन भर मजदूरी करनी पड़ती थी। उसने अपने आँसू पोंछे, उसके हाथ अदृश्य सत्ता के प्रति जुड़ गए" हे प्रभु! मेरा जीवन तेरी दया का प्रमाण है, मैं सदा तेरे चरणों में प्रणाम करती हूँ, आभारी हूँ तेरी, किन परिस्थितियों से निकालकर मुझे कहाँ बैठा दिया।" मन हलका हो गया, कड़ाही में गुझिए तल रही थी वह, जब निलेश का फोन आया था, उसके न आने की बात सुनकर मन ऐसा क्षुब्ध हुआ कि कड़ाही उठाकर फेंक देने की इच्छा होने लगी थी, पर अब मन शांत था।

"मेरे पति-जैसा कौन होगा, जो मजदूरों के सुख में सुखी, दुःख में दुःखी रहता हो। उसने तो वह जीवन जीकर देख लिया है। सात दिन हाड़तोड़ मेहनत के साथ मजदूरी की उम्मीद के सपने परवान चढ़ते जाते हैं, ऐसे में यदि किसी

भी कारण से मजदूरी न मिले, तो कैसा लगता है, पता है उसे!''

एक बार ठेकेदार के घर गमी पड़ जाने के कारण रविवार को मजदूरी नहीं मिली, घर आकर एक-एक नजर मम्मी, पापा और तीनों बहनों के चेहरों पर डाली, वहाँ उसे निराशा का समुद्र ठाठें मारता नजर आया। संयोग से उसी हफ्ते होली का त्योहार पड़ गया था, नमक-भात का ठिकाना नहीं था, जब तीनों छोटी बहनों ने रंग-पिचकारी के लिए मम्मी का भेजा खाना जारी रखा, तब बल भरकर कूटी गईं। अब यह बात और है कि मम्मी भी बहुत देर तक रोती रही थीं।

निलेश को नकद रुपयों की जरूरत है, क्या करूँ, क्या करूँ? जब से नोटबंदी लागू हुई है, हर आदमी परेशान है, उसने तो मौका देखकर जो कुछ पास में था, उसे जमा कर दिया था, फिर हर हफ्ते चौबीस हजार निकालती गई थी, शायद यह रकम कुछ काम आ सके। उसने आलमारी खोलकर रुपए गिने, ढाई लाख थे उसके पास। उसे बहुत अच्छा लगा, चलो कुछ तो समस्या का निदान होगा। अब एक दिन में बिलासपुर से जगदलपुर रुपए पहुँचाने की समस्या थी। कोई ऐसा विश्वासी नहीं दिखा, जिसे निलेश के पास भेजा जा सके।

अभी वह द्वंद्व में फँसी ही थी कि दरवाजे पर किसी की आर्त पुकार सुनाई पड़ी, "दे दो माँ, भूखे को एक रोटी! दे दो माँऽ···ऽ···! भूखे को एक रोटी!"

उसने देखा कि एक बूढ़ा आदमी हाथ में डिब्बा थामें, उसकी ओर बड़ी उम्मीद से निहार रहा हैं।

"हे भगवान्! किसी की उम्मीद ना टूटे!" उसने जैसे अपने आप से कहा और रसोई में जाकर दाल, चावल, रोटी सब्जी एक थाली में परोस लाई, यह तो अच्छा हुआ, जो उसने अभी दोपहर का भोजन नहीं किया था, वरना इसे क्या देती? रही बात अपनी तो कुछ भी खा लेगी।

"लो बाबा! इधर छाया में बैठकर खा लो, मैं पानी ला देती हूँ।" उसने सारी वस्तुएँ एक-एक करके भिखारी के डिब्बे में डाल दी। घर के अंदर से जग में पानी ले आई। पानी देने के लिए दरवाजे पर खड़ी रही। वह ऐसे खा

रहा था, जैसे जनम का भूखा हो। भोजन के अंश उसकी दाढ़ी में उलझ रहे थे। ज्यों-ज्यों भोजन समाप्त होता जा रहा था त्यों-त्यों उसके चेहरे पर संतुष्टि के भाव गहरे होते जा रहे थे। वह कुछ पल के लिए अपनी सारी परेशानियाँ भूल गई।

"बाल-बच्चे कितने हैं बाबा?" उसने यूँ ही पूछ लिया।

"चार बेटे और तीन बेटियाँ हैं माँ"! उसकी आँखों की चमक लौट आई थी।

"सब बड़े हैं?"

"हाँ माँ! सब बाल-बच्चेदार हैं।"

"आप की देखभाल कोई नहीं करता?" वह उदास हो गई।

"अपना चला लें, वही बहुत है माँ, लड़कियाँ अपने घर गईं, बेटे अपनी-अपनी माया में फँसे हैं, मैं कोई उम्मीद भी नहीं करता किसी से, आप के जैसे माई-बाप बहुत हैं संसार में, जब तक चल-फिर रहा हूँ, ठीक ही है।" उसने लंबी साँस ली।

"और आपकी पत्नी?"

"वह मुझे छोड़ गई माँ! पाँच साल हो गए। वह तकदीरवाली थी, मुझे बदा था ऐसे दिन देखना, सब अपने-अपने कर्म हैं माँ।" वह अपनी आँखों की नमी छिपाने के लिए झूठी हँसी हँस रहा था।

"पहले आप क्या करते थे?" शायद वह जानना चाहती थी कि यह आदमी, जो उसकी करुणा का अधिकारी बन रहा है, कहीं व्यावसायिक भिखारी तो नहीं। उसे पता है, आजकल कई लोग भिक्षावृत्ति को व्यवसाय की तरह अपनाते हैं, इनकी अच्छी-खासी आमदनी होती है। कई लोग तो इन्कमटेक्स भी देते हैं। वह चंद पल खामोश रहा, फिर मैली सी आँखें उठाकर उसे देखा। "मैं बड़े-बड़े घर बनाता था माँ! कई-कई मंजिल के घर, छोटे-बड़े, मंदिर, मसजिद, गिरजे, गुरुद्वारे बनाए, राज मिस्त्री था मैं, जिंदगी भर मेहनत करके खानेवाले को सब के सामने हाथ फैलाना पड़ रहा है माँ, भगवान् बुलाता क्यों नहीं अपने पास?" वह फूट-फूट कर रोने लगा था।

सुधा के मनोमस्तिष्क में एक हलचल सी हुई "बटुक मिस्त्री!" वह

दस वर्ष की रही होगी, 'लार्सन टुब्रो' कंपनी के कर्मचारियों की हड़ताल के फलस्वरूप सारे कर्मचारी सेवामुक्त कर दिए गए। पापा क्या करते, आठ आदमी का परिवार पालने के लिए? उन्हें विराट नगर से आए अधिक समय नहीं हुआ था। अपने साथ थोड़े से बरतन-कपड़े लेकर चले आए थे नौकरी के भरोसे। गाँव में आए दिन होनेवाले झगड़ों से बचने के लिए पुश्तैनी घर-खेत छोड़कर मध्यप्रदेश के कोरबा नामक स्थान पर चले आए थे, यहाँ नए बन रहे पावर हाउस में उन्हें सुपरवाइजर की नौकरी मिल गई थी। नए परिवेश में अभी गृहस्थी जम ही रही थी कि कंपनी के सारे कर्मचारी बरखास्त कर दिए गए। पापा ने कुली तक का काम किया परिवार के लिए, परंतु एक की मजदूरी से सबका पेट भरना मुश्किल था, सुधा ने स्कूल छोड़कर काम करना प्रारंभ कर दिया। होली पर मजदूरी मिलने की उम्मीद न देख उसने दूसरे ठीहे में काम करना शुरू किया। उसकी दुःख भरी कहानी सुनकर बटुक मिस्त्री ने उसे काम पर रख लिया था। उसकी उम्र देखकर पहले दिन रेत चालने के काम पर लगाया गया था, आधी छुट्टी तक वह दस-पंद्रह धमेले ही छान पाई थी, मिस्त्री जुगाड़ पर बैठा बिजली की गति से ईंटों के रद्दे-पर-रद्दे चढ़ाता जा रहा था। बटुक उस ठीहे का सबसे तेज-तर्रार मिस्त्री था, उसके साथ चार मजदूर लगते थे, दो रेजा ईंट-मसाला पहुँचाने के लिए और दो कुली रेत-सीमेंट ढोकर मसाला बनाने के लिए। उसकी आँखों में नागवारी के भाव देख उसे भय लग रहा था कि कहीं उसे कल से काम पर आने से मना न कर दिया जाए।"

"सुन न नोनी, जा न मिसतिरी ऊप्पर रंग डारबे, पइसा देही ओ।" एक रेजा थी, उससे फुसफुसाकर कह रही थी। उसके हाथ में रंग था, उसने कुछ देर पहले डाला था उसके ऊपर रंग।

पैसे मिलने के अलावा उसे कुछ समझ नहीं आया, उसने डिब्बे में रंग घोल लिया और जब देखा कि बटुक पूरी तन्मयता से ईंटें जोड़ रहा है, तब पीछे से जाकर उसे लाल रंग से सराबोर कर दिया। पहले तो वह सपकाया, एक बार निगाहें उठाकर उसे देखा, फिर उसकी नजरें झुक गईं, वह गीले कपड़ों की परवाह किए बिना लगातार अपना काम करता रहा। तीसरे दिन

रविवार अर्थात् मजदूरी मिलने का दिन था और सोमवार को होली। मजदूरी मिलने पर उसे ढूँढ़कर उसने दो रुपए पचास पैसे दिए थे। दो रुपए पचास पैसे अर्थात् उसके एक दिन की मजदूरी। उन्हीं थोड़े से पैसों से उसके परिवार ने उस वर्ष होली मनाई थी।

"मैं बटुक नहीं हूँ, माँ मेरा नाम सीताराम था, अब तो नाम भी बदल गया है, सब भिखारी ही कहते हैं।" उसके स्वर में दिल को चीर देनेवाला दर्द था।

"कोई बात नहीं, आप ने अनगिनत लोगों को घर दिया है। स्वयं भले ही बेघर रह गए।" वह बड़ी गंभीरता से कुछ सोच रही थी।

"ऐसा करो बाबा, वो जो मंदिर दिख रहा है न!··· उसी की सीढ़ियों पर रात को सो जाया करो। वह हमारा ही बनवाया हुआ है और हाँ, कल सुबह अच्छी तरह नहा-धोकर तैयार हो जाना, आप को प्रतिदिन मंदिर से ही भोजन मिल जाया करेगा, मैं कह दूँगी पुजारी जी से।" वह हाथ जोड़े जमीन पर झुक-झुककर उसे आशीर्वाद दे रहा था।

"माँ! तेरे पाँव में काँटा न गड़े, भगवान् तेरा सुहाग बनाए रखे। बैठ के नहीं खाऊँगा, मैं मंदिर की सफाई कर दिया करूँगा।" वह असीम कृतज्ञता से उसे देख रहा था।

सुधा ने सारी नकदी सँभालकर कमर में बाँधी और ड्राइवर को बुलाने के लिए फोन कर जगदलपुर जाने की तैयारी में लग गई।

"मैं आ रही हूँ निलेश, न मुझे नक्सलियों का डर है, न चोर-डाकुओं का, बस तुम्हारी चिंता दूर करनी है। तुमने तो कभी सोचा भी नहीं होगा कि घर-खर्च से मैं रुपए बचाती हूँ, मेरी सोच का दायरा बहुत छोटा है निलेश, मैं आज तक अपनी गरीबी से बाहर न निकल सकी, आज भी मेरी जरूरतें अत्यंत सीमित है। हाँ, जो कुछ बनाया है, रख लेती हूँ, न होगा तो इस बार रक्षा के यहाँ चले जाएँगे त्योहार मनाने, जब से ससुराल गई है, माँ न सही, कुछ तो समझने लगी है। इस बार जब आई थी, कितने सच्चे मन से कहा था उसने—"माँ! यदि आप न होतीं, तो पापा कैसे रहते अकेले?"

□

चूहेदानी

मॉल में मिला था, पहले पहल राजेश, पास की सीट पर बैठा सिनेमा देख रहा था, रिया के तो मन बहलाव का साधन ही था सिटी मॉल, जब भी जी ज्यादा उदास होता, इसी तरफ निकल आती, आज सुबह से ही बादल छाए थे, बरसात के अंतिम दिन थे, कभी क्वांरवाली तीखी धूप बिखर जाती, तो कभी घनघोर घटा छा जाती। बादल वाले दिन रिया को शुरू से ही पसंद नहीं थे, बस चुपचाप बिस्तर पर लेटकर टी.वी. देखो या फेसबुक पर चेटिंग करो। नींद आए, सो जाओ, यू ट्यूब देखो! बस इतने में ही दिनचर्या सिमटकर रह जाती है।

खुले दिन में कहीं आओ-जाओ अच्छा लगता है, कुछ समय पहले तक उसके पास समय नहीं रहता था कि अपनी सहेलियों को मैसेज भेज सके और अब समय उसे चारों ओर से जैसे दबोचे रहता है। जब घड़ी देखो, घड़ी की सुई 2 मिनट से ज्यादा हुआ तो पाँच मिनट आगे खिसकी होती है। सोओ तो कितना? बात करो तो कितना, ममा पर तो इतने बड़े घर की जिम्मेदारी है, नौकरों को देखना, खाना बनाना, पापाजी को समय देना, उसके पास तो जरा भी समय नहीं। बड़े दुलार से पाला ममा-पापा ने। वह चार लड़कियों में सबसे छोटी थी। पढ़ाई-लिखाई में ज्यादा मन तो कभी नहीं लगा, बस कक्षाएँ पार करती गई। बड़ी कक्षाओं में रुकी भी, बस इंटर के बाद उसने पुस्तकों से हाथ जोड़ लिया। बड़ी बहने एक-से-एक फन में माहिर थीं। अकसर इनाम लेकर घर आतीं और वह सोचती रहती, मुझे क्या जरूरत है, इस टीना-टप्पर की, हम ऐसे ही किसी से कम नहीं हैं। बाद में तीनों ने अच्छी नौकरियाँ एवं अच्छा

घर–वर हासिल किया। रिया के मन में कोई मैल नहीं था अपनी बहनों के प्रति, उसे ममा–पापा का प्यार जो सबसे अधिक मिलता था। जिस चीज की ओर उँगली उठाई, अगले ही पल उसके हाथ में आ जाती। उसे घरेलू कामों से घृणा थी, यह क्या? घर पोंछो, चूल्हा साफ करो, जूठी थाली उठाओ, कहने पर भी उसने कुछ करना पसंद नहीं किया, चाहे ठीक रहे या बीमार, सब ममा के ही मत्थे?

वजन बढ़ा, किंतु ऊँचाई 4 फुट 9 इंच से ज्यादा नहीं बढ़ सकी, माँ को अपनी गोल–मटोल बेटी पर बहुत नाज था।

"जिहाँ जाही मोर बेटी, राज करही, देख के देबो, छोटा परवार, जिहाँ जियादा जुम्मेदारी झन रहैं।"

पच्चीसवें में दुलहन बनी थी वह; लोगों के अनुसार उसे अच्छा घर और सुंदर वर मिल गया था।

उसने तो बेवकूफ वर और भरा–पूरा घर पाया था। उसे सबसे ज्यादा अवांछित उस घर में उस स्त्री का प्रभाव लगता, जो कमाकर दस आदमी का परिवार चलाती, गधी जैसे सामान ढो–ढो कर लाती और उससे, रिया से अपेक्षा करती कि वह दौड़कर उसके लिए पानी लाए—ठेंगे पर जाए ऐसा प्रभाव, उसे किसी की परवाह नहीं थी, दौड़कर घर, दौड़कर बाहर, गाड़ी खड़ी करती, सामान उतारती और घर की सफाई में लग जाती। हुरती होगी बाहर में, बड़ा गुमान है अपनी मध्यम सुगठित काया पर, कपड़े सलीके से पहनकर आँखों पर चश्मा चढ़ाकर जब गाड़ी स्टार्ट करती तो जैसे रिया के कानों में साँप की फुफकार जहर घोलने लगती, "अब अपना दिन भर घूमे और हम घर में रहकर मक्खी मारें।"

"आज माँ की यह रचना प्रकाशित हुई, आज माँ का यहाँ–यहाँ सम्मान हुआ, यह देखो फोटो!" चेहरे से नूर टपकता रहता था बछड़े के। जहाँ ऑफिस से आया, बस घुसा माँ के आँचल में। लड़ो–झगड़ो, मारो–पीटो, सब सहेगा, डोकरी को हजार गालियाँ दो सुनेगा, लेकिन सामने पड़ते ही माँ! माँ! आजिज आ गया था उसका दिल। वैसे जब उसने अवसर पाया, उसी बेटे से ऐसी लताड़ लगवाई कि कई दिन तक रोती–बिसूरती रही। मन्नत भी माँगी थी

दामिनी माता से कि उसे मेरी जिंदगी से दूर कर दो तो बड़े कान वाले बकरे की बलि दूँगी, किसी ने सुनी उसकी गुहार? तभी तो जब उसने उसे स्पष्ट मना किया, "तू मेरे पति से बातें नहीं कर सकती, चुगली कर-करके मार खिलवाती है, शर्म-हया बाकी हो तो डूब मर चुल्लू भर पानी में, वह गुस्से में वैसे कम ही आती है, परंतु उस दिन तो आगबबूला हो गई, सुजल को खींच ले गई उसकी बगल से।

"ठीक है, तुम्हारा बेटा मेरे पास रहेगा!" वह पागल की तरह चीख पड़ी थी।

"मेरे बच्चे को मुझसे दूर मत करो!"

पूरा बल लगाकर डोकरी को ढकेला था, गिर पड़ी थीं मुँह के बल, उसकी चीख सुनकर बूढ़ा आ गया था, उसने डोकरी की दोनों बाहें कसकर पकड़ ली, बीच-बचाव की नीयत से।

"हटो-हटो, दूर हटो दोनों।"

उसने पलक झपकते ही उसका गला दबाना प्रारंभ कर दिया, उसके गले का मंगल सूत्र टूट कर बिखर गया। उसने लात चलाई, इसने कसकर पेट पर लात मार दी, झोटा पकड़कर बाल उखाड़ लिये, ले बड़ा गुमान है, डाई किए गए लंबेवाले बालों पर। बाल में हाथ उसने भी डाला, किंतु यहाँ तो गिने-चुने बाल हैं, कौन गधे; जैसे बालों का भार ढोता फिरे? सो मुट्ठी खाली रह गई।

रोती रह जिंदगी भर! झगड़े के डर से बताया नहीं अपने बेटे को। क्या बताएगी? वह कहाँ चाहती है कि किसी की जिंदगी सुख-चैन से गुजरे। सासों के शमन के लिए ही पुराने जमाने में ऋषि-मुनियों ने बुढ़ापे में संन्यास का प्रावधान रखा था। बहू को घर की चाबी दो और बुड्ढी निकलो घर से भगवान् की खोज में। अन्य परंपराओं के लिए तो खूब हाय-तौबा मचाएँगे, इसे एकदम भुला दिया है। अब तो जिंदगी भर की अपनी कमाई पर अपना अधिकार जताते हैं, जबकि कहा करते हैं, "सबकुछ बच्चों के लिए ही कर रहे हैं।" झूठे कहीं के, धमका रहा था अमर, जा अपने बाप को बुलाकर चली जा, मैं अपने घर से अलग नहीं रह सकता? रहेगा तो उसका बाप! उसने पारिवारिक हिंसा का आरोप लगाकर अंदर करवा दिया था, पति, सास-ससुर,

जेठ-जेठानी, सभी को। जाएँ वहीं सासपन बघारें, अमर के दोस्तों ने छुड़ाया था जमानत पर सभी को। डोकरी मरी क्यों नहीं? जहाँ चारों ओर प्रशंसा थी वहाँ, थू-थू हो गई, वह तो उनके आने के पहले ही सोनल और सुजल के साथ पिताजी के पास आ गई थी।

लंबी कानूनी लड़ाई के दौरान उसके मन में उनके प्रति कोई सद्भाव नहीं जनम सका, न ही उसकी प्रतिहिंसा कम हुई, कितना कहा उसने कि अलग घर बनाकर रहते हैं, डोकरी के मुँह पर थूकना बंद कर दो, लेकिन माना नहीं, उसे माँ और पत्नी दोनों चाहिए। क्या कभी एक म्यान में दो तलवारें रह सकती हैं? कोई बीमार पड़े, तड़ से सेवा की जिम्मेदारी ले लेगी, त्योहार आए नहीं कि उपहार उठा लाई। औरत है कि भूतनी? न चैन से रहे, न दूसरों को रहने दे। उसे बस प्रशंसा की भूख है। प्रशंसा और श्रेय पाने के लिए ही मरती रहती है। मरे, उसे तो अपना खयाल रखना है, सिर्फ अपना। वह अच्छी तरह जानती है, स्वास्थ्य बिगड़ा तो बस कोई अपना नहीं होनेवाला।

सोनल और सुजल जब कानून के द्वारा अपने पिता को दे दिए गए, तब उसकी आँखें पथराकर रह गईं। आँसू न जाने क्यों रूठ गए थे उससे। आग उठती थी पेट में और हृदय तक जला जाती थी।

"मैंने तो उसके बेटे को लात मार दी, फिर क्यों छीने उसने मेरे बच्चे?" फिर सोचती "ठीक हुआ, ले ले क्रेडिट अब अच्छी तरह! दो-दो बच्चे पालने का, निकल जाएगी सारी समाजसेवा, बहुत घमंड है उसे अपने जाँगर का। खैर, अच्छा हुआ! उसने संतोष की साँस ली थी, कौन अपनाता उसे बच्चों के साथ? मन होता, तो रो लेती, फिर आँसू पोंछकर मन बहलाने के लिए फेसबुक पर चेटिंग करती, कई दोस्त बने, किंतु लेपटॉप से बाहर न निकल सके। वह पासवाले मॉल या सुपर बाजार में समय काटती, उस दिन सिनेमा देखने का मूड हुआ, सो आकर बैठी, पिक्चर चल रही थी—'निकाह'। अपनी ही जैसी कहानी होगी, ऐसा उसे आभास था, किंतु वैसा नहीं निकला—उसका पति अमर न तो हीरो की तरह शक्की मिजाज था, न ही उसने उसे तलाक दिया था, यह तो उसी की जिद थी कि घर से अलग रहेंगे, नहीं तो एकदम अलग हो जाएँगे।

दूसरे विवाह के बाद की कहानी देख-देखकर वह रो रही थी कि बगल में बैठे व्यक्ति ने अपना रूमाल बढ़ा दिया।

"आँसू पोंछ लीजिए, आज के युग में आप जैसी भावुक महिला से मिलकर मैं आश्चर्यचकित हूँ।" राजेश ने बड़े मधुर स्वर में कहा था।

सच कहते हैं, जब कोई चुप करानेवाला हो, तभी रोने का भी मजा है। वह जी भर रोई थी। राजेश ने सहानुभूति जताते हुए जब उसका हाथ थाम लिया था, तब भी उसने कोई एतराज नहीं किया था। उसने रोते-रोते पूरी फिल्म देखी थी, बाद में कैफे में कॉफी पीकर एक नई उम्मीद के साथ वह घर आई थी। ससुराल छोड़ने के बाद पहली बार वह खुलकर हँसी थी। माँ, रोज की तरह अपने काम-धंधे में लगी थी। बड़ी बहन आई हुई थी, उसने उसकी प्रसन्नता का कुछ अंदाजा लगाया था।

"अच्छा किया रिया, जो सारे झंझट से निकल आई। हम तो आज पंद्रह वर्ष से सबकुछ झेल रहे हैं।"

"अब उतार फेंको सारे बंधन, नए रास्ते मिलेंगे!" आज वह मस्ती में जान पड़ रही थी।

"चौदह वर्ष का बेटा है रिया, मेरे बिना रह नहीं सकता, उसके भविष्य को कैसे दाँव पर लगा सकती हूँ, फिर मैं सोचती हूँ ऐसा कैसे संभव हो सकता है कि अन्य लोग हमारी सारी इच्छाएँ पूरी करें, हमारे सारे आवेग सहन करें और हम किसी का जरा भी न सहें।" वह गंभीर चिंतन में थी।

"अरे दीदी, कोशिश करने में क्या है, जब आप माँगेगी ही नहीं तो क्या मिलेगा आपको।" उसने बहन की बातों को हल्के में लिया। राजेश से मित्रता उसे जीने का नया संबल दे रही थी, उम्र थोड़ी ज्यादा थी, किसी कॉलेज में प्रोफेसर था, सीधा-सादा, निश्छल और अच्छी आमदनीवाला। पत्नी दो वर्ष पूर्व किसी बीमारी के कारण स्वर्ग सिधार चुकी थी। बच्चे थे नहीं। बस अकेला रह गया था बेचारा। ठीक है, रिया उसे वह सबकुछ देगी, जिसकी उसे आवश्यकता होगी। सबसे अच्छी बात तो यह कि उसकी माँ बचपन में गुजर चुकी थी। मिलना-जुलना बढ़ता गया, राजेश और रिया एक-दूसरे के काम आने लगे। माँ-पिताजी को भी रिया के पुनः घर बसाने में कोई एतराज नहीं था।

"कभी-कभी मैं यह सोचता हूँ रिया कि तुम जैसी पत्नी को ठुकरानेवाला व्यक्ति कितना बदकिस्मत था। क्या शुरू से ही वह तुम्हारी कोई परवाह नहीं करता था?" राजेश ने उसका हाथ अपने हाथ में लेकर हलके से दबाते हुए पूछा था।

"अब उन कटु स्मृतियों को मत कुरेदो राजेश! मैं उस आदमी को, जो सदा अपनी माँ के कहे पर चलता था, कभी सपने में भी याद करना नहीं चाहती, जिसे अपनी पत्नी की भावनाओं का खयाल नहीं, वैसा पति दुःख के सिवा क्या दे सकता है।" वह गहरे तक पीड़ा में डूब गई थी।

"भूल जाओ, जो बीत गया! हम अपनी नई जिंदगी प्रारंभ करने का विचार करें। देख लो यदि तुम्हें लगता हो कि हमारी निभ जाएगी तो।"

"निभेगी क्यों नहीं? तुम्हारे साथ न निभने का सवाल ही पैदा नहीं होता और है ही कौन, जिससे निभाना मुश्किल हो?" उसके होंठों से निकला था।

एक दिन वह उसका घर देख आई, सुंदर बँगला, राजेश अकेला रहकर भी इतने व्यवस्थित तरीके से रहता है, यह देखकर उसे बहुत अच्छा लगा था। दोपहर का खाना भी दोनों ने घर में साथ-साथ खाया था, उसने पूछा था, "खाना कौन बनाता है तुम्हारा?"

"हैं एक माँजी, वही बनाती हैं।" उसने छोटा सा उत्तर दिया था।

"अरे! नौकरानी पर पूरा घर छोड़े हुए हो तुम तो, क्या वह यहीं रहती है?" उसकी छठी इंद्री ने उसे सतर्क रहने का संकेत किया।

"वे बड़ी विश्वसनीय हैं, चिंता मत करो। फिर तो तुम आ रही हो, इस घर को सँभालने के लिए।" वह सहज था। उसने भी उसे देखने में कोई रुचि प्रदर्शित नहीं की, न ही वह सामने आई, एक खटका सा लग गया था रिया को, "कहीं यहाँ भी तो... ?"

नहीं! नौकरानी बदलने में उसे कितनी देर लगनेवाली थी। पैर तो पड़े उसका इस बँगले में। पिताजी ने भी राजेश को पसंद किया था, साधारण पार्टी का आयोजन कर वरमाला डलवा दी गई थी, एक-दूसरे के गले में। जो कुछ बन पड़ा, माँ-पिताजी ने दिया-लिया भी। सभी के चेहरे पर संतोष था। "चलो, बिगड़ी बात बन गई। रिया को अपना नया घर मिल गया। आज पति

मिला है, कल बच्चे भी मिल जाएँगे।"

जब वे घर पहुँचे, रात आधी ढल चुकी थी, रिया को याद आ रही थी अपनी पहली शादी, बरातियों की शरारतें, अमर की प्यासी आँखें, वह शहनाई, फूलों की सजावट, नाचते-गाते लोग, घर के दरवाजे पर सुहागिनें सज-धजकर आरती उतारने के लिए तैयार थीं, बड़ी माँ ने आरती की थी, वे सहज-सरल व्यक्तित्ववाली गाँव की महिला थीं। उसके समान कंका डायन नहीं, अपने आगे कुछ समझती ही नहीं किसी को, "यह उठाओ, वह उठाओ, यहाँ साफ करो, वहाँ सामान जमाओ।" देती रह गई आदेश। रिया ने हर बार पलटकर वार किया, "तुम्हीं कर लो।" मुझे समय नहीं मिलता, ऐसे फालतू कामों के लिए।

प्रसव के समय दस भुजा बन गई थी जैसे, अस्पताल घर, खाना-पीना, बच्चा-कच्चा सँभालना यहाँ तक कि उसके हाथ-पैर तक मलती थी।

"नवाइन ठीक से नहीं करती, मैं कमर में तेल अपने हाथ से लगाती हूँ।" "अपनी बहू के लिए छट्ठी का खाना मैं ही बनाऊँगी।" जैसा भी बने, अच्छा कहने की मजबूरी, बहुत निभाया रिया ने, "वह सब समझती थी, सबसे महत्त्वपूर्ण बने रहने की चाल थी सब, किसी सास ने आज तक अपनी बहू से प्रेम किया है, जो यह अजूबी करेगी? उसके दिल का कालापन वह बहुत पहले ही समझ गई थी। जब अवसर मिला, अच्छी खबर ली, कई बार तो दो-दो हफ्ते खाट पकड़े रह गई, किंतु हद हो गई बेशर्मी की, उठी तो फिर वैसी-की-वैसी। उसे सौत तक तो कह दिया रिया ने, फिर भी दस-बीस दिन बाद वही बेटा, वही बहू, इसीलिए तो रिया को लगता है उसका शक सच न हो कहीं। कलयुग में कुछ भी असंभव नहीं है। भगवान् करे उन्हें उनके किए की सजा मिले, घिसट-घिसट के मरें माँ-बेटे।

वह कार से उतरी थी, राजेश ने उसके लिए दरवाजा खोला था, न कहीं धुक-धुकी, न कहीं जिज्ञासा, रह तो रही है महीनों से राजेश के साथ, बस फर्क इतना ही है कि अब उनका रिश्ता कानूनी जामा पहन चुका है। अब उसकी कोख से जन्मे बच्चों का जायज पिता राजेश होगा। बच्चों की याद आते ही एक हूक-सी उठी।

"आह! मेरी सोनल! मेरा सुजल! मेरे देखते-देखते पराए हो गए। उन दुष्टों के कारण वह आज बिना बच्चों की हो गई है। उसकी आह जरूर उनका नाश करेगी। किसी दिन अवश्य वह सुनेगी कि डोकरी के मुँह में कीड़े पड़ गए, मर गई सड़-सड़के।

"कहाँ खो गई रिया?" माँ से मिलो।

"माँ से··· ?" उसे जैसे बिच्छू ने डंक मार दिया हो।

"कौन सी माँ, कैसी माँ? तुमने तो कहा था कि तुम्हारे माँ-बाप नहीं है।" कई प्रश्न एक साथ उसके मुँह से निकले। उसने सामने देखा, आरती का थाल लिये एक वृद्ध महिला खड़ी थी, वह उसे बड़ी वात्सल्य भरी निगाहों से देख रही थी। आरती के सुनहरे प्रकाश में उसका चेहरा दमक रहा था।

"रिया कोई भी बच्चा बिना माँ के कैसे बड़ा हो सकता है? ये मेरी यशोदा माँ हैं, इन्हें प्रणाम करो!" ये ही तुम्हारी सासू माँ हैं, माँ-बाप के न रहने पर, पत्नी की बीमारी में और फिर पत्नी के जाने के बाद के समय में इन्होंने ही मुझे जीने का संबल दिया, अपनी कोख के बच्चे की तरह मुझे पाला-पोसा, मैं इनकी राय के बिना कोई काम नहीं करता, अब इनकी पूरी जिम्मेदारी मेरी और तुम्हारी है। ये मेरे लिए जन्मदात्री से भी कुछ अधिक ही हैं। रिया आज जो तुम इस घर की मालकिन बनी हो, यह भी इनकी ही कृपा का फल है, इन्होंने तुम्हारी दुःख भरी कहानी सुनी और मुझे भरोसा दिया कि ये अपनी बहू को इतना प्यार और सम्मान देंगी कि वह अपने सारे दुःख भूल जाएगी।" कहते-कहते राजेश भावविभोर हो गया। उसने झुककर माँ के पैर छुए।

"धोखा!··· !···मेरे साथ धोखा हुआ··· !··· !···" रिया के मुँह से अस्फुट शब्द निकले और वह बेहोश होकर राजेश की बाँहों में झूल गई।

□

खोज सको, तो...

लगभग 6 वर्ष का था, जब उसने पहली बार उसे 'माँ' कहकर पुकारा था। उसकी ममता बह चली थी धारो-धार। एक बार जो कसकर गले से लगाया तो वह उसके आँचल में छुप-सा गया। एक वर्ष तक लगातार उसने उसे दही-बेसन से रगड़-रगड़कर नहलाया था। गोरा रंग शीशे-सा निखर आया था। नाम रखा था—अनुराग, अनुराग श्रीवास्तव। दोनों की प्यास बराबर थी, दूर के रिश्तेवाले भइया-भाभी के एक्सीडेंट में चल बसने के बाद तीन वर्ष का अनु सभी रिश्तेदारों के लिए जैसे भार हो गया था। दस जगह भटकने के बाद उसे अनाथालय में डाल दिया गया। सास रिश्ते को याद रखते हुए दो-चार महीने में एक-दो पैकेट बिस्कुट के दे आया करती। प्यार से सिर पर हाथ फेर दिया करती।

व्यक्ति के नाते-रिश्ते उसके लिए पुकारने के शब्द थे। माँ, पापा, दीदी, भइया, सब थे आश्रम में, परंतु वह अनुभूति नहीं थी, जिसके लिए हर व्यक्ति व्यग्र रहता है। दान-दाताओं, सरकारी मदद आदि से प्राप्त अर्थ का यथा योग्य बँटवारा होता। मैनेजर, क्लर्क, वस्तु परिचायक, रसोइया आदि से होते हुए बच्चों के मुँह तक सूखी रोटी का टुकड़ा आता। छोटी-छोटी वस्तुओं के लिए मार-पीट, गाली-गलौज, लड़ना-भिड़ना और पले-पलाए अनाथालय के कर्मचारियों द्वारा अच्छी प्रकार तोड़ा जाना, यही दिनचर्या थी वहाँ।

वह भी तो तड़प रही थी, आँचल के खालीपन से। साल भर पहले ब्याह कर आई वह मोटी-सी लड़की एक बच्चे की माँ बन गई और वह तब तक महीने के रुकने का इंतजार ही कर रही थी। उम्र के साथ उसके पेट पर भी

तो मोटी चर्बी चढ़ गई थी, परंतु मन मानता नहीं था कि वह अपनी आधी से अधिक उम्र पार कर चुकी है। जब तक बड़े-बड़े बच्चे न हों, कोई औरत अधेड़ कैसे हो सकती है भला? वह सोचा करती।

"बस दूसरों के लिए ही सोठउरा बाँधती रहोगी, छछूँदर भी नहीं जनमेगी इस बूढ़ी काया से, बाँझ-हो-बाँझ! मान लो! अब डॉक्टर क्या कर लेगा, जब भाग्य में लिखाकर नहीं लाई? जरा-सी बात पर इतना कुछ बोल गईं अम्माजी।" वह अंदर कमरे में जाकर देर तक रोती रही। देवरानी पहली बार माँ बनी थी, छठी मनाई जा रही थी। कुआँ पूजते समय वह सुरीले राग से गा रही थी, "जल भरो हिलोरी हिलोरी रेशम की डोरियाँ।" "रेशम डोरियाँ तब निक लागे, जब सोन धइलवा होई रेशम की डोरियाँ।" पूजा खतम हुई-न-हुई वह वहाँ से चलने की तैयारी करने लगी।

"माँ! अमेरिका से एक डॉक्टर आया है, 60 वर्ष की औरत के भी उसने बच्चा पैदा कराया है। मैं तो अभी 42 की ही हो रही हूँ, आप देखना जरा, मैं चलती हूँ।"

"अरे! इतने सारे मेहमान आए हैं, अभी ही जाने की क्या जरूरत पड़ गई, डॉक्टर फिर नहीं मिलेगा क्या?" अम्मा की त्योरियों पर बल पड़ गए थे।

"समय को कोई नहीं जानता अम्मा! डॉक्टर के पास कई दिनों से नंबर लगा रखा है आपके बेटे ने।" वह अपना पर्स लेकर घर से निकल रही थी कि अम्मा कह पड़ी थीं।

"बस आज तू बच्चा लेकर ही लौटना, अकेली आई तो घर में घुसने नहीं पाएगी। सब सुनते हुए बाइक पर पीछे बैठ गई थी वह।

भरी हुई आँखें देखकर सबकुछ समझ गए थे दिनेश।

"तुम कुछ मत सोचो! अम्मा तो हमारी औलाद का मुँह देखने के लिए पगला गईं हैं।" शब्दों से मरहम लगाया था उन्होंने।

किसी कारणवश डॉक्टर से मुलाकात न हो पाई थी, घर का उत्सव, मेहमानों की भीड़ बहुत बेगानी लगी थी उसे, वह दिनेश के साथ देर रात तक पार्क मैं बैठी रही थी, ऊपर से चुप, किंतु मन में तूफानी हलचल लिये, सब के सोने के बाद ही घर जाना ठीक रहेगा, दोनों एक ही बात सोच रहे

थे। "मैं आपके लिए बड़ी अशुभ हूँ, एक औलाद भी न दे सकी अब तक।" पार्क से उठते हुए उसने भरे गले से कहा था।

"माँ की बातों को दिल से मत लगाओ शोभा! शायद उनकी बातें दाता के कानों तक पहुँच ही जाएँ, उसकी हथेली दबाकर दिनेश ने उसे सांत्वना दी थी।

घर पहुँचे तो देखा, सब तो जहाँ-तहाँ सो चुके थे, अम्मा दरवाजे पर टहल रही थीं। "कहाँ गए थे तुम लोग? एक फोन ही कर दिया होता।" उनकी आवाज फटी हुई थी। पछता रही थीं अपने किए पर।

शोभा चुपचाप कमरे में जा रही थी कि माँ ने रास्ता रोक लिया।

"मेरी बात का बुरा मान गई? माफ कर दे बेटी, सठिया गई हूँ बुढ़ापे में। जितनी बातें कहीं, उनमें एक भी क्षमा योग्य नहीं है बेटी, पर तेरा दिल बहुत बड़ा है।" उन्होंने शोभा को अंक में भर लिया था।

"माँ! यह क्या! इतने लोगों के सामने इसे क्या कुछ न कह दिया तुमने? तुम बाज आओ वरना मैं इसे लेकर घर छोड़ दूँगा, फिर खिला लेना पोता!" दिनेश ने कड़ुए स्वर में माँ को उनकी गलती का अहसास दिलाया।

"मान गई थी शोभा, माँ अब तक भूखी बैठीं थीं। तीनों ने भोजन किया था, टूटे मन से। दूसरे दिन माँ कार्यक्रम से बची मिठाइयाँ-पूड़ियाँ लेकर अनाथाश्रम जा रही थीं। रिक्शे पर बैठीं तो सँभाल नहीं पा रही थीं। उसकी ओर असहाय दृष्टि से देखा था और वह बैठ गई थी उनके साथ।

अनाथाश्रम में अंदर प्रविष्ट होते ही छोटे-बड़े बच्चों ने उन्हें घेर लिया था। 'दादी'—अनु माँजी के पास आकर उन्हें प्यार भरी नजरों से देख रहा था। "तेरी बुआ भी आई है।" उसकी तरफ संकेत किया था माँ ने। "बुआ नहीं, मेरी माँ!" वह उसके अंक में समाता चला गया था उसके मातृ-अंगों में सनसनी-सी अनुभव हुई थी, आँखें नम हुईं और दिल की धड़कने तेज हो गई थीं, उसे ऐसा लगा, जैसे दिनभर की लू के बाद शाम को मेघ ने धरती पर शीतल जल के छीटें मारे हों।

"तू कहाँ था अब तक, मेरी याद भी नहीं आई तुझे? तू क्यों नहीं आया मेरे पास अब तक?" वह कुछ निरर्थक से शब्द बुदबुदा रही थी।

"माँ, मुझे छोड़कर मत जाना अब! कितने दिनों से तुम्हें पुकार रहा था मैं। वह आशा भरी निगाहों से उसे देख रहा था। दिनेश और माँ ने पूरा सहयोग किया था, अनु को उसका बनाने में, सारी कानूनी औपचारिकताएँ पूरी कर उन्होंने उसे सदा के लिए अपना बना लिया था। परिवार में थोड़ी-बहुत बातें हुईं, किंतु पति-पत्नी की प्रसन्नता देख सब चुप हो गए थे।

समय लगा था एक अनाथ बच्चे को अपना वारिस बनाने में, वह तो जैसे अपनी सारी पीड़ा भूलकर इतराना सीख गई थी अपने भाग्य पर। अनु ने उनके सूने संसार में खुशियों का खजाना भर दिया था, थोड़ा कुछ रह गया था पाने को, सद्य प्रसूत शिशु का मुख कैसा होता होगा, जब एक औरत अपने बच्चे को जन्म देती होगी, वह क्षण कैसा होता होगा, वह क्षण क्या वैसा ही होता होगा, जब वह अनु से पहली बार मिली थी? "कोई बात नहीं, अनु की औलाद से यह कमी भी पूरी हो जाएगी," वह समझाती थी स्वयं को। पलक झपकते ही जैसे अनु, गोरा-नारा लंबा सा सुंदर युवक बनकर खड़ा था उनके सामने। स्वास्थ्य विभाग का शासकीय कर्मचारी, नौकरी लगी थी कमालपुर के सरकारी अस्पताल में, भेजना पड़ा था अपना बेटा, उसे संतोष था अनु की तरक्की से। अब तो उसके सपने बिना पंखों के न जाने कहाँ-कहाँ की यात्रा करने लगे थे।

"बस, अब बहू ले आओ।" परिवार के लोग छेड़ते।

"आप लोगों का आशीर्वाद रहा तो वह दिन भी आ जाएगा।"

जब भी छुट्टी मिलती, अनु घर भागा आता, दिनेश की तबीयत अब खराब रहने लगी थी। शुगर और हाई बी.पी. ने उनकी हालत बिगाड़ रखी थी। उन्होंने समय से पूर्व ही सेवानिवृत्ति ले ली थी।

"बस, अब अनु की शादी हो जाए तो सब लोग साथ-साथ रहें, इतना बड़ा घर, बड़ा सूना-सूना लगता है। हम चार-छह नाती-पोते लेंगे शोभा! बस जिंदगी का अंतिम चरण गुजार लेंगे हँसी-खुशी।" दिनेश भी विचार बाँटते रहते उससे। हमारी बहू बहुत सुंदर होनी चाहिए, या फिर सुंदर भले ही कम हो, परिवार को लेकर चलनेवाली होनी चाहिए, इस विषय पर अकसर उनमें बहस होती रहती।

"माँ, वह टेंटवाला पूछ रहा है कुछ।" अनुराग था, जून की गरमी में पसीने से लथ-पथ, पार्टी की व्यवस्था में लगा।"

"क्या हुआ, हम अनु की शादी में शामिल नहीं हो सके। शानदार पार्टी करेंगे, पोते का अन्नप्राशन है, कोई हँसी-खेल है क्या।" स्वर से ऐसा लगा था, जैसे इस डाल से उस डाल कूदता बंदर, एक डाल छोड़कर दूसरी पकड़ने की विवशता को भोग रहा हो, उसने डाल पकड़ने में देर की नहीं कि जमीन पर आ पड़ेगा और डाल से छूटे बंदर को बंदर-समाज कभी स्वीकार नहीं करता।

"क्या हुआ अनु ने हमें अपनी शादी में नहीं बुलाया? हम बहू को पूरे मन से अपनाएँगे, समुद्र की तरह बनकर, जिसमें सारी नदियाँ आकर मिल जाती हैं अपना अस्तित्व भूलकर।"

छह माह का बेटा हो गया अनु का और उन्हें पता तक नहीं था, वह तो कमालपुर के किसी आदमी से बाजार में उसकी भेंट हो गई, तब सारी बातों का भेद खुला, उसे तो जरा भी विश्वास नहीं हुआ, भले ही पेट की मजबूरी के कारण उनका बेटा उनसे दूर रहता है, परंतु जब आता है, उसकी गोद में ही सोता है अब तक, इतना बड़ा छल वह कर ही नहीं सकता। विश्वास-अविश्वास के झूले पर हिचकोले खाते वे कमालपुर पहुँचे थे।

एक अधेड़ उम्र की बेवा ने दरवाजा खोला था, उसकी आँखों में प्रश्न थे, "आप कौन हैं, कैसे आए हैं?"

"क्या यह अनुराग श्रीवास्तव का मकान है?"

"हाँ, पर मैंने आप लोगों को पहचाना नहीं।"

"हम उनके माता-पिता हैं, आप कौन हैं?" शोभा ने पूछा था।

"आइए, आइए, पहले अंदर आइए।" वह दरवाजे से हट गई थी। सुंदर सजा ड्राइंग रूम, सब-कुछ व्यवस्थित, जैसे ही वे सोफे पर बैठे, अंदर से छोटे बच्चे के रोने की आवाज आई।

"लगता है उसने सच ही कहा था।" शोभा बोल पड़ी।

"पहले सच सामने तो आने दो।" दिनेश अभी भी भ्रम में थे।

वह औरत ट्रे में पानी ले आई।

"लीजिए पानी!"

"पहले बताइए हमें, अनुराग कहाँ है?"

"वह तो ड्यूटी पर गया है?"

"आप उसकी कौन हैं?"

"जी मैं उसकी···सास हूँ।" वह कुछ सकुचाती हुई-सी बोली थी।

"यह कैसे हो सकता है? हमारे बेटे ने हमें इतना बड़ा धोखा दिया!" शोभा की आँखों के आगे अँधेरा छा गया, वह गिरने को हुई।

"बहनजी, सँभालिए स्वयं को, मनुष्य परिस्थितियों के आगे विवश होता है।" वह शोभा को सँभालने में लगी थी। थोड़ी ही देर में अनुराग ने ड्राइंग रूम की कॉलबेल बजाई।

दरवाजा उढ़का भर था, अंदर का दृश्य देखकर वह सकते में आ गया। "अरे क्या हुआ मेरी माँ को?" पापा, आप लोग बिना किसी सूचना के कैसे आ गए?" वह एक तरफ शोभा को सँभाल रहा था, दूसरी तरफ दिनेश से प्रश्न पूछ रहा था।

"यही जो कुछ देखना बाकी था, उसे देखने आ गए, तुमने तो हमें जीते जी मार दिया अनुराग, क्या हमारी ममता में कहीं खोट रह गया था?" उनकी आवाज आर्द्र हो उठी।

"पापा! पहले माँ को सँभालते हैं, फिर क्या मजबूरी थी, बताऊँगा आप को।" "आरती! ग्लूकोज का शरबत ले आओ माँ के लिए"! वह चिल्लाया था। एक हाथ में शरबत का गिलास और दूसरे में बच्चे को लेकर आई वह।

"पापा! अपने पोते को सँभालिए जरा!" उसने बेतकल्लुफी से बच्चा उनकी गोद में डाला और शोभा के मुँह से गिलास लगा दिया। थोड़ी देर लगी थी उसे प्रकृतिस्थ होने में।

"एक बार हमें बताया तो होता तुमने कि तुम अपनी पसंद से शादी करना चाहते हो, देख तो लिया होता हमारा मन! क्या हमारी खुशी तुमसे अलग थी अनुराग? वह कराह रही थी।

"माँ! हमने गलती की थी और इस आपके पोते के लिए हमें शादी करनी पड़ी। मुझे मालूम था माँ, तुमने मेरे लिए क्या कुछ नहीं किया, यदि

इसे कुछ हो जाता तो शायद मैं कभी भी आप से क्षमा नहीं पा सकता था।"

"बेटा! यदि हम तेरी खुशी में शामिल होने लायक नहीं थे, तो कम-से-कम जब तेरा बेटा बहुत बीमार था, तब तो फोन कर दिया होता," दूसरे दिन कहा था शोभा ने।

"उस समय कितना अकेला हो गया था माँ, लगता था भगवान् मुझे मेरे कर्मों की सजा दे रहे हैं, जैसे मैंने आप लोगों का दिल दुखाया, वैसे ही इधर भी पा रहा हूँ। मैं हर दिन बेचैन रहा माँ, यह सोचकर कि कहीं पापा-मम्मी को सदमा न लग जाए ये सब जानकर।"

बड़ा सा आँगन, चारों ओर बने आठ कमरे, सारा घर सुव्यवस्थित, सुंदर सलोनी-सी बहू, दौड़-दौड़कर सेवा कर रही थी, पापा, पापा करते मुँह नहीं थक रहा था उसका। उसने अपने काम से छुट्टी ले ली थी, "मेरे सास-ससुर आए हैं, उनकी खातिरदारी करनी है।" वह तरह-तरह के व्यंजन बना रही थी।

"हाँ, ऐसी ही बहू की कल्पना तो की थी हमने, सुंदर-सुशील और परिवार को लेकर चलनेवाली, सुना है उसकी माँ के पास दस एकड़ खेत भी है। अच्छी तकदीर है हमारे अनु की। हाँ, हम खोजते तो भी इतना अच्छा रिश्ता न मिलता, फिर हीरे जैसा पोता, सारे सुख अचानक दे दिए भगवान् ने।"

दिनेश पोते को पाकर पिछला बीता कल भूलना चाह रहे थे, परंतु स्वर में यह उदासी कैसी, उसके मन में भी काँच की किरच जैसा कुछ काट रहा था धीरे-धीरे··· "क्या नहीं मिला?" पूछा उसने अपने मन से, 'क्या बेटे का बसा संसार बरदाश्त नहीं हो रहा है, ईर्ष्या हो रही है?'

"अरे नहीं-नहीं, बेटे की खुशी न भाए, यह कैसे हो सकता है, बेटे का सेहरा देखने के लिए तो कब से उसकी आँखें तरस रही थीं, फिर पोता, वह तो ईश्वर का वरदान ही है, जैसे, दिनेश के क्रोध की दवा बन गया है वह तो।"

"बिना कोशिश के मिल गया इतना कुछ, इसीलिए मन कसक रहा है क्या?" उसने पुनः अपना मन टटोला।

"ऐसा भी क्यों हो? यह तो ईश्वर की कृपा है, बचपन में बहुत दुःख

झेला था उसके अनु ने, उससे मिलने से पहले, बाद में तो उसने दिनेश को भी कभी उसे डाँटने-डपटने नहीं दिया था। उसने अवसर भी नहीं दिया, जिस राह पर चलाया, उसी पर चल पड़ा, परंतु जीवन का इतना अहम फैसला और वह दरकिनार हो गई, अनु के प्यार के लिए वह सारी दुनिया से लड़ जाती।"

"तो क्या लड़ने का मौका नहीं मिला, इसलिए मलाल है?" मन ने व्यंग्य किया। ठीक है, अब यदि नहीं अपनाते तो फिर से हो जाएँगे पहले जैसे अकेले, बुद्धिमानी इसी में है कि इनके मन में अपना प्रेम बढ़ाया जाए, विश्वास जगाया जाए। पति-पत्नी कमा रहे हैं, प्रगाढ़ प्रेम में आबद्ध, बच्चे को बहू की माँ सँभाल रही है, हमें चिंता ही क्या है, बस अपने घर में रहो, अपने में मस्त। चिंता हमें तब भी क्या थी, जब अनु हमारी जिंदगी में नहीं था। जिम्मेदारियों की जंजीर पकड़कर ही तो मनुष्य उम्र के पहाड़ चढ़ता है। सुख-दुःख के मेले उसे प्रेरणा देते हैं, आगे बढ़ने के लिए, अपनी मंजिल पाने के लिए। जिम्मेदारी निभाने की चिंता न हो, तो जीवन निरुद्देश्य न हो जाएगा? इसी मायाजाल में बँधने के लिए तो हम दर-दर भटके थे, एक औलाद चाहिए थी हमें।

"हमारी संपत्ति की अनु को तो कोई आवश्यकता नहीं है शोभा। सोचता हूँ किसी संस्था को दान कर दूँ, जो कुछ आज तक बचाया है।" उसी की भाँति दिनेश के मन में भी कुछ चल रहा था लगातार···।

"देखिए! यहाँ की वस्तुएँ यहीं रह जातीं हैं, यह तो पता ही है, अब इससे क्या फर्क पड़ता है कि इसका मालिक कौन होता है। मन छोटा क्यों करते हैं? सब ठीक हो जाएगा, उसे हमारी न सही, हमें तो उसकी जरूरत है।" उसने दिनेश को समझाने की कोशिश की थी।

"माँ, यहाँ बैठो न मुन्ने को लेकर, पंडितजी पूजा कराएँगे, हाँक लगाई थी अनु ने। उनका शौक पूरा करने के लिए ही आज आरती ने सोलह सिंगार किया था, उनके जाननेवाले पहली बार उनकी बहू को देख रहे थे। मेहमान सारे अनचीह्ने थे, इसलिए हाथ जोड़े उसने अपने होंठों पर एक नकली मुसकान चस्पा कर ली थी।

वह बैठी थी बच्चे को गोद में लेकर, परंतु वह जोर-जोर से रोने लगा,

उसे सँभालना मुश्किल हो गया, वह रुआँसी हो गई। उसकी नानी उसे लेकर आराम से पूजा में बैठी। वह गेट पर जाकर मेहमानों का स्वागत करने लगी।

"बड़ी तकदीर है आपकी, बिना खोजे इतनी सुंदर बहू मिल गई।" जैसे ही कोई बधाई देता, उसके दिल में हूक सी उठती। मेहमानों से घिरे बैठे थे दिनेश।

"शादी का पूरा खर्च अन्नप्राशन में ही खर्च कर दोगे, ऐसा लग रहा है श्रीवास्तवजी, बड़ा सुंदर आयोजन है और वह जो बड़ी-बड़ी पुतलियाँ नाच रही हैं, वे तो बड़ी मन भावन हैं।"

"हाँ भाई, एक ही तो बेटा है मेरा, बचाकर क्या करूँगा?" वे उत्तर देते।

"माँ! कहीं कोई कमी है क्या, मुझे लग रहा है तुम कुछ खोज रही हो? क्या चाहिए, बोलो, ले आऊँ!" अनु अब भी उसका मन पढ़ना भूला नहीं है। उसे जरा-सा अच्छा लगा।

"कुछ खोज तो रही हूँ बेटा।"

"क्या माँ?"

"शायद अपने बेटे के जीवन में, उसके घर में, उसके सुख-दुःख में अपना स्थान!" उसकी पीड़ा डी.जे. की कर्कश ध्वनि में तिरोहित हो गई।

"तो क्या तुमने मुझे क्षमा नहीं किया माँ?"

"मैं तुमसे नाराज ही कब थी? मैं तो बस, तुम्हें अपने हाथों से दूल्हा बनाना चाहती थी, आरती उताकर अपनी बहू को गृह-प्रवेश कराना चाहती थी, मैं चाहती थी कि मेरा पोता सबसे पहले मेरी गोद में आँखें खोले, उसके जन्मोत्सव में सोहर गाकर पितरों को आमंत्रित करना चाहती थी, शायद यही कुछ खोज रही हूँ मैं, खोज सकते हो तो खोज लाओ। लगता था, जैसे उसकी आवाज किसी गहरे कुएँ से आ रही है।

"और अब बुलाइए बच्चे के दादा को, अन्नप्राशन का मुहूर्त आ गया है।" पंडित ने पुकारा और अनु उसका प्रश्न अनुत्तरित छोड़कर पापा की ओर चल पड़ा।

□

माटी कहे कुम्हार से…

खड़…खड़…खड़…स्ट्रेचर की कानफोड़ू आवाज सुनकर स्नेहा की नींद उचट गई, उसका सारा शरीर काँपने लगा। पेट में उथल-पुथल होने लगी। सेमी प्राइवेट रूम का एक बिस्तर खाली था, उसी पर कोई नई पेशेंट आ रही थी लेबर ओटी से। पेशेंट तो बेहोश थी, वार्ड बॉय और हाउस कीपर ने मिलकर उसे उतारा और खाली बिस्तर पर लेटा दिया। वह कराह रही थी बेहोशी की हालत में। उसके पीछे-पीछे गोद में बच्चा लिये एक उम्रदराज महिला ने कक्ष में प्रवेश किया। अटेंडर के खाली पड़े बिस्तर पर बैठ गई थी वह, बच्चे को लिये-लिये।

"क्या हुआ?" उसने अनायास ही उस महिला से पूछ लिया।

"बेटी है।"

"पहली है?"

"नहीं, चौथी।"

"चौ…ऽ…ऽ…थी ऽ…ऽ… ? जाँच नहीं करवाई क्या?"

"क्या करते जाँच करवाकर? प्रसाद समझकर ले लिया, जो मिला।" महिला की आवाज गंभीर थी, लग रहा था जैसे कुछ कामना के विपरीत हो गया हो, वह अपने आप को सँभाले हुए थी।

"आप बहुत दु:खी हो रही हैं?" उसके स्वर में स्वत: सहानुभूति घुल गई।

"मेरा भगवान् जानता है, मुझे बच्ची होने का कोई गम नहीं है, देखिए न, तीन बच्चियाँ नॉर्मल हो गईं, इसके समय ऑपरेट करना पड़ा, वह तो भगवान्

का लाख-लाख शुक्र है कि मेरी दोनों बच्चियाँ सही सलामत हैं।" उसने लंबी साँस ली। नवजात बच्ची सो रही थी, सद्यः प्रसूता की कराह धीमे-धीमे बिखर रही थी कमरे में।

"ये आप की कौन··· ?"

"मेरी बेटी है सबसे छोटी, यह पुरातत्त्व अधिकारी है, दामाद भी ऊँचे पद पर हैं, इसकी बड़ी बेटी कॉलेज में पढ़ रही है। इस उम्र में बच्चा चाहने का कोई सवाल ही नहीं था, किंतु आनेवाले को कौन रोक सकता है! आ.ही गई।"

"स्नेहाऽ···ऽ! आँखें बंद करके सो जाओ, तुम्हारे लिए नींद आवश्यक है।" इस खटर-पटर में देवकी की भी नींद खुल गई, अस्पताल में वैसे भी कौन सो पाता है! पाँचवें दिन स्नेहा की तबीयत थोड़ी ठीक थी, सो देवकी भी जरा आराम करना चाहती थी। अब तक तो जैसे गले पर तलवार लटक रही थी। यदि स्नेहा को कुछ हो गया होता तो सारी बदनामी उसी की होनी थी। सास-ससुर तो थे नहीं, दोनों जेठ अपनी-अपनी नौकरी पर गाँव से दूर रहते थे, पुस्तैनी मकान में वही तो रहती थी अपने पति-बच्चों के साथ। सारे रिश्तेदारों की आव-भगत, नेवता-हँकारी, सबकुछ उसी की तो जिम्मेदारी है। ननदों का क्या, जरा सा ससुराल में जी ऊबा, चलो पाँड़ेपुर, भाभी सबकुछ करेगी ही। यह स्नेहा तो और! ससुराल में इसके पैर टिकते कहाँ हैं! जब मायके में किसी की नहीं सुनती तो ससुराल में क्या सुनती होगी? लगी आधी रात को चबड़-चबड़ करने, ससुरालवालों को छोड़कर सारी दुनिया इसकी सगी है। वह मन-ही-मन बड़बड़ाई। अब उसने स्नेहा की ओर मुँह कर लिया। नई पेशेंट को अभी डीप चढ़ रहा था, लाइट तो बुझने से रही! स्नेहा ने कंबल खींचकर मुँह ढक लिया और नींद को बुलाने लगी, परंतु उचटी नींद फिर आती कहाँ है! उसकी आँखों के आगे सोना-मोना के चेहरे नाचने लगे। कितनी प्यारी बच्चियाँ हैं! बात करती हैं तो लगता है, जैसे फूल झड़ रहे हों! अभी आठ वर्ष की ही तो है सोना और मोना पाँच की, दुनिया-जहान की बातें सुन लो! ऐसी ही तो वह भी होती! वही जो छोटे-छोटे टुकड़ों में दिखी थी, जिन्हें पहचानना मुश्किल था···नहीं···नहीं मुझे अपना बीता हुआ कल याद

करने की आवश्यकता नहीं है, जो शेष है, उसे ही समेटना है अब तो, वह न जाने किस जन्म की दुश्मन थी? किस पाप का बदला लेने आई थी उसकी कोख में? रोज हजारों औरतें ऐसा करती हैं, जैसा उसने किया, किसी को पता भी नहीं चलाता, सारा बखेड़ा उसी के साथ होना था। उसने अपनी पीड़ा में आराम पाने के लिए सारा दोष उस अजन्मी बच्ची के सिर मढ़ दिया, जो स्वयं उसकी क्रूरता की शिकार हो गई थी।

हाँ, अब तो दूसरों के साथ वह भी स्वयं को डाँटने के लायक ही रह गई है। बी.एस-सी. पास किया था उसने, अच्छे मार्क्स आए थे, वह कॉम्पटीशन की तैयारी करना चाहती थी अपनी सहेलियों की तरह।

"जा, वहीं जाकर करना, जो कुछ करना हो! हमारी और भी लड़कियाँ हैं, रिटायर होने के पहले सभी को निपटाना है हमें। अच्छे ब्राह्मण हैं, दस बीघा खेत है, पढ़ा-लिखा लड़का है, सास बिजनेसवाली है, माँग-जाँच कुछ है नहीं, चार आदमी का छोटा सा परिवार रहेगा, और क्या चाहिए तुझे?" पापा ने डाँट दिया था।

सबकुछ सच ही निकला, दस बीघे खेत में जाओ, गेहूँ उगाओ! कमी क्या है? सास की नर्मदा के किनारे जबलपुर के रामघाट पर माला-फूल की दुकान है। ससुर गाँव में खेत-खार घर-द्वार देखते हैं। पढ़े-लिखे पति को आज तक कोई ढंग की नौकरी नहीं मिल सकी। आज यहाँ तो कल वहाँ, हजार-दो हजार महीने के लिए बारह से पंद्रह घंटे रोज झख मारता रहता है। बिना नागा पढ़े-लिखे होने का ताना सहो। डोकरिया न जाने कहाँ से हाथ देखना सीख आई है, लोग भीड़ लगाए रहते हैं दुकान में। आँख के अंधे गाँठ के पूरे लोगों की कमी कहाँ है अपने देश में? न जाने कैसे जोड़-तोड़ करके जबलपुर में एक छोटा सा मकान खरीद लिया है, बस वही सोलह आना है, दुकान का भी बहाना ही है, छाती पर मूँग दलती यहीं जमे रहने का। बेटा तो हई है लल्लूलाल, पल्लू पकड़े रहता है माँ का। अब तो सोना-मोना भी दादी-दादी करती घूमती रहती हैं, नाश्ता दादी के हाथ से, खाना दादी के हाथ से, बाल वे ही अच्छा बनाती हैं। स्कूल उन्हीं के साथ जाना है, लोग उनकी इज्जत करते हैं। सोना रात में उन्हीं के साथ सोती है, वे कहानियाँ सुनाती हैं।

"जाओ तुम लोग भी, उसे किसी से कुछ लेना-देना नहीं है।" चिढ़कर उसने मन-ही-मन कहा था।

एक मुट्‌ठी भात के लिए मैके में भारी नहीं है स्नेहा, माँ-बाप की जायदाद में बेटी का इतना तो हक बनता ही है। रहो तुम लोग दादी-पापा के साथ, पढ़ो-लिखो, चाहे जहन्नुम में चली जाओ! जब अपना मन परेशान रहता है, तब कुछ भी अच्छा नहीं लगता। बड़ी गोड़धरिया के बाद एक प्राइवेट स्कूल में नौकरी भी लगी तो सारा कस-बल निकल गया। सुबह सात से दोपहर तीन बजे तक स्कूल में पढ़ाओ, बाद में पालकों से संपर्क करो, रात में मूल्यांकन की कॉपियों की जाँच! अपना जीवन तो रह ही नहीं गया हो जैसे। बच्चियों को देख-देखकर तो वह और चिड़चिड़ाती, उनके सिवा और था भी कौन, जिस पर वह अपनी खीज निकालती? ऐसे में वे और दादी के निकट होती गईं। जैसे ही स्कूल की छुट्‌टी हुई, वह निकल गई पाँड़ेपुर के लिए, इस बार तो जाते समय बताया भर था कि वह जा रही है, और नहीं तो क्या? दस साल हो गए शादी हुए, कब तक कहीं आने-जाने के लिए रिरियाती रहे! अपना भी कोई वजूद है या नहीं?

उसका पाँड़ेपुर पहुँचना हुआ कि देवकी भाभी का अपने मायके जाना हो गया। उनके भतीजे की शादी पड़ी थी। यह तो वैसे ही हो गया, जैसे कोई नमाज बख्शवाने जाए और रोजे गले पड़ जाए। गाँव में इन दिनों काम की भरमार रहती है। फसल की कटाई-मड़ाई, मजदूरों का दाना-पानी सबकुछ सुरक्षित रखना, भाई बेचारे की सालभर की कमाई थी, भाभी को समझ में नहीं आया तो क्या वह भी नासमझ बन जाए? हल्की सी नींद आई थी, फिर खुल गई, बगल में बच्ची काँय-काँय कर रही थी। उसकी नानी उसके कपड़े बदल रही थी।

एक हूक सी उठी उसके दिल में। अब कोई कभी इस कोख में पैर नहीं पसारेगा, वह अधूरी औरत हो गई, जिस अंग के कारण औरत मर्द से भिन्न होती है, वह उसे खो चुकी है। न नौ माह का लाड़-प्यार, न देख-भाल, न घर के कामों से छुट्‌टी, अब से कभी कोई नन्हे-नन्हे हाथ उसके स्तनों से खिलवाड़ नहीं करेंगे, उसके आँचल से अब कभी अमृत नहीं झरेगा। उसका

जीवन एक न भरनेवाले सूनेपन से सदा के लिए घिर गया। उसने पेट से आग का गोला गले की ओर चढ़ता अनुभव किया। आँखों से गरम-गरम आँसू बह चले। उसने सिसकी रोकने के लिए अपना मुँह दबाया, बनावटी दोषारोपण, सत्य के प्रकाश में अँधेरे की भाँति नष्ट हो गया। जाग जाएगी देवकी भाभी तो फिर दस बातें सुनाएगी। जब डाँट की जरूरत थी, तब किसी ने नहीं डाँटा उसे, हो सकता था शायद तब वह अधूरी औरत बनने से बच जाती। उसने नाभि के नीचे हाथ फेरा। दस-बारह टाँके लगे थे, पूरे पेट पर पट्टी बँधी थी। डॉक्टर कहते हैं, धीरे-धीरे खाली जगह भर जाएगी, भर तो जाएगी, पर क्या वह पुनः माँ बन सकेगी? भले ही जरूरत न हो, हैं न उसकी दो-दो बेटियाँ सोना और मोना, उनके बाद उसे और नहीं चाहिए था कुछ, इसीलिए तो···।

ऐसा तो नहीं था, स्वयं से झूठ बोलने से क्या फायदा? उसे वह नहीं चाहिए था, जो उसके पेट में था, उसे वह चाहिए था, जिसकी कमी थी उसके जीवन में।

हजार सावधानियों के बाद भी होनी को कौन टाल सका है? भले ही लांछन किसी को भी लगे। वह फोन पर कैसे कहे कि पुनः उसके पाँव भारी हैं। दोनों लड़कियों की पढ़ाई का खर्च उठाने में ही राजेश्वरी के दाँतों पसीना आ रहा था, एक और लड़की···ऽ···ऽ! आगे-पीछे सोचते-सोचते दिन निकलते गए। मायके में अकेली थी, वह खाट पकड़ लेती तो घर कौन सँभालता! देवकी भाभी जब तक आई, सुरक्षित मुक्ति का समय बहुत दूर जा चुका था। सोनोग्राफी की रिपोर्ट देखने के बाद उसकी खोपड़ी भक्क से उड़ गई; उसे एक ही बात समझ में आई थी कि चाहे जैसे हो, इस कलंक को धो डालना चाहिए।

"जो लगेगा, दूँगी मैडम, मुझे इस भार से मुक्त कर दीजिए!" उसने अपनी शादी का कंगन डॉक्टर के हाथ में रख दिया था।

"देखिए, आपकी प्रॉब्लम मैं समझ गई हूँ, परंतु रिस्क लेना संभव नहीं है। मैं दवाई दे देती हूँ, अपने आप साफ हो जाएगा। आप हमारा नाम किसी से नहीं बताएँगी, दवा लेने की बात आप स्वयं भी भूल जाएँगी।" डॉक्टर ने सरगोशी की थी। वह इसी तरह की सेवा के लिए जानी जाती थी, बहुत माल

बनाया था उसने थोड़े ही समय में। कल तक जहाँ उसका अस्पताल किराए के एक कमरे में लगता था, आज उसका तीन मंजिला सर्व सुविधा युक्त अस्पताल है। उसने राजनैतिक सुरक्षा प्राप्त करने में सफलता पाई है। स्नेहा जैसे मामले में ही एक महिला की मौत होने के कारण वह विशेष चर्चा में आ गई थी, किंतु वाह रे जुगाड़! आठवें दिन वह जेल से बाहर थी, अस्पताल का काम यथावत् चलने लगा था।

सबकुछ मालूम था उसे, आखिर करे क्या? और किसी ने घास जो नहीं डाली उसके आगे। और कोई ले न ले, उसे तो रिस्क लेना ही पड़ा। चार दिन तक वह दर्द से तड़पती रही। इंतजार करती रही कि रक्त के रेले के साथ वह पिंड भी बाहर आ जाएगा, जो उसके जीवन में हजार समस्याएँ लेकर आनेवाला है। भाभी ने जब सारा माजरा समझा, तब सिर थामकर बैठ गईं।

"अब क्या जवाब दूँगी तुम्हारी सास को? बड़ा पाप हो गया। कहेंगी, तुम्हारी लापरवाही से बच्चा खराब हो गया। कुछ किया तो नहीं तुमने? मुझे ठीक-ठीक बताओ!" उन्होंने उसे झिंझोड़ दिया था।

"कुछ नहीं किया, भाभी! अपने आप दर्द शुरू हो गया।" उसने दाँतों पर दाँत चढ़ाकर दर्द बरदाश्त किया था। उसके माथे पर पसीने की बूँदें झलक रही थीं।

"हमें तो कुछ समझ में नहीं आ रहा है—क्या करें क्या न करें, तुम्हारी ससुराल फोन कर देते हैं।" भाभी एकदम से घबरा गई थीं।

"नहीं भाभी, वहाँ फोन मत करो! मैं ठीक हो जाऊँगी, हो सके तो मुझे अस्पताल ले चलो!" कहते-कहते वह चक्कर खाकर गिर पड़ी। उसके दोनों पैरों के बीच जमीन पर चमकीला लाल रक्त फैल गया था। देवकी ने जबलपुर फोन कर दिया। दूसरे ही दिन राजेश्वरी पाँड़ेपुर पहुँच गई। कैवल्य रह गया बच्चियों के पास।

धुलाई करके उसकी कोख की सफाई कर दी गई, वह घंटों बेहोश रही।

"माँजी, आप लोग भी गजब करते हैं। मेल बेबी का चाह में पाँच महीने के फिमेल बेबी को मार दिया! उसका सब अंग बन चुका था। काट-काटकर निकालना पड़ा। सड़ गया था बच्चा पेट में ही। कम-से-कम एक सप्ताह

पहले गोली खिलाई है आप लोगों ने। धिक्कार है ऐसी औरत लोगों को, जो पेट में लड़की को मार देती हैं। मन तो हो रहा है, पुलिस बुलाकर आप लोगों को जेल भेज दूँ।" साउथ इंडियन डॉक्टर राजेश्वरी को दरवाजे पर खड़ी देख उसी पर बरस पड़ी। वह हाथ जोड़े सबकुछ सुन रही थी।

"मैडम! मैं बहुत आभारी हूँ आपकी, आपने मेरी बहू को बचा लिया।"

"ठीक है, ठीक है।" डॉक्टर बुरा सा मुँह बनाए असीम व्यस्तता के भाव प्रदर्शित करती चली गई थी।

कुछ नहीं पूछा था उस समय राजेश्वरी ने, घर आने पर अच्छी खबर ली—"बहुत मजा आया न मुझे हत्यारी साबित करके? तुमसे किसने कहा था बच्चा गिराने के लिए? तुम पालती क्या उसे? नहीं लेना था तो पहले से होशियार रहती! तुम्हारे पापा ने यदि गेहूँ न बेचे होते तो तुम्हें बचाने के लिए किसी पराए के आगे हाथ फैलाना पड़ता हमें। न कुछ सोचना न समझना, बैग उठाई और मायके! रहो यहीं अब, मैं बच्चियों को सँभालूँगी या तुम्हारी सेवा करूँगी?" वह दूसरे ही दिन उसे छोड़कर चली गई थी जबलपुर।

स्नेहा के शरीर से बहुत सारा खून बह गया था, उसकी रंगत हल्दी के समान पीली पड़ गई थी। दवाई चल रही थी। इस बीच कैवल्य का कई बार फोन आया। वह भी उससे सख्त नाराज था, बस एक ही बात रटे जा रहा था, "तुमने ऐसा क्यों किया? जैसे दो पल रही हैं, वैसे ही तीन भी पल जातीं।"

"तुमने भी तो दो-दो बार मुझे गोलियाँ खिलाईं, तब कुछ नहीं हुआ? और जब मैंने स्वयं खा ली तो पाप हो गया?"

"सप्ताह-दो सप्ताह और पाँच महीने में तुम्हें कोई अंतर ही नहीं लगता? अब तो मेरा मन भी तुम्हारी ओर से उचट गया है, जब तुमने इतने बड़े फैसले में मेरी राय जानने की जरूरत नहीं समझी, तब अकेले जीवन भी जी सकती हो।" उस दिन की बात ने तो स्नेहा के आत्मविश्वास को जैसे तोड़कर रख दिया। आँसू बहाने के सिवा अब और क्या रह गया था उसके जीवन में? कभी मन होता, दवाइयाँ खाना बंद कर दे, जीवन वैसे ही समाप्त हो जाएगा या फिर नींद की ढेर सारी गोलियाँ खाकर जान दे दे, रोज हिम्मत जुटाती, लेकिन कुछ कर नहीं पाती। कभी बेटियों का भोला चेहरा आँखों के सामने

झूल जाता, कभी पति का, कभी मन होता सबकुछ छोड़कर कहीं दूर चली जाए, फिर लगता, घर से बाहर एक जवान औरत को नोचनेवाले अनेक भेड़िए हैं, वह कैसे बचेगी उनसे? और भी दुर्गति हो जाएगी।

भाभी के व्यवहार में भी वह अंतर देख रही थी। अब पहले सब लोगों को खिला-पिला लेती, तब उसका ध्यान स्नेहा की ओर जाता। ठीक है भाई, बाहर जानेवालों का इंतजाम तो पहले करना ही होगा। वह न उसकी जिम्मेदारी थी और न ही उसके दिल में स्नेहा के लिए प्रेम था। उसे तो लगने लगा था कि अपने मन का करके इसने अपनी जिंदगी तबाह कर ली। इसके माँ-बाप इतना तो नहीं छोड़ गए कि इसे जीवन भर ढोया जा सके।

उसके शरीर में एक अनोखा परिवर्तन आने लगा, उसके उदर में कुछ बढ़ने लगा। पेट में जानलेवा दर्द के साथ जब-तब बदबूदार रक्तस्राव होने लगता। उसके चीखने-चिल्लाने से त्रस्त होकर भइया एक दिन उसे अस्पताल ले गए, डॉक्टर ने साधारण जाँच-पड़ताल के बाद कुछ दवाइयाँ देकर विदा कर दिया। उसका पेट लगातार बढ़ रहा था, छूने पर ऐसा लगता, जैसे तीन महीने का भ्रूण हो, वह बेहद हैरत में थी। बराबर रक्तस्राव हो रहा था, फिर क्या बिना बीज के फल लग सकता है। उसे चलने-फिरने में भी परेशानी होने लगी थी।

एक दिन वह बहुत देर तक अपने स्त्री-जीवन पर आँसू बहाती रही, ब्राह्मण परिवार में जन्म लेने के कारण सरकार ने हर जगह पीछे कर रखा है उन्हें, आरक्षण के कारण सरकारी नौकरी मिलती नहीं। लड़का हो तो जैसे-तैसे जी ले, लड़की की उचित व्यवस्था न हो तो जिंदगी भर का रोना! जैसे-तैसे पढ़ाओ-लिखाओ, एक-एक पैसा जोड़कर शादी करो, ससुराल में भी आजन्म दासता। कौन सा सुख भोगने के लिए लाती अपनी बेटी को इस संसार में? जा बेटी! थोड़े समय में ही मुक्त हो गई! माफ करना अपनी माँ को! मैं भी आती हूँ तेरे पास! उसने सोच लिया, और नहीं सहना है, एक बार सास को सुना दे खरी-खरी, बस अलविदा इस संसार से।

उसने राजेश्वरी का नंबर मिलाया।

"हलो!" उधर से राजेश्वरी की आवाज सुनाई दी।

"मैं बोल रही हूँ, मम्मीजी, प्रणाम करती हूँ।"

"भगवान् तुम्हें सद्‌बुद्धि दे!" राजेश्वरी के स्वर का रूखापन महसूस किया उसने।

"मम्मी! आप बहुत नराज हैं न मुझसे! आज तक मैं कभी आप को संतुष्ट नहीं कर पाई। आप मेरी इतनी खराब हालत देखकर गईं और एकदम भूल गईं, शायद मेरी जगह आपकी बेटी होती तो आप ऐसा न करतीं। ठीक है, जो आप ने किया, अच्छा ही किया। मुझे मेरी बच्चियों से दूर किया, पति से दूर किया, अब निकल जाती हूँ आप की दुनिया से।" उसकी सिसकी निकल गई, गला भर आया।

"अरे सुनो तो! मैंने तो तुम्हें आराम करने के लिए वहाँ छोड़ा है। मेरी सेवा से तुम भी तो कभी संतुष्ट न हो सकी! नहीं तो बार-बार मायके ही क्यों भागती? बेवकूफी की बातें मत सोचो, जो भी पहली गाड़ी मिले, उससे तुरंत निकल लो जबलपुर के लिए। गाँव में क्या इलाज होगा? हम जाएँगे, फिर तुम्हें लेकर वापस आएँगे, इससे कोई फायदा तो है नहीं! पुरानी बातें भूल जाओ! जो गया, वह वापस तो आ नहीं सकता!" उनके मुँह से एक नि:श्वास खारिज हुई।

राजेश्वरी ने मुरली को भी फोन किया कि स्नेहा को तत्काल पहुँचा जाओ।

देवकी के लिए तो यह आदेश मुँह माँगे वरदान से कम नहीं नहीं था। "चलो-चलो, जो लगता है, लगने दो, ट्रेन से ले जाना तो बहुत मुश्किल है, किराए की कार ले आओ।" उसने मुरली भइया को भेजकर सारी व्यवस्था करवाई। दूसरी सुबह तक वह अपनी ससुराल में थी। भइया तो पहुँचाकर चले गए। भाभी को मम्मी ने जाने नहीं दिया।

"मुझे किसी का भरोसा नहीं रह गया। कल को आप कह सकती हैं कि बिना इलाज के हमारी ननद को मार डाला सास ने। आप यहीं रहो, जब तक तबीयत नहीं सुधरती इसकी।" सास ने कहा।

"ऐसी बात नहीं है, मम्मीजी, आप की बहू है, जैसा चाहें वैसा करें, रही बात रहने की तो आप जानती ही हैं, घर में करने-धरनेवाली मैं ही हूँ, बच्चे पढ़

रहे हैं, मेरा वहाँ रहना आवश्यक है।" भाभी ने दबे स्वर में कहा था।

"हाँ, अब सही कहा आपने, मेरी बहू है, मैं ही सबकुछ करूँगी, मुझे आपके सहयोग की आवश्यकता है। जब हम अस्पताल चले जाएँगे, तब सोना-मोना का साथ दे देना, जैसे ही यह थोड़ी ठीक हो जाए, चली जाना।" मम्मी की मैत्रीपूर्ण वाणी सुनकर भाभी रुक गई थीं।

फिर तो जो प्रारंभ हुआ, इस अस्पताल से उस अस्पताल का चक्कर तो अघा गया स्नेहा का मन। कोई कुछ बताता कोई कुछ। निष्कर्षतः ज्ञात हुआ कि गर्भाशय में बच्ची के सिर की हड्डी छूट गई थी, वह बढ़ने लगी है, जिससे पेट में दर्द हो रहा है। वही आँतों को दबा रही है। गर्भाशय में गंभीर संक्रमण हो चुका है, यदि तुरंत ऑपरेशन करके गर्भाशय निकाल नहीं दिया गया तो स्नेहा का बचना नामुमकिन है। वैसे तो राजेश्वरी को वह फूटी आँख नहीं सुहाती, किंतु जाँच के परिणाम को सुनकर उसका चेहरा धुआँ-धुआँ हो गया। मन की व्याकुलता चेहरे पर छलक आई। 'हो सकता है, इलाज में लगनेवाले खर्च से डर रही हो। डॉक्टर ने खर्च भी तो तीन लाख बता दिया है, कहाँ रखी होगी डुकइया इतना रुपया? झूठी शान को बनाए रखने में तो लगी रहती है जी-जान से।' जब कभी अपनी पीड़ा से किंचित् आराम पाती, तरह-तरह की बातें सोचा करती स्नेहा। कैवल्य अब एकदम शांत था। घर के काम में माँ की मदद करता, बच्चियों को तैयार कराकर स्कूल भेजता, जहाँ-जहाँ स्नेहा जाँच के लिए जाती, साथ-साथ लगा रहता। इतना लगाव अब से पहले कभी अनुभव नहीं किया था उसने अपने पति से। उसे लगता था, ससुराल के सारे रिश्ते-नाते स्वार्थ के हैं, वह मरे या जीए, इन्हें कोई फर्क पड़नेवाला नहीं है, किंतु अब इनके चेहरे पर छाई मुर्दनी कोई और ही कहानी कह रही है। एक बार जब कैवल्य को चोट लग गई थी, तब भी इसके चेहरे का नक्शा ऐसा ही था। इसी तरह बेचैन थी। तो क्या उसे भी ये लोग प्यार करते हैं?

"कहीं ये लोग मँजे हुए कलाकार तो नहीं? शायद सोच रहे होंगे, इसे मरना तो है ही, क्यों न अपने किए पर पछताती मरे? किंतु मन इस बात को मानने के लिए तैयार नहीं होता, नाटक कोई घड़ी, दो घड़ी करेगा, लगभग पूरा महीना हो गया पाँड़ेपुर से आए, माँ-बेटे लगे हैं सेवा में, कभी आँखें लाल

रहती हैं तो कभी खाना रखा रह जाता है। रोते हैं, लगता है उसके लिए या फिर इलाज के लिए रुपयों का जुगाड़ न हो रहा होगा, चाहे जो हो, इनकी परेशानी का कारण तो वही है न ऽऽ ?"

"अरे! ये क्या? सोना-मोना को क्या हुआ? ये खून से लथपथ कैसे हो गईं? मम्मी-पापा सिर पटक-पटककर रो रहे हैं अपनी पोतियों के लिए, हमारा तो वंशनाश हो गया भगवान्! हमारी बहू अब कभी माँ नहीं बन सकती। सोचा था, चलो दोनों पोतियों को देखकर जी लेंगे, सत्यानाश हो उस ट्रकवाले का, जिसने इनकी ऑटो को टक्कर मार दी। अब हम क्या करें भगवान्? किसके सहारे जीएँ?" मम्मी को रोते उसने पहली बार देखा था, बड़ी कड़क औरत हैं, आँसू की इतनी मजाल कहाँ कि उनकी पलकों की दहलीज लाँघ सकें? वह रोना चाहती थी अपनी सोना-मोना के लिए, किंतु कंठ से आवाज ही नहीं निकल रही थी। उसने पूरा जोर लगाया, "हाय मेरी बच्चियाँ ऽ···ऽ! अब मैं किसके लिए जिऊँगी? भगवान् मुझे उठा ले!" उसने अपने ही हाथों से कसकर अपना गला दबाने का प्रयास किया, किंतु कुछ न हो सका।

"सोना-मोना के लिए तो इतना रो रही है, और जिसे गर्भ में ही मार दिया उसका क्या? ले भोग बेटी को मारने की सजा! अब इस जन्म में तुझे कोई माँ नहीं कहेगा!" किसी की आवाज गूँजी थी उसके कानो में।

"हाँ! मैंने पाप तो बहुत बड़ा किया, परंतु इसमें उनका क्या दोष? मुझे क्षमा कर दो हे ईश्वर! मेरी सोना-मोना को जीवन-दान दे दो!" वह हाथ जोड़कर विनय कर रही थी।

"स्नेहा! स्नेहा! ये क्या कर रही हो?" उसने चौंककर आँखें खोलीं। राजेश्वरी उसकी आँखें पोंछ रही थी।

"कोई डरावना स्वप्न देखा क्या?"

"हाँ मम्मीजी, बहुत डरावना! सोना-मोना कहाँ हैं?" उसने काँपती आवाज में पूछा, उसकी आँखें भय से फैली हुई थीं।

"ये देखो! संडे के कारण इनकी छुट्टी है आज, लेती आई तुमसे मिलाने।" राजेश्वरी ने नहाई-धोई साफ-सुथरी बच्चियों को धीरे से उसकी बाँहों में सरका दिया।

"तुम्हारी भाभी कहाँ गई तुम्हें अकेली छोड़कर?" उसने कमरे में चारों ओर निगाहें दौड़ाईं। देवकी हाथ में चाय का गिलास लिये आ रही थी।

"ये क्या देवकी! मैंने तुम्हारे भरोसे छोड़ा है अपनी बहू को, तुम उसे अकेली छोड़कर···!" राजेश्वरी ने वाक्य अधूरा छोड़ दिया।

"रातभर सोई नहीं थी आज, सुबह-सबेरे जरा सी आँख लगी थी इसकी। मैंने सोचा कि सो रही है, तब तक एक कप चाय ले आऊँ अपने लिए, बस अस्पताल के दरवाजे तक गई थी।" वह सकपका गई थी। प्रातः के आठ बज रहे थे। नई पेशेंट सो रही थी, स्नेहा अपनी बेटियों को सीने से लगाए धार-धार रो रही थी।

"मेरी सोना, मेरी मोना, भगवान् तुम्हें सलामत रखे! मेरी उमर भी लग जाए तुम्हें, मेरे पापों की छाया भी न पड़े तुम्हारे ऊपर!" वह अस्फुट स्वर में बुदबुदा रही थी।

"क्या देखा सपने में? बड़ी भावुक हो रही हो!" राजेश्वरी ने पूछा।

"जबान से नहीं कह सकती, मम्मीजी, मैंने जो देखा, वह हद से ज्यादा भयानक था। यह तो अच्छा हुआ, जो आज आप इन्हें लेती आईं, वरना न जाने मेरी क्या हालत होती?"

"जो कुछ देखा हो, भूल जाओ! अंदर से टाँके अभी हरे होंगे, उनमें तनाव नहीं आना चाहिए, वैसे भी इस समय देखे गए सपने का कोई मतलब नहीं होता, यों ही जो दिमाग में रहता है, सपने में दिखने लगता है।" राजेश्वरी ने बड़ी सहजता से स्नेहा को सँभाला।

आज पाँच दिन हो गए उसका ऑपरेशन हुए, गर्भाशय निकाल दिया गया उसका, "तो क्या वह औरत नहीं रह गई? अधूरा हो गया उसका जीवन?"

यही बात बार-बार उसे उद्वेलित कर रही थी।

"यहाँ लेटे-लेटे न जाने क्या-क्या सोचती रहती हो, स्नेहा? जो हुआ उसे भूलने की कोशिश करो! एक अनावश्यक पड़ा अंग, जो सड़कर तुम्हारी जान लेने पर आमादा था, शरीर से निकाल दिया गया, अब तुम हमेशा निरोग रहोगी। अब तो संकट टल गया। दो-तीन दिन में तुम्हें घर ले जाएँगे यहाँ से छुट्टी कराकर।"

"क्या आपने अपना फैसला बदल दिया? आप तो मुझे अपने घर में नहीं रखना चाहती थीं नऽ···ऽ ? मेरी भूल भी वैसी ही थी, आप की कोई गलती नहीं, मम्मीजी, मैंने अपनी बेवकूफी से आप सबको कितनी परेशानी में डाल दिया।" वह पीड़ा भरे स्वर में बोली, उसके होंठों पर एक दर्दभरी मुसकान थी।

"फैसला नहीं बदला बेटा, घर ही बदल दिया, यहाँ से तुम सीधे अपने नए घर चलोगी।" वह राजेश्वरी की बात का अर्थ न समझ सकी।

"ममा! उस पुराने घर को दादी ने बेच दिया, अब हम किराए के नए घर में शिप्ट हो गए हैं।" सोना ने चहककर बताया। उसे धक्का लगा, एक मकान ही तो था संपत्ति के नाम पर, और उसे भी बेच दिया मम्मी ने।

"यह क्या किया आपने, मुझ जैसी नालायक बहू के लिए बेघर हो गईं?'' स्नेहा ने आश्चर्य से नजरें उठाकर अपनी सास को देखा; उसकी सीपी सी आँखों से मोती झरने लगे।

''क्या करती, बेटी और घर में से एक को चुनना था मुझे।"

□

राख के नीचे

वह धीरे-धीरे उसका तलवा सहला रहा था। "अपने पाँव नीचे मत रखना मिती, मैले हो जाएँगे। मैं तो हिंदुस्तान का राजा हूँ, तुम्हें सदा फूलों पर चलाऊँगा, हजारों नौकर-चाकर तुम्हारे इशारे के इंतजार में खड़े रहेंगे। फूलों को भी तोड़कर लाना नहीं पड़ेगा, जहाँ तुम मुझे देखकर मुसकराईं कि अपने आप फूलों की वर्षा हो जाएगी।" वह उसके होंठों को चूम रहा था।

"हाँ, मेरे प्यारे चंदन, मैं तुम्हारे राज्य की अकेली महारानी! बस कुछ ही महीने…।" लाल-नीले-पीले रंग के वलयों का ऊपर-नीचे होता नर्तन, दोनों एक-दूसरे का हाथ थामे आकाश में उड़ चले थे। बादलों के पार जहाँ परियाँ नाच रही थीं, मधुर संगीत बज रहा था। हौले-हौले सुबह हुई, पंछी जागे। "उठो, ऐ सोनेवालो, भोर जगाए।" अरे, यह क्या? बार-बार यही लाइन! वह हड़बड़ाकर उठ बैठी।

"यह कौन आ मरा सुबह-सुबह और वह कहाँ चला गया? जरा दरवाजा भी नहीं खोल सकता! कितना सुहाना सपना था, ओह!" उसके पूरे अंग में झुरझुरी सी हो रही थी, उस पर सपने का प्रभाव पूरी तरह छाया हुआ था। जरा सा आँखें खोलकर उसने अपने गाउन की तलाश की, वह दूर पलंग के दूसरे किनारे पर पड़ा हुआ था। इस बीच कभी गाना बजता, जो उसके डोर वेल का रिंग टोन था, कभी दरवाजे पर थाप पड़ती।

"आ रही ऽ…ऽ…ऽ हूँ!" उसने अनमने स्वर में आवाज का उत्तर दिया। उसके चेहरे पर नागवारी के भाव स्पष्ट दृष्टिगोचर हो रहे थे।

उसने बगलवाले कमरे से दरवाजे की ओर बढ़ती पदचाप सुनी। "अब जा रहा है, जब मेरा सपना टूट गया!" वह गुस्से से बड़बड़ाई, "हाय! सिर दर्द

से फटने लगा।" उसने अपना सिर दोनों हाथों में लेकर दबाया।

वह लुंगी के ऊपर शर्ट पहनता दरवाजे की ओर बढ़ रहा था। दरवाजा खोला तो सामने कल्पना मैडम अपना बड़ा सा बैग सँभालती खड़ी थीं।

"आइए, आइए मैडम! आज सुबह-सुबह कैसे आना हुआ?" वह दरवाजे से हट गया।

"सुबह ही है अभी तक, दोपहर के एक बज रहे हैं।" मैडम अंदर आकर सोफे पर बैठ चुकी थीं।

"अच्छा हो, उसी से बात करती रहे, नंबर वन की माथा है डोकरी! सब बनावटी बालों में एक भी बाल सफेद नहीं मिलेगा। लगता है, हर हफ्ते पार्लर जाती है। दाँत भी अवश्य नकली ही होंगे। साड़ी की कलफ देखो, एकदम कड़क! अच्छी छनने लगी है दोनों की, अच्छा है, छने, अपने को क्या? अपन तो बस दिन गिन रहे हैं, इधर अठारह साल पूरे हुए उधर उड़न ऽ ऽ छू!" उसने एक बेफिक्री की अँगड़ाई ली और मुँह धोने के लिए वॉशरूम चली गई।

"मिति नहीं दिख रही है?" उन्होंने उसके कमरे की ओर अपनी निगाहें घुमाईं।

"उसका अभी उठने का टाइम कहाँ हुआ है? पूरी रात मोबाइल पर लगी रहती है, जब नींद खुलती है, तब सुबह होती है। आपकी आवाज सुनकर उठी है, ऐसा लगता है।" उसकी आवाज में वही तिरस्कार था, जिसे सुनकर मिति का आधा खून जल जाया करता है। वह रात भर जागे या दिन भर सोए, किसी को क्या मतलब है? अपना दिन भर छछूँदर की तरह छुछुआता है तो कौन कहने जाता है? जिसे पाएगा, बस उसकी ही शिकायत करेगा गोबर जैसा मुँह बनाकर। उसकी तो तकदीर ही फूटी थी, जो माँ चली गई उसे छोड़कर। इतनी स्वस्थ, इतनी सुंदर! देखकर कोई कह नहीं सकता था कि पचास के लपेटे में है, वैसा ही सुव्यवस्थित रहन-सहन, उनका सिंदूर-टीका मलिन कभी नहीं देखा था मिति ने। पता नहीं कब उठती थीं, कब सोती थीं? उनके रहते इसकी भी पहचान कहाँ हो पाई थी? वैसे यह पहले भी उसे घूर-घूरकर देखता था। कहता भी था, "मेरे भानजे को पाल क्या दिया, तुम्हारा हक बन गया अपने मायकेवालों को रखने का। इससे मेरा

कोई खून का रिश्ता नहीं है। तुम लाद रही हो मुझ पर इसे।"

कहता तो सच ही है, इससे उसका खून का क्या, कोई रिश्ता नहीं है। यह उसका मौसा लगता है तो क्या हुआ, इससे बड़ा दुश्मन भी कोई नहीं दुनिया में। एक तो उसके माँ-बाप उस हिंसा के शिकार हो गए, जिसकी किसी को उम्मीद भी नहीं थी। छोटे चाचा ने दिन-दहाड़े घर में घुसकर खाना खाते पिताजी एवं गिलास में पानी ढालती माँ को गोलियों से भून डाला था। वह संभव के साथ पड़ोस में खेल रही थी, घटना की खबर सारे मोहल्ले में आग की तरह फैल गई। पड़ोसन ने उन्हें ऐसा छुपाया कि हत्यारा उन्हें ढूँढ़ता ही रह गया, वह पूरा वंश नाश करके उनकी संपत्ति हड़पना चाहता था। बाद में जब वह कुछ दिनों के लिए जेल गया, तब बड़ी मौसी उसे ले आईं और छोटी संभव को ले गई।

तीन साल छोटा है मिति से। अब तो वह भी बड़ा हो गया होगा। छोटी मौसी उसे अपने साथ जापान ले गईं, आज तक दुबारा भाई-बहन एक-दूसरे से नहीं मिल सके; शायद इस डर से भी कि कहीं दुश्मन उसकी जान के पीछे न पड़ जाए। छोटी मौसी न स्वयं कभी देश लौटीं, न संभव को ही भेजा। वह अपने माता-पिता के अंतिम दर्शन भी नहीं कर पाई थी। बहुत दिनों तक तो लगता था, सब झूठ कह रहे हैं। वे हैं इस दुनिया में, लेकिन सच से कब तक आँखे मूँदे रहा जा सकता था?

"अरे, कहाँ हो भई मिति बिटिया? जल्दी से इधर आ जाओ, मैं तुम्हारी पसंद के दही-बड़े बनाकर लाई हूँ।"

यह पहले-पहल उसे ही मिली थी आनंद मेले में, उसने अपनी सहेलियों के साथ पॉपकॉर्न का स्टाल लगाया था। वह मेले में किसी संस्था के बच्चों को लेकर आई थी। माँ के न रहने की बात जानकर एकदम से चिपक ही गई। आज तक कुँआरी घूम रही है। लगता है, अभी तक इसकी तलाश जारी है अपने जीवनसाथी की। 'ठाकुर साहब-ठाकुर साहब' करती रहती है। देख ही रही है, अच्छे पद पर काम कर रहा है। घर-द्वार सब जमा-जमाया है। आज भले ही बाप-बेटी अपने-अपने खाने का इंतजाम अपने हिसाब से करते हैं, घर में सब वस्तुएँ बिखरी पड़ी हैं। संडे छोड़कर नौकरानी के लिए दरवाजा खोलनेवाला कोई नहीं रहता था, इसने चिढ़कर उसे छुड़ा दिया था, वह जो निलेश सिंह

ठाकुर कहलाता है। हाँ···ऽ···ऽ··· ! पूछे न ऊछे, मैं दूल्हे की चाची, अब ये आ रही हैं माँ बनने। उसने घृणा से मुँह में भरा टूथ पेस्ट थूक दिया। लगता है, कुछ खिचड़ी-विचड़ी पकने लगी है। अभी मात्र तीन महीने ही हुए हैं पहचान हुए और किसी-न-किसी बहाने से हर रविवार को आने लगी है। यह तो जब से बीवी मरी है, एकदम से पागल हो गया है। दो-चार दिन वह स्कूल क्या नहीं गई, नाम ही कटवा दिया।

दो साल हुए माँ को गए, स्तन कैंसर से मरी थीं। इलाज में तो कोई कमी नहीं की थी इसने, मुंबई ले-लेकर जाया करता था। दो-दो, तीन-तीन बार ऑपरेशन हुआ, बड़े कष्ट से मुक्ति मिली थी उन्हें जीवन से। वह अपने दुःख में ऐसा डूबा कि भूल ही गया मिति को। यों कहें तो उसने उसे अपनी जिम्मेदारी समझा ही कब था? बस पल रही थी कुत्ते-बिल्ली की तरह। माँ ही पैरेंट्स मीटिंग में जाती, रिपोर्ट कार्ड साइन करती, ट्यूशन छोड़ने जाती। स्कूल के लिए तैयार करती, यह तो अकसर लड़ा करता था, "मेरे भानजे ने तेरे ही कारण घर छोड़ा है। तू यदि उसे माँ का प्यार देती तो क्या कारण था कि शादी होते ही एकदम बेगाना हो गया?" वह रोती थी, "बस मेरी यही गलती है कि मैंने बाँझ होने के बाद भी माँ बनने की कोशिश की। अपनी ननद के बेटे को माँ बनकर पाला, जब वह बीमारी से हार गई, मानस के पापा अपने को सँभाल नहीं सके। दो माह बाद ही मानस को अकेला छोड़ गए, तब मैंने उसे गले से लगाकर पाला। अब जब मेरी बहन के साथ इतना बुरा घट गया तो क्या उसके बच्चों को सहारा देना हमारा मानवीय कर्तव्य नहीं है? हमारा मन भी लगा रहता है।"

"अरे, मिति बेटी! कितनी देर लगाती हो फ्रेश होने में?" वह आवाज दे रही थी।

"आप लोग लीजिए न आंटी, मैं आ रही हूँ।" उसकी नजर चाय के बरतन पर पड़ी, न जाने कब से गंदा जमा पड़ा था। अपने तो धो-धाकर बना लेते हैं। अब यह देखेगी तो अच्छा नहीं लगेगा। लोगों को न जाने कितना शौक होता है दूसरों के जीवन में झाँकने का। कैसे माँजूँ? माँ ने तो कभी कुछ करने ही नहीं दिया। बीमार रहती थीं, फिर भी उसे खेलने-कूदने, पढ़ने-लिखने का बराबर अवसर दिया करती थीं। "तू, पढ़ लिख ले! जो कुछ सीखना हो, सीख ले, घर

के काम तो जीवन भर करने हैं। वो सब तो मैं तुझे एक महीने में सिखा दूँगी।" चली गई माँ! अब तो उसकी मिति के समान बुरा कोई रह ही नहीं गया संसार में। उसकी आँखें भर आईं अपने पुराने दिन याद करके।

"अरे, तुम चाय के बरतन माँज लाई?" वह किचन तक आ गई थी। उसके हाथ में पेपर प्लेट थी, जिसमें उसने दही-बड़े रखे हुए थे। पेपर प्लेट वह अपने साथ ही लेकर आई थी। पहली बार नहीं आई थी इस घर में।

ठीक है न आंटी, आप बैठिए नऽ!" उसकी निगाहें संकोच से झुकी हुई थीं। यदि वह चाहती तो इधर-उधर फैली अपनी किताबों, कपड़ों और बरतनों को उनके स्थान पर रख सकती थी। पलक झपकते तो नहीं बीत जाएँगे कुछ महीने। क्या सबकुछ जैसे-का-तैसा छोड़कर चली जाएगी चंदन के साथ?

"अरे! आओ न, एक साथ बैठकर खाते हैं।" उनका प्रबल आग्रह देखकर मिति को उनके साथ आना पड़ा।

"लीजिए न, आप भी।" मिति ने झुकी निगाहों से कल्पना आंटी को देखते हुए आग्रह किया।

"बस ले रही हूँ।" किसी नवोढ़ा की तरह चम्मच से छोटे-छोटे टुकड़े उठाकर खाने लगी वह।

"बहुत अच्छे बने हैं, आपने बड़ी मेहनत की।" वह रुचि लेकर खा रहा था।

वाह! कैसे बिछा जा रहा है। और किसी की मेहनत की तारीफ करते तो मुँह में दही जमी रहती है, अभी परसों की ही तो बात है, पड़ोसन के बहुत समझाने पर उसने ड्यूटी से आते ही उसके हाथ में चाय की प्याली थमाई थी, जिसे देखते ही वह भड़क उठा था, "किसने कहा तुझसे चाय बनाने के लिए? हाँ, तेरी उस दिन की बात सुनने के बाद तूने कैसे सोच लिया कि मैं तेरा दिया कुछ भी खाऊँगा-पिऊँगा? तू तो मुझे खाने में जहर मिलाकर देना चाहती है नऽ?" वह कलेजा फाड़कर चीख रहा था।

"तो थूक दे चाय में! मेरी बात तो याद है तुझे और तूने क्या रिपोर्ट लिखवाई थाने में? मैंने तुझ पर रेप केस का आरोप लगाने की धमकी दी है, मेरा तेरा कोई खून का रिश्ता नहीं है। मैं तेरी गोद ली हुई संतान हूँ, जिसका

कोई डॉक्यूमेंट्स नहीं है। तू तो मुझे बाल-संरक्षण गृह भेजना चाहता था नऽ ? मुझे घर से निकालकर रँगरलियाँ मनाना चाहता है ?"

ऐसा ही नाटक करना था तो पहले ही क्यों रखा ? मुझे मार डालता, हत्यारे ! जीकर ही क्या कर रही हूँ ? वह अपने कमरे में लेटी बहुत देर तक रोती रही थी। बार-बार थाने में पड़ी डाँट उसके कानों में गूँज रही थी।

"आपको शर्म आनी चाहिए, अपनी ही बेटी के खिलाफ शिकायत दर्ज कराते हुए। इसने यदि झूठी रिपोर्ट कर दी, तब भी आप लंबे से नप जाएँगे। यदि किसी भी प्रकार की प्रतारणा की शिकायत मिली तो आप पर विभागीय व्यक्ति होने के नाते भी कोई रियायत नहीं की जा सकेगी।" उसके चेहरे पर जैसे बारह बज रहे थे। उसके सड़ियल स्वभाव से सब पूर्व परिचित थे।

"जहाँ भी रहा, अपने नीचेवालों का जीना हराम किए रखा। पुलिसवाले चौबीस घंटे के नौकर हैं, लगातार काम करते रहो। दारू-गाँजे से कमाई मत करो। बताए कोई इनसे कि पुलिसवालों के घर-द्वार नहीं होते क्या ? क्या समाज में सिर उठाकर जीने का उनको हक नहीं है, क्या पुलिस के छोटे से वेतन में बच्चों को ऊँची शिक्षा दिलाई जा सकती है ? यह तो साफ साजिश है, सिपाही का बेटा सिपाही और अफसर का बेटा अफसर बनाने की। इसीलिए तो भगवान् ने संतान का मुख नहीं दिखाया। एक को पाला भी था तो लात मारकर रफूचक्कर हो गया। अब आया है पंजे में।" उसने सुना था, ड्यूटीवाले आपस में बातें कर रहे थे। उसे एक अनजानी पीड़ा ने अपनी गिरफ्त में ले लिया था। हाँ, उसके थाने जाने का लाभ उसे इस प्रकार मिला कि तब से उसने उसके खाने-पीने या मोबाइल के लिए खर्चा देने में आनाकानी नहीं की। बस बाहर निकलने से मना कर दिया। नंबर वन का शक्की है। उसे लगता है, अड़ोस-पड़ोसवाले मिति को बिगाड़ देंगे। अब कुछ बोलता भी नहीं, मत बोले, यहाँ किसे गरज पड़ी है ऐसे कूड़मगज से बात करने की ? रहा समय कटने का सवाल, तो वह फेसबुक पर बड़े आराम से कट जाता है। कभी यूट्यूब खोल लो तो जो चाहो वो देखो। हाँ, परेशानी हो जाती है कभी-कभी एडल्ट विडियोज देखकर, तब के लिए नींद की गोलियों का इंतजाम रखना पड़ता है।

"आप बैठिए ! मैं जरा एक पैकेट दूध लेकर आता हूँ चाय के लिए।" वह

अपने कपड़े से पैसे निकाल रहा था।

"अजी! आप कहाँ जा रहे हैं? हमारी मिति बेटी ले आएगी।" उसने अपने बैग से निकालकर सौ रुपए का एक नोट मिति की ओर बढ़ा दिया।

कोई नई बात नहीं है। जब आती हैं, कुछ-न-कुछ घटा ही रहता है। वह इतनी भी नासमझ नहीं है, अपने बीच से उसे हटाने का बहाना है सब। उसे क्या, अच्छा ही है, अवसर का लाभ उठाकर वह भी चंदन को बुला लेती है मिलने के लिए। आज तो वह शहर से बाहर है। ऊब मिटाने के लिए उसने एक अँगड़ाई ली और दरवाजा उढ़काते हुए बाहर निकल गई। डेयरी घर से लगभग पाँच सौ मीटर की दूरी पर थी। वह आराम से गई-आई। आस-पास के घरों तथा काम करते मजदूरों पर नजर डालती। दो बजे की धूप उसके दाएँ अंग को तपा रही थी। नवंबर के शुरुआती दिन थे, किंतु ठंड अभी विधिवत् प्रारंभ नहीं हुई थी। उसने सुना है, मौसम-चक्र बदल रहा है।

दरवाजा उसी प्रकार उढ़का था, जैसा वह छोड़ गई थी। उसने बिना आवाज किए अंदर जाने लायक दरवाजा खोला और सीधे अपने कमरे में चली गई दूध लिये-लिये। बगलवाले कमरे से धीमी, किंतु स्पष्ट आवाजें आ रही थीं—

"और तो जो भगवान् ने किया, उसे कोई बदल नहीं सकता; किंतु मैं इस लड़की से बहुत परेशान रहता हूँ। एक भी बात नहीं मानती। बताइए, जब घर में कोई महिला नहीं है तो कौन सिखाएगा भला-बुरा उसे? कुछ कहने की कोशिश करता हूँ तो गलत भावना मन में लाती है। सच कहूँ तो इस लड़की ने कभी मुझे बाप का दर्जा दिया ही नहीं।"

"रो ले, रो ले नया मुरगा पाया है नऽ! मैंने तो तुझे बाप नहीं समझा, तू ने ही कब मुझे अपनाया?" वह किचन में जाकर चाय का पानी चढ़ाने लगी। सोकर उठने के बाद चाय मिल जाए तो तबीयत फड़का-फाइट हो जाती है।

"बच्ची है ठाकुर साहब, समय आने पर सब ठीक हो जाएगा।" उसने सहानुभूति भरे स्वर में कहा।

"क्या सुधरेगी मैडम, पहले जमाने में इतनी उम्र में लड़कियाँ अपनी ससुराल जाकर पूरा घर सँभालती थीं और इसे देखिए, दोपहर ढले सोकर

उठती है। पूरी रात मोबाइल पर न जाने क्या करती रहती है? देखते-देखते मेरा घर श्मशान हो गया। थोड़ा-थोड़ा सीखती, तब भी कम-से-कम अपने लिए तो पका-खा लेती। नौकरानी लगाओ तो दरवाजा नहीं खोलती, मैं ठहरा नौकरीवाला इनसान, वह भी पुलिस की नौकरी; जिसमें घर-परिवार के लिए कोई समय नहीं होता।"

"कभी कुछ सिखाने की कोशिश की? माँ थी तो उसने भी कभी कुछ करने न दिया और तू तो बस रोना भर जानता है, कुछ सिखाता तो जरूर सीख जाती। और अच्छा ही किया न सीखकर। मैं क्या तेरे लिए खाना बनाऊँगी? जा-जा मुँह धोकर रख। चाहे जितना रो ले, तेरे लिए तो कुछ नहीं करूँगी।" कोई सुने-न-सुने, वह हर बात का उत्तर नहीं में देती जा रही थी।

"ठाकुर साहब, जहाँ समस्या है, वहाँ समाधान भी है। आप इसकी शादी कर दीजिए।"

"ऐसी बिगड़ी लड़की को किसके पल्ले बाँध दूँ, मैडम? फिर अभी यह अठारह की कहाँ हुई है?" उसके स्वर में उसकी हताशा बोल रही थी।

"कोई करे, न करे, वह तो करेगा न; जिससे यह रात भर बतियाती है। उसका नाम चंदन है। मेरी जान-पहचान का है, बड़ी उम्र का आदमी है, इसे सुधारकर रख देगा। धनी बाप का अकेला बेटा है, पढ़ा-लिखा भी है। वह भी खुश और हम भी खुश। आप कहें तो बात करूँ, उसका बाप तो दोनों तरफ का खर्चा दे देगा हँसी-खुशी। हर्रा लगे न फिटकरी, रंग चोखा आए। फिर यदि आपको पसंद आएगा तो मैं आपका उजड़ा घर बसाने की जिम्मेदारी ले लूँगी।"

"इतना सबकुछ है तो अब तक कुँआरा क्यों बैठा है?"

"कुँआरा कहाँ? पहले दो शादियाँ हो चुकी हैं। जिसके भाग्य में सुख नहीं होता, उसकी मति मारी जाती है। दोनों भाग गईं इसका घर छोड़कर। और कुछ नहीं, जरा बातें ज्यादा करता है। बड़ी ऊँची-ऊँची, कभी ताजमहल खरीदने की बात करेगा तो कभी लाल किला। मिति जाए भोगे अपने भाग्य का सुख। वहाँ न किसी काम की कोई फिक्र रहेगी, न जिम्मेदारी। सब काम के लिए अलग-अलग नौकर लगे हैं। मुझे तो लगता है, हमारी मिति के लिए सब प्रकार से उचित रिश्ता है। न हो तो अभी सगाई करके छोड़ दीजिए, कुछ माह बाद जब

अठारह की हो जाएगी, तब शादी कर देंगे। मुझे तो बस आपकी ही चिंता लगी रहती है।" मैडम की आवाज अत्यंत मधुर थी।

बड़ी प्यारी लगी थी मिति को वह। उसके चंदन से उसका विवाह करा रही थी। कोई लाख बुराई करे, चंदन तो उसकी हर अदा का दीवाना है। इतना सुंदर, शिक्षित और कमाऊ है वह। जब तक साथ रहता है, लगातार उसकी प्रशंसा करता रहता है। चंदन से मिलाने के लिए वह फेसबुक की सदा आभारी रहेगी। रही बात शादी की तो पैसेवालों की दो क्या, चार भी हो सकती हैं, वैसे भी आजकल लड़कियों में हसबैंड चेंज करने का ट्रेंड है। वे छोड़कर नहीं गईं, उन्होंने मिति का रास्ता साफ किया। वह तो मिति के सारे दर्द की दवा है। शादी के बाद उसका अपना संसार होगा, जहाँ की वह मालकिन होगी। वह सबकुछ सीखेगी। उसे सजा देने का इनका सपना कभी पूरा नहीं होगा।

"हुम्म! बड़ी उम्र का आदमी है, जिसकी दो-दो औरतें भाग चुकी हैं, वह मेनिया का शिकार है। बहुत अच्छा रिश्ता ढूँढ़ा है, मैडम मेरी बेटी के लिए, क्या मेरे पास उसकी शादी के लिए पैसे नहीं हैं? क्या वह मेरे ऊपर भार है? अब मेहरबानी करके यहाँ से तशरीफ ले जाइए, वरना मैं आपकी सारी चिंता झाड़ दूँगा। उस अधेड़ उम्र के पागल से अपनी बेटी ब्याहने से अच्छा तो मैं उसे किसी कुएँ में धकेल दूँगा। जाइए, दफा हो जाइए।" उसकी चिल्लाहट से पूरा घर झन्ना उठा। उसकी तेज आवाज में धीरे-धीरे एक कंपन शामिल होता अनुभव किया मिति ने।

"हाय! चंदन पागल है, कितना बड़ा धोखा हुआ उसके साथ?"

"सोच लीजिए अच्छी प्रकार, आपकी बददिमाग बेटी के लिए इतना अच्छा रिश्ता फिर नहीं मिलेगा। फिर आपके साथ इस उम्र में कौन घर बसाने आएगा?" वह इस अप्रत्याशित व्यवहार से सकते में आ गई थी।

"अरे! भाड़ में जाए यह रिश्ता और चूल्हे में जाओ तुम! जल्दी भागती हो या उठाऊँ पुलिसिया जूता…ऽ…ऽ…ऽ… ?" वह बल भर चीखा।

दुम दबाकर भाग रही थी वह।

"पा…पाऽ… !" अस्फुट स्वर निकला मिति के मुँह से।

□

सुबह से शाम

उसने अपनी खोजी नजर उस चाय की दुकान पर डाली, "मर गए साले सब-के-सब, ऐसा भी कहीं त्योहार मनाया जाता है? सारी दुकानें बंद करके मस्ती करने में लगे हुए हैं, पूरी रात बीत गई हरामखोर हुड़दंगियों को अस्पताल पहुँचाते-पहुँचाते। कम-से-कम बीस को तो उसने ही पहुँचाया, कितनी भीड़ थी अस्पताल में, ओह! अगर हम भी इन्हीं की तरह त्योहार मनाने लगें, तब क्या हो, देखो तो दलिद्दर लोग कैसे पूरी दुकान गंदी छोड़कर भागे हैं? भट्ठी पर कुत्ता सो रहा है, सो ले बेटा, सो ले! तेरा ही तो राज है, यहाँ तो चाय के लिए जी तरस रहा है।" वह चाय की तलब से अपने को बेचैन अनुभव करने लगा। वैसे तो कई लोगों से उसकी पहचान थी, किंतु पुलिसवालों से पहचान कैसी होती है, वह अच्छी तरह जानता है, एक तो त्योहार का दिन! ऊपर से सबेरे का समय, ज्यादातर लोग दिन भर के थके देर रात को सोए होंगे, कौन उसे अपने दरवाजे पर देखकर प्रसन्न होगा? उसने मन को मारा। सात बजे होंगे सुबह के, सड़कें, गलियाँ वीरान थीं, जगह-जगह रंग गुलाल से धरती लाल थी। चौक-चौराहों पर होलिका-दहन के अवशेष बिखरे पड़े थे। कहीं राख, कहीं सुलगती लकड़ियाँ, कहीं शराब की बोतलें, दो दिन पहले से शराबबंदी है, फिर भी न जाने कहाँ से मिल जाती हैं इतनी बोतलें? वह धीरे-धीरे टहलता हुआ पूरे मोहल्ले की टोह लेता रहा। नगर निगम के नल में पानी आने लगा था, उसने मुँह-हाथ धोकर अपनी थकान मिटाने का प्रयास किया। अभी तो वातावरण में शांति छाई हुई थी। नल के पास पड़ी टूटी चूड़ियों से उसे कल का वह भयावह मंजर याद हो आया, जिसे देख उसकी बुद्धि चकरा गई थी। दो आदमी एक औरत को अपनी-अपनी ओर खींच

रहे थे। रात के करीब दस बजे होंगे, वह माँ भद्रकाली मंदिर के प्रवेश द्वार के पास चबूतरे पर बैठा जरा-सी कमर सीधी कर रहा था कि किसी महिला की आवाज उसके कानों से टकराई।

"मोला जान देवा ददा हो तूँहर पाँव परत हौं··· !"

"कतेक मुस्किल म इहाँ तक लाए हन, छोड़ेच बर ? चुपे चुप रहे र···! अमरा देबो तोर घर, किल्ली पारबे त नरी मसक देहूँ।"

"मामला संगीन मालूम पड़ता है।" उसने तत्काल अपने हैंडसेट पर पुलिस कंट्रोल रूम का नंबर डायल किया।

वे मोटर साइकिल पर थे दो युवक और एक युवती, किसी बात पर उनमें झिकझिक हो रही थी।

"तैं एही मेर रव यार! में ऐला ठिहा म अमरा के आवत हँ, तिहाँ तोहु ला लेगहूँ!" उसकी जबान लड़खड़ा रही थी।

"नहीं यार, तीनों झि एके संग जाबो, बने तो जावत हन।"

"तें समझस नहीं यार, ओदे पुलिसवाला है, तुरंत रोक लिही, अइसे मोर बाई हे कइके लेग जाहँव। "

"अरे किधर जाते हो ? " वह लपकता हुआ उनके पास तक पहुँच गया था।

वे हड़बड़ा गए थे।

"कुछू नहीं साहेब! एहर अपन मन के हमर संग जावत हे।" उसे छोड़कर दोनों एक साथ बोल पड़े। औरत की सिसकियाँ तेज हो गईं।

"अपने से जा रही है तो रो क्यों रही है ?" उसने कड़क कर पूछा।

"खाबे-पीबे तेला कव साहेब, हमर तिहार झन बिगाड!" उनमें से एक बोला। वह खुशामदी लहजे में दाँत निपोर रहा था। औरत कातर निगाहों से उसे देख रही थी। वह उनके निकट चला गया था। "लाओ दस हजार और जल्दी भागो यहाँ से!" वह फुसफुसाया था।

"अतेक तो नईं हे साहेब, सौ-पचास ह, बन जाही।" उनके पसीना छूटने लगा था ठंडी रात।

"जानते हो कितनी सजा होगी औरत को बुरी नीयत से अगवा करने

की?" वह आराम से गाड़ी का हैंडल पकड़े हुए था। इसी बीच उसने गाड़ी बंद कर के चाबी निकाल ली थी। अभी मोल-भाव चल ही रहा था कि पुलिस का डग्गा आ गया। अगले पाँच मिनट में उन्हें लेकर पुलिस की गाड़ी जा चुकी थी। वह संतोष की एक अधूरी साँस ले पाया था कि मारपीट वाले पहुँच गए।

"चलो कट गई रात, बस अब आधे घंटे में उसकी छुट्टी हो जाएगी। उसने एक गहरी साँस अपने फेफड़े में भरी। पूर्व दिशा की ओर उसकी नजरें उठ गईं। आदित्य अपना सिंदूरी बाना उतारकर सुनहली चादर ओढ़ चुके थे। उसे बहुत अच्छा लगा।

"आज तो छुट्टी है यार! सुलोचना कई दिनों से भिड़ी है गुझिए, फाफड़े, सलोनी, नमकीन और न जाने क्या-क्या बनाने में। ड्यूटी की ऐसी मजबूरी कि खाना खाने के लिए भी घर न जा सका। आज तो पुलिसवालों की होली है, पब्लिक से ज्यादा ही धमाल होगा। आई.जी., डी.आई.जी., एस.पी. आदि सारे अधिकारी-कर्मचारी एक साथ मिलकर होली खेलते हैं। उनकी पत्नियाँ भी आती हैं सामुदायिक भवन में होली खेलने। सुलोचना को तो पहले ही पकड़ ले जाती हैं सब। नाचने-गाने में उसका कोई जवाब जो नहीं है।

आठ बजते ही वह मोटर साइकिल से घर के लिए चल पड़ा। मन में लड्डू फूट रहे थे। वह कार्यक्रम बनाता जा रहा था दिन भर का। विभाग में सभी एक-दूसरे को भइया-भाभी कहते हैं, आज तो जो मिल जाए रंग दो! साल भर का भाभी कहना किस दिन काम आएगा?

घर पहुँचकर नित्य क्रिया से निवृत्त हो वह अभी नाश्ता ही कर रहा था कि सुलोचना ने बाल्टी भर रंग डालकर सिर से पाँव तक सराबोर कर दिया। वह कुछ कर पाता, इससे पहले ही वॉशरूम में घुसकर दरवाजा अंदर से बंद कर लिया। लाख प्रयत्न बेकार गए दरवाजा खुलवाने के।

"अच्छा किया न धोखे से रंग डालकर? जब मिलोगी, तब बदला लूँगा, याद रखना।" वह अंदर से ही··ही··ही··ही··ही करके हँसती रही।

"घर छोड़कर कहाँ जाएगी, देख लूँगा आगे-पीछे।" मन-ही-मन

सोचते हुए उसने अपने कपड़े बदले, सफेद कपड़ों पर ही तो रंग दिखते हैं। गुलाल का पॉली बैग अपने हाथ में लिया, कुछ रंग, पैंट की जेब में रखा और घर से निकल गया। वह रक्षित आरक्षी केंद्र बेमेतरा की ओर जाने की सोच ही रहा था कि उसकी नजर जगमोहन पांडे पर पड़ गई। वे धुले कपड़े पहने कनपटियों के पास शेष बचे बालों में कंघी किए खरामा-खरामा पुलिस लाइन की ओर बढ़ रहे थे।

प्रारंभ भइया से ही करता हूँ, एकदम छोटे भाई की तरह मानते हैं। "प्रताप बच्चों को स्कूल छोड़ दो। प्रताप मेरी उमर हो गई कुछ करने की हिम्मत नहीं होती, कल परेड में जरूर टोकाटाकी हो जाएगी, मेरे जूते ठीक से चमक नहीं रहे हैं। बाबू जरा बरियार हाथ लगा देते तो अच्छा हो जाता। प्रताप! जरा अपनी भौजाई को पिक्चर में बैठा आते, मेरी ड्यूटी है और यह है कि कान खाए जा रही है।" वह सोचता, बुजुर्ग आदमी हैं, चलो कर देते हैं सेवा। उन्हीं के कारण उसे तंबाकू की डिबिया रखने की जरूरत नहीं पड़ती थी, जब मन हो माँग लो! नींद से उठकर भी तंबाकू देने में कभी नहीं चिड़चिड़ाए। वह जरा तेज गति से उनकी ओर बढ़ा।

"भइया! आ रहा हूँ ···!"

"अरे नहीं···!" उनके कदम तेज हो गए।

यह भी उनके पीछे लपका। वे और तेज हुए। यह भी लगभग दौड़ पड़ा। "अरे रुको! भाग क्यों रहे हो, आपको खा जाऊँगा क्या?" वह जोर से चिल्लाया।

"रंग मत लगाना! मेरा सिर दर्द होता है।" एक बार पीछे देखकर वे चिल्लाए और घूमकर और तेज भाग चले। सड़क के दोनों ओर खड़े लोग इस दौड़ में शामिल होकर चिल्लाने लगे थे।

"पांडेजी और तेज और तेज, वह आप के पीछे है···!"

"प्रताप और तेज! भागने न पाएँ बूढ़ऊ! लपक लो ···!"

"बाप रे! बुरे फँसे···!" लेकिन एक बात तो हुई, इनकी असलियत का पता चल गया। बूढ़ा हूँ, कह-कहकर खूब बेवकूफ बनाया इन्होंने। अब देख ही लेता हूँ, कहाँ तक दौड़ते हैं, वह और जिद्द में आ गया। सड़क के किनारे

के दर्शक बदलते गए। सिमगा जानेवाली सड़क पर वे भागे जा रहे थे। "कहीं गिर न पड़ें बूढ़ऊ", वह डर भी रहा था। उसकी साँस धौंकनी की तरह चल रही थी। पाँच किलोमीटर से कम क्या दौड़े होंगे अब तक ? वह बस एक हाथ की दूरी पर रह गया था उनसे। "हाँ! कहाँ जाओगे बचकर ? ये आए हाथ में, बस चार अंगुल की दूरी रह गई। यह क्या, बिजली की गति से वे पलटे और उसे कमर से कसकर पकड़ लिया। फिर क्या उठा-उठाकर तीन पटखनियाँ दे दी। उसकी हड्डियाँ चरमराने लगीं। गुलाल का बैग न जाने कहाँ गिर गया, वह रिरियाने लगा। छोड़ दो भइया, अब नहीं माँगूँगा तंबाकू। मैं नहीं जानता था कि आदत लगाकर मेरी ये हालत करोगे।"

"रे पागल, तू तंबाकू माँगने के लिए इतनी दूर दौड़ गया ? वे पछतावे में पड़ गए। होली के कारण सड़क पर कोई वाहन भी दिखाई नहीं दे रहा था। बड़ी देर बाद एक एंबुलेंस गुजरी, उसे ही रोककर दोनों पुलिस लाइन आए। पुलिस ग्राउंड में होली का जलसा अपने शबाब पर था। अभी-अभी आई.जी. साहब की मिसेज आई थीं, पुलिस बैंडवाले जोर-शोर से बजा रहे थे—

"साँची कहें तोरे आवन से हमरे,
अंगना में आई बहार भउजी।"

सभा-भवन के अंदर से ढोलक, झाँझ, मंजीरे की आवाज आ रही थी। अवश्य सुलोचना पहुँच चुकी होगी। वह कान देकर उसका स्वर पहचानने का प्रयास कर रहा था कि तब तक दो जवान पांडेजी को पकड़कर उनकी चिकनी दाढ़ी में रेतवाली गुलाल रगड़ने लगे थे। "ठीक हुआ! बड़े भागनेवाले बने थे।" उसके कलेजे में ठंडक पहुँचे, इसके पहले ही वह भी दो जवानों की गिरफ्त में था। विरोध किया तो शर्ट-पैंट तार-तार हो गए। रंग-अबीर से पूरा ढँक गया वह। कुछ कहता, इसके पहले ही वे उसे छोड़ किसी और की ओर बढ़ गए थे।

"दो तो बज ही गए होंगे, चलूँ जरा भाभी से भी मिल लूँ, इन्हें तो अभी एकाध घंटे फुरसत नहीं मिलेगी।" मैदान में लाइन से लगी कुरसियों पर लोग बैठे हुए थे, एक खाली कुरसी पर जगमोहन पांडे बैठ गए थे। "इनका बदला उनसे लेता हूँ।" सोचता हुआ वह सबकी बेखयाली का लाभ उठाकर ग्राउंड

से बाहर आ गया। सड़क पर भी कुछ लोग पानी-कीचड़-गोबर आदि से त्योहार मना रहे थे। लगा कि किसी ने पहचाना नहीं उसे। पांडेजी के घर का दरवाजा उढ़का हुआ था। घर के अंदर से मालपुए सिंकने की मीठी-मीठी मनभावनी सुगंध ने याद दिलाया कि उसे जोर की भूख लगी है। भाभी-भाभी पुकारता वह अंदर घुस गया। "अरे! आप तो चिन्हा ही नहीं रहे हैं!" उन्होंने संशयपूर्ण निगाहों से उसे देखा।

"देखिए अभी कुछ डालिएगा नहीं! कड़ाही चढ़ी है।" कहती हुई वह वॉशरूम में घुस गईं।

"नहीं कुछ नहीं लाया, आप चिंता न करें!" कहते हुए उसे अपने पीछे आते देखकर वे कछुए की तरह अपने सारे अंग घुटनों के बीच समेट, सिर को आँचल से अच्छी प्रकार ढाँककर बैठ गईं, उसे अपने निकट आया देख सिर भी घुटनों के बीच कर लिया। उसने बड़े आराम से जेब से पक्का चूड़ी रंग निकाला और उनके सिर पर पूरा पैकेट खाली कर दिया। उसके बाद आँगन में बनी टंकी से एक बाल्टी पानी निकालकर उनके ऊपर उड़ेल दिया। वे कुनमुनाईं, उन्हें गीले कपड़ों में देखने की दबी हुई इच्छा लिये एक पल वह वहाँ रुका था, तब तक पांडेजी का बेटा न जाने कहाँ से दौड़ा-दौड़ा आया और उसके ऊपर फिनायल की पूरी बोतल उड़ेल कर तेजी से बाहर भाग गया।

"यह क्या डाल दिया रे चिरकुट? मारे बिना छोड़ूँगा नहीं!" वह हवा की तरह उसके पीछे भागा।

"वह तो गधे के सिर से सींग की तरह गायब हो गया था। अपना घर देखा तो ताला बंद था। फिनायल की तीखी गंध से उसका सिर चकराने लगा था।

"एक नंबर का हरामखोर है। साला पूरा बाप पर गया है। अगर भाभी का मोह न होता तो इनके दरवाजे पेशाब करने भी न आता।" वह मन-ही-मन बड़बड़ाता ग्राउंड की ओर लौट गया। वहाँ अब होली के गीतों पर डांस हो रहा था। देखनेवाले तालियाँ बजा रहे थे। भाँग के ड्रम के पास बहुत भीड़ लगी थी। उसने गुस्से-गुस्से में बिना गिने कई गिलास खाली किए, तब कहीं

जाकर मूड होलियाना बना। वह भी नाचनेवालों में शामिल हो गया, लेकिन एक बात उसकी समझ में नहीं आई कि नाचनेवाले नाक बंद करके उससे दूर क्यों हुए जा रहे हैं?

"क्या लगा लिए जवान? एस.पी. साहब पूछ बैठे थे।

"ओ मेरा भतीजा चिरकुट! बहुत बदमाश है सर!" नजरें झुकाए वह उनसे दूर चला गया था।

"अरे बजाओ, भई बाजा! क्यों रोक दिया ऐं? चलो बजाओ।" उसकी जबान लड़खड़ा रही थी।

"चलो प्रताप! अब नहाते हैं, सब लोग चले गए।" जगमोहन पांडे की आवाज उसने पहचान ली। एकदम भूत बने हुए थे।

"नहीं! अभी तो मैं नाचूँगा!"

उसने अपनी बाँह छुड़ाने का प्रयास किया।

"छुड़ा लोगे क्या, साले मरते तक भांग पी लिया, अब होश कहाँ से रहे?"

"चल रहा हूँ भइया, छोड़ो न!" उसने पूरा बल लगाकर खुद को छुड़ाया।

सब चले गए, तब भी वह इमली की छाया में बैठा रहा "सुलोचना को जरा भी उसकी फिक्र होती तो इतनी देर तक यहाँ न बैठी होती, जानती है, मैं कल रात से भूखा हूँ, ठीक है, थोड़ा और इंतजार कर लो! भाभी भी तो औरत ही हैं, कैसे घर में काम कर रही हैं, ये तो लता मंगेशकर हैं न!" मन की भड़ास निकालता रहा वह। जब शाम घिरने लगी, तब वह घर की ओर चला।

दरवाजे पर सुलोचना खड़ी थी, पक्का उसी का इंतजार कर रही थी। वह नहा धो चुकी थी, रंग अभी पूरे नहीं छूटे थे, चेहरे पर विचित्र-सी चित्रकारी नजर आ रही थी। वह बस थोड़ी ही दूर रह गया था कि रंग से सराबोर एक आदमी आया और सुलोचना के सिर पर अबीर की पन्नी उलट दी, वह उसके चेहरे पर गुलाल मलने लगा।

"अरे! हटो-हटो, मैं नहा चुकी हूँ, दिखाई नहीं देता क्या?" उसने पूरे बल से नशे में चूर उस सींक से पतले आदमी को दूर फेंक दिया और अपना

चेहरा साफ करने का असफल प्रयास करने लगी।

क्रोध से उसकी कनपटियाँ जलने लगीं, "पति के लिए दरवाजा बंद और दूसरों के लिए अजंता की मूरत बनी खड़ी है।"

"कौन है बे, ऐसे ही लगाया जाता है महिलाओं को रंग?" उसने उसे कमर से पकड़ लिया और सड़क के समांतर बहनेवाली बड़ी नाली की ओर ले चला, जिसे कल से ही कुछ होलियारों ने नाली का पानी बाँधकर एकत्र कर रखा था।

"में नोहर सिंग हौं भइया, सालोसाल तूंहर घर-बाहिर सफाई करथौं अतका हक तो हे न मोर?" उसकी आँखें नशे की खुमारी के कारण मुँदी जा रही थीं, जबान लड़खड़ा रही थी।

"ले न!! भाभी च काबर? भइयो संग होली खेले के पूरा हक हे तोर।" उसने उसे पूरा-का-पूरा नाली में उतार दिया।

"सुबह से शाम हो गई, दस मिनट भी रहे घर में? ऐसा ही आदमी लिखा था करम में, बैठकर काट दिया होगा भाभी के पास। न जाने कौन सी बात है, जो कभी खत्म होने का नाम ही नहीं लेती।" उल्टे बाँस बरेली जाते देख वह चुपचाप वॉशरूम में घुस गया।

□

कहाँ गई सुनैना

उसे हाथ पसारकर भीख माँगना स्वीकार नहीं, परंतु जीविका का कोई साधन भी तो नहीं। एक स्वीकार्य मार्ग मिल ही गया था। प्रात: स्नान-ध्यान, पूजा-पाठ से निवृत्त हो एक थाली में कृष्ण भगवान् की आरती लेकर मंदिर के प्रमुख द्वार की ओर निकल जाती, मंदिर के दाहिनी ओर विशाल 'इंटरनेशनल धर्मशाले हैं! जहाँ थोड़ी-थोड़ी देर में यात्रियों के जत्थे आते रहते हैं। चबूतरों से सुसज्जित कचनार के वृक्षों की सघन छाया में बैठकर किंचित विश्राम करते हैं। वह उनकी आरती उतारकर श्री कृष्णजन्मभूमि की पावन धरा पर उनका स्वागत करती है। गुलाल का टीका लगा देती है, यात्री स्वेच्छा से उसकी थाली में चंद सिक्के डाल देते हैं, जो पच्चीस-तीस रुपए तो हो ही जाते हैं, इन्हीं से तो जीवन चल रहा है, माना कि भोजन-शयन की व्यवस्था मंदिर ट्रस्ट से होती है, परंतु और आवश्यकताएँ? उनके लिए तो कुछ करना ही पड़ता है, साथ के सब लोग मथुरा के अन्य मंदिरों के सामने हाथ पसारते हैं, ताकि तेल साबुन, चाय नाश्ते का खर्च पूरा हो सके, यूँ कपड़ों की तो कोई चिंता नहीं करनी पड़ती, श्रद्धालुजन देते रहते हैं।

उसने आरती दिखाई, चेहरा देखना जरूरी तो नहीं, परंतु तिलक लगाते समय नजरें यदि उसके माथे पर ठहर गईं तो उसकी क्या खता? वह धक्क से रह गई, "अरे! ये यहाँ कैसे आ गए, क्या उसे खोजते, अरे नहीं, दस साल से खोज ही रहे हैं क्या? चेहरा मोहरा जस-का-तस रखा है, आँखों पर सुनहरी फ्रेम का चश्मा, गले में मोटी सी सोने की चेन, कलाई पर नए फैशन की

घड़ी, शानदार हलके नीले रंग का सफारी सूट पहने वह अधेड़ पुरुष सब ओर से बेफिक्र लग रहा था। उसने उसकी ओर देखे बिना ही दो रुपए का सिक्का निकालकर आरती की थाली में डाल दिया था।

"सारे तीर्थों की ऐसी की तैसी कर रखी है इन भिखारियों ने" उसने उसे सुनाकर कहा।

"कुछ भिखारी भी तो भरे-पूरे घरों से निकल कर आते हैं।" उसके होंठों से वाक्य खारिज हुआ। वह उस पुरुष के साथ की युवती, युवक और दस वर्षीय बालक पर दृष्टि डालती आगे बढ़ गई थी। स्वर शायद पहचाना-सा लगा था उसे। उसकी खोजी नजरों ने उसका पीछा किया था शायद, वह मंदिर के पीछेवाली गली में जाकर कहीं गुम हो गई थी।

"क्या हो गया पापाजी, किस उलझन में पड़ गए?

"कुछ नहीं! इस औरत की आवाज कुछ जानी-पहचानी सी लगी है"! वह गंभीर था।

"होता है पापाजी, कभी-कभी"। युवती ने अपने हैंड बैग की चेन बंद करते हुए लापरवाही से कहा। युवक बालक के साथ उलझा हुआ था।

"पापा! जैसे कृष्णजी की गोपियाँ थीं, वैसी ही मुझे भी चाहिए, दिला देना ना··· !"

"तुम्हें बाद में समझाऊँगा, तुम्हारे स्कूल में हैं न··· ? गर्ल्स, वे ही तो गोपियाँ हैं खेला करो उनके साथ!"

"चलो लाइन में तो लगो, नहीं तो लाइन लंबी हो जाएगी!" युवती ने उन्हें अपनी ओर आकर्षित किया।

"हाँ चलो जल्दी!" युवक हड़बड़ाता हुआ बच्चे के साथ लाइन में लग गया। नीचे से वह तेज कदमों से अपने डेरे की ओर बढ़ रही थी, 'पक्की बात है, वह वही है, जिसके गले में कभी उसने जयमाला डाली थी, जिसके साथ तीस वर्षों तक संसार चलाया था। उसे कैसे भूल सकती है, जिसे नौ माह तक अपनी कोख में महसूसा था पल-पल? अपने हृदय का अमृत पिला-पिलाकर बड़ा किया, आज भी बसी है बचपन की वह मूरत उसकी आँखों में। सारा काजल फैल जाता था उसके गोल-से मुखड़े पर।

बड़ी-बड़ी झालर माथे को चूमती होती, कहीं से भी खेल-कूद कर आता, उसके सीने से चिपक जाता "माँ! तेरे बिना कहीं कुछ अच्छा नहीं लगता मुझे"!

"सोम, मेरे लाल! तेरे बिना मेरी भी गति नहीं है।" वह उसके मुखड़े पर चुंबनों की बरसात कर देती।

उसे याद है, सोम के स्कूल का वह पहला दिन, उसकी गोद से बलपूर्वक निकालकर स्कूल की आया के हवाले किया था शेखर ने। जब तक वह आ नहीं गया, आँखें पोंछती एकटक दरवाजा ताकती रही। शेखर ने डाँटा भी था, "अब बड़ा हो रहा है सोम, इतना मोह करोगी, तो वह पढ़ कैसे पाएगा?"

बीसियों रिश्ते ठुकाराए थे उसने अपने सोम के। "सुंदर-सुशील उच्च शिक्षित अच्छी सेलेरीवाला नौजवान, उम्र के पच्चीसवें पड़ाव पर ही सारी सफलताएँ उसकी झोली में आ गिरी थीं। शेखर ने भी बहुत कुछ बनाया था। पुस्तैनी जायदाद तो जो थी, सो थी ही। सोने की गृहस्थी थी उसकी, उसका घर सभी प्रकार की आधुनिक सुविधाओं से सुसज्जित था। उस घर की वह एकछत्र महारानी थी।

"खाना बनाने में सुनैना का जवाब नहीं, घर का रखरखाव हो या बच्चों की परवरिश, सुनैना सब में फिट है, मेरी अच्छी तकदीर थी, जो ऐसी बहू मुझे मिली"। उसने अनेक बार अपने कानों से सुना था, अम्मा को पड़ोसियों से कहते हुए। शेखर खाने-पीने का शौकीन ठहरा, सुनैना ही सँभाले उसे, दस बजे रात को उड़द दाल के बड़े की फरमाइश कर देगा, कैसे उसकी दाल फूलती है, कैसे भूखे शेर को गरमागरम बड़े परोसे जाते हैं। ये तो वही जाने। शेखर कहीं जाए, कुछ भी करे, कभी हो-हल्ला नहीं मचाती। ज्यादा हुआ तो कह देगी "मेरे भाग्य में जो होगा, कहाँ जाएगा? या मेरी सेवा में ताकत होगी, तो वे मेरे ही रहेंगे"।

"अरे बहना! आज कैसे जल्दी आ गई आरती दिखाकर, कोई बड़ा दानी मिल गया क्या?"

बड़ी मुँहफट है निर्मला भगतिन, उड़ती चिड़िया के पर गिन लेती है। सुनैना को गठरी के पास गुमसुम बैठी देख पूछ ही लिया।

देशभर से पहुँचे बेसहारों के लिए श्री कृष्ण जन्मभूमि मथुरा की ओर से एक बहुत बड़े क्षेत्र में टीन-शेड बनाया गया है। स्त्री-पुरुष सब साथ रहते हैं। अपनी मर्यादाएँ आप बाँध ली हैं। एक तरफ पुरुष तो दूसरी ओर महिलाएँ, सब अपनी-अपनी चादर पर सोते हैं। पाकशाला से भोजन करके आ जाते हैं, सुबह सारे सामानों की गठरी बनाकर एक-एक खंभे से टिकाकर रख देते हैं, सिमटी-सिकुड़ी जिंदगी देव के चरणों में स्थान पाकर चल पड़ी है सीधी राह पर।

कोई जिम्मेदारी नहीं, किसी की पुकार नहीं, किसी को इनकी जरूरत नहीं। राग-द्वेष से मुक्ति तो खैर यहाँ भी नहीं है, किसी को ज्यादा दान मिल गया, बाकी लोग जल उठे, किसी को बुखार आ गया, बाकी कहने लगे, "ले ज्यादा उड़! आ गया न बुखार? इसीलिए कहते हैं अपनी उम्र देखकर चल! त्योहार तेरे लिए ही तो आया था, नाचती रही पूरी रात भूतनी बनी।"

आदत पड़ गई है सुनैना को इन सबकी, सच पूछें तो अब ये लोग ही उसका परिवार हैं। ये न बोलें तो वह गूँगी होकर रह जाएगी, दूसरा दिन होता, तो वह भी नहले पे दहला देती निर्मला भगतिन को, "हाँ… ! तेरा खसम मिल गया था, कहने लगा, तुम मेरी साली हो, लो माल पर हाथ फेर ल्यो"।

परंतु आज तो जैसे वह भँवर में फँसी तेजी से गोल-गोल घूम रही थी। दस साल बाद आज अचानक दिख गया था उसका अपना परिवार, नहीं अपना कहाँ? कभी था अपना नहीं, तब भी अपना नहीं था, भ्रम था सुनैना को कि पति-पुत्र, बहू सब उसके हैं, उस घर की वह धुरी है, सबकुछ उसके ही इर्द-गिर्द घूम रहा है, परंतु क्या यह सच था?

सुजाता को उसी ने पसंद किया था अपने सोम के लिए, पढ़ी-लिखी सुंदरता की मूरत आधुनिकता के रंग में सिर से पैर तक रंगी हुई, नए डिजाइन के कई-कई जोड़े गहने बनवाए थे उसने। विभा को जितना दिया था, उससे अधिक ही दिया बहू को। बेटी तो पर घर गई, बहू से ही तो घर-आँगन रोशन होगा। वही उसका वंश चलाएगी, उसे भोजन-पानी देगी, उसका भार हल्का करेगी। एक बेटा, एक बेटी, बस्स! भगवान् से इतना ही बनाए रखने की पार्थना की थी उसने।

"सुजाता, मेरी फाइल देना! मेरे कपड़े! मेरा टिफिन, मेरे मोजे, मेरा नाश्ता!"

सोम हड़बड़ाकर रख देता घर भर को।

"आ बेटा! मैं नाश्ता लगा देती हूँ!"

"नहीं माँ! तुम आराम करो! सुजाता दे देगी"।

वह दिन भर सोम के फोन का इंतजार करती, जब भी लगाती व्यस्त की आवाज आती, सुजाता दिन भर कान से मोबाइल चिपकाए रहती।

"ये लो ताजे फल, ये लो ताजी सब्जियाँ, तुम्हारी नई ड्रेस, तुम्हारी नई कार की चाबी, मेरे खयाल से कलर तुम्हें अवश्य पसंद आएगा।" शेखर ने अपनी घूर्णन कक्षा बदल ली थी।

"सुजाता बेटा, नाश्ता देना, खाना देना, मेरे कपड़े, चलो, घुमा लाएँ तुम्हारे मायके से, ये लो किराए के रुपए, इस माह से हजार रुपए बढ़ा दिया है हमने, सँभालकर रख देना!"

उससे न जाने कौन सी भूल हो गई, जिसके कारण इन दोनों ने उसका नाम लेना ही छोड़ दिया। ये सारे काम तो वह करती आई थी। वह कहीं खड़ी, कहीं बैठी उनका मुँह निहारा करती, कोई कुछ कहे, उससे कुछ माँग ही लें, उसे देखकर शेखर की निगाहें न जाने क्यों झुक जातीं, उसे कुछ समझ में नहीं आता।

"सब्जी में कोई स्वाद नहीं, कपड़े वॉशिंग मशीन में पड़े हैं दो दिन से, महरी ने सारे बर्तन जूठे माँजे हैं आज और तुम हो कि बिना साफ किए उसी में परोसे जा रही हो! रसोई में सारी वस्तुएँ बिखरी पड़ी रहतीं हैं, कभी समेट भी लिया करो, ऐसे ही बनती है कटहल की सब्जी? नमक भी बराबर नहीं है।" वह घर में रहती थी, इसलिए सुजाता के काम करने का ढंग उसकी नजरों के सामने आ जाता था। एक दिन तंग आकर उसे कहना पड़ा था।

"मम्मी! आप मुझे न सिखाएँ तो ही अच्छा है! कभी ठीक से रखा घर-परिवार? सब तरसते रहे अच्छे खाने के लिए, इसीलिए तो सब आप को दुत्कारते रहते हैं, अब कभी इस तरह की बात सुनी तो अच्छा नहीं होगा··· !" सुजाता ने करारा उत्तर दिया।

वह तो 'बहूरानी' का जवाब सुनकर जैसे आकाश से गिरी। क्रोध से उसका सारा वजूद जल उठा। उसे विश्वास था कि इस उद्दंडता के लिए न इसे इसका ससुर माफ करेगा, न ही पति। क्या-क्या सपने सँजोए थे, सब मिट्टी में मिल गए। वह सोच-सोच कर आँसू बहाती रही।

"पापा! मम्मी मुझे हर्ट करती रहती हैं, कहती हैं मुझे कुछ आता ही नहीं"। वह तीन साल की बच्ची की तरह मचलकर उससे लिपट गईं।

"मैं उसे डाँटूँगा बेटा, पुराने जमाने की है न··· ! कूढ़मगज, पढ़ी-लिखी तो है, लेकिन उस समय की पढ़ाई भी तो वैसी ही थी।"

वह कुछ कहती, इसके पहले ही चढ़ दौड़ा शेखर, "अपनी होशियारी अपने पास रखो, कभी कुछ बनाया ढंग का, अब जब सलीकेदार बहू मिल गई है तो बहुत सुघड़ बन रही हो? वह तो हम जैसे थे, जो किसी तरह निभाया अब तक।"

"निभाया आप ने? मैं तो सोचती थी कि आप मुझे··· ! बड़े नाटकबाज हैं आप तो इतने बड़े सत्य को किस सरलता से छिपा लिया।" उसने लुटे-पिटे स्वर में कहा। अपने कमरे में आकर वह देर तक रोती रही, किसी ने उसकी ओर ध्यान नहीं दिया।"

"आज मेरा मित्र आ रहा है खाने पर, कुछ अच्छा सा बना लेना सुजाता बेटी और हाँ इन्हें तो रसोई में घुसने भी नहीं देना, वरना सारा गुड़-गोबर करके रख देंगी! उसके आत्मसम्मान पर ऐसे आघात सुबह से शाम तक लगते ही रहते थे।

"पापा! मम्मी के मायके से पैठन की साड़ी मिली है, मुझे दिलवा दो···न···पापा!" वह ललचा गई थी।

"दे दो न, तुम्हें पहनना भी तो नहीं आता ठीक से, सुजाता एक तो साड़ी पहनती नहीं, आज कह रही है तो दे दो।" शेखर ने जाने-अनजाने फिर प्रहार किया। फिर स्वयं ही उठाकर साड़ी उसे दे दी। जैसे-तैसे साड़ी पहनकर वह रसोई में गई, फर्श बुहारता आँचल तेल की कड़ाही में डूब गया। उसने साड़ी उतारकर जो फेंकी, तो दुबारा उठाकर नहीं रखी। वह दिल पर पत्थर रखकर रह गई। यदि सुजाता ने उससे कहा होता, वह स्वयं ही उसे ठीक ढंग से साड़ी पहनाती, परंतु बकौल शेखर के उसे तो साड़ी पहनना आता ही नहीं। उसके

दिल की धड़कनें अपने आप बेकाबू हो जातीं, ऐसा लगता, जैसे बस अब उससे कोई गलती हुई, अब शेखर ने उसकी लानत-मलानत की। अब सुजाता फुसफुसाई, अब सोम ने उसे देख बुरा सा मुँह बनाया।

"माँ ने खा लिया?" सोम पूछता है।

"उनको किसकी परवाह है? खा-पीकर सो रही हैं।''

"ठीक है, हमारे लिए निकालो।"

"मम्मी ने खाया?" शेखर पूछता है।

"नाश्ता भारी हो गया था पापा, फिर आप तो जानते ही हैं, उन्हें मेरे हाथ का बना खाना पसंद भी नहीं आता और कुछ-कुछ बनाकर खाएँगी।"

उसके शरीर का रक्त सूख रहा था। सब पराए लगने लगे थे, उसके दिल में चौबीस घंटे एक आग जला करती, कौन है अपना, क्या अपनेपन के बिना भी कोई जी सकता है? हाँ···! क्यों नहीं? जैसे वह जी रही है। यदा-कदा उसके मुँह से किसी फिल्म के गाने की पंक्तियाँ निकल जातीं, "कैसे जीते हैं भला लोग मुहब्बत के बिना।"

"यह क्या रेंकती रहती हो? जरा शर्म करो, घर में इतनी अच्छी बहू है, क्या सोचेगी तुम्हारे ऐसे चरित्र देखकर?" शेखर के कानों में उसकी गुनगुनाहट पड़ी थी।

"यही तो मैं आप से पूछना चाहती हूँ, क्या आप को बार-बार अपनी पत्नी का अपमान करते हुए शर्म नहीं आती है?" धीमे किंतु जहरीले स्वर में कहा था उसने।

"अब जबान भी चलाने लगी! मैं नहीं सह सकता यह सब, रहना है तो रहो, नहीं तो मायके जाओ!" शेखर चीख रहा था।

अपना घर छोड़कर मैं कहीं नहीं जाऊँगी! आप का चरित्र भी देख रही हूँ मैं, जरा भी परवाह है मान-मर्यादा की, धर्म-कर्म की? चार दिन की आई बहू हर प्रकार से सास से श्रेष्ठ हो गई! चलो मान लिया श्रेष्ठ है, तो दुनिया में और कोई जीने पाएगा या नहीं? मुझसे अब और बरदाश्त नहीं होता, अपनी बेटी से तो इस प्रकार नहीं लिपटते थे, फिर यह क्या लगने लगी आपकी? उसने अपनी आवाज चबाते हुए कहा।

बहू-बेटे अपने कमरे से ही सारा झगड़ा सुन रहे थे।

"पापा! पापा! मम्मी ने आज मुझ पर सबसे गंदा ब्लेम लगा दिया, मैं इस घर में एक पल भी नहीं रहूँगी!" सुजाता रोती हुई आकर खड़ी हो गई थी।

"हाँ पापा! मम्मी का व्यवहार अब सहन नहीं हो रहा है, हम दूसरी जगह अपना इंतजाम कर लेते हैं"। क्रोध के कारण सोम की आँखें लाल हो रही थीं।

"नहीं सुजाता! अगर कोई इस घर से गया, तो यह बदजात औरत जाएगी, इसके दिल में ऊपर से नीचे तक पाप भरा है, खुद ही कहा था कि सुजाता हमारी बहू नहीं, बेटी बनकर इस घर में रहेगी, अब जल रही है ईर्ष्या की आग में। अभी तक इसी के आगे-पीछे घूमते रहते थे न, हम बाप-बेटे, इसीलिए मगरूर हो गई है।

"निकालकर देखो मुझे घर से, तुम्हारी काली करतूतें बताती हूँ सबको"। वह भी अपना आपा खोकर दहाड़ी।

"क्या बताएगी तू बोल! बोल! क्या देख लिया तूने? क्या तू अपने बेटे को गले नहीं लगाती, क्या उसे चूमती नहीं, मैं कैसे सहता हूँ?" शेखर ने तड़ातड़ उसके गालों पर थप्पड़ बरसाए, घसीटकर कमरे में ले गया और अंदर से दरवाजा बंद कर तब तक पीटता रहा, जब तक थककर निढाल न हो गया। उसे अधमरी हालत में छोड़कर वह बाहर निकल गया।

बाप-बेटे सुजाता का मन बहलाने की कोशिश करते रहे। रोती कराहती कुछ-कुछ वह भी सुनती रही।

"ऐ भगतिन! चलो, चलो, केशवदेवजी के मंदिर में साड़ी-चद्दर बँट रही है, सब गए।" निर्मला भगतिन लगभग उसे खींचती हुई ले चली थी।

जन्मभूमि मंदिर के मुख्य द्वार से लेकर केशवदेव तक लंबी लाइन लगी हुई थी। पुलिसवाले अच्छी प्रकार जाँच कर अंदर जाने दे रहे थे, इस द्वार से लगा हुआ ही दूसरा द्वार है, यहाँ से महिलाएँ अंदर जातीं हैं, इधर भीड़ अपेक्षाकृत कम थी। उन्हें तो वैसे भी कोई रोकता नहीं हैं। वे सीढ़ियाँ चढ़कर जब ऊपर पहुँचीं, तब प्रातः के आठ बज चुके थे, मंदिर से सटी मसजिद के पीछे से कबूतरों का झुंड इधर आया और दुकानों की छत पर बिखरे दानों

पर एक साथ बैठ गया, सभी दाना चुगने लगे। जैसे ही दाना फेंकनेवाले ने हाथ उठाया, वे बिना आवाज के पंख फड़फड़ाते उड़ गए, कुछ मसजिद पर बैठ गए, कुछ पुनः दाना चुगने आ गए। उस दिन सोमवार था, केशव देवजी कामदार श्वेत वस्त्रों से सुसज्जित थे, उनके मुकुट में श्वेत रत्न जड़े हुए थे। गले में श्वेत पुष्पों की माला शोभा पा रही थी। मंदिर के अंदर भजन हो रहा था, ढोलक, झाँझ, मजीरे बज रहे थे। भक्तजन नृत्य कर रहे थे।

'कैसे आऊँ रे कन्हाई तेरी गोकुल नगरी, बड़ी दूर नगरी, बड़ी दूर नगरी।

रात में आऊँ तो कान्हा डर मोहे लागे, दिन में आऊँ तो देखे सारी नगरी, बड़ी दूर नगरी।"

ठाकुरजी के पास बैठे पुजारी पंचामृत बाँट रहे थे। उन दोनों ने खोजी निगाहों से चारों ओर देखा, गोवर्धनजी की ओर साड़ी-चादरें बँट रही थीं, वे दोनों लाइन में लग गईं।

"अरे! ये तो वे ही लोग हैं। शेखर कैसे पुण्यात्मा की तरह गरीबों को दान कर रहा है, सोम देता जा रहा है, सुजाता सब को नमस्ते कर रही है।

"वाह रे··· ! धर्मात्मा! मुझे नहीं चाहिए इनकी भीख।" वह धीरे से लाईन से निकल कर ऊपर जानेवाली सीढ़ियों की ओर जाकर बैठ गई।

वह खोई-खोई आँखों से गोवर्धनजी की ओर देख रही थी।

"जैसे-के-तैसे रखे हैं अब तक, कलयुग में पाप करके आदमी बढ़ता है। अब तो बीच में कोई नहीं रह गया कलह करानेवाला, धन की कमी है ही नहीं, बस राज कर रहे है।" सोच तो वह उस दिन की तरह ही रही थी, किंतु हृदय-दाह आज उतना नहीं था, ईश्वर का प्रसाद खाते-खाते बड़ी सहनशीलता आ गई थी।

"जरा बच्चे को पास से देख लेती! सोम जैसा ही है या सुजाता की तरफ ज्यादा गया है ? मन में अभिलाषा जाग्रत् हुई।

"जिस रास्ते जाना नहीं, उसका पता पूछने की क्या आवश्यकता, अपनी कोख का जाया अपना न हुआ, तो दूसरा क्या अपना होगा ?" उसने बलपूर्वक नजरें घुमा लीं दूसरी ओर।

"लेकिन बच्चे ने क्या बिगाड़ा है ? सारे बच्चे केशवजी के ही रूप हैं।"

उसने चोर नजरों से बच्चे की ओर देखा, "नाक-नक्श तो एकदम सोम जैसा पाया है, हाँ, रंग अलबत्ता सुजाता का है।'' उसके सीने में ममता का ज्वार-सा उठा, 'काश कि एक बार अपने पोते को गले से लगा पाती!'

कपड़े बाँटने का काम समाप्त हो चुका था, अब वे इसी ओर आ रहे थे, उसने साड़ी के पल्लू से अपना चेहरा ढँक लिया, जैसे कोई ग्रामीण महिला हो।

"हे केशवदेव! जीवन में हुए पापों से मुझे मुक्त करो, मैंने सुनैना के साथ बड़ी ज्यादती की।" शेखर के कदम केशवदेव के सामने ठिठक से गए थे, उसके मुँह से आह निकल रही थी।

"पापा! पछताने से क्या लाभ? जो होना था, सो हो गया, आपका उनसे उतना ही साथ लिखा था।" सुजाता सयानेपन से समझा रही थी।

"मैं माँ की पीड़ा नहीं समझ सका पापा, यह तो नीरू के होने के बाद पता चला कि माँ-बाप के लिए औलाद क्या चीज होती है"। सोम पछतावे भरे स्वर में कह रहा था।

"पर गई कहाँ सुनैना? इतना खोजा, कहीं पता नहीं चला, मैंने उसे निकाला अवश्य था घर से, परंतु यह नहीं जानता था कि वह सचमुच चली जाएगी, ऐसा तो मैं उसे डराने के लिए अकसर कहा करता था।"

"पापा, उस दिन क्रिकेट मैच हो रहा था न भारत-पाकिस्तान का, हम तीनों देखने में मगन थे, मम्मी को खाना वगैरह बनाने के लिए कह दिया था मैंने, उन्होंने जैसा उनसे बना, बनाया था। बार-बार बुलाने पर भी हम खाने की टेबल पर नहीं गए, दस बज गए थे, रात को आप झल्लाए, हमारे मुँह से भी कुछ निकल गया। मुँहजोर तो थीं ही, उन्होंने भी कहा-सुना, बस पापा आपने उन्हें बाहर निकालकर दरवाजा बंद कर लिया। सुजाता के मुँह से उस दिन की घटना का सहज वर्णन सुनकर उसके हृदय का घाव पुनः रिसने लगा।

"मैच तीन बजे सुबह तक चला, उसकी कचर-कचर में भारत हार गया। मैंने सोचा था, वह दरवाजे पर बैठी होगी, खोलकर देखा तो वह वहाँ नहीं थी, तभी से तो खोज रहे हम लोग? उसके मायकेवालों ने आकाश-पाताल एक कर दिया, उन्हीं के कारण तो पाँच वर्ष जेल में सड़ना पड़ा।"

शेखर जैसे स्वयं से बातें कर रहा था।

"आयं···एं···एं···शेखर पकड़ा गया था?" उसने खुद से प्रश्न किया।

उन्होंने तो साफ कह दिया कि सुनैना की हत्या शेखर ने की है। वह उसे प्रताड़ित करता था और वह जो सड़क के किनारे जली हुई लाश मिली थी, न जाने कैसे सुनैना की चूड़ियाँ वहाँ टूटी हुई मिल गईं! बाप रे, बाप! मैं भला किसी को जला सकता हूँ, क्या वह भागती नहीं? हाँ, ऐसा हो सकता है कि गुस्से में उसने स्वयं ही आत्मदाह कर लिया हो, चाहे जो हुआ हो, कारण तो मैं ही हूँ न? उसकी गलती तो न कानून देखेगा, न भगवान्, न समाज, दिन-रात का कलह अच्छे-भले को पागल कर देता है।' शेखर ने निःश्वास छोड़ी। उसकी पीठ सुनैना की तरफ थी। शायद वह अपने प्रश्नों के उत्तर भगवान् से प्राप्त करना चाह रहा था।

"पापा, जो बीत गया, उसे भूल जाइए, सब भाग्य का लिखा है।" सोम समझा रहा था।

"सच कह रहे हो शेखर! दिन-रात का अपमान, उपेक्षा वह भी उनसे, जो जान से ज्यादा प्रिय रहे हों, अच्छे-से-अच्छे आदमी को विक्षिप्त बना देता है। उस रात कितने मन से तुम्हारे लिए कचौरी और खीर बनाई थी मैंने, उठकर खा नहीं सके! कहते तो वहीं लाकर खिला देती, सारी मेहनत का पुरस्कार दिया तुमने मुझे घर से निकालकर। अँधेरी बरसाती रात में तुमने उस सुनैना को घर से निकाल दिया, जिसे दिन में भी अकेले कहीं जाने नहीं देते थे। चिल्लाकर रोई थी वह, कौन सुनता? सभी घरों से मैच की तेज कमेंट्री सुनाई दे रही थी। वह अपना होश खो बैठी थी, उसने अपनी चूड़ियाँ तोड़कर फेंकी, बाल नोचे, सिंदूर-टीका पोंछ लिया।

"आज से मैं किसी की पत्नी नहीं रही। उसने अनजाने ही रेलवे स्टेशन का रास्ता पकड़ लिया, स्टेशन पर एक रेलगाड़ी छूटने को तैयार थी। भीड़ में शामिल हो, वह गाड़ी में चढ़ गई। उसके पास एक फूटी कौड़ी भी नहीं थी। शरीर पर पहने गहने उसने पहले ही उतारकर फेंक दिए थे। भूलते-भटकते पता नहीं किस प्रकार वह मथुरा पहुँच गई, लोग कहते हैं, दो वर्ष तक यहाँ के धमार्थ चिकित्सालय में उसका इलाज चला था।

"यह पहेली समझ से बाहर बनी हुई है, यदि वह जली लाश सुनैना की थी तो पोस्टमॉर्टम रिपोर्ट में वह कम उम्र की औरत की लाश क्यों पाई गई? यदि लाश दूसरे की थी तो सुनैना के गहने, चूड़ियाँ, मंगल सूत्र वहाँ कैसे आए?" वह अपना माथा हथेली से रगड़ रहा था।

"रिपोर्ट सही थी, शेखर वह लाश सुनैना की नहीं थी, उसी की तरह कोई दूसरी होगी जिसे उसके पति ने मारकर जलाया होगा"। वह घृणा से बुदबुदाई।

"कोई श्राप नहीं दूँगी शेखर, पर इतनी आशा अवश्य करूँगी कि परम पिता तुम तीनों को अगले जन्मों में किसी औरत की कोख न दे; शरीर धारण करने के लिए।"

"प्रश्न जहाँ का तहाँ है, वह कहाँ है, प्रभु, तुम ही बता दो! उसके मिले बिना सब मुझे हत्यारा ही समझेंगे।" शेखर ने केशवदेव की ओर देखकर हाथ जोड़े थे।

"अब तुम्हें सुनैना कभी नहीं मिलेगी शेखर, तुम हत्यारे ही समझे जाते रहोगे।" उसकी आँखों से दो बूँद आँसू निकलकर हथेलियों में समा गए।

□

पहला दिन

उस दिन भी वह साढ़े चार बजे उठी, आदतन उसके मुँह से निकल पड़ा—"सर्व मंगल मांगल्ये शिवे सर्वार्थसाधिके, शरण्ये त्रयम्बके गौरी, नारायणी नमोस्तुते।"

उसने अपनी हथेलियाँ खोलकर हस्त-दर्शन किए, जो कर्म के आधार हैं, जो प्राणी के लिए ईश्वर के समान सहयोगी हैं, उसे कुछ याद आया, बिना किसी सोच के आँसू की कुछ बूँदे हथेलियों पर गिर पड़ीं। कल विदाई के समय सहकर्मी शिक्षिकाओं के सीने की गरमी का ताजा एहसास हुआ, दिमाग में एक प्रश्न उठा, "आज कहाँ जाना है?" साथ ही आईने पर नजर गई, सिर के··· झिंथराए बाल, जिनमें सफेदी की मात्रा ज्यादा थी, आँखों के नीचे हल्की स्याही और सामने के दाँत की खाली जगह।

"यह क्या हो गया उसे?"

जीवन ठहरता तो नहीं? यह निर्बाध रूप से अपने गंतव्य की ओर बढ़ता ही जाता है। कल सुबह की स्थिति कुछ दूसरी थी, "बस, आज भर सबसे अच्छी साड़ी पहन ले, मैंचिंग की चूड़ियाँ डाल ले। आज के बाद तो ये ज्यादातर आलमारी की ही शोभा बढ़ाएँगी। कहाँ जाना होगा नियम से? दिल की धड़कन बढ़ी हुई थी। लगता था, जैसे अब कुछ घंटों में ही वह जादू की छड़ी अपना प्रभाव खो देगी, जिसे घुमा-घुमाकर उसने अपने लिए सर्व सुविधायुक्त अपना संसार बसाया था। उसके कदम बोझिल थे, किसी बहाने से उसकी आँखें बरसना चाहती थीं। उसने रोज की तरह नाश्ता किया, जान-बूझकर कुछ देर से स्कूल पहुँची, उस दिन 31 मार्च होने के कारण छात्रों

के परीक्षा परिणाम घोषित होने थे। शिक्षिका बहनें कार्य पूर्ण करने में लगी थीं। वह प्रत्येक कक्षा में जाती, भर नजर बच्चों को देखती, छठी कक्षा में तो जैसे उसके आने के बारे में किसी ने कुछ ध्यान ही नहीं दिया। सब आपस में बातचीत करने अथवा तू-तू, मैं-मैं करने में निमग्न थे, उसके मन में हिलक उठ रही थी। अब कल से वह इनकी शिक्षिका नहीं रह जाएगी। उसने संकेत भी किया।

"आज मेरा अंतिम दिन है स्कूल में, तुम लोग जरा शांत हो रहो।"

"तैं नई आबे त पूरा स्कूल बंद हो जाही।" मुँहलगे छात्र सुजल ने लापरवाहीपूर्वक कहा और पुनः बातचीत करने लगा। उसने आज किसी को न डाँटने का विचार बनाया था, सत्र का अंतिम दिन था, किसी का मन पढ़ाई में नहीं लग रहा था। उसने चॉक लेकर श्याम पट पर प्रश्न लिखा, "अनुशासन क्या है?" हल्ला बंद हो गया।

सभी सोचने लगे। कुछ ने खड़े होकर उत्तर दिया, जिसे उसने अनुशासन की परिभाषा लिखकर पूर्ण कर दिया। थोड़ी देर बाद वह आठवीं कक्षा में गई, विद्यार्थियों को आगे की पढ़ाई के संबंध में कुछ आवश्यक जानकारी दी। उनका दुःख भी उसके ही समान था। वे स्कूल छोड़कर जा रहे थे, वह भी स्कूल से सदा के लिए जा रही थी। वे मौन वेदना सहते रहे। कमल नाम का विद्यार्थी उसके लिए विगत तीन वर्षों से समस्या बना हुआ था, आदतन अनज्ञाकारी, न पढ़ना, न तो किसी को पढ़ने देना, उसका सिद्धांत था। बहुत बार समझाया, लेकिन वह किशोर अपनी सोच के अनुसार जीनेवाला है, उसे स्कूल से निकालने की धमकी दी गई। वह कई हफ्ते स्कूल नहीं आया, हारकर उसे ही मनाकर लाना पड़ा। उसने पता लगाया, शराब के कारण कर्जे के बोझ से दबे उसके पिता ने दो वर्ष पूर्व आत्मघात कर लिया था। माँ मजदूरी करके बच्चे पाल रही है। उसका छोटा भाई सहदेव स्कूल से जाने के बाद इधर-उधर कुछ काम करके चार पैसे कमाता है। उसकी पारिवारिक पृष्ठभूमि जानने के पश्चात् वह उसे और अधिक चाहने लगी थी। कल वह स्कूल नहीं आया था, उसने उसके भाई को भेजकर मिलने के लिए बुलवाया। बड़ी मुश्किल से आया।

"मेरा आज अंतिम दिन है कमल, यदि मुझसे तुम्हारे प्रति कभी ज्यादती हो गई हो तो मुझे माफ कर देना, किसी भी प्रकार अपनी पढ़ाई जारी रखना।" उसका गला भर्रा गया था, वह होंठों पर झूठी मुसकान लिये सुनता रहा, जैसे ही वह चुप हुई, वहाँ से चला गया। सातवीं के छात्रों से भी उसने इसी प्रकार विदा ली। उसका हृदय खंड-खंड हो रहा था। जिस स्कूल में लगातार आठ वर्ष तक आती रही। उससे हमेशा के लिए दूर होना उसके लिए दूध पीते बच्चे को माँ की गोद से छीन लेने जैसा लग रहा था। उसे विदा करने के लिए संकुल प्रभारी श्री अशोक तिवारी और संकुल समन्वयक श्री योगेश पांडेयजी आए हुए थे। जलपान के बाद बहनों ने उसे सिंदूर तिलक से अभिषिक्त कर श्रीफल का उपहार दिया। बहन शकुंतला ने रामचरितमानस (मझला साइज) पुस्तक रहल के साथ उसे भेंट की। प्रभा शुक्ला ने सुंदर सा पेन दिया। उनका उपहार उसे अत्यंत प्रिय लगा।

"चलो, अब चलते हैं, बहनजी को विदा कर दें!'' मीना बहनजी ने कहा। हेड मास्टर, नायक बहनजी, आनंद बहनजी, सभी उसके साथ शाला प्रांगण में आए, जहाँ उसकी प्लेजर खड़ी थी, उसने कातर दृष्टि से शकुंतला मैडम को देखा और अचानक उसकी बाँहें फैल गईं। उनकी आँखों से गंगा-जमुना बह निकली। सभी से भेंटकर उसने स्वयं को संयमित किया। निगाहें झुकाईं और अपनी गाड़ी स्टार्ट कर बरसती आँखों से देखते हुए अपने स्कूल से सदा के लिए विदा ले ली। घर तक वे बरसती आईं।

चूँकि गरमी इस वर्ष अन्य वर्षों की तुलना में कुछ अधिक ही पड़ रही है, अप्रैल प्रारंभ नहीं हुआ और कई रातों से गरमी के मारे नींद नहीं आ रही है। उसने केशरवानी को सारे कूलर ठीक करने हेतु दे रखे थे। वह एक सप्ताह से नदारद था, अतः उसके घर जाकर अपना काम पूरा करने के लिए कहा। घर आई तो पति महोदय ने माहौल हल्का करने के लिए हल्की-फुल्की बातें प्रारंभ कीं। उसके ज्येष्ठ पुत्र एवं पुत्रवधू मिठाई, फूल-माला, बुके आदि लेकर आ गए। विगत 6 माह से उनसे उसका अनबोला चल रहा था। इस अवसर पर उनके आने की उसे जरा सी भी संभावना नहीं थी, सभी लोगों ने टीका लगाकर पुष्प भेंट कर स्वागत किया। वह लगातार रोती रही। एक

बात जान लें, उसके आँसू बहुत कम निकलते हैं। हर अवसर पर धैर्यपूर्वक व्यवहार करना उसके व्यक्तित्व की विशेषता है। कुछ दिन पहले उसे शक हो गया था कि आँखों में आँसू सूख जाने की बीमारी तो नहीं हो गई? चलिए इस समय वह शक तो दूर हो गया। उसका बड़ा बेटा सेवाकाल की विशेष घटनाओं का वर्णन कर रहा था। सम्मानपूर्वक सेवा समाप्ति पर मित्रों से भी बधाई संदेश प्राप्त हो रहे थे।

कल का दिन तो ऐसा था, जैसे छोटे बच्चों का होता है, जागती तो रोती, थकती तो फिर सो जाती। संध्या काल में अपने आराध्य श्री आंजनेय के पूजन-दर्शन हेतु मंदिर गई थी। उस अयोग्य की उँगली पकड़कर सारी मुश्किलें पार करानेवाले पिता वे ही तो हैं, अश्रुपूरित नेत्रों से उनकी महिमा का गुणगान किया। एक ऐसी बालिका, जो पाठशाला जाने के लिए तरसा करती थी, उसे पढ़ने-लिखने का ऐसा अवसर दिया कि वह जीवन के चौतींस वर्ष शिक्षिका के रूप में कार्य कर आज सेवानिवृत्त हो गई। इस बीच उसे एक भी स्पष्टीकरण देने की नौबत नहीं आई। अत्यंत मान-सम्मान से शिक्षक, राज्यपाल एवं राष्ट्रीय शिक्षक सम्मान से नवाजा गया उसे। सारा विभाग उस पर गर्व करता रहा।

"हे पिता! मेरी उँगली थामे रहना, आज मैं अकेली हूँ। मुझसे मेरा काम छूट गया है, जिसे मैं अपने जीवन से ज्यादा महत्त्व देती हूँ।" वह हनुमानजी की प्रतिमा की ओर देखती मौन अश्रु बहाती रही।

समय तो किसी के लिए रुकता नहीं है। वह बीते दिनों की याद करती, कभी सोती, कभी जागती रही थी और आज का यह दिन—प्रातः भ्रमण पर जाना कुछ समय से अनियमित हो गया है। नींद समय से न खुली तो बस घर भर की ही होकर रह जाती। उसने स्वयं से वादा किया था कि पहले दिन से ही प्रातः भ्रमण को नियमित कर लेगी। अब पहले की तरह भाग-दौड़ नहीं होगी, यदि पैदल न चली, तो बेतहाशा वजन बढ़ जाएगा, जो स्वयं में हजार बीमारियों की जड़ है। वह नित्य क्रिया से निवृत्त हो, एक कप हर्बल टी लेकर घूमने निकल पड़ी। सड़कें, पेड़-पौधे, जाने-पहचाने लोग, सब अनजाने से लगे। फिर जब चेहरे पर नजरें गड़ाकर देखा तो लगा कुछ नहीं बदला। मेक्सी

पहने हाथ में तार खुँसी डंडी लिये ऊँची-ऊँची डालों से फूल चुराती महिलाएँ, अपने प्राण प्रिय श्वानों की जंजीरें थामे चोर नजरों से इधर-उधर देखते या उसके जोर से खींचते, चले जाते लोग, बस कृपा तो उन्हीं पर बरसेगी, जो या तो सो रहे होंगे या घूमने निकल गए होंगे। वह उसकी परिचिता! जिससे उसकी पहचान मैट्रिक की परीक्षा के दौरान हुई थी। उस समय भी वह नगर निगम में लिपिक का काम करती थी। जो अब तक कुँआरी है, बाद में उसे न जाने कहाँ से ब्रह्मज्ञान प्राप्त हुआ कि उसने मनुष्य की बजाय जानवरों पर प्यार लुटाना अधिक उपयुक्त समझा। उसके घर में कई कुत्ते हैं, जिन्हें वह अपना सगा मानती है। उन्हें आदर से संबोधित करती है। पहले उन्हें खिलाकर स्वयं खाती है। स्मृति वन के रास्ते में अपने दो-तीन कुत्तों की जंजीरें पकड़े वह ऐसी प्रसन्न नजर आती है, जैसे प्राचीन काल में राजकुमारियाँ अपने मनोरंजन के लिए अश्वों की वल्गा सँभाले रथारूढ़ होकर अकेली भी यात्रा पर निकल जाती थीं। ऐसा उसने कई टीवी सीरियल में देखा है। वह उस दिन भी सारी दुनिया से निर्लिप्त अपने सगे-संबंधियों को मार्ग विभूषित करवाने ले जा रही थी। उसके चेहरे पर रात्रिकालीन आलस्य के साथ चिकनाई चमक रही थी, जो चेहरे के हल्के पड़ चुके चेचक के दागों के कारण फिसल पड़ने से बच रही थी।

"नमस्तेजी।" उसने जबरिया उसका ध्यान अपनी ओर आकृष्ट किया।

नमस्ते करती वह खींची चली गई। सोच-विचार में उसे किंचित् विलंब हो चुका था। सूर्य का सिंदूरी वृत्त पूर्व की ओर उदित हो रहा था। उसने कदम रोककर श्रद्धापूर्वक विश्वदेव को प्रणाम किया। वे पेड़ों के झुरमुट से आहिस्ता-आहिस्ता बाहर निकल रहे थे। बहुत सारे लोग वापस लौट रहे थे, जिनका उसने अभिवादन किया, उत्तर पाया, बाकी तो अपने रास्ते आए-गए।

सबकुछ तो ज्यों का त्यों है, वही बदल गई है, वह अब भूतपूर्व शिक्षिका हो चुकी है। जहाँ भी रहती, मनोमस्तिष्क में यह सतर्कता रहती थी कि ड्यूटी पर पहुँचना है। छुट्टी के लिए आवेदन पत्र देना है, समय पर स्कूल पहुँचना है, डायरी बनानी है, कॉपी जाँचनी है, प्रश्न निकालना है, वही कोना तो रिक्त हो गया है, इसलिए इतनी दुःखी है। शुभचिंतकों ने अपने-अपने अनुभव

के आधार पर सेवा-समाप्ति पर मिलनेवाली धनराशि के सदुपयोग के मार्ग सुझाए। सभी का एक मत था कि अपने निर्वाह हेतु रुपए सुरक्षित रखे जाएँ, उसे लगा, जैसे ऐसा सोचकर वह उन लोगों के प्रति अत्याचार करेगी, जिनके बलिदान के बिना वह अपनी नौकरी नहीं निभा सकती थी। जब उसने मिनी पी.एस.सी. पास कर नौकरी प्राप्त की थी, तब तीनों बच्चे छोटे थे, बड़ा आठ वर्ष, मझला छह वर्ष और सबसे छोटा डेढ़ वर्ष, उसने दो बच्चों को स्कूल भेजकर तीसरे को गोद में उठाए स्कूल जाना प्रारंभ किया था। कितने उदास हो गए होंगे बच्चे? माँ घर में नहीं है, यह भावना ही बच्चे को हद से ज्यादा अकेला कर देती है। छोटे बेटे को कंधे पर उठाए, उसका बास्केट एक हाथ में पकड़े, वह पहले मेन हास्पिटल जाकर इंजेक्शन लेती, क्योंकि उस समय वह कमर दर्द से पीड़ित थी। फिर सिटी बस में चढ़कर पाँच कि.मी. दूर विद्यालय पहुँचती, नए परिवेश में बच्चा बड़ा असहज अनुभव करता। वह पूरे दिन उसके कंधे से चिपका रहता, उसे लिए-लिए ही वह कक्षा एक के विद्यार्थियों को पढ़ाती। घर आती तो स्कूल से आकर दोनों बच्चे दरवाजे पर बैठे होते, उसका कलेजा मुँह को आ जाता। नहीं हो पाएगी नौकरी! बच्चों को बहुत कष्ट हो रहा है। फिर भी उस समय को सबने मिलकर काटा, बड़ी सहजता और प्रसन्नता से, शरीर में शक्ति और मन में उमंग थी उसके, उसे अपने बच्चों का भविष्य गढ़ना था। बड़े होते बच्चों ने उसे भरपूर सहयोग दिया। नौकरी के आर्थिक संबल ने उन्हें सम्मानजनक मुकाम पर पहुँचाया, तो फिर जमा राशि पर एक का ही अधिकार लूट नहीं तो और क्या है।

उसने सभी को बराबर हक देने का फैसला कर लिया था।

स्मृतिवन से आकर नहा-धोकर अनजाने ही तैयार हो गई। गाड़ी स्टार्ट कर चल पड़ी, उसने अपने आपको विद्यालय से थोड़ी दूर पर पाया। सचेत होकर पुनः वापस लौट आई। पूरे दिन इस बात को स्वीकारने में लगी रही कि वह अब सेवानिवृत्त हो गई है।

गुजरा किसी तरह सोते-जागते पहला दिन, कितना अंतर है दो पहले दिनों में? सेवा का पहला दिन, मुख्यालय से पाँच कि.मी. दूर पतिदेव के साथ सिटीबस में बैठकर प्रातः 10 बजे पहुँची थी अपने स्कूल। बस में यात्रा

करने की कोई वैसी आदत नहीं थी, बिना कुछ पकड़े ही बच्चे को लेकर खड़ी हो गई। लगा गिर पड़ेगी, बस के गेट पर एक मध्यम ऊँचाई की सौम्य आकृतिवाली उम्रदराज महिला ने बच्चे को अपनी गोद में सँभाल लिया। वे स्वर्गीया सुशीला पांडेय बहनजी थीं। वे भी प्रा, शाला, कोनी में पदस्थ थीं, वहीं जा रही थीं।

जैसे नसों में धीरे-धीरे ग्लूकोज चढ़ता है, वैसे ही हौले-हौले आत्मगौरव की भावना जन्म लेकर पुष्ट हो रही थी। वह उसे धारण करती जा रही थी। नौकरी से मिलनेवाले आर्थिक संबल पर उन सब की आशाएँ टिकी हुई थीं। वह दिन भी आज की तरह ठहर-ठहर कर बीत रहा प्रतीत हो रहा था, घर में रहते हुए दोपहर में एक घंटे आराम करने की आदत थी। बच्चा भी कुछ देर सोता था। यहाँ कैसे सोएँ माँ-बेटे? एक पानी की खाली टंकी थी। उसने उस पर लकड़ी का श्यामपट बिछाकर उसी पर अपने बच्चे को सुलाया था। शाला प्रांगण में नीम के पेड़ के नीचे खड़े श्री अरविंद कुमार राम ने उसे चाय पीने का आमंत्रण दिया, चाय क्या थी, मानो ईश्वर का प्रसाद ही था। उसे बड़ी ताजगी का अनुभव हुआ।

गौरव की भावना अब दयनीयता में बदल रही है, तोड़ रही है अंदर-अंदर।

दोपहर को भाई का फोन आया था, उसने भी अनिंद्य सेवा समाप्ति पर बधाई दी, उसे उसके अवसाद का अंदाजा था, इसीलिए उसने उसे कुछ याद दिलाने की कोशिश की। उदास क्यों होती है दीदी? सेवानिवृत्ति की तारीख तो सेवा प्रारंभ में ही लिख दी जाती है, इसे भी सहजता से ले, फिर तेरे पास तो काम का अंबार है, अपनी रचनाएँ पूरी कर! घूमने-फिरने जा। गरीब बच्चों को उपचारात्मक शिक्षा देने की जो तेरी योजना थी, उस पर काम कर। एक काम से निवृत्ति हुई है, बल्कि यूँ कहें कि कार्य ने अपना रूप बदला है। यह तो सोच, यदि बड़े अपना स्थान रिक्त नहीं करेंगे तो नई पीढ़ी को काम कैसे मिलेगा?

उसकी अंतिम बात वास्तव में दमदार थी, पीड़ा का अंत तो नहीं हुआ, लेकिन नियति को स्वीकारने का बल अवश्य मिला। संध्या के साथ कर्तव्य

के नए आयाम उपस्थित हुए। उसने गाय को दाना-चारा दिया। दूध की बाल्टी साफ की। भोजन में कुछ ठीक-ठाक बनाने के बारे में सोचने लगी। कुछ याद न आया, फिर वही खालीपन चारों ओर से डसने लगा। वह शाम की उदासी को अपने हृदय में उतरती अनुभव कर रही थी। पहले तो शाम के समय कार्यों की बरात उमड़ आती थी। जैसे ही स्कूल से आओ, गायें आकर खड़ी हैं, पूरा घर बिखरा है, तब तक कोई मिलने आ गया। कोई चाय के लिए चिल्ला रहा है, इधर भोजन बनाने में विलंब हुआ जा रहा है। मुँह धोना तो दूर, लघुशंका के लिए जाने का वक्त भी नहीं रहता था। किचन समेटते रात के ग्यारह बज जाते, नई आई पत्रिकाओं को पढ़ने के लिए जी तरसकर रह जाता। लेटते ही निद्रा के आगोश में अपनी सुध-बुध खो देती। आज भी वे सारे काम हैं, किंतु कल कहीं जाने की जल्दी नहीं है। इसलिए कुछ करने का मन भी नहीं है। वह बैठी खिड़की से डूबते सूर्य को देख रही थी। सिंदूरी गोला अग-जग को बलिदानी केसरिया रंग में रंग रहा था।

"अभी तो सूर्यास्त में विलंब है। सब तरफ उजाला है, फिर यह मन में अँधेरा क्यों हुआ जा रहा है? झूठा है मन, उसने स्वयं को प्यारी सी डाँट लगाई।"

"मैडम अब तें हमला पढ़ा! अब तें हमला पढ़ा! तैं कहे रहे रिटायर होहूँ त तुमन ला पढ़ाहूँ! एदे आ गयन मैडम। हम कमजोर हन हमर डहर कोनो नई देखैं।" कुछ छोटे-बड़े बच्चे, मैले-कुचैले बच्चे, बोरी का बस्ता लिये बच्चे दौड़े चले आ रहे थे उसकी ओर। अरे! ये तो घर के सामनेवाले नीम के पेड़ के नीचे बैठ रहे हैं। "ऐ··· ! देखो तो मेरा चशमा किधर है? बच्चे आ गए हैं पढ़ने, जब तक उजाला है, तब तक पढ़ा दूँ इन्हें।"

□

दान-दहेज

अच्छा घर-बार, धन-दौलत, नौकरी-चाकरी, छोटा-परिवार, एक शब्द में कहें तो जैसा वह सोचा करती थी, वैसा ही सबकुछ। राकेश इंजीनियर है, माता-पिता, सरकारी नौकरीवाले, बहनें दोनों ससुराली, उसने अपने जानिब वह सब पता लगाया था, जिसे रिश्ते के लिए आवश्यक माना जाता है, आज के युग में भी राकेश हर प्रकार के नशे से दूर था। माता-पिता से दूर न जाना पड़े, इस विचार से अपना काम प्रांरभ किया था। जरा मन पीछे हटा, एक साथ रहना, यानी हिमानी के ऊपर जिम्मेदारी का दबाव। रोक-टोक! कौन सी बड़ी बाधा थी? शादी के साल भर बाद ही उसने इससे भी बड़ी बाधा को नहीं उखाड़कर इतनी दूर फेंक दिया था कि दुबारा कभी उसकी हवा तक न लगी। आकाश क्या कम मातृभक्त था? पिता के न रहने पर बस माँ-बेटे ही तो रह गए थे परिवार के नाम पर। दोनों में एक-दूसरे के प्राण बसते थे, लेकिन उसने पार की न इतनी बड़ी बाधा। वैसे ही हिमानी भी साल के अंदर ही या तो अपने घर में अकेली अपने पति के साथ रहती या अपना घर बना लेते दोनों।

पर यह क्या हो रहा है? यहाँ से लड़की पसंद करके, कुल-गोत्र, राशि-वर्ण, नाड़ी-योनि, पूछ-पूछाकर गए, कुंडली के छत्तीस गुण मिलते थे। हिमानी के मुरझाए चेहरे पर प्रसन्नता की चमक देखी थी उसने।

"माँ, मेरे जाने पर घर कैसे चलेगा?" उसने उदास होकर पूछा था, सोचे भी क्यों नहीं? दस वर्ष से कमाकर घर चला रही है। शिवानी और भवानी पढ़ाई पूरी करके चार पैसे कमाने के लिए हाथ-पैर मार रही हैं। किसी प्रकार

अपना खर्च निकाल ही लेती हैं। आधार स्तंभ तो हिमानी ही है। आकाश को घर बैठे लगभग दस-ग्यारह वर्ष हो गए, जो कुछ मिला, उससे यह एक घर खरीद लिया था। थोड़ी-बहुत पेंशन है, चल रही है गाड़ी। तीनों बेटियाँ बेहद समझदार हैं। उन्हें अपनी आर्थिक स्थिति का अंदाजा भलीभाँति है। मरे लड़केवाले मानें तो घर बेचकर करनी होगी शादी। कैसी तो हो गई हिमानी, अठारह बीस की उम्र में जैसे फूल खिलते थे उसके चेहरे पर। आँखें हँसती रहती थीं जैसे। कोई मोहक सुगंध झरती रहती थी उसकी देह से, धीरे-धीरे बदल गई वह। अब तो सदा गंभीर रहती है। ऑफिस से आई, कमरे में घुसी। न अधिक बातचीत, न कोई फरमाइश। जो कुछ मिला, खा-पीकर चली। बेचारी! अपनी उम्र में किसे नहीं लगता? उसकी तो तीनों बेटियाँ तीस के पार हो चुकी थीं। बेटे का मुँह देखने की चाह में तीन देवियाँ आ गईं। उसके बाद तो न जाने कैसे स्वयं ही पूर्ण विराम लग गया था। वह तो अभी पाँच साल पहले तक प्रतिमाह अपने शरीर में कुछ अलग प्रकार का परिवर्तन खोजा करती थी, अब तो हो गया, जो होना था। सब मनसूबा बेकार निकला। फोन आ गया।

"आपकी लड़की तो हमें पसंद है, परंतु हम ऐसे घर से लड़की लाना नहीं चाहते, जिस घर में दादा-दादी न हों, हमें माफ कीजिएगा।" कटे पेड़ की तरह बिस्तर पर गिर पड़ी थी वह, ऐसा पहली बार हुआ हो, यह भी तो नहीं है। तीसरी बार है, उसकी शादी का लगते-लगते टूट जाना।

अजीब बदलाव आ रहा है लड़केवालो में! पहले दान-दहेज, सुंदर पढ़ी-लिखी लड़की, बारातियों के स्वागत-सत्कार की बात होती थी। अब घर में दादा-दादी! चाहे स्वयं अपने माँ-बाप के साथ न रहते हों। सब बहाना है, अवश्य किसी दुश्मन ने शादी काट दी है।

हिमानी के दादा को तो वह नहीं ला सकती, लेकिन दादी? उसे ला सकती थी, पता नहीं, अब वहाँ रहती है या नहीं। वह कहाँ आएगी? जब इतने दिनों में कभी नहीं आई, न खोज-खबर ली तो अब क्या रहेगी आकर? सुनकर उसे तो खुशी ही मिलेगी। बेटे को देखकर शायद पिघल जाए। कोशिश करनी होगी। लोगों की सोच नहीं बदली जा सकती। सोच यह कि जिस परिवार में

सयानों का स्थान रहता है, उस परिवार की लड़कियाँ अपनी ससुराल में भी बुजुर्गों की सेवा करती हैं, यह उनके संस्कार में होता है। हालाँकि यह सिद्धांत पूर्णरूपेण सच नहीं है, उसकी माँ ने तो पगली सास की अंत तक सेवा की। क्या मजाल, जो बाहर निकलने दे? चाहे वह कितना ही चीखे-चिल्लाए, घर गंदा करे या गालियाँ दे, वह सब सहती थी। लोग कहते—पागलखाने भेज दो, परंतु वह नहीं मानी, घर पर ही दवाई होती रही, बहुत कुछ ठीक भी हो गई थी दादी।

परंतु उसे तो न जाने क्यों आकाश और अपने बीच सास बरदाश्त ही न हुई। पहले दूसरे दिन से ही जल में तैरती काई की तरह किनारे करना शुरू कर दिया था उसे। पहले-पहले शर्मिंदा सा आकाश बगलें झाँकता रहता, उसकी प्यारी पत्नी सारिका फूट-फूट कर रोती होती, माँ गुस्से से उबलती होती, वह किसे सँभाले, किसे छोड़े? फिर उसने डाँटकर माँ को चुप कराना और सारिका को सांत्वना देना प्रारंभ किया था। उसकी दृष्टि में माँ का अत्याचार बढ़ता ही गया था। सारिका के आँसू झूठे नहीं हो सकते थे न?

"माँ यहाँ लेटी क्या कर रही हो?" वह हिमानी की आवाज सुनकर चौक उठी। वह आ गई है अपने काम से। आजकल किसी कंपनी में काम कर रही है। आते ही एक बार माँ को अवश्य पूछती है।

"माँ क्या हुआ?"

वह उठी थी, बेटी को एक गिलास पानी देना उसका फर्ज बनता है। उसके मुँह से कुछ नहीं निकल सका।

"क्या हुआ माँ, बोलो न, लड़केवालों का फोन आया क्या?" वह माँ का चेहरा देख परेशान हो उठी थी।

"कहते हैं, जिसके घर दादा-दादी न हों, उस घर से लड़की नहीं लेंगे। बताओ भला जिसके घर दादा-दादी न हों, उसकी लड़की क्या कुँआरी रहेगी?"

"चिंता मत करो माँ! जहाँ भाग्य होगा, वहाँ शादी लगेगी ही।" उसने सयानों की तरह समझाया। "वैसे माँ! हमारी तो दादी थी न··· ?" उसका प्रश्न सारिका को हिला गया।

"थी बेटी! हो सकता है अभी भी हो। उसके मन में कोई खोट न होता तो क्या घर छोड़कर चली जाती? लगभग पैंतीस साल हो गए घर से निकले, कभी बेटे की भी सुध नहीं ली। वैसे यदि वो घर में होती तो और कोई रिश्तेवाले घर की ड्योढ़ी न चढ़ते।" वह हिमानी के लिए चाय-पानी ले आई थी। उसने देखा भी नहीं माँ की ओर। बहुत रोना-धोना मचा था।

"तुम्हारी गलती की सजा मुझे मिल रही है माँ! तुम्हें बना के रखनी थी न अपनी सास से? अब हम तीनों बहनें, कहो तो किसके घर बैठें जाकर?" वह रोए जा रही थी।

"शांत हो जा बेटी! जिन्होंने तुझे ठुकराया है, वे बड़े अभागे हैं। उनकी सोच की बलिहारी है। उन्हें बहू नहीं, नौकरानी चाहिए, जो जीवन भर उनका गू ढोती रहे। अच्छा हुआ, जो उन्होंने मना कर दिया, वरना जीवन भर का रोना हो जाता।" सारिका अब दूसरे ढंग से समझा रही थी हिमानी को।

और भी अच्छे-अच्छे रिश्ते आए, किंतु बात न बनी। नाना-नानी, दादा-दादी की खोजबीन में यह तो नहीं कहा जा सका कि लड़की की दादी अब इस संसार में नहीं हैं? सबकुछ सुनते हुए भी आकाश चुप रहे। जब सारिका एकदम से झल्ला गई, तब धीरे से कह दिया—

"उस दिन भी तुम्हारे ही मन की चली थी, जब माँ रोती हुई दस बजे रात को घर से निकली थी। मैं कुछ कर सका था क्या? तुम तो हाथ में मिट्टी तेल का डिब्बा लेकर खड़ी थी—यह घर से निकले या इसी समय जल मरूँगी, फिर रहना जेल में माँ-बेटे एक ही संग। हम तो लाचार हैं तुम्हारी योजनाओ के आगे। वह और जल-भुनकर राख हो गई थी। उसे पता ही न चला था कि उसका पति मन में उसके प्रति ऐसी भावना रखता है।

"बताओ पापा! बेटा होकर कभी खोजा दादी को? माँ तो परकोठिया थी, आप तो उनके बेटे थे?" हिमानी ने कठघरे में ले लिया था उसे।

"पता क्यों नहीं लगाया? इसी शहर के राजेंद्र नगर में डॉक्टर बलदेव के यहाँ रहती हैं। वे लोग उसे बहुत मानते हैं, कभी-कभी मिलता हूँ तो गले लगाकर पूरे टाइम रोती रहती हैं।"

"अच्छा, तो इतना बड़ा धोखा किया तुमने मेरे साथ, कभी हवा नहीं

लगने दी कि तुम उसके बारे में कुछ जानते हो, उसके सारे करम भूल गए, शर्म नहीं आती है उसका बेटा कहलाने में?" सारिका नागिन-सी बल खा गई।

"हाँ, आती है शर्म उसका बेटा कहलाने में, मैं ऐसा बेटा हूँ, जिसने अपनी माँ को घर से निकलकर परायों के घर आश्रय लेते देखा है, कुछ न कर सका मैं। जेल जाने से डरता था न और तुम्हारे हाथ में तो हमेशा··· ?"

आकाश ने जरा व्यंग्य से कहा।

"पापा, चलिए! हम दादी को लेकर आएँगे, बात शादी की नहीं है, हमें अपनी दादी चाहिए! माँ यदि नहीं मानती है तो हम तीनों भी घर छोड़कर निकल जाएँगी।" हिमानी की आवाज में दृढ़ता थी।

"हम सब मर जाएँ तो भी नहीं झुकेगी वह।" सारिका ने हारे हुए स्वर में कहा।

"पापा, हम कल चलेंगे दादी से मिलने?" हिमानी ने अपना फैसला सुनाया जैसे।

"माँ सबसे पहले निकलकर ऑटो में बैठ जाना न··· ! वरना अब तुम्हारे अकेले होने की बारी आ गई है।" हिमानी का स्वर···तल्ख···था।

"राणो! तुम्हें मैंने बेटे से कम नहीं माना, भतार पाने के लिए इस तरह उतावली हो जाओगी, यह तो कभी सोचा भी नहीं था मैंने?" सारिका ने अपने दोनो हाथों से अपना सिर दबाया।

रात भर उसे नींद नहीं आई, लड़कियाँ कुँआरी नहीं, बेवा जैसी दिखने लगी हैं, समय पर ही सब अच्छा लगता है। इनका बनाना है तो यह भी सही, इसीलिए जिंदा है आज तक मेरे जी का कंटक। कहते भी हैं न, वक्त पर गधे को भी बाप कहना पड़ता है। चलूँ, पैर पकड़कर मना लाऊँ, नहीं तो लड़कियाँ बेहाथ हो जाएँगी, आ गई तो काम होते ही, फिर वही रास्ता दिखा दूँगी। नहीं आई तो ये जो ज्यादा चपड़-चपड़ कर रही हैं, हमेशा के लिए चुप हो जाएँगी। आदमी हारता अपनी कोख से ही है। मैं ही मूर्ख थी, जो जानते-बूझते इन्हें संसार में ले आई, इसीलिए तो लोग बहा देते है नाली में, लगता जो कुछ लगता, आज यह दिन तो नहीं देखना पड़ता। वह पूरी रात सोचती रही।

जाते-जाते बड़ी उदार होकर माफ करती गई थी, अब समझ में आया, उसने बड़ी होशियारी से मुझे श्राप दिया था। तुमने मेरे साथ जो भी किया, अपनी समझ से ठीक ही किया। तुम मेरे अरमानों का फल हो, मैं तुम्हें माफ करती हूँ! भगवान् करे, तुम्हें ऐसे दिन कभी न देखने पड़ें। अब समझ में आया, उसका तात्पर्य था तू बेटे की माँ न बन सके, बेटा नहीं होगा तो बहू कहाँ से आएगी, फिर घर से कौन निकालेगा?

उसी के श्राप का फल है, वरना तीन में एक भी लड़का दे देते भगवान् तो क्या ये लड़कियाँ इतना चढ़ पातीं? वह अकेले में आँसू ढारती रही।

हिमानी-शिवानी आज काम पर नहीं गईं। हिमानी ने जल्दी से कुछ नाश्ता बनाया, आकाश और सारिका दवाई खाते हैं, ब्लडप्रेशर की, वह तो एकदम शांत थी। तैयार हुई जैसे-तैसे, क्या कोई शादी में जाना है, जो तैयार होकर जाए, खुदा ना खाश्ता यदि आ ही गई तो इस छोटे से घर में कहाँ रहेगी? पता नहीं, कौन-कौन सी बीमारी हो गई होगी, कहीं खाँसी हुई तो पूरा घर थूक-थूककर भर देगी। कैसे बोलेगी उससे इतने दिनों बाद, ऑटो में बैठी वह सोच रही थी।

राजेंद्र नगर पंद्रह कि.मी. दूर है शिवाजी नगर से। जब वे डॉ. बलदेव के शानदार भवन के सामने पहुँचे तो देखा कि एक युवक एक वृद्धा को साथ लिए धीरे-धीरे टहल रहा है लान में।

दरवाजे पर ऑटो से इन लोगों को उतरता देख वह गेट के पास आ गया था। सब एक-दूसरे का मुँह ताक रहे थे कि वृद्धा बोल पड़ी—आकाश मेरा बेटा! उसने आगे बढ़कर आकाश को गले लगा लिया। उसकी ऊँचाई बहुत कम हो गई थी, कमर झुक गई थी, चेहरे पर झुर्रियों का साम्राज्य था, सिर के बाल बगुले के पंख जैसे हो रहे थे। आकाश की कमर से लिपटी वह रोने लगी थी, जार-जार।

"मेरी तकदीर ही खोटी है बेटा, तुझे रोज-रोज देख भी नहीं सकती, कितने दिनों बाद आया है इस बार। भूल ही गया था मुझे," अन्य लोगों की उपस्थिति की बात वह भूल गई थी, ऐसा लग रहा था।

"आइए न आप लोग अंदर!" युवक ने उन्हे अंदर बुलाया।

तीनों युवतियाँ एक साथ वृद्धा से लिपट गईं।

"दादी, दादी हम आपकी पोतियाँ! आपको लेने आई हैं," हिमानी ने उसके झुर्रियों भरे माथे को चूमते हुए कहा।

"मेरी पोतियाँ, हे भगवान! कहीं मैं खुशी से मर न जाऊँ?" वृद्धा की स्थिति अजीब हो रही थी, एक बार हँसे, एक बार रोए।

सभी आकर लॉन में पड़ी कुरसियों पर बैठे, सारिका अब तक चुप थी। "दादी, हमें तो कल ही आप का पता चला है और आज लेने आ गईं, तैयार हो जाइए घर चलने के लिए।" हिमानी चंचल हो रही थी।

"अपनी माँ से पूछा बेटी?" वृद्धा ने धीमी आवाज में कहा।

"माँजी, मुझे माफ कर दीजिए, मैं अपनी गलती की सजा भुगत रही हूँ। शादी नहीं हो पा रही है इनकी। लोग पूछते हैं कि इनकी दादी कहाँ है? आप घर चलिए।" सारिका ने वृद्धा के पैर पकड़ लिये।

युवक ने उनके लिए जलपान का प्रबंध किया। आगे-पीछे की बातें होती रहीं।

"यह मेरा बेटा सोमू है, डॉ. सोमनाथ, बहुत बड़ा डॉक्टर है, अपने पापा से भी बड़ा! जब मैं इस घर में आई, यह एक वर्ष का था, इनके माँ-पिताजी डॉक्टर हैं, उन्हें रात हो या दिन, जब मरीज आए, अस्पताल जाना पड़ता था। डॉ. साहब ने इसे पालने के लिए मुझे अपने घर में शरण दे दी, उन दोनों को मेरे हाथ का भोजन बेहद पसंद है। यह तो आज भी मेरे बिना नहीं रह पाता, देखो घर के सब लोग गरमी की छुट्टी मनाने शिमला गए हैं और यह घर पर ही रुका है। ड्यूटी भी देख रहा है और मुझे भी।" वृद्धा अब सँभल चुकी थी। डॉ. सोमनाथ चुपचाप सुन रहा था।

"माँजी, अब हमें इनकी नौकरी की आवश्यकता नहीं है। आपकी उम्र हो गई है अब घर चलिए।" सारिका ने अधिकारपूर्वक कहा।

"आंटीजी जरा सोच-समझकर बात कीजिए! ये मेरी दादी हैं, नौकरानी नहीं। ये कहीं नहीं जाएँगी, आप लोग इज्जत के साथ वापस चले जाएँ।" डॉ. की आवाज तल्ख हो उठी।

"दादी, हमारी शादी नहीं हो रही है आपके बिना, क्या हम पूरी जिंदगी

कुँआरी रहें, हमारी क्या गलती है, फिर मम्मी भी तो आप से माफी माँग रही है न··· ?" हिमानी उनसे फिर लिपट गई।

"आकाश बेटा! तू मुझे लेने आएगा, मैं इसी दिन के इंतजार में जी रही थी, तुझे किसी भी रूप में मेरी आवश्यकता अनुभव हुई, यही मेरे लिए बहुत है। मेरी प्यारी बहू मुझे बुलाने आई, जीवन का अर्थ पूर्ण हो गया मेरे।" उनका कंठ अवरुद्ध हो गया था, आँखों से अश्रु धार बह रही थी।

"दादी! सोचना भी मत जाने के बारे में, यदि गई तो मैं समझूँगा कि तुम्हें मुझसे प्यार नहीं, मेरी सेवा से तुम संतुष्ट नहीं।"

"तुमने सोच कैसे लिया कि मैं उस घर में वापस जाऊँगी, जहाँ से मुझे दुश्चरित्र ठहराकर निकाल दिया गया था। वह चिट्ठी तुम्हीं ने रखी थी न बहूरानी?"

मेरे बेटे की नजरों में मुझे गिराने के लिए, मेरा दुर्भाग्य! मेरे बेटे ने भी नहीं सोचा कि भरी जवानी में वैधव्य का अभिशाप ढोते इसकी माँ ने इसे किस दुःख से पाला? अधेड़ उम्र में···वह प्रेम की पींगे कैसे बढ़ा सकती थी?

"और किसी तरह इनके ऊपर कोई असर होता न देख मुझे वैसा करना पड़ा, मुझे माफ कर दीजिए माँजी।" सारिका अपराधी की तरह निगाहें झुकाए हुए थी।

"सुनो बहूरानी, तुम्हारे पाप की सजा अपनी पोतियों को नहीं दूँगी, इसलिए जब लड़केवाले आएँ, तब मुझे फोन कर देना, ड्राइवर छोड़ देगा मुझे। जरा भी पता नहीं चलेगा कि तुमने षड्यंत्र करके अपनी सास को घर से निकाल दिया है, परंतु एक वादा करो बच्चियो!"

"क्या दादी माँ " तीनों एक साथ बोलीं।

"तुम तीनों ससुराल जाकर अपनी माँ का आचरण न दोहराओगी।"

□

तुम मुझ में रहते हो

कल से लगातार थोड़ी-थोड़ी देर में मोबाइल की घंटी बज रही है। पूजा घंटी बजते ही छटपटा उठती है, आँखों में नमी तैर आती है और वह फोन काट देती है। मुँह में ओढ़नी भरकर रोती है। क्या बात है? कुछ समझ में नहीं आता। कई बार तो उसने स्वयं मोबाइल उठाकर दिया बात करने के लिए, उसने लेकर परे रख दिया, फिर वाइब्रेशन मोड में रख दिया, उसका···हिलकना···देखकर कलेजा दहल रहा है। कल से ही क्या हो गया, इस हँसती-खेलती लड़की को? पहले तो कभी उदास होना ही नहीं। हर डाँट पर हँस देना, छिपाकर आँसू पोंछ लेना उसकी आदत है। अभी देख रही है, कुछ दिनों से लड़की खोई-खोई रहती है। खाने-पीने में ध्यान नहीं देती, जिस काम में हाथ लगाया, उसे चुपचाप करती जाती है। फोन ज्यादा आने लगे हैं। सहेली के घर ज्यादा जाने लगी है, अरे! अरे! हाँ कोई है तरंग नाम की धनाढ्य परिवार की बेटी, कॉलेज में पढ़ती है, पूजा के साथ। जब देखो, तब बुलाती रहती है।

''आओ, एक साथ मिलकर परीक्षा की तैयारी करते हैं।" फिर तो जैसे बिजली लग जाती है उसके हाथों में, फटाफट झाड़ू-बुहारू करके भोजन बनाकर, चाची से इजाजत ले लेती है। ''घर के बगलवाले होटल में पार्टी चल रही है, कुछ घंटे पढ़कर आ जाती हूँ।'' कल्याणी तो बस कल्याणी है। सारा कुछ हुआ मिल रहा है, कॉलेज में प्रोफेसर है। थकी-हारी आई, बस थोड़ा आराम चाहिए होता है उसे भी। विश्वास है उसे अपनी पूजा पर, फिर

वह जानती ही है, पढ़ाई दो जन में ज्यादा अच्छी होती है, बहुत जरूरी होने पर ही रोकती है पूजा को। यह लड़की पूरे परिवार की धुरी है, सुबह से ही सब की चाय, नाश्ता, टिफिन का इंतजाम, उसकी दवाई, कल्याणी की उस दिन पहनने की साड़ी का पूरा सेट जमा कर रखती, इन सब कामों में कई बार वह जैसे-तैसे कपड़ों में कॉलेज जाती। लोगों की नजर तो उसकी मुसकान से ही बँधकर रह जाती होगी। ज्यादा सहेलियाँ भी नहीं हैं, यही है, जो तरंग कहलाती है, जिसने न जाने क्या पाया पूजा में, एकदम गुड़ चींटा हो गई है।

उसने तो बरसों पहले अपनी जबान सी ली थी। ऐसी ही तो थी हू-ब-हू दुबली-पतली-सी। "लड़की, तू दाँत बंद करेगी या मैं दाँत तोड़ दूँ तेरे?" खीझकर माँ कहती और बदले में खिलखिलाकर वह बाहर भाग जाती। लगता, जैसे पंख उड़ने को बेताब हैं। उड़े और गगन के तारों को छू कर आ जाए, उड़े और सुंदर-सुंदर फूलों को चूमकर वापस आ जाए, फिर उड़े और उदास लोगों को गुदगुदाकर भाग आए। बहुत सारे लतीफे थे उसके स्मृति कोष में। फिर एक दिन कुछ ऐसा हुआ कि दिमाग में धूल भरी आँधी चली, उस झंझावात में कोई फूला-फला कामना तरु, धराशायी हो गया, हँसी उसके नीचे दबकर दम तोड़ गई। अब मरी हँसी तो जिंदा हो नहीं सकती, न पानी बरसा, न बादल छँटे, धुंध अब भी छाई रहती है। उलझन में फँसाए, अपने साथ कभी दूर अतीत में ले जाती है, तो कभी वर्तमान से मुँह छिपाकर घूँघट डाल लेती है।

"तेरे मस्त मस्त दो नैन, मेरे दिल का ले गए चैन, मेरे दिल का ले गए चैन।" पूजा के मोबाइल की रिंग टोन है यह। कल्याणी के आने का समय था न, इसलिए मोबाइल ठीक करके रख दिया था उसने।

वह फिर से रोनेवाली है, ऐसा लगा। "ले! ले!...उसने अपनी बड़ी-बड़ी भाव विहीन आँखें फैलाकर अपनी घनेरी पलकें झपकाईं और पूजा के कान से मोबाइल लगा दिया, "हैलो! हैलो पूजा!"

"हाँ बोलो!"

"पूजा, मुझसे क्या गलती हुई? कुछ तो बताओ! मैं मर रहा हूँ तुम्हें देखने के लिए।" वह सुन रही थी उस ओर की आवाज।

"मैंने तुमसे कभी ऐसा कुछ नहीं कहा, जानते हो मेरे घर की परिस्थितियाँ? जिसने मुझे मान-सम्मान दिया, पाला-पोसा, मैं उन्हें निराश नहीं कर सकती।" वह सिसक रही थी।

"चाहे मैं कुछ भी क्यों न कर लूँ! मुझे पता नहीं था पूजा कि तुम मुझसे प्यार नहीं करती वरना कभी ऐसे सपने न देखता, मेरी जिदंगी में तुम्हारे सिवा कुछ भी नहीं है, न आगे, न पीछे। यदि तुम आज शाम सात बजे सोहनी-महिवाल पार्क में नहीं मिली तो समझो मेरा मरा मुँह देखोगी।'' उधर से फोन काट दिया गया।

वह फोन हाथ में लिये रो रही थी।

"और तू, यदि ऐसी न होती तो मैं इतनी मजबूर न होती, किसी का इतना एहसान न होता इस जिंदगी पर, जिसे चुकाए बिना मैं मौत को भी गले नहीं लगा सकती। तू ऐसी है, छोटा भाई नासमझ है, आठ-नौ साल का प्यारा सा बच्चा, पापा इतने सीधे-साधे कि बस कुछ कहा नहीं जाता। जिस औरत के चेहरे पर उन्होंने कभी मुसकान नहीं देखी, उसके साथ जीवन गुजार रहे हैं चौबीस वर्ष से। वह तो चाची जब अकेली हो गई थी, चाचा की अचानक मृत्यु से, तब दोनों परिवारों ने एक-दूसरे को बिना किसी लिखित अनुबंध के स्वीकार कर लिया था। इस तरह पल रहे हैं हम लोग।"

नैना माँजना-धोना, घर की साधारण साफ-सफाई में पहले भी मदद करती थी, पूजा जैसे-जैसे बड़ी होती गई, कल्याणी घर की जिम्मेदारियों से मुक्त होती गई।

वह न रहे तो क्या चाची घर-बाहर करती हुई सँभाल लेगी उसके माँ बाप और भाई को, क्यों और कितने दिन सँभालेगी भाई? जब वही उनके मान-सम्मान को धूल में मिला देगी। अभी तो एक-एक पैसा जोड़ रही हैं, कहती हैं मेरी पूजा ने बड़े दु:ख उठाए हैं मायके में, इसकी ससुराल अच्छी ढूँढूँगी।

उस तपस्विनी को क्या वह खून के आँसू रुलाएगी?

"मैं नहीं आऊँगी, नहीं आऊँगी, कभी नहीं आऊँगी।" वह तकिये पर सिर पटक-पटक कर रो रही थी।

वह आम की फाँकों जैसी आँखें फाड़े देख रही थी सकपकाई हुई। दिमाग में छाए धूल भरे बादल कुछ घने और आर्द्र हो गए, "क्या, क्या, क्यों? उसने पूजा का कंधा धीरे से पकड़ लिया।

उसने अपने आँसू पोंछे।

"कुछ नहीं, कुछ नहीं।" वह सामान्य होने की कोशिश करने लगी।

वह अपनी पतली-पतली गोरी-गोरी अंगुलियों से उसके आँसू पोंछने लगी।

"रहने दे! मुझे कुछ नहीं हुआ और जो हुआ, सब तेरी वजह से हुआ। जब तू ऐसी थी, तब बच्चे पैदा क्यों किए?" उसने चिढ़कर अश्लील प्रश्न किया, वह जानती थी उसे सुख-दुःख उस तरह नहीं व्यापता, जिस तरह अन्य लोगों को।

"जाएगी? जा! मैं रहती हूँ घर में।" नैना ने आज बड़ी समझदारी की बात की थी।

"नहीं जाना मुझे कहीं।" वह चीख पड़ी। मैं अपने परिवार से प्रेम करती हूँ। वह सोच रही थी, उसके सिवा उसके आस-पास कोई नहीं है। नैना की भला क्या गिनती थी उसकी नजर में।

धूल के बादल और घने हुए, बेचैनी सी लगने लगी, किसी प्रश्न का उत्तर देना तो आवश्यक नहीं था उसके लिए, आज क्या, कभी भी। हाँ, आज का प्रश्न उसकी बेटी की ओर से था।

पता नहीं, कहाँ से ठंडी-ठंडी हवा चलने लगी, मनो-मस्तिष्क में धूल के बादल उड़ने लगे। कुछ उजाला सा होने लगा।

गोरे रंग की एक चंचल-सी लड़की, पीठ पर बालो की दो चोटियाँ, दोनों हाथों में दबी सीने से लगी कॉपी-पुस्तकें, पलकें झुकी रहतीं रास्ते

भर। कॉलेज के रास्ते की ओर घूमनेवाले लड़के हार गए थे इस लड़की से। देखती ही नहीं किसी की ओर तो क्या दिखाया जाए। सहेलियों के साथ खिल-खिल, बाकी समय मुँह बंद। बी.ए. फाइनल की परीक्षा के फार्म भरे जा रहे थे, क्लर्क की टेबल के चारों ओर लड़कियों की भीड़ जमा थी। उसके दाएँ कंधे से सटी खड़ी रही थी वह। बहुत देर बाद उसने ध्यान से देखा था उसे, कनपटियों को छूती भौंहों को ऊपर उठाकर उसने सारे कागजात आगे सरका दिए थे। सबकुछ ओके था, फॉर्म जमा हो गया था। वर्ष भर में ढेरों मौके आए पास आने के। वह गज भर की चौड़ी छातीवाला, सुहानी नाक और साँवले रंग का छह फुटा जवान था, क्लीन शेव्ड चेहरे पर हमेशा गंभीरता ओढ़े रहता, लड़कियों के कॉलेज में ही···ही···ही···हा-हा ···हा कैसे चलता? झुकी निगाहों से देखा करता उसे, कहीं हलचल मचने लगी थी उसके दिल में। समझ न पाई कि पहलू में अनजानी जलन क्यों हो रही है? बहुत कुछ इसी की तरह। हँसना कम हो गया था, काम-काज में मन नहीं लगता, पढ़ाई पूरी हुई, मार्कशीट बाँट रहा था जय। बहुत देर से खड़ी थी वह। सभी लड़कियाँ चली गईं, शाम का धुँधलका उतरने लगा कॉलेज के प्रांगण में।

"मैं कल ले लूँ क्या सर?" उसने ऊबकर पूछा था।

"अरे नहीं! यह लीजिए आपकी मार्कशीट, बी.ए. प्रथम श्रेणी में लाने के लिए बधाई नैना, मेरी ओर से तुच्छ भेट!" उसने जल्दी से अपनी जेब से एक खिला हुआ लाल गुलाब निकालकर मार्कशीट के साथ ही उसे दे दिया।

"थैंक्यू सर! उसकी निगाहें झुकी हुई थीं।

"मैं तुम्हें बहुत पसंद करता हूँ नैना!" उसने उसे एक बार नजर भर के देखा, फिर निगाहें झुका लीं। उसके होंठों की थरथराहट महसूस की थी नैना ने।

शादी पक्की हो गई थी उसकी, जय हर बार अपनी यादें ताजी करने आ जाता, केटरिंगवालों का मुखिया जय, फोटोग्राफर जय, बरात की गवानी में सबसे आगे जय, फोटो खींचते समय कहा था एक बार "मेरी जिदंगी की अंतिम

खुशी है नैना तुम्हारी शादी, मैं तुम्हारे बिना जी नहीं सकूँगा, यदि मुझे जिंदा देखना चाहती हो तो चलो मेरे साथ, मैं तुम्हें अपनी जान से ज्यादा चाहता हूँ।"

"देखिए यह सब आपको शोभा नहीं देता। मैं बड़े परिवार की लड़की हूँ, मेरा कोई भी गलत कदम मेरे पीछे के दर्जनों लोगों का जीवन चौपट कर देगा। मुझे क्षमा कीजिए, यदि आप खुश न रहेंगे तो मैं भी अपनी जिंदगी की खुशियों का स्वागत कैसे कर सकूँगी?" उसने पूरी तरह संयम रखा हुआ था।

फूलों से सजी कार पर वह बैठी थी, उसने घूँघट की ओट से किसी की तलाश की थी, नीम के तने का सहारा लिये वह कार की ओर ही देख रहा था।

पूरे मन से उसने शादी को स्वीकारा था, किंतु दिल के अधिकांश हिस्से में अँधेरा छाया था।

जब चार दिन बाद पग फेरे के लिए मायके गई, तब समाचार मिला—उसी के कॉलेज में पढ़नेवाली छोटी बहन से। "दीदी! दीदी! वो जो सर थे न, जय सर।"

"हाँ-हाँ! क्या हुआ उन्हें? उसका दिल धड़क उठा था।

"तेरी शादी के दूसरे दिन उन्होंने फाँसी लगा ली थी, कहते हैं किसी से चक्कर था? धता बताकर वह किसी दूसरी ओर चली गई थी।"

जैसे कोई भारी चीज सिर पर गिर पड़ी हो। धूल भरा बवंडर हलचल मचाने लगा, तभी से उसके दिमाग में। आँखों का सूनापन, लगता है, जैसे कोई भाव ही नहीं है जीवन में। धुँध और घनी हुई, फिर कुछ पिघलने लगा, आँखों से बहने लगा, गले से सिसकियाँ फूट पड़ीं।

"तू मत रो? जाकर मिल ले! मैं सँभाल लूँगी आगे।" उसने पूजा को अंक में भर लिया। संभवत: यह पहला आलिंगन था, जिसमें ममत्व की उष्मा थी।···

"ऐं···माँ रो रही है, अरे माँ रो रही है, कोई देखो! माँ रो रही है।" पूजा के आँसू मुसकरा पड़े।

"तू जा न, मैं हूँ न।" नैना ने फिर कहा, "कहाँ माँ?"

"वहीं जहाँ, वह बुला रहा है। सचमुच उसने कुछ कर लिया तो?"

"कौन माँ?"

"वही, जिसका फोन सुनकर कई घंटे से रो रही है।" उसकी आवाज जैसे गहरे कुएँ से आ रही थी।

"मुझे उस पागल की बात की कोई परवाह नहीं, आज तो मैं खुशी से खुद पागल हो जाऊँगी, ऐसा लग रहा है। इतने दिनों बाद मेरी माँ की आँखों में आँसू आए हैं। पत्थर की मूरत जी उठी है, हनुमान को प्रसाद चढ़ाऊँगी। आज तो जमीन पर लोटते हुए मंदिर तक जाऊँगी।" वह नैना को बेतहाशा चूम रही थी।

"तू जाती क्यों नहीं, कहीं देर हो गई तो?"

"माँ मैं सिर्फ-और-सिर्फ अपने पापा-मम्मी, भाई और चाची से प्यार करती हूँ, उनके मान-सम्मान को ठेस पहुँचाने के लिए मैंने जन्म नहीं लिया। बाकी किसी के कुछ भी कहने से मुझे क्या लेना-देना।" वह अपने स्वर की उदासी छिपाने का भरपूर प्रयास कर रही थी।

"यदि ऐसा है तो उसकी बातें सुनकर इतना रो क्यों रही थी? मेरी कसम खाकर बोल!"

"क्योकि मैं उससे भी··· ?"

पूजा की नजरें जमीन देखने लगीं।

डोरबेल बजी थी उसी समय, कल्याणी आ गई थी कॉलेज से।

"चाची! चाची! माँ अपने आप अच्छी हो गई, अच्छी बातें कर रही है।" वह कल्याणी से लिपट गई थी।

"कल्याणी, कल्याणी! तुमने इस बच्ची को माँ बनकर पाला है, इसे इसकी खुशी से मिला दो, एक और नैना के जन्म को रोक लो कल्याणी।" नैना उसके पैरों से लिपटी, आँसू भरी निगाहों से उसे देखती पूजा की खुशियों की भीख माँग रही थी।

"अरे बाबा! इतने सारे आश्चर्य! मुझे कुछ समझने दोगी तुम दोनों, क्या चमत्कार हो गया घर में? दोनों रो रही हैं, न जाने क्यों?" कल्याणी ने अपनी कनपटियाँ अपने दोनों हाथों से दबा लीं।

"चाची यह लो पानी, बैठो पहले यहाँ?"

पूजा ने ठंडे पानी का गिलास कल्याणी के हाथ में दिया और पकड़कर सोफे पर बैठा दिया।

"बताओ अब!"

"चाची, अचानक माँ रोने लगी, फिर मुझे गले लगाकर बोली, कल्याणी से तेरे लिए प्रार्थना करूँगी। एकदम समझदारी की बातें चाची!" पूजा की आवाज आवेश में तेज हो रही थी।

"आइए डॉक्टर मनोज! मेरी बधाई स्वीकार कीजिए। कल्याणी ने आवाज देकर जिस युवक को बुलाया, उसे देखते ही पूजा की हड्डियों में ठंडी सिहरन दौड़ गई।

"अरे बाप रे! यहाँ कैसे आ गया यह?"

"सुनो, यदि कुछ भी ऊट-पटांग कहा न, तो तुमसे पहले मैं छत से नीचे कूद जाऊँगी। मैं नहीं जानती चाची इसे। इसकी बातों का विश्वास न करना।" पूजा ने अपने स्वर में सच्चाई भरने का प्रयास किया, किंतु सफल नहीं हो सकी।

"पूजा! मैं तुम्हारी माँ का डॉक्टर हूँ, इन्हें देखकर तुम मुझे माफ कर दोगी ऐसी उम्मीद है मुझे। एक हू-ब-हू परिस्थिति निर्मित करने के लिए मैंने तुम्हारा इस्तेमाल किया।" डॉ. मनोज हाथ जोड़कर खड़े थे।

"तो क्या सारा कुछ नाटक था? आप को तो एक्टर होना चाहिए डॉक्टर!" पूजा के चेहरे पर हवाइयाँ उड़ने लगीं।

"मैंने पहली बार बिना दवा के एक मरीज को ठीक किया है, पूजा तुम्हारा सहयोग याद रखूँगा।"

"डॉक्टर साहब, मेरी बेटी के दिल से खिलवाड़ करके आपने अच्छा

नहीं किया।" नैना के चेहरे से बेटी का गम झलक रहा था।

कल्याणी अंदर से एक लिफाफा ले आई, "डॉक्टर साहब आप की फीस।" उसने लिफाफा डॉक्टर के हाथ में थमा दिया।

"डॉक्टर साहब हम आपके सदा ऋणी रहेंगे, आप ने मेरे घर की खुशियाँ वापस लौटाई हैं।" वह विनम्रता से हाथ जोड़े खड़ी थी।

"जाओ पूजा! डॉक्टर साहब को दरवाजे तक छोड़ आओ।" कल्याणी ने जान-बूझकर पूजा को भेजा।

"सर! आप कहते हैं इस केस में मेरा सहयोग महत्त्वपूर्ण है, किंतु पूरी फीस लेकर चलते बन रहे हैं, क्या यह उचित है?" पूजा ने बंकिम मुसकान चेहरे पर लाकर कहा।

"तो क्या चाहिए तुम्हें, बोलो?"

"एक वादा!"

"कैसा वादा?"

"आप अपनी शादी में मुझे अवश्य बुलाएँगे, मैं आपकी दुलहन को अपने हाथों से सजाकर आपके कमरे में भेजना चाहती हूँ।" उसके स्वर में संसार भर की पीड़ा रची-बसी थी।

□

आएँगे फिर लौटकर

जीवन में पहली बार होली पर वे दोनों बच्चों से दूर थे। जब तक नौकरी में रहे या तो गाँव चले जाते या गाँववाले उनके पास आ जाते। अम्मा-बाबूजी की हार्दिक इच्छा रहती थी कि होली अपने गाँव में ही मनाई जाए। जयंत ने उनकी इच्छा का हमेशा आदर किया। वह तो जब बच्चे बड़े हो गए और अम्मा-बाबूजी भी परलोकवासी हो गए, तब सबका गाँव में इकट्ठा होना कम हो गया। अपने बच्चों में किसी की परीक्षा तो किसी का इंटरव्यू पड़ गया। कभी अपनी ही हिम्मत न पड़े खाली पड़े घर में जाकर त्योहार की पूरी व्यवस्था करने की। ननदों का स्थान बहू-बेटी न ले सकीं, बहू मायके जाना पसंद करती और बेटी अपनी ससुराल, शादी के बाद वर्षों वे दोनों ही केंद्र में रहते थे। सारा परिवार उनके चारों ओर चक्कर लगाता रहता था। बाद में वे किनारे हटते गए, केंद्र में मधु और मुक्ता आ गए, उनकी पसंद का खाना बनने लगा, उनकी पसंद से मेहमान आने-जाने लगे और आज तो केंद्र भी वे ही हैं और परिधि भी।

कल रात जयंत को अचानक ऐसी खाँसी शुरू हुई कि चैन लेना नामुमकिन हो गया। खाँसते-खाँसते परेशान हो रहे हैं, पूरी रात वह कभी पानी गरम करके लाती, कभी पीठ सहलाती, कभी दौड़कर खेत देख आती। बाउंड्री नहीं बन पाई है अभी तक। लोगों के पशु छुट्टा चरते हैं, अपनी फसल बचाने के लिए रखवाली ही एक मात्र चारा है। वैसे लकड़ी के बड़े-बड़े बिजूके बनवाए हैं। उन्हें जगह-जगह खड़ा कर दिया है। वे आदमी के कपड़े पहने हाँडी के ऊपर मुरेठा बाँधे हाथ में डंडा थामे आदमी का भ्रम पैदा करते हैं। कुछ पशु मनुष्य की होशियारी समझ जाते हैं और अवसर पाकर सारी फसल चौपट! खाना भर

ही नहीं है, रौंदकर पूरा सर्वनाश कर देते हैं। पता नहीं, किस तरफ से नील गायों का झुंड आता है। पलक झपकते ही पूरा खेत खाली कर जाता है। उन्हीं के डर से तो आज दो महीने से वह लाठी लेकर खेत में पड़ी पुरानी कार में ही आराम करती है। ठीक से नींद भी नहीं आती। हर आधे घंटे में उठती है, टॉर्च जलाकर दूर-दूर का जायजा लेती है। जहाँ कोई काली छाया हिलती-डुलती सी लगती है, वह 'हो रे!' की तेज आवाज के साथ लाठी लेकर बिना ऊपर-नीचे देखे, उस दिशा में दौड़ पड़ती है। दिन में जयंत देखते रहते हैं, किंतु रात भर जागना उनके बूते का नहीं था। फिर उसके रहते वे क्यों तकलीफ उठाएँगे, सेवा करना तो पत्नी का कर्तव्य है न! अब तो रात की ठंड भी कम हुई है, पूस माघ की हाड़ जमा देनेवाली ठंड में दमे के मरीज कितने दिन डटे रह सकते थे? दिन में देख लेते हैं, यही बहुत है। घर की साफ-सफाई, भोजन-पानी, गाय का दाना-चारा सबकुछ तो उसी के माथे है।

कल रात होली जली थी, उसने बस्ती के आस-पास के खाली स्थानों में आग की बड़ी-बड़ी लपटों के साथ मनुष्यों की हर्ष-ध्वनि सुनी, नगाड़ों की थाप के साथ होली गीतों की मद्धिम स्वर-लहरी सुनते हुए गेहूँ के खेतों के ऊपर से हवा के साथ-साथ बादलों के रथ पर सवार चाँद चहल-कदमी कर रहा था। पूर्णिमा की चाँदनी हरे-भरे पेड़ों की फुनगी पर चढ़ी नीचे झाँक रही थी। उसे बड़ा अच्छा लगा था सारा वातावरण। उस तरफ, जहाँ उसके खेत की सीमा महावीर के खेत को छूती है, पलाश के कई बड़े-बड़े पेड़ हैं, इस समय तो पत्रहीन टेसू के फूल शाखों पर केसरिया चादर ओढ़े इठला रहे हैं। खेत से लगा हुआ आम का एक बाग है, वहाँ बड़े सबेरे से कोयल कूकने लगती है। ठंड कम होने से थोड़ी राहत महसूस हुई थी कि देश के उत्तरी इलाके में बर्फ गिरने के कारण यहाँ भी बादल छा गए। एक झोंका पानी भी बरस गया। ठंड वापस आ गई। जयंत चले गए थे, होलिका दहन स्थल की ओर। सारी उम्र तो नौकरी के कारण कभी शामिल नहीं हो पाए। खदान की कालिमा में सिर पर बत्ती बाँधे अपने परिवार के लिए उजाले का एक टुकड़ा ढूँढ़ते रहे। एस.ई.सी. एल. में छुट्टी के दिन काम करने पर तीन गुना वेतन मिलता है, जो ही चार

पैसे बने, क्या रखा है त्योहार में? दोनों बच्चों की पढ़ाई-लिखाई, पिताजी की हमेशा की बीमारी, ऊपर से रईसोंवाले शौक! तीज-त्योहार पर बहनें आस लिये आ जाती थीं, न्योता-हँकारी, कुछ-कुछ बढ़ती महँगाई। इसी प्रकार कौड़ी में कसीदा काढ़ते कैसे पैंतीस वर्ष गुजर गए, पता ही न चला। अब जब सेवानिवृत्त हुए हैं तो सबकुछ याद कर रहे हैं। बच्चों के बिना कुछ बनाने का मन नहीं था उसका, किंतु इनका खयाल करके थोड़ा-थोड़ा सबकुछ बनाया, थोड़े गुझिए, थोड़ी मठरी, थोड़ी पपड़ी, पसंद तो सब है, परंतु शुगर खाने दे तब तो! लाख सावधानियों के बाद भी दमा उभर ही आया, खदान के घूल, धुएँवाले वातावरण का उपहार है यह बीमारी। अधिकतर क्या 99 प्रतिशत कर्मचारी इस बीमारी से ग्रस्त हो जाते हैं। अभी-अभी जरा सी आँख लगी है। उसने तीन-चार तकिए लगाकर उन्हें अधलेटा सुला दिया था। खाँसी कम हुई तो वह धीरे से दरवाजा उढ़काकर बाहर आ गई। दबे पाँव झाड़ू-बुहारू, दाना-चारा, बरतन-भाँडा आदि करने लगी। अभी वह गाय का दूध निकालकर फारिग हुई थी कि दरवाजे पर आवाज हुई, उसने दरवाजा खोलकर देखा, तो मोती खड़ी थी, सिर से पाँव तक गुलाल में रँगी।

"मोंही पोदीना देई देव अम्मा! तुम्हार बेटवा परे हें उल्टी-टट्टी होय लागि ही"—उसके बिना पूछे उसने अपना मकसद बता दिया। इसका पति छेदी खेती का काम देखता है। न जाने क्या खाया-पिया, तबीयत खराब कर ली। कहाँ मदद करता कुछ, तो लो और देखो, उसने मन ही मन कहा।

"लई लेव उठी हवय।" उसने हाथ के इशारे से नल के आस-पास फैले पोदीने की ओर संकेत किया।

तुम्हरे पापा भी तो परे हैं, रात से। मारे खाँसी के दम नहीं ले पा रहे हैं। उसने मोती को बता दिया। वैसे तो रात में पचीसों बार मधु को फोन लगाया, परंतु टावर न मिलने के कारण बात नहीं हो पाई, लड़का आए तो इलाज-पानी का इंतजाम हो। यहाँ तो दूर-दूर तक कोई कहने लायक आबादी नहीं है। बस, इक्का-दुक्का घास-फूसवाले झोंपड़े हैं। पचास कि.मी. आगे शहडोल और उतने ही पीछे अनूपपुर। ये शहर भी ऐसे नहीं हैं, जहाँ स्वास्थ्य-सुविधाएँ बेहतर

हों। अच्छा इतना ही है कि मेन रोड के पास ही यह फार्म हाउस है। अभी दो साल पहले तक तो यह भूखंड भी पूरा का पूरा बंजर पड़ा रहता था। बरसात में कुछ जंगली पौधे उग जाते थे, जो ठंड के प्रारंभ में ही सूखकर धरती की गोद में छिप जाते थे। जब पहले-पहले वह जयंत के साथ इसे देखने आई थी, पहली नजर में ही नापसंद कर दिया था। हारी-बीमारी में आदमी किसे पुकारे? वही भय आज सत्य साबित हुआ। न तो बेटी के पास फोन लग सका, न बेटे के पास। चिरमिरी में होते तो वह अकेली भी अस्पताल ले गई होती अब तक। यहाँ न गाड़ी, न घोड़ा, खाँसते-खाँसते कभी कुछ हो गया तो वह क्या मुँह दिखाएगी दुनिया को? जयंत ने जब इस खेत को खरीदने की ठानी, तब दोनों बच्चों ने विरोध किया। ''पापा अब तो आप लोगों को डॉक्टर के नजदीक रहना चाहिए। इससे अच्छा शहर में एक घर ले लीजिए, बड़े बच्चे पढ़ेंगे और आप लोगों की सेवा भी करेंगे।" ये बिदक गए थे। "अपना मत देखो न!···हमें खेत, खलिहान, जंगल पहाड़, पानी, गाय, बछड़ा चाहिए। हमें कुछ नहीं होगा। हमारे शास्त्रों के अनुसार भी अब हमारी वानप्रस्थ की उम्र है। हाँ, इतना कर सकते हैं कि तुमसे जितना हो सके, हमें सुविधा संपन्न बना दो।" जयंत ने दो टूक बात की थी।

बेटे-बेटी की पढ़ाई-लिखाई, शादी-ब्याह, अच्छे रोजगार का इंतजाम करने के बाद वे बची जिंदगी अपने हिसाब से जीना चाहते थे। वह तो फिर हर हाल में उनके साथ थी, तभी से, जब से फेरों का अर्थ जाने बिना उनके साथ सात फेरे लिये थे। उसने एक ही अर्थ समझा था, जैसे आज उनके पीछे-पीछे चल रही है, सबके सामने वैसे ही पूरी जिदंगी चलना है, बस उसका यही एक कर्तव्य है। तेरह साल की कच्ची उम्र थी उसकी। कक्षा सात में पढ़ रही थी। जयंत मैट्रिक करके निकले थे उसी वर्ष। दोनों के लिए विवाह एक उत्सव था, जिसमें घर-परिवार, हित मित्र, जात-परजात मिलकर एक लड़के से एक लड़की का जीवन सदा के लिए जोड़ देते हैं।

ससुराल आने के दूसरे ही दिन पारिवारिक रस्म के अनुसार वह सिर पर गोबर लेकर खेतों की ओर चली थी, जयंत कंधे पर कुदाल लिए उसके साथ-साथ चले थे। उनके साथ बाजे-गाजे के साथ घर-परिवार, टोले-मोहल्ले की

औरतें शगुन के गीत गाती चल रही थीं। उसने कामदार साड़ी पहन रखी थी, पतली कलाइयाँ, सुहाग की लाल चूड़ियों से भरी हुई थीं। पहली-पहली बार घूँघट डाला था, वह हवा के साथ उड़-उड़ जाता था, पाँव में पाजेब थी, चप्पल नई होने के कारण बार-बार लगता, वह अब गिरी, तब गिरी। बड़ी ननद सँभाल लेती थी अपनी गोद में। खेत में विधिवत् पूजा-अर्चना हुई, जयंत ने पाँच कुदाल मारकर प्रतीकात्मक खुदाई की और उसने गोबर फेंककर खेत को आवश्यक भोजन कराया। उसने घूँघट उठाकर देखा था, दूर-दूर तक फैले खेत, जिनमें जानवर चर रहे थे, एकदम उजाड़ पड़े हुए थे। गेहूँ की कटाई हो चुकी थी, उसकी एक फुट की खूटियाँ सिर ताने खड़ी थीं। उन्हें बचा-बचाकर चलना पड़ रहा था। वह भी गाँव की लड़की थी। खेतों तक दौड़ते हुए आना-जाना उसका प्रिय खेल था। बाबू के लिए लोटे में चाय लेकर जाती, जब वे खेतों में कुछ काम कर रहे होते, कटाई के समय मजदूरों को गुड़-पानी देने जाती। खलिहान की रखवाली में भी सहयोग करती, क्योंकि तब तक स्कूल की छुट्टी हो चुकी होती, उसकी तरफ के खेत सिंचित थे, दोनों फसलें होती थीं। अधिकांश खेतों में बोर खुदे हुए थे। यहाँ तो गोबर डालकर आने के बाद दुलहन के सिर पर पीतल का कलश रखे, यही टोली गाते-बजाते पुनः लगभग दो किलोमीटर तक पानी लाने गई थी, एक प्राकृतिक नाला था, वहीं का पानी आस-पास के गाँववाले बारह महीना पीते थे। दूल्हे ने कलश भरकर दुलहन के सिर पर चढ़ाया था, जिसे प्यास लगी थी, पानी पी रहे थे, जिनके हाथ में कोई बरतन था, उसमें राह के लिए भर लिया था पानी।

जब से शादी के कारण मेहमान आए थे, बैलगाड़ी में पानी के बड़े-बड़े बरतन रखकर ले जाते और भरकर ले आते थे, घर के मर्द लोग। साधारण दिन में यह औरतों का दायित्व था कि वे मुँह अँधेरे से आवश्यकता भर पानी ढोने लगें। उसने भी तो ढोया था कुछ वर्ष। वह तो बाबूजी की खदान में नौकरी थी, कहे-सुने, लाजे-लिहाजे उन्होंने दुआर पर कुआँ बनवा दिया, भले ही तीन सौ फुट नीचे पानी मिला, किंतु एकदम मीठा! इस एक ही पुण्य ने उनके सारे पाप धो दिए। अरे नहीं, यही क्यों, जब मेडिकल अनफिट हुए, तब नौकरी भी तो

मधु को दी, बाकी चाहे जैसे भी रहे हों। गाँव से निकलकर खदान में मजदूर बने थे, खदान के अंदर पीठ पर कोयला ढोने का काम मिला था उन्हें। ड्यूटी से लौटते हुए भठ्ठी से पीकर आते। गिरते-पड़ते, गाली-गलौज करते, बड़बड़ाते। मनहरण पांडेय, जिनके पुरखे गाँव भर के लोगों से पाँव पुजवाते थे, कथा-भागवत् में जाते थे, आज ऐसा दिन आया कि कोयला ढो रहे हैं। इसी कुंठा ने उन्हें आदतन शराबी बना दिया। शराब के साथ मांस भी तो चाहिए, कहते हैं दोनों भाई-भाई है। आस-पास के गाँवों की कई औरतों से उनकी यारी थी। वे छुट्टी के दिन घर आतीं। दिन-रात पत्नी की तरह घर-बार सँभालतीं और दूसरे दिन अपनी बिदा बिदागरी लेकर घर चली जातीं, ऐसे में कैसे बरक्कत होती घर में? सास घर-परिवार, खेत-खार सँभाले गाँव में रहती, उसने समझा था पति की कुंठा का रहस्य! जब कभी घर आते, कुएँ पर ले जाकर मलमल कर नहलाती-धुलाती। सारे कलुष-कल्मष धोकर वह अपने पति को निष्पाप कर देती, कभी किसी प्रकार की शिकवा-शिकायत या लड़ाई-झगड़ा करते किसी ने भी नहीं सुना था उन्हें। असिंचित क्षेत्र में खेती से क्या उपजता? साल भर उन्हीं में लगे रहो! खाद डालो, जोताई करो, बीज बोओ, पानी नहीं गिरा। सूख गया। ज्यादा गिर गया तो गल गया। दाने पड़ने के समय एक पानी के लिए मार खा गई फसल, हुई भी तो चार माह से ज्यादा नहीं चलती। ऐसे में नौकरी का ही तो सहारा था।

चारों ननदों की शादी के लिए खेत बेचने पड़े उन्हें, पढ़ाई बीच छोड़कर जयंत को भी काम में लगना पड़ा। जब सभी लोग चिरमिरी में रहने लगे, तब कुछ सँभलने लगी गृहस्थी। जयंत के मन में अपने खेतों की कसक चुपचाप जिंदा रह गई थी। मधु की पढ़ाई बड़े-बड़े शहरों में हुई थी। बेटी माया को डॉक्टर बनने का शौक था, सो उसे डॉक्टर बनाया, मधु खदान में ही लेबर ऑफिसर बन गया। बहू भी पढ़ी-लिखी और समझदार मिल गई। माया ने अपने लिए डॉक्टर पति पसंद किया। अब वे दिल्ली के एक बड़े अस्पताल में अपनी सेवाएँ दे रहे हैं। ओह! बेटी-दामाद डॉक्टर और बाप लग रहा है बिना डॉक्टर के··· !

अच्छा माया को फोन लगाती हूँ, शायद लग जाए। दूध की बाल्टी लिये वह तेज कदमों से कमरे की ओर बढ़ी, जयंत की खाँसी की आवाज सुनाई पड़ रही थी। उजाला हो चुका है, काम करनेवाले तो आज छुट्टी पर हैं, उन्हें बुलाया भी नहीं जा सकता, क्योंकि उनके होशोहवाश पर तो महुए की बेटी का राज होगा, किसी की आवाज उनके कानों में पड़ेगी ही नहीं। गाय को दाना दे ही दिया है उसने। बस अब चाहे जैसे हो, जयंत को अस्पताल ले जाना आवश्यक है। नहीं होगा तो किसी बस में बैठाकर शहडोल तक ले जाएगी, फिर वहाँ किसी अस्पताल में भरती कर देगी, यूँ तो नहीं देख सकती उन्हें। शायद अब मधु को फोन लग जाए, यहाँ टावर की समस्या तो रहती ही है।

"आख्! आख्!...वे सीना पकड़े छटपटा रहे थे। वह दौड़ी थी उनकी ओर।

"तुझे तो काम से फुरसत नहीं, मैं नहीं रहूँगा तब लिए रहना खेत-खार!" उन्होंने बड़ी मुश्किल से अटक-अटककर कहा।

उसने उनका सिर अपने सीने पर रख लिया और सीना सहलाने लगे।

"क्या करूँ भगवान्?" उसे बेचैनी ने घेर लिया।

"कुछ तो करना ही होगा।" उसने जैसे कुछ निश्चय किया। धीरे से जयंत का सिर तकिये के सहारे टिकाकर माया का नंबर मिलाने लगी, संयोग से फोन लग गया।

"हैलो।"

"हाँ, मम्मी प्रणाम, कैसे हैं आप लोग?" उधर से माया बोल रही थी।

"आशीर्वाद बेटा! इधर पापा को दमे क्रा दौरा पड़ गया है, मधु को फोन लग नहीं रहा है। कोई साधन नहीं मिल रहा है, कैसे अस्पताल ले जाऊँ?" उसकी आवाज भर्रा गई। अब तक थमी भावनाएँ बह चलीं?

"मम्मी, घबराओ नहीं, उन्हें किसी भी तरह लेकर शहडोल पहुँचो, सड़क पर लिफ्ट लेने की कोशिश करो! मैं अभी निकल रही हूँ वहाँ के लिए, मधु भइया से भी बात कर लेती हूँ।" माया ने फोन रख दिया।

वह चप्पल पहनकर सड़क की ओर चल पड़ी। जयंत को लगातार खाँसी आ रही थी।

"रुकिए! रुकिए!" यह तो निकल गई, जीप थी कोई परिवार जा रहा था कहीं।

वह आ रही है कार, वह सड़क के बीच खड़ी होकर रुकने का संकेत करने लगी, परंतु कार फुटपाथ पर उतरकर आगे बढ़ गई। गाड़ियों का आवागमन आज एकदम कम है। त्योहार के दिन भला कौन ड्यूटी पर जाएगा और कौन यात्रा करेगा ? उसे निराशा घेरती जा रही थी, उसे सड़क पर खड़े हुए लगभग आधे घंटे हो गए, कोई उसकी विपदा सुनने के लिए नहीं रुका।

एक भरा हुआ ट्रक आता देखकर वह हाथ फैलाकर खड़ी हो गई, गाड़ी रुक गई। खिड़की से एक दाढ़ीवाले ने झाँककर संकेत से गाड़ी रोकने का कारण पूछा, "भइया, मेरे पति बहुत बीमार हैं, उन्हें शहडोल तक ले चलो! मुँहमाँगा किराया देंगे।" वह हाथ जोड़कर गिड़गिड़ा रही थी।

"परंतु इस ट्रक में बीमार कैसे जा पाएगा, कोयले का ट्रक है, जा तो मैं शहडोल ही रहा हूँ, यदि आप को असुविधा न हो तो आ जाइए।" उसने गाड़ी सड़क के किनारे लगाई।

वह दौड़ी कमरे की ओर, मोबाइल, ए.टी.एम. और कुछ जो नगद था, बैग में डाला, जयंत को सँभालकर पलंग से उतारा और कमरे में ताला डालकर उन्हें सँभाले धीरे-धीरे सड़क की ओर बढ़ी।

ट्रक ड्राइवर गाड़ी से उतरकर उनके पास आ गया था, उसने जयंत को सँभाल लिया।

रिटायरमेंट के बाद मिली सारी पूँजी लगाकर यह खेत खरीदा था जयंत ने। बोर करवाया, दो कमरे बनवाए, दिन-रात मेहनत की दोनों ने, अपने सपनों का संसार बसाने के लिए। जहाँ दो साल पहले बंजर था, वहाँ आज गेहूँ की फसल लहलहा रही है। मजदूरों की यहाँ सहूलियत है। पिछड़ा इलाका होने के कारण रोजगार-धंधे बहुत कम हैं। आस-पास के गाँववाले उनके यहाँ से पीने का पानी ले जाते हैं, परे हारे गाय का दूध, रुपया-पैसा देने से कभी पीछे नहीं हटे जयंत, लेकिन आज जब उन्हें सहारे की जरूरत है, कोई दिखाई नहीं दे रहा है। बेटे की राय से नहीं चले, इसलिए शायद वह भी मन में खुन्नस रखता हो या फिर हो

सकता है, वह हमें फोन लगा रहा हो, जब टावर नहीं है तो वह भी क्या जाने।

"आप तो हमारे लिए भगवान् बन गए भैया!" वह कृतज्ञ स्वर में बोली थी, उसे लग रहा था जयंत की तबीयत अवश्य सुधर जाएगी।

"सबकुछ अल्लाताला की मर्जी से होता है बैनजी, आप लोगों के त्योहार के कारण कोई ड्राइवर नहीं आया, माल पहुँचाने की इमरजेंसी आ गई, तब मैंने सोचा, स्वयं ही चलना चाहिए।" वह सँभालकर जयंत को गाड़ी की तरफ ला रहा था।

"यहाँ हमारी मदद के लिए आप को भगवान् भेज रहे थे भइया।"

"हाँ! अब तो मुझे भी ऐसा ही लग रहा है।"

उसने गाड़ी से एक बड़ा सा पेंट का खाली डिब्बा निकाला और उसी पर पैर रख कर उन दोनों को सामने की सीट पर बैठा लिया

"आपको डर तो नहीं लगेगा मेरे साथ?'' हलके से मुसकराकर उसने पूछा।

"आपको देखकर डर दूर भाग गया।"

वह जयंत को पकड़कर बैठ गई। दरवाजा फटाक से बंद कर दिया, ट्रक मालिक ने।

"चलें!"

"हाँ!"

उसने गाड़ी स्टार्ट की।

"अरे-अरे रोको गाड़ी! अरे शीला! वह देख, हमारे खेत में नील गायों का झुंड घुस आया है!" अक्ख-अक्ख, जयंत खिड़की से बाहर देख रहे थे, उसने एक बार खिड़की से बाहर देखा, सचमुच बीस-पचीस नील गायें उसके खेत को चर रही थीं।

अब तक ट्रक में ब्रेक लग चुका था।

"चलिए भइया, जितना तेज चल सकते हैं!" उसने उधर से आँखें फेर ली थीं।

□

पग फेरा

ब्रह्म मुहूर्त के आगमन की सूचना में पक्षी आपस में चुहल करने लगे थे। शहनाई पर एक दर्दीली धुन बजाई जा रही थी।

"बाबुल की दुआएँ लेती जा, जा तुझको सुखी संसार मिले
मैके की कभी न याद आए, ससुराल में इतना प्यार मिले।

प्रभात भारती के आँसू अब तक सूखे नहीं थे।

"दहेज का सारा सामान इस गाड़ी में करीने से रखवाओ अशोक!" उसने टेंटवालों से बातचीत में उलझे बड़े लड़के को सचेत किया। फूलों से सजी मखमली स्टेज की परतें उधेड़कर नग्न प्लेटों को एक-दूसरे के ऊपर सजा दिया गया था। कालीन समेटे जा चुके थे। भोजन की ओर देखें तो सारी मेजें सफेद गंदे कपड़ों के कफन ओढ़े अपने उठाए जाने की प्रतीक्षा कर रही थीं। सारा सामान गाड़ियों में भरा जा रहा था। लग्नवाटिका प्रातः आठ बजे तक छोड़ देनी थी अनुबंध के अनुसार।

"अशोक के नीचेवाली टेबल, वहीं तो बैठी थी मीनू अपने पति नवल के साथ। वीडियो शूटिंगवालों ने वाटिका के एकांत कमरे में दोनों के ढेरों क्लोजअप लिये थे। वहीं से मीनू का हाथ पकड़े निकला था नवल। मुसकराती-शरमाती दुलहन को उसकी सहेलियों ने उत्साहित किया था। उधर दूल्हे के भाई और मित्र उसे हिम्मत दे रहे थे।

"अब बन्नी हमारी है।"

"अब बन्ना भी हमारा है।"

दोनों ने एक-दूसरे के मुँह में मिठाई डाली थी। कहीं कुछ दरका था उसके भीतर।

उसे दु:ख नहीं मानना चाहिए, यही तो वह चाहता था एक लंबे समय से कि उसकी मीनू को एक मजबूत सहारा मिल जाए। जन्म से लेकर आज तक हाशिये से बाहर आने की लगातार कोशिश करती रही वह, परंतु सफल न हो सकी थी। तीन बच्चे पहले ही थे उनके और की न आवश्यकता थी, न इच्छा। कहने को लड़की-लड़के दोनों ही थे उसके, जो गाँव में रहते थे। परिवार नाम के पाप का उससे मेल ही क्या? प्रारंभ से ही शहर में रहकर पढ़ा था। दयानंद भारती जब सड़क के किनारे बैठकर जूते सिलता था, तब से ही उसे मानता था।

हमारे पुरोहित का नाती है, वे तो हमारे हाथ का पानी तक नहीं पीते थे, हमारा भाग्योदय हो गया, जो यह लड़का हमारे घर खाने-पीने लगा।" वह कहा करता था। आरक्षित कोटे से उसके तीनों लड़के सरकारी मुलाजिम हो गए थे। परिवार में एकता थी। दयानंद भारती ने एक बड़ा सा बँगला खरीद लिया। उस समय बेटों ने बाप की सड़क के किनारेवाली दुकान बंद करवा दी। बनारस जैसे शहर में इतना बड़ा घर होना अपने आप में कुछ मायने रखता था।

दयाराम सुख की साँस लेते हुए कहता, "सब महात्मा गाँधी का प्रताप है, वरना हम कभी मणिकर्णिका घाट पर गंगा स्नान नहीं कर पाते, न उन्होंने देश की आजादी के लिए इतना संघर्ष किया होता और न ही हमारी दशा सुधरती। बस पूर्वजों की भाँति गाँव भर के मरे जानवर उठाते रहते। सारी चेतना ऊँची जातवालों से बचकर चलने में ही लगी रहती।" आज भी उनके सामने बराबरी पर बैठा नहीं जाता। आज भी प्रभात को पायलागी कहना नहीं भूलता वह, परंतु लड़के-बच्चे एक साथ खेलते-कूदते गाली-गलौज करते हैं, एक-दूसरे का जूठा खाते हैं, वह एक छोटी सी कोठरी किराए से लेकर रहता था, पढ़ने के लिए। गाँव में ढंग का स्कूल ही कहाँ था, जो पढ़ता। किसी तरह खिचड़ी पकाकर खा लेता था। ऐसे समय में दयानंद के परिवार

से मिला अपनापन उसे बहुत सहारा दे रहा था। मांस-मदिरा का शौक उसे तभी लग गया था, जब वह हाई स्कूल में था। बच्चे चिल्लाएँ, चाहे दुनिया, मुँह की लगी भला छूटती है? अब तो चौबीस घंटे बस उसी का सहारा रह गया है। ये क्या? शराब की बुराई किए जाते हैं! आखिर भगवान् ने कुछ सोच-समझकर ही तो दुनिया में शराब जैसी चीज बनाई होगी, अब बनी है तो पीने के लिए ही तो? मर जाएँगे साले बचा-बचाकर! क्या जाने कैसा अनुभव होता है, कितनी ताकत मिलती है शराब से? चाहे तो चूहा भी शेर को गालियाँ दे सकता है। जिनके आगे निगाहें नहीं उठतीं, पीने के बाद तो उनकी माँ-बहन सब अपनी खास रिश्तेदार हो जाती हैं। सरकार का भी पूरा राज दारू से ही तो चल रहा है। देवता भी कहाँ रहते हैं सोमरस के बिना? ये तो जिनकी तकदीर में पीना नहीं लिखा है, वे ही चिढ़कर इस दैवी उपहार की निंदा करते हैं।

"पापा! आप यहाँ खड़े किसका इंतजार कर रहे हैं? सारे रिश्तेदार चले जा रहे हैं मिल तो लीजिए जाकर, उधर गेट पर कुरसी लगाकर बैठ जाइए।"

अशोक अभी-अभी दहेज की गाड़ी रवाना करके आया था।

"अरे! मैं यहीं खड़ा मीनू की वापसी का इंतजार कर रहा हूँ बेटा!" सचमुच उसे उसकी वापसी की प्रतीक्षा थी। खर्च बचाने के लिए कहें या फिर नव-दंपती को एक-दूसरे के सान्निध्य में रहने का मौका देने के उद्देश्य से अब ब्याह में ही गवन की रस्म का प्रतीकात्मक निर्वहन कर दिया जाता है। दुलहन को लेकर गाड़ी कुछ दूर जाती है। फिर वापस आ जाती है। दुलहन गाड़ी से उतरकर कोहबर तक जाती है, पानी पिलाया जाता है उसे। वह फिर सबसे मिलती, पहले की तरह परिवार की पूर्व विवाहित लड़कियाँ पकड़कर उसे गाड़ी पर चढाती हैं। उसकी आँखों से बहते आँसुओं से लड़का जरा भी प्रभावित नहीं हुआ। चाहे खर्चे के लिए भले ही कुछ दे देता हो; उसके शौक से कभी प्रसन्न नहीं हुआ वह।

"अरे इतनी बड़ी जिंदगी जब काट दी, इसी के सहारे तो क्या अब छूटेगी

किसी के कहने-सुनने से, जाओ! राम का नाम लो! कल दिन भर अन्न नहीं खाया उसने, उपवास करके ही कन्यादान किया जाता है। ठीक है, अन्न नहीं खाया उसने, शरबत पिया, भले ही सड़े अंगूर का हो, था तो शरबत ही, यह तो मन मानने की बात है। नाम चाहे जितने रख लो। सब कहते हैं, पीने से आदमी अस्वस्थ हो जाता है, आओ! कर लो मिलान! अभी 17 ग्राम हिमोग्लोबिन है, माना कि शुगर-बी.पी. के कारण आँखें धोखा दे गईं हैं। लिवर भी खराब हो रहा है। एक मुट्ठी दवाइयाँ नाश्ते के पहले और बाद में लेनी पड़ती हैं, परंतु इससे क्या? आजकल तो जो नहीं पीते, वे इससे भी ज्यादा बीमार पड़ते हैं। आज जीता कौन है साठ से ज्यादा? वह तो पैंसठ का हुआ जा रहा है। दस लोगों में व्यक्तित्व का प्रभाव वैसा ही है, जैसा नौकरी के समय हुआ करता था। उसने सब का काम कर देने का वादा किया। बार-बार किया। मीठे स्वर, मधुर मुसकान और साथ ही जाम! बड़ा कहलाने के लिए आवश्यक ट्रिक था उसके पास। एक तो फर्राटेदार अंग्रेजी, मोहक व्यक्तित्व और दूसरे दोस्तों के साथ समय गुजारने की आदत। उसे सम्मान मिलता आया है, अपने आस-पास के लोगों से। ये तो लड़के हैं, जो धेले की इज्जत नहीं करते। न शराब से मतलब है, न समाज से। ये क्या कर पाएँगे? उसे तरस आता है उन पर। कमाने लगे हैं, उसका चलता तो गाँव के स्कूल में प्राइमरी पास कर कहीं इस खेत, कहीं उस बाड़ी, कभी शराब तो कभी जुए के अड्डे पर डोलते होते। वह तो पिताजी की बरजोरी कहो या इनकी तकदीर कि शहर में आकर रहने का मौका मिल गया, तब वह उत्तर प्रदेश हथकरघा उद्योग बनारस में क्लर्क था, उस समय दयाराम का बड़ा बेटा राधारमण वहाँ मैनेजर था। उसी की मेहरबानी और कूटनीति से वह मजदूर यूनियन का नेता बन गया। दोनों तरफ से खूब कमाई की थी उसने। उसी समय उसकी जिंदगी में आई थी नीरा, मलयानिल सी सुगंध बिखेरती। वह ऑफिस में झाड़ू-पोंछा करती थी। उसका साड़ी पहनने का अंदाज, बराबर प्लेट्स पर लगा पिन, हाथों में चार-चार चूड़ियाँ, माँग में छिपा रहनेवाला सिंदूर, वह दुबली-पतली गोरी-नारी स्त्री थी।

घनी बरौनियाँ झालर की तरह आँखों पर झुकी रहती थीं। चुपचाप काम करती बड़ी अच्छी लगी थी वह उसे।"

उसने अपनी ओर से पहल की थी।

"आप किस मजबूरी में यह सब करती हैं, आपके पति··· ?"

"उनका काम ठीक से नहीं चलता।" वह हाथ बाँधकर खड़ी थी।

"यह तो लंगूर के पहलू में हूर जैसी बात हो गई। उसके साथ भी तो ऐसा ही हुआ। इतना सुंदर, सुशिक्षित और कमाऊ वह और पल्ले बाँध दी गई एक एल.पी. लड़की (लिख लोढ़ा, पढ़ पथरा)। सुनने में आया है, उसके गाँव में स्कूल ही नहीं है।

वैसे प्राकृतिक सौंदर्य से रीती नहीं है माला, किंतु सलीका? एक बार हुआ यूँ कि माँ ने बड़ी साध से उसे बनारसी साड़ी पहना दी और दोनों को मोटर साइकिल से बाहर घूम-फिर आने को कहा। उसने अनेक प्रयास किए, किंतु वह साड़ी न सँभाल सकी। इधर पिन लगाए, तो उधर गिर जाए। इधर खोंसे, तो उधर जमीन में लसरने लगे। किसी प्रकार थोड़ी दूर गया, फिर हाथ खड़े कर दिए, "माँ! कहीं साड़ी-वाड़ी फँस गई और गिर-गिरा गई तो और परेशानी हो जाएगी।" उसने निगाहें झुका रखी थीं।

और एक यह है, कितना सुव्यवस्थित व्यक्तित्व! बातचीत में कितना सलीका है। मन में ऐसे धँसती जा रही है, जैसे केक की मलाई में जेली।

कहीं चौकीदारी करता था उसका पति। उसके घर से निकलते ही महाशय पहुँच जाते और आने से पहले उसका बिस्तर खाली कर देते।

वह ऑफिस में भी उसके आस-पास मंडराया करती। मुँहा-मुँहीं बात फैलने लगी।

"अच्छा फँसाया है। हाँ, काम से क्या? माल तो उम्दा है। सफाई मोंटू से करवाता है, फूल उससे बदलवाता है। नाजुक जो है, फूलों-जैसी!"

"दिमागवाली है, दिन-रात कमा रही है।"

"अरे! आग लगे ऐसी कमाई में, अपने आदमी को धोखा दे रही है।"

"धोखा क्या, वह भी जानता होगा, ये झुमके, ये नई-नई साड़ियाँ, क्या चपरासन की कमाई से आ रही हैं?

जब वक्त मिलता, यही बातें होतीं। जाति-बिरादरी में जातिवाली पत्नी, जो गाँव में रहकर बच्चे पाल रही थी और शहर में मन पसंद अंतरंग सखी! पाँचों अंगुलियाँ घी में थीं प्रभात भारती की। अब तो चोरी का खटका भी छूट गया था। जीवन सहज हो चला था। तनख्वाह का तीन-चौथाई घर भेज देता, बचे पैसे के साथ ऊपरी आमदनी से अमृत पान करता।

रस भरे गिलास में एक दिन छिपकली गिर पड़ी। वह निकला न था कि उसका पति आ गया। उसे धक्का देते हुए चादर लपेटकर वह भागा था। दिल की धड़कनें जैसे फेफड़ा फाड़ देने पर उतारू हों। भयभीत वह, उस दिन घर में ही दुबका रहा। रात होते ही गाँव के लिए निकल पड़ा। आश्चर्य हुआ घरवालों को उसे अचानक आया देखकर। किसी से बिना कुछ बताए, वह सबसे मिलता-जुलता रहा। उसी बेचैनी की देन है—मीनू। पत्नी के सीने में मुँह छिपाकर वह निर्भय हो गया था। गाँव से ही एक माह का मेडिकल भेज दिया था। जब वापस आया, तब पता चला कि नीरा अब इस संसार में नहीं रही। उसे उसके पति ने बहुत मारा था उस दिन। नौकरी छोड़ देने के लिए कह रहा था। दूसरे दिन जब वह ड्यूटी से आया, नीरा अपनी साड़ी का फंदा गले में बाँधकर पंखे से झूल रही थी। उसके हाथ में एक कागज था, जिसमें लिखा था 'सर की कोई गलती नहीं है, उन्हें मैंने बुलाया था।' उसके शरीर पर लगे घावों के कारण पुलिस को हत्या की शंका थी। उसका पति शक के आधार पर उस समय भी जेल में ही था।

वह डरते-डरते ड्यूटी पर आया था। उसने देखा कि मामला शांत हो चुका है उसने चैन की साँस ली थी। नौ माह बाद मीनू के जन्म की सूचना मिली थी उसे। समझ में नहीं आया रोए या गाए, नौकरी का भी क्या ठिकाना? राधारमण ने नौकरी दिलाने के लिए उसे अपना भाई बना लिया था। सारे प्रमाण-पत्र नकली बनवाए गए थे, जिन पर उसके पिता का नाम दयानंद

भारती लिखा हुआ था। उसे जाति बदलते ही आरक्षण का लाभ मिल गया। उसने अपना नाम प्रभात पांडे से बदलकर प्रभात भारती रख लिया था। वैसे भी उसे अपना छोटा नाम प्रभात ही पसंद था।

"चलो, चिंता की कोई बात नहीं है, माँ–बाप हैं, वे सब सँभाल लेंगे। विभाग में तीन से अधिक बच्चेवालों को कई सुविधाओं से वंचित रखा जाता था। लोग गँवार अलग से समझते थे। इस परिस्थिति के लिए उसकी बीवी एकदम सही है, न कोई गिला न शिकवा! न कोई माँग, पहुँच गए तो गद्गद! चले आए तो बड़ी–बड़ी आँखों में बहते आँसू, पता नहीं क्या है उसमें? उस पर सौ जान से न्योछावर हैं, आज भी माँ–पिताजी। नीरा कांड में पुलिस के शक की सुई उसकी ओर भी उठी थी, पिताजी को कुछ भनक लगी थी शायद, उन्होंने छोटे भाई के साथ उसके परिवार को उसके पास भेज दिया। बड़ी मुश्किल से राधारमण ने उसे पुलिस के पंजे से छुड़ाया था। "इस सीधी–सादी बहू और नन्हे–नन्हे बच्चों का मुँह देखकर बचाना पड़ रहा है इसे तो, वरना सड़ने देता जेल में।" उसने बड़ी घृणा के साथ कहा था और बाद के वर्षों में उसने उससे दूरी बनाए रखी। अनचाहे भार से वह बुरी तरह दब गया था। दोनों लड़कों की पढ़ाई बनारस में बहुत खर्चीली हो गई थी। बड़ी लड़की तो गाँव में ही रह गई थी। मीनू बहुत छोटी थी, वह जैसे–जैसे होश सँभालती गई, उसके तन–मन से चिपकती गई थी। शराब की बढ़ी हुई तलब से परिवार बदहाल था। मीनू अपने छोटे–छोटे हाथों से गिलास लाती, मिक्स्चर का पैकेट लाती, वह चाहे जितनी गालियाँ दे, कभी उससे नाराज नहीं होती थी। वह लगभग बारह साल की थी, जब उसे चौतरफे दबाव में आकर नौकरी से वी.आर.एस. लेना पड़ा। विभाग में फर्जी कर्मचारियों की गहन जाँच हो रही थी सी.बी.आई. द्वारा। बनारस छोड़कर कहाँ जाए? दयाराम भारती के परिवार के सिवा उसका कौन सा सहारा था। अपनी सगी औलाद जैसा माननेवाला दयाराम भारती स्वर्गवासी हो चुका था। राधारमण एक बड़े राजनेता का दामाद बन गया। अब पुराने संबंधों को ढोना उसके लिए भी मुश्किल ही था।

उसके बच्चे पढ़ाई छोड़कर छोटा-मोटा काम करने लगे थे। नौकरी के बदले मिले पैसे से उसने बड़ी बेटी की शादी निपटा दी थी। बस, अब एकदम खाली हाथ था। मीनू देखती, उसकी शराब की छटपटाहट, उसे लगता शराब न मिली तो बाप मर ही जाएगा।

"पिओगे पापा, अपनी पसंदवाली?" उसने पूछा था उससे एक दिन।

"कहाँ मिलेगी मीनू?" उसने आशा भरी निगाहों से देखा था उसे।

"मैं लाई हूँ, ये लो!" उसने कमीज उठाई और सलवार में खोंसी ब्लेक डॉग की शीशी निकाल कर दे दी। दाँत से डॉट तोड़कर नीट ही पूरी शीशी खाली कर उसने तृप्त और उपकृत निगाहों से उसे देखा था, चौबीस घंटे के उपवास के बाद मिली थी उसे दारू।

"कैसे जुगाड़ हुआ मीनू, तुम्हारे पास पैसे कहाँ से आए?" उसने होंठ पोंछते हुए पूछा था।

"उसकी चिंता आप मत करो पापा! किसी से उधार लिया है मैंने, बाद में चुका दूँगी। काम मिल जाएगा कहीं-न-कहीं।" उसने संयत स्वर में कहा था।

उसे कहाँ चाह थी मीनू के चेहरे पर फैली थकावट देखने की। कुँआरी लड़कियोंवाली चमक कहाँ थी उसके मुख पर?

"बड़ी होशियार हो गई है मेरी मीनू! किसने दे दिया तुझे उधार? सारे जाने-पहचाने लोग तो हमें कर्ज दे चुके हैं। कहाँ से नया दाता मिल गया?

पत्नी भी बोलने लगी है अब तो "लो! और पार्टी करो, पेटी भर शराब लाओ, नहाओ उसी से, दिन भर में लड़के सौ दो सौ कमाकर लाते हैं तब तो अन्न मिलता है।" सब समय का फेर है रे! नहीं तो मिमियाया करती थी बकरी की तरह।" वह मन ही मन कहता।

"ये क्या पापा, सुबह-सुबह होंठों पर जीभ फेर रहे हैं, देर हो गई क्या?" अशोक चिढ़ रहा था उसे देख-देखकर।

सभी चिढ़ते हैं अब तो, वह बेकार हो चुका है, अशोक ही तो पूरे घर

का खर्च सँभाले हुए है। 32 की हो गई थी मीनू, उसने तो उसकी डोली उठने की उम्मीद ही छोड़ दी थी।

"इसकी शादी नहीं करोगे क्या, जिंदगी भर बेटी की कमाई खाओगे?" माला बराबर लड़ती मीनू के लिए।

"नहीं यह रावण है, कौन करेगा इससे शादी? बस ऐसे ही ठीक है।" वह चिढ़कर कह देता। वास्तव में उसे लगता था मीनू के जाने के बाद इस घर में कोई उसका खयाल नहीं रखेगा। अशोक ने किसी तरह जोड़-तोड़कर बनारसी साड़ियों की एजेंसी ले ली है। भाई-बहन उसी में लगे रहते हैं। अब तो लगभग ठीक चल रहा है सबकुछ। मीनू की सुंदरता में क्या कमी है? माँ-बाप का मिला-जुला रूप है वह। स्कूल जाकर तो जो पढ़ी, गाँव में ही पढ़ी। बनारस में तो सभी लोग ज्यादातर रोटी के ही पीछे लगे रहे, मीनू के पास बी.ए. की डिग्री है और वह बिल्कुल असली है। कई ऐसे स्कूल चल रहे हैं, जहाँ परीक्षा कोई और देता है डिग्री किसी और को मिल जाती है। मीनू को बातचीत में कोई नहीं पकड़ सकता, शहरी रख-रखाव और तहजीब ने उसे अत्याधुनिक रूप दे दिया है।

उसी का तो चमत्कार है कि यह शादी लग गई। माना कि चालीस का हो रहा है प्रदीप, परंतु देखने में तो मीनू के बराबर ही लगता है। इतने लोग थे, क्या किसी ने जोड़ी पर अंगुली उठाई? वह भी बी.ए. पास है। उनका भी साड़ियों का ही धंधा है। पढ़ी-लिखी पत्नी धंधे में हाथ बँटाएगी, यही सोचकर उसने दान-दहेज, घर-द्वार किसी चीज पर ध्यान नहीं दिया। उसे तो सुंदर सुशील और शिक्षित जीवनसाथी की कामना थी, यहाँ तक कि शादी का अधिकांश खर्च वह स्वयं उठा रहा था, वरना लग्न वाटिका में शान से कन्या दान करना तो असंभव जैसा ही था। उसने संतोष की एक लंबी साँस ली।

सभी कुछ रखा जा चुका था, सारे मेहमान विदा हो गए थे। अंतिम गाड़ी में घर के लोग निकलनेवाले थे।

"वे लोग आए क्यों नहीं अब तक मीनू को लेकर पगफेरे के लिए?" वह उदीयमान सूर्य की किरणों से बचने के लिए अपनी आँखों को हथेलियों की ओट में छिपाए उस रास्ते पर नजरें टिकाए हुए था, जिससे दो घंटे पहले मीनू अपने पति के साथ फूलों से सजी कार पर बैठकर गई थी।

"वह नहीं आएगी पापा, उन लोगों का कहना है कि शादी, गवन और पगफेरा तीन-तीन रस्म एक साथ हमारे यहाँ नहीं होती। घर से पगफेरा कराएँगे।" छोटे लड़के ने बाँह पकड़कर गाड़ी पर बैठा दिया था।

"जल्दी चलो यहाँ से, नहीं तो किराया बढ़ जाएगा!" अशोक के हाँक लगाते ही गाड़ी आगे बढ़ चली।

तीसरे दिन आई थी मीनू, अशोक गाड़ी लेकर गया था लिवाने। सुहाग की प्रसन्नता खोज रहा था वह उसके चेहरे पर।

"पापा!" वह दौड़कर उसके गले से लिपट गई थी।

"क्या बात है मीनू, इतना तो तू पहली विदाई के समय भी नहीं रोई थी, सब ठीक तो है न बेटी?" उसकी आँखों के आँसू पोंछता पूछा था उसने।

"पापा! कुछ भी ठीक नहीं है, अलग-अलग नामों से सारी औरतों से शादी करके उनसे कमाई करता है। मुझे मुक्ति नहीं मिली पापा!" वह जार-जार रो रही थी।

"नहीं! उनका तो साड़ियों का कारोबार है।"

"वह तो दुनिया को दिखाने के लिए है।"

"ये लो पापा! आप के लिए लेती आई हूँ, वहाँ ढेरों बोतलें सजी हैं, ग्राहकों की खातिरदारी में लगती हैं। उसने डिप्लोमेट की बोतल प्रभात के हाथ में थमाई और आगे बढ़कर माँ के गले लगकर रोने लगी।

□

कहाँ जाऊँ?

लाची का दिल भर गया था पोती के यहाँ रहने से, जब देखो, तब दामाद दारू पीकर गरियाता रहता।

"दाइज म लाने हे डोकरी ला, चार पइसा के फायदा नहीं, मुँह मरई हे।" वह कल्ला के रह जाती उसकी बातें सुनकर। छह माह हो गए उसे दसमत दमोदर के घर रहते, भले ही आज एक-एक कौर पर ताने मिलते हों, उस रात, जब अचानक उसे दिल का दौरा पड़ा था, तब ये ही तो उसे लेकर सरकारी अस्पताल गए थे। जैसे बना, वैसे सेवा-टहल की। डॉक्टर कह रहे थे कि आश्चर्यजनक है इसका बच जाना। दसमत तो अभी भी नून-बासी, जो जुटता है, उसे खिलाती-पिलाती रहती है। उसने भी तो बड़ी मुश्किल से इसे बचाया था, दो साल की थी, जब सुमता ने आत्महत्या कर ली थी। कोई जाने, न जाने, वह जानती है उसकी आत्महत्या का कारण। सबसे छोटी बेटी थी वह उसकी। आठवीं में थी, तभी से उसके पाँव बहक गए थे, उसे वह सबकुछ चाहिए था, जो सहेलियों में उसका महत्त्व बढ़ा सके, अच्छे कपड़े, गाहे-बगाहे कीमती चॉकलेट की पार्टी, मोबाइल, मॉल में घूमने के किस्से आदि।

कई बड़े घरों के बिगड़े जवान होते लड़के उसकी झोपड़ी में छिपकर गांजे का कश लिया करते थे। क्या करे जीने के लिए? जब से जांगर थका, डोकरा न जाने कहाँ से दो-चार पुड़िया लाकर बेच लिया करता था। वह ठहरी बनिहारिन, दिन भर घर से बाहर ही बीत जाता, न जाने किसके बहकावे में आ गई सुमता? उसने पढ़ाई छोड़ दी और शाम रात को रुपए लेकर आने

लगी। पूछने पर हत्थे से उखड़ जाती।

"जब मेरा शौक पूरा नहीं कर सकते तो पूछने का क्या अधिकार है, मैं कहीं से लाऊँ?"

उसके सूखते मुँह और चौड़ी होती कमर को देखकर उसने समझ लिया था कि लड़की का शौक अच्छी तरह पूरा हो गया है। उसने स्वयं देहाती दवा खिलाकर उसका पेट उतारा था गरियाते हुए।

उसने अपने एक दोस्त से शादी कर ली। उसके पति को उसके पुराने शौक से कोई एतराज नहीं था, बस पैसा मिलता जाए दारू-मुरगे के लिए। साल भर में दसमत का जन्म हो गया। दूसरे साल फिर से…!

"चलता धंधा रोकना ठीक नहीं। तू कोई कोठा खोलकर तो बैठी नहीं, काम चल गया तो चल गया, ग्राहक इधर-उधर हो गए तो फिर से जुटाने में मुश्किल होगी। जैसी तू इज्जतदार, वैसे ही तेरे ग्राहक!" बहुत मारा था, उसके पसंदीदा प्यारे पति ने। जुए-दारू के लिए कहाँ जाए वह अपनी हड्डियाँ घिसने?

उम्र भले ही बाइस की हो, वह बुरी तरह थकने लगी थी। बच्चा गिराना भी क्या सरल था? खर्च लगता, सो तो लगता ही, ग्राहक को कच्ची देह पसंद नहीं आती, यह तो दसमत के समय ही समझ गई थी वह। आठ माह का पेट लेकर कितना कमाए? गुस्से और आत्मग्लानि के चलते उसने अपने आप को आग के हवाले कर दिया था। नन्ही दसमत के कारण वह फिर से लइकोरी हो गई थी। करम ठोंक लिया था उसने, क्या करे? जब अपना ही सिक्का खोटा था तो औरों का क्या दोष? सियान के जाने के बाद वह अब तक कई घरों में काम करती थी, वह तो बीमारी…! सही कहते हैं आजकल अमीर-गरीब, जवान-बूढ़ा नहीं देखती बीमारी। हाँ, लेकिन इस बिन माँ की बच्ची के पेट के लिए तो उसे हिम्मत करनी ही थी। कमर दर्द से कराहती रहे या बुखार में तपती रहे, काम से नागा नहीं करती, यूँ भी इतनी बूढ़ी नौकरानी कोई रखना नहीं चाहता, लगता एक फूँक में उड़ जाएगी। दो बड़ी बेटियों की ओर उसने मदद की उम्मीद से हाथ फैलाए थे। "पाल लो बेटी तुम्हारी बहन की निशानी है, समय जाते

देर कहाँ लगती है। यह भी काम करने लगेगी। जैसे तुम्हारे बच्चे पल रहे हैं, वैसे ही यह भी पल जाएगी। मैं तो अपने ही पेट के लिए नहीं जुटा पाती भोजन, इसे कैसे पालूँगी?"

"तू ज्यादा पालनहार न बन, जिसकी औलाद है, उसे सौंप दे। जो इसके भाग्य में होगा, हो जाएगा। यहाँ अपने तो पाले नहीं जाते, एक और सिर का बोझा बढ़ा रही है।" दोनों की राय लगभग एक ही थी। दामाद की नीयत से वह भलीभाँति परिचित थी, जानते-बूझते कैसे दे दे गाय को कसाई के हाथ में? दसमत की दादी आई थी उसे देखने, उससे भी उसने हाथ जोड़कर विनय की थी। "समधिन आप की पोती है दसमत, ले जाइए इसे अपने घर, तब तो पहचानेगी न अपने परिवार को। मेरे पास तो कुछ भी नहीं है इसके लिए। कैसे क्या करूँगी। आप के पास सबकुछ है, नून-बासी खाके पल जाएगी।"

"तुमको लाज नहीं लगती मरी हुई बेटी की औलाद को अकेले छोड़ने में? धोखे से चरकट को हमारे बेटे के पल्ले बाँध दिया था। मनमानी चाल चलनेवाली औरतों का यही हश्र होता है। अपनी जिद में अपनी जान से गई, अब दूसरी शादी का खर्च कौन देगा, हमीं कौन से धन्ना सेठ हैं, बताओ? बनिहार आदमी, कमाते-खाते हैं।"

"थी तो सचमुच गलत, पर उसकी कमाई तो तुम्हारा बेटा ही खाता था। काम करता तो वह क्यों उल्टे-सीधे काम करती? आज बच्ची छोड़कर मर गई तो कोई जिम्मेदारी लेने को तैयार नहीं है।" वह राग धर के रोने लगी। उसकी समधिन पल्ला तान के भागी अपने घर।

टोले-मोहल्लेवालों ने दसमत के बाप सनेही को बुलाकर डाँट-डपट लगाई।

"सीधे-सीधे लड़की को ले जा, नहीं तो जेल में चक्की पीसते नजर आओगे। लड़की की हत्या का मुकदमा लगा देंगे तुम्हारे खिलाफ।" वह थोड़ा सकपकाया था।

"ठीक है, दाई पाले बच्ची को खरचा दूँगा। और जब अपने हाथ-पैर की हो जाएगी तो अपने पास ले भी जाऊँगा।'' उसने जान छुड़ाने के लिए

कह तो दिया, लेकिन उसके घर का दरवाजा ही भूल गया। चला गया उत्तर प्रदेश कमाने। एक साल बाद आया तो उसके साथ उसकी चूरिहाई पत्नी थी। मिलने आया था वह उसके साथ। जी-भर के खरी-खोटी सुनाई थी उसने। वह ही-ही करके हँसता रहा। थोड़ी देर बेटी को खिलाया और हाथ में दस रुपए का एक नोट देकर चला गया था। उसने समझ लिया था कि दसमत उसी के हिस्से की है। उसको साथ लिये-लिये घरों में काम करने जाती, दूसरों के फटे-पुराने माँग जाँचकर पहनाती। वह बड़ी जल्दी-जल्दी बढ़ रही थी। चार वर्ष की होने पर दौड़-धूप कर हाथ-पाँव जोड़कर उसका नाम सरस्वती विद्या मंदिर में करवा दिया। अत्यंत गरीब होने के कारण उसे सरकारी छूट का लाभ मिल गया।

नौवें साल में ही जो रंग चढ़ा तो बड़े-बड़े घर के बच्चे फेल उसकी सुंदरता और सलीके के आगे। "जो गलती अपनी बेटी के साथ हुई, वह इसके साथ न होने देगी" यह प्रण किया था उसने। मोहल्ले के लोग दसमत को सुमता की निशानी समझकर बहुत मानते थे। सनेही भी आता जाता रहता था। एक दिन वह अपनी पत्नी के साथ घर आया और जबरन दसमत को अपने साथ अपने गाँव ले गया। पढ़ाई के बीच में उसे ले जाना लाची को अच्छा नहीं लगा था। एक तो वह उसके बिना रहने की कल्पना से भी दूर थी दूसरे बिना किसी प्रोग्राम के इस तरह ले जाना जैसे छीनकर ले जा रहा हो। वह पूरे दिन रोती रही थी। न जाने क्यों मन किसी अज्ञात आशंका से बैठा जा रहा था। दसमत की भोली बातें याद आती रहीं। न कुछ खाने का मन हुआ, न पीने का। काम पर भी नहीं जा सकी।

तीसरे दिन दसमत की सौतेली माँ अपने भाई के साथ ऑटो से उसके घर आई। उन्होंने पकड़कर दसमत को उतारा।

"हाय, क्या हो गया मेरी अच्छी-भली बच्ची को?" वह सुध-बुध भूलकर दौड़ी और दसमत को गोद में लेकर बेतहाशा चूमने लगी। उसे जगह-जगह चोट लगी थी। एक आँख फूलकर बंद हो गई थी। पलक काली पड़ गई थी।

"बताओ तुम लोग, कैसे हुई इसकी यह हालत?" वह वहशियाने

अंदाज में चीख रही थी। उसके समधियाने का सरपंच ऑटो से उतरा था। उसने बताया, "दाई बड़े भाग्य से तुम्हारी बच्ची बच सकी है, इसके बाप ने इसे तीन लाख में बेच दिया था। जब यह जाने से मना करने लगी, तब देखो, कैसे अधमरा करके मारा है। ये कहो कि उसकी माँ इस सब में शामिल नहीं थी। उसने ही मुझे बुलाया। हमने उसे थाने पहुँचा दिया है। दाई इस लड़की को अब कभी इसके बाप के साथ मत भेजना।" टोले-मोहल्लेवाले जुट आए थे। सनेही मिल जाता तो जिंदा न बचता, उनके गुस्से को देखकर ऐसा लग रहा था। तबसे तो हर पल अपनी पलकों में छिपाकर रखा था लाची ने अपनी दसमत को।

अपने हिसाब से शादी भी अच्छे घर में ही की है। दामाद का अपना व्यक्तिगत हाथ ठेला है, चाहे तो दिन भर में पाँच सौ कमाकर ला सकता है। घर में सब कमाने-खाने लायक हैं, दसमत के ऊपर किसी की जिम्मेदारी नहीं है।

अच्छा है दामाद भी, वह तो सड़ा हुआ महुआ है, जो बक-झक कराता है। वह दरवाजे पर बैठी गुन रही थी। शाम ढल चुकी थी। दामाद काम से वापस आ चुका था।

"अब इस डोकरी का क्या करें? कुछ सोचो, वरना मैं पागल हो जाऊँगा इसे देख-देखकर।"

"लाठी डिब्बा धरा देते है। माँगेगी, खाएगी।" दसमत चिढ़ रही थी।

अरे बाप रे! ये लोग कौन हैं, जो उसे लाठी-डंडा पकड़ाने चले हैं, वह जैसे आकाश से गिरी।

"मैं क्यों माँगूँगी भीख? मुझे तो मोहल्लेवाले हाथो-हाथ रखते हैं, अपने घर जाऊँगी! झोपड़ी सही, महल से कम नहीं है। भूखी सही, सो तो सकती हूँ आराम से, सियान की कमाई समझो या पेंशन, बेजा कब्जे में बना लिये थे दो कमरे, सीट डालकर, अब कौन हटा सकता है? बिजली, पानी, सड़क सब बन गया है। सरकारी निराश्रित पेंशन और सस्ता चावल मुझे मिलता है। अब यहाँ एक पल भी नहीं रह सकती!" वह अपनी सारी मजबूरियाँ भूलकर दम भर चिल्ला रही थी।

"दसमत, ए दसमत! मुझे मेरे घर पहुँचा दे बेटी! और नहीं सहा जाता। मैं तेरे पाँव पड़ती हूँ!" अब वह गिड़गिड़ा रही थी।

"घर! कौन सा घर, वह तो कब का बिक गया, इतने दिन से खा क्या रही है? अपने डउका की कमाई, कमा के धर गया है न?" दामाद की बात सुनकर उसके पाँव तले से जमीन खिसक गई।

"बता दसमत! किससे पूछकर मेरा घर बेचा है तुम लोगों ने?" उसकी आवाज आस-पास के माहौल में फैल गई।

"नानी क्या पता था, तू बच जाएगी? वैसे तू घर मुझे ही देनेवाली थी।" दसमत निर्लज्जता से उसकी आँखों-में-आँखें डाल कर बोली।

"तो अब कहाँ जाऊँ मैं?" गिर पड़ी जमीन पर वह।

□

वसूली

वह रोज स्कूल के अंदर आकर ऑफिस में बैठ जाता था।

"तुम लोग इतनी तनख्वाह पाते हो, बच्चों को ठीक से पढ़ाते नहीं। इनको कुछ नहीं आता। आगे शिकायत करूँगा। सब जगह महीना बँधा-बँधा है, पंचायत का, खाते हो, कोई बात नहीं! सब के बाल-बच्चे हैं, हम लोग दिन-रात सेवा में लगे रहते हैं, अपना घर-बार छोड़कर, तो क्या मूर्ख हैं? मेरी हैसियत अभी जानते नहीं हो, एक इशारे पर पसान में नजर आओगे, यहाँ जो बैठकर मोटा माल ले रहे हो सरकार से। हमारे गाँव के लिए मास्टर की कमी नहीं है। एक इशारे पर साखन को हटा दिया और धजाराम को सरपंच बना दिया। कइसे दीदी! कुछ गलत कह रहा हूँ तो माफ करना।" वह अपनी बात की स्वीकारोक्ति के लिए शिक्षिकाओं की ओर देखता। सब लोग उसकी बात सावधान होकर सुनते।

"तुम लोग भी कुछ करो, नहीं तो सरपंच से तुम्हारे रजिस्टर पर दस्तखत नहीं करवाऊँगा, फिर कैसे मिलेगी तनख्वाह? खा-खा के मोटा गए हो। यहाँ गाँव के आदमी को काम नहीं मिलता, बाहरवाले मौज कर रहे हैं।" और भी तरह-तरह की बातें, कक्षा में लड़ते-भिड़ते बच्चों को छोड़कर सब सुनते, जो वह कहता।

कई बार उसने कब्जुल वसूल रजिस्टर वापस करवा दिया, किसी-न-किसी बहाने से। कभी अक्षर साफ नहीं हैं, तो कभी सील ठीक से नहीं लगी है।

समय से कब्जुल वसूल ऑफिस न पहुँचने पर वहाँ से फटकार मिलती।

वेतन विलंब से मिलता। हेड मास्टर सोहन शर्मा ने कार्यालय से संपर्क करके रास्ता निकाला जिसके अनुसार यदि सरपंच हस्ताक्षर न करे तो लिखकर भेज दे, सरपंच का हस्ताक्षर करने से इनकार। वेतनवाली समस्या हल होने के बाद स्टाफ ने चैन की साँस ली। उसने भी पैंतरा बदला, अब आए दिन शराब के नशे में दो-चार लोग घुस जाते, ऑफिस में घुसकर कागज-पत्र इधर-उधर करते। कहते, "हम शाला विकास समितिवाले हैं, हमें जाँच का अधिकार है।" उनकी बदतमीजी देखकर शर्माजी ने शिक्षिकाओं को निर्देशित किया कि आप लोग इन्हें देखकर अपने कक्ष का दरवाजा बंदकर अपना काम करती रहें, मैं इनसे निबट लूँगा। इस उपाय से वे तिलमिलाकर रह गए, उनका मकसद ही था शिक्षिकाओं से बदसलूकी करके अपना मनोरंजन करना। हेड मास्टर जब इस गाँव में पदस्थ हुए, उस समय की स्थिति बड़ी दयनीय थी। सभी शिक्षक अपनी-अपनी सुविधा से आते-जाते। एक तो दर्ज ही बहुत कम था, जो था, वह भी पढ़ाई से वंचित था। दो बड़े-बड़े कमरे, एक छोटा सा ऑफिस, कमरों के सामने बरामदा, बस इतने में ही पाँच कक्षा के बच्चे बैठते थे। उनका भी वही हाल, आओ-जाओ घर तुम्हारा ही है। एक शिक्षक बराबर चाय की केतली चढ़ाए चाय बनाता रहता। शिक्षिकाएँ या तो स्वेटर बुनतीं या घर के काम स्कूल में निबटातीं।

स्कूल के सामने लगभग दो एकड़ का खेत था, जिसकी आमदनी से स्कूल का खर्च चलाया जाना था। उस समय सरकारी मेंटेनेंस का रुपया शाला विकास समिति की सहमति से खर्च करने की शासकीय बाध्यता थी, यहाँ बाध्यता की कोई बात ही नहीं थी। सबकुछ सहज था। खेत की कमाई, मेंटेनेंस का रुपया मिल-बाँटकर खाया जाता था। शिक्षक पंचायत का हिस्सा देकर अपना निजी काम करते थे। स्कूल की खपरैल वर्षों से सुधारी नहीं गई थी। हैंड पंप न जाने कब से बिगड़ा पड़ा था, बच्चे तालाब से पानी पीकर आते, कभी एक-दूसरे पर पानी फेंकते, कभी पानी में गिर जाते। पक्की सड़क से स्कूल की इमारत लगभग पाँच सौ मीटर दूर थी। कच्ची-चिकनी मिट्टीवाला रास्ता, जहाँ पानी गिरे, भयानक कीचड़ हो जाए। साइकिल कंधे पर उठाकर लानी पड़े। पैदलवालों के जूते-चप्पल में पाँच-पाँच किलो मिट्टी

लिपट जाए। गिरते-पड़ते स्कूल पहुँचे तो पैर धोने के लिए पानी बच्चे तालाब से ही लेकर आते थे। वे जूते-चप्पल से मिट्टी छुड़ाकर धो लाते थे। जहाँ पानी गिरने की संभावना दिखी कि छुट्टी की घंटी बजी। आँगन से ज्यादा पानी कमरे में ही गिरता। बच्चे एक-दूसरे को धकेलकर आगे निकलने के चक्कर में एक-दूसरे को गिरा देते। शिक्षकों के पास शिकायतें आतीं, किसी को छड़ी पड़ती, किसी को फटकार। शर्माजी ने सारी अव्यवस्थाओं को दूर करने के लिए स्कूल को अनुशासन में बाँधा, यहाँ तक कि एक मिनट लेट होने पर अपनी भी हाफ सी.एल. लगाने लगे। मरम्मत के लिए आई सरकारी रकम से स्कूल का छप्पर सुधरवाया, हैंड पंप की मरम्मत करवाई। इससे खउवा पार्टी तिलमिलाई हुई थी। ज्ञानदास नाम था उसका, सरपंच धजाराम का दायाँ हाथ। लेन-देन की सारी सेटिंग वही करता था। कहाँ से पैसा मिल सकता है, सूँघता रहता था। गाँव में जितने अपराध होते, वह छिपा ले जाता, "पुलिसवाले कुकुर मन खाहीं तेखर ले हमीं काबर नी खा लेई।" गाँव भर को पता है कि सेवाराम को उसके बहू-बेटे ने दुर्गा अष्टमी की रात साबल से मार डाला था। सबेरा होते ही सेवाराम की लाश जला दी, हत्या का स्थान ऊपरी मिट्टी निकालकर लीप-पोत दिया गया। साबल वेल्डिंग मशीन से गला दिया गया। बदले में सेवाराम का खेत ज्ञानदास के बेटे के नाम आ गया। घर में अवैध दारू बेचनेवाला धजाराम अपने मोहल्ले का पंच था। गाँव के ज्यादातर लोग उसके घर हाजिरी देते थे। उन्हीं की कृपा से उप-सरपंच बना। ज्ञानदास उसका लँगोटिया यार था। उप-सरपंच की कमाई उसे कुछ जँची नहीं। वह सरपंच के पीछे हाथ धोकर पड़ गया। उसके इशारे पर गाँव की ही एक लड़की ने उस पर बलात्कार के प्रयास की शिकायत ग्राम सभा में की। वह तो थाने जा रही थी, ज्ञानदास ने समझाइश देकर उसे सरपंच से एक मोटी रकम दिलवाई। सभी सदस्यों को अपनी ओर मिलाया।

ऐसा सरपंच कैसे रह सकता है गाँव में, जो हमारी बहू-बेटियों की अस्मत से खेलने का साहस करे। इसे हटाकर धजाराम को सरपंच बनाते हैं, यह हमेशा हम जैसा कहेंगे, वैसा ही करेगा। पीओ-खाओ जी भर के "जा रे मेलू, मेचका घर के जम्मों मुरगी मन ला ले नान। सब झिन-मिल के खाबो तिहाँ काली

धजाराम हमर नवा सरपंच होही। इहाँ के बात ला कहूँ गोठियाही चाहे बोट नई दिही धजा भइया ला तेन अपन दई बहिनी ला धरही।" दारू–मुरगी के बाद कसम तो रिवाज निभाने के लिए दे दी ज्ञानदास ने। दूसरे दिन बहुमत के साथ धजाराम सरपंच और ज्ञानदास महा–सरपंच बन गया। बस, अब उगाही चल रही थी। उसके लिए साम, दाम, दंड, भेद की नीति अपनाई जा रही थी।

शिक्षक भी अपने नाम के एक ही थे, सब सुनते रहे, लेकिन फूटी कौड़ी भी नहीं दी। हेड मास्टर विचारों के पक्के थे। ठीक है, बैठाए रहो, मत काम करने दो, हमें तो अपने वेतन से काम है।

लगा, जैसे वह हार मान गया। अब आता तो पैर छू–छूकर माफी माँगता, "गुरु का स्थान तो भगवान् से भी ऊपर है। आप लोग हमारे गाँव की मर्यादा हैं, मैं अपनी सगी बहनों से ज्यादा आप लोगों को मानता हूँ। पहले का सरपंच पूरा खा गया, उसे आप लोगों की तकलीफ दिखाई नहीं दी। जरा सा पानी गिरा नहीं कि घुटने भर पानी स्कूल में, पानी निकास का साधन है ही नहीं, मोहल्ले भर का पानी यहीं जमा होता है। अब हमारे हाथ में ताकत आई है तो सबसे पहले आप लोगों का ही काम होगा। कल से स्कूल के नए कमरों की नींव पड़ेगी।"

"ये दे पट्टा देवत हन सस्ता म, तूंहूँ मन ले लेवा लेह त!" एक दिन उसने कृपालु होकर कहा था।

"बाहर से आते हो, इसीलिए देर से पहुँचते हो, यहाँ रहोगे तो डंडा मारकर समय पर स्कूल लाएँगे।"

"हम लोगों को मिलेगा भइया?" पूजा और आरती मैडम एक साथ बोल पड़ीं।

"हाँ! काहे नहीं मिलेगा, हम देंगे तो? उसके लिए पुख्ता उपाय करना होगा। पहले यहाँ का राशन कार्ड बनवाओ! वोटर लिस्ट में नाम जुड़वाओ, फिर हम पट्टा देंगे मेन रोड पर, कोई हटा नहीं सकता, ऐसा पक्का पट्टा बना देंगे। वह दोनों शिक्षिकाओं के दिल में उतरा जा रहा था।

उसकी कानी आँख और चेचक के दागों से भरा चेहरा सारी दुनिया में सबसे सुंदर दिखाई दे रहा था।

"कितना लगेगा?" आरती मैडम की आँखें में चालाकी से चमक उठी थी।

"तीन डिसमिल पचास हजार, पहले तैयारी कर लो, फिर बात करेंगे।" वह अपने शब्दों से उनके कानों में शहद घोल रहा था।

"हमारे पास शहर में घर है भइया, धोखा तो नहीं होगा न?" पूजा मैडम ने उसकी आँखों में आँखें डालकर इठलाते हुए अपनी शंका जाहिर की।

"अरे दीदी! कुछ नहीं होगा, कौन जाँच करने के लिए फुरसत में है?"

"दौड़ो! फॉर्म भरो! कार्ड बनवाओ, वोटर लिस्ट में नाम जुड़वाओ, पैसा निकालो यहाँ-वहाँ से, अपने साथ मायके का भी कल्याण करो।" दाँत निपोरे-निपोरे लगता होंठ अब फैले ही रह जाएँगे। दोनों ने दो-दो प्लॉट के लिए एक-एक लाख जमा किए।

पीले रंग का, मोटे-मोटे, काले-काले अक्षरों में लिखा गया पट्टा देखकर दोनों ने जैसे जीवन धन पाया। "ईंट लाओ, सीमेंट लाओ, मजदूर खोजो, सीट लाओ, दरवाजा लाओ, छपाई करो, लिपाई करो, दोनों गरमी की छुट्टी भर बवंडर की भाँति पूरे शहर में मँडराती रहीं। किसी ने घर के के लिए कुभाषा का प्रयोग क्या कर दिया कि इस जमीन पर बने घर पहले भी तोड़े जा चुके हैं, दोनों ऐसी व्याकुल हुईं कि पाँच-पाँच हजार रुपए पटवारी को भी दे आईं, किसी प्रकार की गड़बड़ रोकने के लिए।

जुलाई में जब स्कूल खुला, तब इनकी मेहनत का फल देखकर एक शिक्षक के मुँह से हठात् निकल गया 'वीर भोग्या वसुंधरा'।

रेशमी कपड़े भेंट किए थे उन्होंने अपने ज्ञान भइया को, एहसान से दबे-दबे।

"घर को किराए पर देकर कुछ कमाने के बारे में सोच ही रही थी कि एक दिन स्कूल जाते समय उन्होंने जो देखा उसे देखकर उनके दिमाग में एक्सीवेटर का कान फोड़ू शोर हलचल मचाने लगा। आँखों के आगे अँधेरा छा गया। मैदान में ईंट, सीमेंट, लकड़ी फटे दरवाजे-खिड़कियाँ, सब टूटे-फूटे एक-दूसरे के ऊपर-नीचे गिरे-पड़े अपने नाम को रो रहे थे। बहुत सारे लोग उन्हें ढोकर अपने घर ले जा रहे थे।

"ए"' ! हमारा सामान है, कैसे लिये जा रहे हो? वे गाड़ी से उतरकर गिरती–पड़तीं पटवारी के यहाँ पहुँचीं। पहले दो दिन तो उससे भेंट ही नहीं हुई। जब मिला तो इनका रोना–धोना देखकर उसके मुँह से निकल पड़ा, "क्या करें मैडम, ओ जो काना चेचक दागवाला है न! एकदम से पीछे पड़ गया।" ''हटाओ इनको जल्दी, पचास हजार तनख्वाह पाती हैं। गाँव की जमीन पर दादागीरी से कब्जा कर लिया है, मैं नहीं गया तो कलेक्टर साहब के पास चला गया। तभी तो नगरनिगम वाले रातोरात ढहाने पहुँच गए।" उसने अपना पल्ला झाड़ लिया।

ज्ञानदास का काम जोरों पर चलने लगा था। "ए ही हो तो रातोरात गाँव की जमीन मुक्त कराए।" नए पट्टे बिक रहे थे धड़ाधड़, स्कूल की इमारत अधूरी रह गई थी, एलॉट नहीं आ रहा था। सड़क बनाई थी, वह बह गई, वे क्या करें? आजकल पानी का भी तो कोई भरोसा नहीं रहता। वह निर्द्वंद्व है।